D0554837

Ellen S. Woodward

Twentieth-Century America Series
Dewey W. Grantham, General Editor

Ellen Sullivan Woodward, sometime in the late 1920s
(Courtesy Albert Y. Woodward, Jr.)

Ellen S. Woodward
New Deal Advocate for Women

Martha H. Swain

UNIVERSITY PRESS OF MISSISSIPPI
Jackson

Library of Congress Cataloging-in-Publication Data

Swain, Martha H.
    Ellen S. Woodward : New Deal advocate for women / by Martha H.
Swain.
      p.   cm.—(Twentieth-century America series)
    Includes bibliographical references (p.   ) and index.
    ISBN 0-87805-756-0 (alk. paper)
    1. Woodward, Ellen S. (Ellen Sullivan) 2. Women social reformers—
United States—Biography. 3. New Deal, 1933–1939. I. Title.
II. Series.
HQ1413.W68S93 1995
361.7′4′092—dc20
  [B]   94-35499
                                                 CIP

British Library Cataloging-in-Publication data available

With love
for
Margaret and Mimi

Contents

Preface

People who know that I have been writing a biography of Ellen Sullivan Woodward may read this book and cite it less as biography and more as another New Deal administrative history. That is why it bears the title it does. After Woodward was widowed, her work absorbed her life. Even her social and professional organization contacts were work-related. She was a workaholic because, as a conscientious official, she had little choice but to master the details of her agencies: first, the Mississippi State Board of Development (1926–1933); then three successive New Deal work-relief programs (1933–1938); followed by the Social Security Board (1938–1946); and, finally, the Office of International Relations of the Federal Security Agency (1946–1953). Upon leaving the Works Progress Administration for the Social Security Board, she wrote a friend, "It has been hard to sever the old ties for I have simply lived my work for the past five and a half years."[1]

Anyone who has ever "worked" RG 69 at the National Archives, the records of the Federal Emergency Relief Administration, the Civil Works Administration, and the Works Progress Administration knows that one could spend a lifetime examining the manuscripts of the Division of Women's and Professional Projects alone. During all the spring and summer breaks I spent over a period of ten years delving into RG 69, I barely touched the surface. Under the direction of Richard Crawford and Aloha South, however, I have obtained maximum results for my time and am grateful to them for their patience and expert's knowledge of the holdings. The day-by-day records are a maze of details and administrivia that is exasperating for a researcher. How much more frustrating must they have been to relief officials? Those readers who believe this study is needlessly cluttered with too many routine matters must take it on faith that I have omitted much more than I have included.

There are historians I respect who are critical of the New Deal work programs for women because the projects did not meet the needs of a vast number of impoverished women.[2] Detractors and skeptics would have had women perform work other than traditional "women's work," or they would have had work relief comply with labor market theories current then and now. I have tried to show that Woodward and her staff recognized serious limitations within the programs, but that they were dealing with hard political realities of the day. Reading the incessant stream of letters to WPA officials from a hostile public and an antagonistic business community alongside frequent communiques from congressional harpies and the sine qua nons of a vigilant President and a watchdog Bureau of the Budget becomes a real downer. Holger Cahill, director of the WPA's Federal Arts Projects, remembered, "There was a dead cat coming in the window every few minutes."[3]

I argue that Woodward's achievements were considerable in view of the constraints on her efforts to win a modicum of economic security for women through New Deal work programs and within the fledgling Social Security system. I am convinced that Woodward's liberal bent and humanitarianism were based in her observation of poverty and a lack of economic opportunity for women in her home state of Mississippi. Critics who fault her work program for women for a lack of boldness may come to understand her practice of attempting the "art of the possible." To those historians who correctly discern forces of social control in local relief administrations that mitigated against the poor and minorities, I can say that I have never found a shred of evidence that Woodward held to any illiberal tenets.[4]

I first learned about Ellen Woodward while researching a dissertation on Mississippi Senator Pat Harrison, who trusted implicitly her good judgment. Then I had an opportunity to meet a number of older colleagues of my twin, Margaret, formerly a child welfare specialist with the Mississippi Department of Public Welfare and now a social work educator. Her early supervisors, pioneers in public welfare in Mississippi, knew Woodward and experienced the electrifying effect she had on early professionals in the state.

What is remarkable about Woodward is that her advancement was based almost entirely on her own self-education in public affairs. She received no formal education beyond the age of fifteen and had been married half her life when she was widowed at age thirty-seven in 1925. Other than a short time as a music teacher, she had never worked for pay. And yet, eight and a half years later, in September 1933, she was in Washington in a post ranked the second highest held by a woman in the Roosevelt administration; furthermore, she had no political constituency or national personal recognition. Thus I hope that readers will understand my compulsion to treat in some detail her odyssey from the parlors of clubwomen friends all the way to the inner offices of important federal agencies during two presidential administrations.

Woodward kept her papers and records of her work; they are now in the Mississippi Department of Archives and History. Imbued with a sense of history, she knew she lived in important times and hoped one day to write her own story. The papers describe more than her own work; they document the activities of a large circle of women in club work, political affairs, and government service. Her papers, however, contain no family correspondence and in only a few letters to friends does she reveal any of her personal anxieties. She left no journal or diary. Only the memorabilia in one large scrapbook indicates a private life among a group of devoted friends.

Crucial to Woodward's entry into public affairs was the emergence of a strong women's club movement in Mississippi that was representative of clubs elsewhere working for change in tradition-bound communities. Woodward used the General Federation of Women's Clubs and the National Federation of Business and Professional Women to promote the reform agenda she advocated. Always generous to her club companions, she made a way for many of them to be employed in the agencies in which she worked. Hence, I have tried to give historical visibility to many of Woodward's contemporaries. The richness of her papers makes that goal easily attainable.

The inner workings of the New Deal's work program for women have never been described in any detail, although some scholars have written of the vicissitudes of the projects for domestic workers. I am indebted to the historians cited in the footnotes and the essay on sources who have written accounts of the New Deal in various cities, states, and the South, and whose mining of project records at those levels for their own studies has benefited mine.

The Division of Women's and Professional Projects could not have succeeded without the many women who served as regional supervisors and as state directors, and in Washington as technical consultants, clericals, or speechwriters. I have tried to bring to the fore those women whose diligent work has gone unrecorded in the histories of the New Deal. They are the unsung heroines who made it all work. At one time, I thought I could demonstrate the career advancement among social workers through a longitudinal study of the state directors. Too many decades have passed and too many have died or are simply unknown by the people in the state departments of health and human services who have answered my queries. I have located only one surviving director. Today, at age eighty-five, Helen Twombly McAleney believes that she was the youngest of all the directors when she became head of the program in Maine in 1937. She has vivid memories of getting New Deal programs across in a Republican state. She had the "devil's own time," but she succeeded admirably.[5]

Woodward came to know a number of Southern women beyond the close coterie of Mississippians. North Carolina's Harriet Elliott, May Thompson Evans, and Gladys Tillett were all prominent in the Women's Division of the Democratic National Committee, another organization whose history is recounted in some detail in this book. Other Southern women emerged as leaders in New Deal agencies or Democratic women's circles thanks in part to Ellen Woodward. I hope that I have contributed some knowledge about the activities of the post-suffrage generation of Southern women. I want also to correct the bias toward Eastern women, whose achievements have dominated social welfare and reform history simply because not much has been written about Southern women of distinction during the era of the New Deal, World War II, and the immediate postwar years. More than anything else this book points to the centrality of Eleanor Roosevelt, to whom Woodward once wrote, "A new day has come to women in Government and out, since you championed our cause."[6]

Ellen Woodward's importance lies not only in her own role as a spokeswoman for many issues regarding women's economic security and political advancement, but also in her foresightedness to document three decades of women's reform activities. I am convinced that she is an important figure in that history.

Acknowledgments

This book has been made possible through the assistance of many people. Archivists at many repositories helped me locate material and then patiently brought out box after box. I have already described the help of Richard Crawford and Aloha South at the National Archives. Shelley Featherson, formerly with *Prologue*, introduced me to the photographs on stack 14 of the National Archives where Jonathan Heller, Patricia Richter, and Karen Yaffe helped me gather the large collection I now have of almost 400 photographs of the WPA Women's and Professional Projects and of the Social Security Board. The late Abe Bortz, Social Security historian, gave me guidance when I went to see him at the SSA headquarters in Woodlawn, Maryland, and opened to me his oral histories with Social Security principals. A chance meeting at the National Archives with Social Security scholar Edward Berkowitz proved enormously beneficial.

In Jackson the cordial and receptive present and former staff of the Mississippi Department of Archives and History has made my long stays there a real pleasure. Particularly, Michelle Hudson, Anne Lipscomb, Bill Hanna, and Vera Richardson made innumerable trips into the stacks to bring out boxes or acquaint me with the rich holdings of the MDAH. Charlotte Capers, who knew Ellen Woodward personally, was at the MDAH when I first began my work there and provided great personal inspiration for what I knew would be a long period of research. Jerome Deyo and Joseph Marshall, at the Franklin D. Roosevelt Library, are responsible for the valuable material I located there while on an Eleanor Roosevelt Institute grant. Lorraine Brown personally drove me from Washington out to George Mason University and the archives of the Institute on the Federal Theatre Project and New Deal Culture, a trip financed by a George Washington University/Smithsonian Institution Short-Term Visitor grant. Elizabeth Shenton helped me with arrangements during a visit to the Arthur and Elizabeth Schlesinger Library at Radcliffe College. Clarke A. Chambers and David Klaassen answered my inquiries and gave me invaluable assistance at the Social Welfare History Archives, University of Minnesota, which I visited under an NEH Travel to Collections grant. At the State Historical Society of Wisconsin, Cindy Knight was especially helpful. Archivists of special collections that I could not personally research have responded promptly to my inquiries. I thank Betty H. Carter for locating excellent material in the Harriet Elliott Papers in the Walter Clinton Jackson Library at the University of North Carolina at Greensboro, and Mark Switzer at Knox College for providing the Chloe Owings file. In addition, I received grants from the Harry S. Truman Library Institute for work at the Truman Library. Awards from the American Philosophical Society, the Albert Beveridge fund of the American Historical Association, and the Texas Woman's University organized research program enabled me to make the early trips to the National Archives.

Many people have been gracious in telling me of their personal association or friendship with Ellen Woodward. As readers will see, Lucy Somerville Howorth has made it possible for me to learn, as I have never learned quite so correctly before, that manuscripts do not tell the whole story by a long shot. I write this in her ninety-eighth year; her recollection of events and conversations is as sharp and detailed today as it was when she first began to tell me in person, by telephone, and by correspondence about Ellen Woodward ten years ago. I owe her a debt of gratitude beyond the power of description.

So, too, am I thankful to others who knew Woodward and have told me much: Maurine Mulliner, May Thompson Evans, Dorothy Lally, Grace Allen, Otis Harden, Wilbur Cohen, and others who are named in the essay on sources. Woodward's niece and nephew, Dorothy Fair Brown and Davis L. Fair, Jr., talked to me at length and provided family photographs. I am saddened that Albert Y. Woodward, Jr., who died in 1990, did not live to see this book, for he greeted me in Washington during my early trips there and told me much about the Louisville years. He, too, provided photographs. Otis Harden made available the photograph of his wife.

I want especially to thank two friends whose writings and discussions have helped me immensely. Blanche D. Coll welcomed me in Washington and told me a great deal about the early history of public welfare; she also made available a typescript of her forthcoming study on public assistance. Blanche is exemplary in her willingness to share her knowledge and research. I first met Elsie L. George in 1978, and have benefited both from conversations with her and her dissertation on the women appointees of the Roosevelt and Truman administrations. Elizabeth Snapp, director of the Texas Woman's University Library, encouraged her staff to buy for me numerous books and dissertations that I needed. Interlibrary loan librarians Jimmie Lyn Harris and Mary Anne Sawers never even murmured about the innumerable requests I made of them; they are due much credit for my research in secondary sources and in unpublished dissertations.

Friends in my department at TWU have encouraged me throughout my work on this book and have been tolerant of me those many times when I have been cranky due to the slowness of my writing. Were it not for the extreme patience of our secretary, Kerrie Alexander, I would never have learned even the rudiments of word processing. It is she and Jami Reever, our very able student assistant, who did all the print-outs. If it had not been for them, this book would not now be in your hands. Jami also helped me proof early copy. Other friends, particularly Dottie DeMoss, Joanne Varner Hawks, and the late A. Elizabeth Taylor, have sustained me with the kind of friendship that daily adds humor, warmth, and encouragement. Dottie, along with Vicki Ratcliffe, too many times to count, has come to my house to care for my pets so I could have some peace of mind about them during long absences.

I am indebted beyond means of expression for years of encouragement from Dewey W. Grantham, editor of the *Twentieth-Century America* series. He read a massive first draft and offered wise counsel on how to reduce a behemoth manuscript to give more focus to Woodward. Also, I am very grateful to Susan Ware who provided exceedingly generous, detailed, and practical suggestions for making Woodward more central in my work. This is a far better book than it once was because of Professors Grantham and Ware. I thank Blanche Coll, Margaret Ripley Wolfe, Lucy Somerville Howorth, Maurine Mulliner, Amalie Fair Robinson, and Marion Walters, my graduate student, for reading chapters dealing with topics in their fields of personal knowledge and expertise. Because of the careful work of copyeditor Roy A. Grisham, Jr., this is a far more lucid and precise book than it once was.

I dedicate this book to my sisters, Mary Elizabeth (Mimi) and Margaret. Margaret has made many trips to Jackson with me and helped in countless ways, but especially in rechecking notes. I am grateful for the materials she has plied me with on Mississippi social welfare history. It was through my older sister, Mimi, that I first learned to love history. Neither has ever wearied of hearing about "the book," and I love them both very much.

Martha H. Swain
Denton, Texas
Spring 1994

Abbreviations

AAUW	Papers of the American Association of University Women (microfilm)
AES	Arthur and Elizabeth Schlesinger Library, Radcliffe College (Cambridge, Massachusetts)
AJA	Arthur J. Altmeyer Papers, State Historical Society of Wisconsin (Madison)
BPW	Archives of the National Federation of Business and Professional Women (Washington, DC)
COHC	Columbia Oral History Collection
DD	*Democratic Digest*
ER	Eleanor Roosevelt Papers, Franklin D. Roosevelt Library (Hyde Park)
ESW	Ellen Sullivan Woodward Papers, Mississippi Department of Archives and History (Jackson)
ESWP	Ellen Sullivan Woodward Papers, Arthur and Elizabeth Schlesinger Library, Radcliffe College (Cambridge, Massachusetts)
FDR	Papers of Franklin D. Roosevelt, Roosevelt Library (Hyde Park)
FDRL	Franklin F. Roosevelt Library
FERA OSF	Federal Emergency Relief Administration Old Subject File, RG 69, National Archives (Washington, D.C.)
FERA NSF	Federal Emergency Relief Administration New Subject File, RG 69
FERA Ss	Federal Emergency Relief Administration State series, RG 69

HLH	Papers of Harry L. Hopkins, Franklin D. Roosevelt Library (Hyde Park)
IW	*Independent Woman*
LC	Library of Congress
LSH	Lucy Somerville Howorth Papers, Arthur and Elizabeth Schlesinger Library (Cambridge, Massachusetts)
MDAH	Mississippi Department of Archives and History
MWD	Papers of Mary Williams (Molly) Dewson, Franklin D. Roosevelt Library (Hyde Park)
NA	National Archives (Washington, DC)
NAW	*Notable American Women*
RG	Record Group
SHC	Southern Historical Collection, University of North Carolina (Chapel Hill)
SHSW	State Historical Society of Wisconsin (Madison)
SSB	Social Security Board, Record Group 47, National Archives
SWHA	Social Welfare History Archives, Walter Library, University of Minnesota (Minneapolis)
WD-DNC	Papers of the Women's Division, Democratic National Committee, Franklin D. Roosevelt Library (Hyde Park)
WPA GSF	Works Progress Administration, General Subject File, RG 69, National Archives
WPA Ss	Works Progress Administration, State series, RG 69, National Archives

Ellen S. Woodward

CHAPTER 1

There's No Town Like
Louisville: 1906–1926

"Advice to Wives: Go Get a Job" ran the headline of a newspaper story on Ellen Sullivan Woodward in April 1938. "I honestly believe that the working wife is the happiest woman in the world and the most successful wife and mother," she told the feature writer who had come to interview the federal official whose own job the press rated second only to that of Secretary of Labor Frances Perkins among the positions held by women under appointment from President Franklin D. Roosevelt.[1] As director of the Division of Women's and Professional Projects of the Works Progress Administration, Woodward had been in Washington for almost five years. She would remain in Washington for the next twenty years. Since 1933, she had made it her goal to see that women heads of households got jobs. Economic security for women would remain her focus when Woodward became a member of the Social Security Board in 1938, and beyond, when, after World War II, she directed a division of the Federal Security Agency.

Although she might speak thus that day in 1938, "I say frequently to the bride of this year or any other year, 'Go get a job,' " no one had said that to her thirty-two years earlier when she was a nineteen-year-old bride in Louisville, Mississippi. But then, there was a marked contrast between the comfortable life that was hers as a well-placed young matron in 1906 and the circumstances wives and mothers confronted during the Great Depression of the 1930s. It was a far cry, as well, from Woodward's casual life as a clubwoman in a small Southern town to a job in the nation's capital that won for her a ranking in 1945 among "Washington's Ten Most Influential Women."[2]

Clearly, Ellen Woodward had the advantages that accrue to those who are to the manor born. Her distinguished family included men who had been political and military leaders for four generations. Through her mother she was a direct descendant of John Adair, a major with South Carolina regiments during the American Revolution who later became both a governor of Kentucky and a U.S. senator,

1

and a brigadier general under Andrew Jackson at New Orleans.[3] John and his wife Katherine were the parents of Margaret Adair, who married William Preston Anderson in 1814. To the Andersons was born, in 1815, a daughter named Nancy Belle, who, with her husband James Murray, made her home in Hernando, Mississippi. The Murrays had two daughters, Ellen and Belle, both of whose future husbands became U.S. senators.[4] In 1886, Ellen married Joseph Weldon Bailey, a native of Crystal Springs, Mississippi. The Baileys located in Gainesville, Texas, where Joseph was elected to Congress in 1891 and to the Senate in 1901. Belle married William Van Amberg Sullivan, whose parents were May Clark and John Isaac Sullivan. It was to Dr. Sullivan, a member of the Mississippi secession convention of 1861 and a Confederate surgeon, that Ellen Woodward traced her lineage as a United Daughter of the Confederacy; as a descendant of the venerated John Adair she was a Daughter of the American Revolution.

Born near Winona, Mississippi, in 1857, and schooled in the town of Sardis, William Van Amberg Sullivan attended the University of Mississippi. In 1875, he became the first law graduate of Vanderbilt University, completing what must have been an abbreviated course since the University had opened only that year. (In all likelihood, he simply "tested out" of some courses by oral examination.) Two years after graduation, William Sullivan began a successful trial law practice in Oxford, Mississippi, and in 1878 married Belle Murray. They were the parents of five children: two sons, William Van Amberg, Jr. and Murray, were followed by three daughters, Belle, Ellen, and Elizabeth (or Bessie).[5] The middle daughter, named Ellen Bailey for her aunt in Texas, was born on 11 July 1887.[6]

In 1895, when Ellen was not quite eight years old, her mother died of tuberculosis, leaving the children (William, the oldest, was fifteen) in the care of their father. The family lived near the town square in Oxford in a two-story Victorian frame house not far from the small brick cottage that served as Sullivan's law office.[7] Especially devoted to her father, Ellen persisted in trailing him to his office and into the courtroom, reciting at home what she heard in court. Her father admired her grace and spirit; when she was ten years old, he told a colleague that his little Ellie had "no such thing as fear of anyone in [her] composition."[8]

Sullivan's public role as a school trustee, city alderman, and delegate to the Democratic national conventions in 1892 and 1896 generated parlor talk that Ellie found fascinating. Her home schooling in politics expanded considerably when her father went to Congress in 1897 and moved his family to Washington for a term in the House of Representatives. His tenure in the House was cut short when Governor Anselm J. McLaurin appointed him to the Senate upon the death of Edward C. Walthall. The new senator, described by the openly biased *Oxford Globe* as "bright, quick, energetic, bold, eloquent [and] brainy," was the youngest senator thus far to serve from Mississippi.[9] When the state legislature convened early in 1900, it elected Governor McLaurin to the six-year term that would have been accorded General Walthall had he lived. His Senate career thus aborted, Sullivan returned to resume his law practice in Washington; his family now included a new wife, Marie Newman Atkins, a Washington widow whom he married in 1900. What sort of relationship Ellen, then thirteen, had with her stepmother is not known. Her son's recollection was that she was "very fond of Marie," and later grateful for her loyalty and care of Sullivan during a lingering illness. Sullivan died in March 1919.[10]

Ellie first attended the Oxford Graded School and continued her education in Washington (although there is no record of where she

William Van Amberg Sullivan and his daughters (l. to r.), Ellen Bailey, Elizabeth (Bessie), and Belle, on the porch of their home in Oxford, Mississippi, about 1895 (Courtesy Davis L. Fair, Jr.)

was enrolled; most likely, the "Washington College" from which she held a diploma in music was the school she attended during 1897-1901). She was sent to Sans Souci Female Academy, in Greenville, South Carolina, for the 1901–1902 term. The new school, which apparently opened around 1900, was owned and directed by a congressional colleague of Ellen's father, William Hayne Perry, and his wife, Louise, the daughter of yet another of Sullivan's associates, Alabama congressman John Hollis Bankhead. The academy was maintained in the former home of the South Carolina Unionist governor, Benjamin F. Perry.[11] Grounds landscaped with trailing vines, arbor vitae, magnolias, and oaks made a handsome setting for a fashionable school, but there are no records of Ellie's studies there. She made no public comment on her year at Sans Souci, nor, apparently, did she maintain contact with any of her classmates. She did not return in the fall of 1902, perhaps because of Congressman Perry's death that summer; thus her formal education was over when she was only fifteen. She had wanted to go to college, she confessed years later, but her father had been "aghast" at the idea and of the mind that college "ruined a woman's charm."[12] Senator Sullivan did not, however, banish his daughter from the political deliberations conducted in the Sullivan home. "I grew up in an atmosphere of politics," she told a group of Democratic women in 1938, "where governmental affairs—local, state, and national—were constantly discussed."[13]

As a teenage girl in Oxford, Ellie enjoyed the gaiety and camaraderie of social outings related to the University of Mississippi and its fraternities. The three Sullivan daughters, the object of much attention from the university boys, were "noted for their beauty, charm, and vivacity" and were the chief attraction for visiting baseball and football teams, or so an old friend remembered. Another recalled Ellie's "belledom and beauty as a girl [and the] auburn hair and fair skin."[14] In 1902, Belle, the oldest sister, married Davis L. Fair, an Ole Miss student leader, football team manager, and baseball captain. Although no romance developed for Ellie in Oxford, she did become acquainted with numerous law students with whom she later served in the Mississippi legislature and the state's economic and civic development. Bessie, the younger sister, married a young Memphis man, Boyce Cannon, in 1905.

Ellie had a number of girlfriends who lived in nearby towns whom she entertained when they came to visit in Oxford.[15] In turn, she spent much of her time with them in Greenwood, Macon, Columbus, and Jackson and with her father's sister in nearby Holly Springs.

Longer intervals with Belle and Davis at French Camp and with Bessie and Boyce in Memphis filled her days.[16] It was during the 1905 winter party season in Memphis that Ellie made her debut at a dance given under the auspices of the Chickasaw Club.[17] The Fairs having moved to Louisville in 1904, it was probably while visiting with them that Ellen met and courted Albert Young Woodward, a Louisville native eight years her senior. A graduate of the University of Mississippi and already an established attorney, Albert Woodward was the son of a prominent physician and the scion of an old Louisville family. Captain M. A. Metts, Albert's grandfather and a pioneer Louisvillian, had served in the Confederate Army and both branches of the Mississippi legislature. On 27 June 1906, Ellen and Albert were married at the Gayoso Hotel in Memphis. They left the next day for their new home in Louisville.[18]

As a young wife barely nineteen years old, "Miss Ellie," as the townspeople soon knew her, quickly made a place for herself in society and church. She sang soprano in the Methodist choir when she was not playing the organ. She also taught Sunday School and was for years president of the Methodist Women's Missionary Society. She was a charter member and regent of the Katherine Adair chapter of the DAR and helped organize the local Order of the Eastern Star, of which she became worthy matron.[19] In January 1909, she and Belle Fair joined the charter group that founded the Fortnightly Club. For the next quarter century, the federated club movement would be Ellen Woodward's forum and the agendas of Mississippi women's organizations the focus of her civic work.

The ladies of the club first elected Woodward president in 1912; she regularly led programs and read papers on a broad range of subjects pertaining to history, politics, and the arts. "Mrs. A. Y. Woodward's paper on the 'Historical Homes of Mississippi' was one of the most interesting and instructive it has been the Club's pleasure to listen to," the Fortnightly reporter posted in the society column of the local paper in 1914.[20]

Such amenities as the Fortnightly members displayed must have been welcomed in the town of Louisville, which in the first decade of the new century had no public water, electricity, or gas distribution and no improved streets other than a few thoroughfares "oiled" to reduce the amount of dust. Despite the lack of paved streets, the Fortnightly Club never failed to meet, although it might resort, as it did one rainy afternoon, to the use of the railroad depot bus to collect the entire membership for a meeting. "We always managed," reminisced a charter member after nearly fifty years of club activity.[21] The ten miles of concrete sidewalks, a waterworks system, electric lights, and an ice plant that Louisville boasted by 1916 were civic improvements for which the Fortnightly Club claimed partial credit.[22] Definitely growing, the town could, by the 1920 census, claim a population of almost 1,800, more than three times the 505 persons enumerated in 1900.

In 1910, Ellen Woodward, now the mother of Albert Junior, born on 27 August 1909, gave a paper on the topic, "Is Woman's Invasion a Fad?" "Splendidly prepared," so the weekly *Winston County Journal* reported, it was one of the papers chosen for discussion at the special annual meeting to which husbands were invited.[23] Although it is not likely that she intended her talk to be a personal statement, for the next fifteen years Louisvillians saw Ellen Woodward as a driving force in community life. President of the Fortnightly Club again in 1915, she directed "Clean Up Days" and oversaw club collections of books and money for the public school library. That year she was one of the "enthusiastic ladies" present when the stockholders of the Winston County Fair created a Ladies Department—Mrs. Albert Woodward, chairman—so that the fair might "take on a new life."[24]

In 1916, "good roads" became a new interest for Woodward, and she prepared a paper on the topic for her club. A member of the Louisville Good Roads Association, she appeared at open meetings to advocate improved streets for the town and graded farm-to-market roads in the county. Home and lawn improvement was another goal. She and Belle Fair were among the townspeople who "motored" to the Mississippi Agricultural and Mechanical College in Starkville, seeking ideas to landscape home and school grounds.[25] In 1917, at the urging of Woodward and Fair, the Fortnightly Club became a pioneer among Mississippi federated clubs in its endorsement of the rural extension work just getting underway under the Smith-Lever Act passed by Congress in 1914.

To be sure, Fortnightly Club efforts were modest; nevertheless, the members managed to raise funds to supplement the first salaries of county agricultural agents and home demonstration workers. Its rural outreach program included serving buffet luncheons in the lobby of the county courthouse to rural youths who came to town on Saturdays, assisting with exhibits and demonstrations at the county fair, facilitating curb market operations in town, and conducting contests and schools of instruction for rural home modernization. Sensitive to the comfort of women shoppers from the country, Woodward chaired a citizen's committee to provide public restrooms in the business district. Probably her most significant work in the rural communities was a campaign among farm wives to win their compliance with the much-resisted tick-eradication law enacted in 1916 by the state legislature. On her own initiative, she went into the county to convince farm women that germ-free milk was worth the cost of treating the cattle.[26] Ironically, her well-remembered forays into the countryside made her an ally of Governor Theodore G. Bilbo, whose defeat for reelection in 1917 has been attributed to the unpopularity of the tick law. Will Hight, editor of the *Winston County Journal* and a hearty champion of all Mrs. Woodward did, described her as "one of our State's most brilliant and lovable women . . . deeply interested in all that goes to make for the best interests of her people."[27]

Civilian mobilization for World War I prompted Louisvillians to a flurry of activity. Citizens who met at the courthouse in July 1917 to form a Red Cross Society named Ellen Woodward vice president and her husband to the executive committee. As the Winston County chairman of the Women's Committee of the Council of National Defense, Woodward, through the *Journal*, appealed for every woman to register her capabilities to "help Mississippi get a line on its woman power" during the week of 14 September, the day declared by the state governor as Woman's Service Day. In January 1918, she reported to a district meeting of the women's CND committee that met on the campus of the women's Industrial Institute and College in Columbus that seventy-nine Winston County women had responded. There is, however, no record of what they proposed to do if summoned to duty. In spite of the fact that the Mississippi Women's Committee, of the Council of National Defense, received no funds from the male-dominated state committee—benign neglect was the story of almost all the women's auxiliaries of the CND—a contemporary participant, Ida Clyde Clarke, praised its "fine example of perfect coordination. "Women of the fair Magnolia State," she wrote, "are looking out beyond the old dried up shell of indifference and lethargy . . . and are making of themselves real and potent factors in the Nation's crisis, and preparing themselves to do citizen's duty."[28]

Through her defense work, Ellen met women from outside her federated club circles and developed new perspectives on women's work and service. Quick to learn, she found that the material sent from the national office of the Women's Committee, headed by Dr. Anna Howard Shaw, illuminated new roles for women leaders in social betterment. As a county chairman, Woodward made it her task to analyze the status and opportunities for women in food production, furthering home economies, and industrial work (admittedly not pertinent to Winston County). Under the rubric of "preservation of the social fabric," she was to plan programs for health and child welfare; the latter became the subject of her talk at a district meeting of CND women at Macon in May 1918. In expediting the goals of the Women's Committee, Ellen called on every Louisville housewife to cooperate with county agents and home demonstration workers in converting vacant lots into war gardens.[29] In all probability, the war efforts of the women of Louisville and Winston County amounted to little in the overall scheme of things, but for Ellen, experiences on the home front provided a valuable lesson she would someday put to use.

The federated women's clubs' crusade for victory provided another avenue for Woodward's war work. At its War Service Convention in the fall of 1917, the president of the National Federation of Women's Clubs outlined for Mississippians the work of the Council of National Defense while the Mississippi president, Mrs. Edward McGehee of Como, in a patriotic speech termed the federation a "training camp." Members kept their knitting needles in action throughout the sessions, applauding Mrs. McGehee's announcement that the federation's state endowment fund was now invested in Liberty Loan bonds. As president of the fourth district of the Mississippi GFWC in 1918, Woodward presided over a "war service" session that met in Louisville in June. She promoted the purchase of Liberty Bonds, sang solos at Red Cross fundraisers, and spearheaded the Fortnightly Club's call for a daily angelus when Louisville church bells would summon townspeople to pray for peace. When the war ended and Winston Countians formed an "After-War Reconstruction County Council" to weigh postwar needs for new schools and roads, improved farms and public health, and the employment of veterans, the Woodwards were involved (Albert became vice chairman of the council).[30]

If Ellen Woodward was all that Will Hight claimed she was—"a brilliant woman [whose] love for civic pride and improvement has been a great benefactor to the city"—her status and influence were nonetheless appreciably enhanced by the political and professional standing of her husband. When they were married in 1906, he was a town magistrate, soon thereafter becoming mayor. In 1914, in a campaign managed by his wife, he was elected chancellor of the Sixth Mississippi Chancery Court District. During his five years on the bench, Albert Woodward consistently drew praise for his "clean administration of the laws"; there were no scandals involving his court. Thus, Judge Woodward's announcement in November 1919 that "health and financial conditions demand that [he] resign" stunned his constituents. He was never a vigorous man, and frequent travel on the judicial circuit was becoming more onerous as the years went by. The Woodwards placed their furniture in storage, sold a few household goods and Ellen's Paige automobile, and left by train for Okmulgee, Oklahoma, where Albert expected to establish a remunerative law practice and recoup some of the loss of income incurred during his years on the chancery circuit. Frequent notices in the *Journal* of tax delinquencies, bankruptcies, and store closings were testamentary that the postwar recession had reached Louisville and diminished Woodward's prospects for restoring his law practice to its former level. Oil strikes in eastern Oklahoma enticed the Woodwards to the west rather than to Greenville, Mississippi, where opportunities also beckoned. With its gambling halls, saloons, and air of a boomtown, Okmulgee proved a big disappointment. Having decided that Okmulgee was not a "family town," the Woodwards returned to Mississippi and to Greenville, where Albert formed a partnership with a former Louisville associate. It was January 1920, a time of unprecedented prosperity, with the high price of cotton continuing to reflect wartime demands. In April 1920, cotton reached a high of forty-two cents a pound, which motivated farmers to plant their largest crop since 1914.[31]

Greenville, located on the Mississippi River and known as the queen city of the rich Mississippi Delta, was in 1920 a progressive town with a population of about 11,500. For the Woodwards, life there was gracious and rewarding, both socially and professionally. They bought a house and were welcomed into a social coterie known as the "South Broadway Street gang." Ellen affiliated with the DAR, and she and Albert soon became charter members of the newly founded Greenville Music Club. Only six months after their arrival in Greenville, the society columnist gushed: "Greenville should feel grateful to fate for sending such an attractive woman as Mrs. Woodward to live in our midst." Judge Woodward's election as city attorney added to the community stature that the couple enjoyed.[32]

Soon Ellen was active in the sewing circle of the Methodist Women's Missionary Society. Although the organization produced some garments and goods for church bazaars, it was primarily a study group that encouraged missionary work overseas. Only a month after inaugurating the fall 1920 season with a talk entitled "Woman's Work," Ellen led the program of study at the biweekly meeting—"in her characteristic charming manner," the local newspaper reported. The next year, she was a Greenville delegate and opening speaker at a district WMS meeting.[33] Through the Missionary Society, Woodward came to know Nellie Nugent Somerville, the foremost woman lay leader of the Greenville Methodist district. As early as 1893, Somerville, at the annual meeting of the home mission society of the North Mississippi conference, had summoned Methodist women to social reform: "Motherless humanity needs your womanly care." In all probability, Woodward's social conscience developed from her experience in the Methodist church and from her contact with dynamic women such as Somerville who sought an equal voice for women in church governance. Similarly, it may be presumed that she was sensitive to the stirrings for racial justice among Methodist women and that she followed the proceedings of the interracial conference held in Memphis in October 1920 under the auspices of the Commission on Interracial Cooperation. Methodist publications, particularly the *Christian Advocate*, were standard reading in the Woodward home. Since 1916, Methodist women, through the churchwide Women's Missionary Council, had committed themselves to mission studies on social action such as the abolition of child labor and illiteracy, provision for juvenile courts, and enforcement of laws regulating the liquor traffic. There can be no question that there was a religious base to Ellen Woodward's reform impulse.[34]

Somerville's influence on Woodward extended beyond the church. When the Woodwards arrived in Greenville in 1920, Somerville, a neighbor on Broadway Street, was lobbying the woman suffrage amendment before the legislature in Jackson, which defeated the measure. In the spring the leading woman's club in Greenville, the Civic Improvement Club, shifted its focus from suffrage, the matter "being no longer an issue," to the "general line of civic work." This shift led to a City Beautiful campaign. By the time the campaign got underway, Woodward had been invited to membership in the club and was promptly elected corresponding secretary. Somerville, a perennial officer in the club, was then serving as vice president. Designated a "captain" in the City Beautiful crusade, Woodward was detailed to handle the problem of neglected vacant lots.[35] Before the campaign concluded, the Woodwards had left Greenville, but Ellen would not forget the strategies she had learned.

Nor would she forget the response of Greenville women to the downturn in the local economy in the postwar years. "Our people [have] suffered so severely from the unprecedented deflation in the price of cotton—the money product of the Delta," an editorial in the *Greenville Daily Democrat-Times* lamented in July 1921, the summer that cotton prices plummeted to nine and a half cents a pound. Conversely, consumer prices were up, prompting the Civic Improvement Club to investigate the rising cost of milk, ice, and laundry services.

Disgruntled members called for a housewives' strike against merchants who were "out of line." Editor L. Pink Smith of the *Democrat-Times*, sympathizing with housewives, observed during the summer of 1921 that national income tax returns revealed that many single women were self-supporting or were heads of families, and that hundreds of thousands of married women were now working to support their families. The facts, Smith argued, proved that the "old fond notion that man is the wage earner" was an "economic fallacy."

Ellen Woodward did not yet have to work outside her home, although she had taught public school music for a time in Louisville. Still, the recession did not leave the Woodwards unscathed. The problems it precipitated for the brokerage firm in Minneapolis managed by Bessie's second husband, Edward Hamilton Dutcher, led the couple to relocate in Miami and plunge into real estate development. Over Christmas 1921, Ellen and Albert Junior visited the Dutchers in Minneapolis. Bessie needed Ellen's counsel and companionship, just as Ellen later would need Bessie. The next summer, having decided to leave Greenville and its economic slump, the Woodwards returned to Louisville, where "Mr. Woodward has large business interests . . . and finds it urgent to be located."[36]

Ellen had liked Greenville very much, but, she remarked upon their return, "there's no town like Louisville." Now living in what the *Journal* called "the handsomest home in our city," the Woodwards resumed the life they had left two years earlier.[37] For Ellen that meant the Fortnightly Club. In 1923, she initiated its most ambitious project to date, a citywide clean-up campaign, the development of a city park and playground, and the conversion into a community center of an old Masonic hall and former schoolhouse dating from 1851. A meeting she chaired at the Methodist Church launched the projects under the auspices of the newly formed City Beautiful Association. Woodward directed the CBA until 1928, when the leadership passed to her sister, Belle Fair.[38]

Independent of the Fortnightly Club, Ellen organized a group of women to monitor sessions of the city council and county board of supervisors. It was the type of activity a League of Women Voters would have engaged in; but there was no League in Louisville (nor had there been one in Greenville).

Woodward may have taken her cue from the *Mississippi Woman's Magazine*, which often featured the work of Nellie Nugent Somerville, who outlined a "practical study of citizenship" before a convention of the Mississippi Federation of Women's Clubs, in November 1922. If Woodward read *The Woman Voter*, published as the voice of the new Mississippi League of Women Voters (and it is likely that she did), she would have had at hand the specific questions Somerville advised women activists to ask elected officials regarding political machinery, election laws, and the administration of local government. Although at first the women of Louisville intimidated male officials, they were eventually invited to enter into discussions. "I've always been particularly interested in women of the South," Woodward reflected a decade later, "because people have the idea they should sit at home. . . . when Southern women get first hand knowledge of conditions, they'll do something."[39]

In August 1923, Albert Woodward, now the Louisville city attorney, won election to the Mississippi House of Representatives from Winston County. Both Woodwards were in Jackson from January through March 1924. Jackson was an exciting place for legislative wives; there were numerous social functions and opportunities to entertain hometown friends and family who were in the city for politics, business, or shopping. Ellen, who always met people well, renewed friendships and met new members of Mississippi's officialdom. In April, Governor Henry L. Whitfield named her to a four-year term as trustee of the Matty Hersee Hospital, a state-charity facility at Meridian. It was her first appointment to a state agency. She remained on the board until September 1925, following her election to the legislature.[40]

At twilight on 6 February 1925, when Judge Woodward had failed to arrive home from his office downtown, Ellen and Albert Junior drove to meet him. They found him lying on the curb near their home, dead from a heart attack. Her husband's premature death and her widowhood at age thirty-seven left Ellen at loose ends. She did not face immediate financial problems, but neither was she left in circumstances that would preclude her never having to work. Ellen postponed making decisions until after she visited her Aunt Ellen Bailey, now living in Dallas. After returning to Louisville, she and Albert Junior left for Miami in early April to visit Bessie and consult with the Dutchers about Ellen's financial affairs. Successful for a time in residential construction and sales along Miami Beach, the Dutchers convinced her to remain there, and Albert enrolled at Miami High School. Ellen became a broker and dabbled in real estate. For years thereafter, she retained a few tracts of land she had bought and built an apartment house, both for investment income and as a possible retirement home.[41] Over the next three decades, she returned to this house for vacations and during periods of poor health.

Other events soon changed the direction Ellen had taken. Six weeks after her husband's death, a group of voters published an open letter in the *Winston County Journal*, urging "Ellie" to permit her name to be placed on the ballot in the August primary that would nominate someone to complete her husband's term. Within days the *Jackson Daily News* predicted that, as a "woman of exceptional ability," she would have no opposition. While Ellen remained reluctant to seek the post, the *Journal* kept open her option to announce her candidacy. On 10 May she did so through an open letter written from Miami. Will Hight proclaimed Ellen "far superior to any lady we have ever known [and] equal to most men when it comes to handling matters of this kind." Home in Louisville in July and August, Ellen told the voters of the county that she only wished to complete her husband's term, adding that she would not seek election in her own right.[42]

She defeated her one opponent—S. D. Rodgers, of Noxapater—a former unsuccessful legislative candidate by a vote of 955 to 451, carrying thirteen of seventeen ballot boxes, overwhelming Rodgers 460 to 99 in Louisville, and even winning a majority in Noxapater. There was no campaign issue in the August primary other than "Ellie's" desire to carry on her husband's work. Victory in hand and facing no opposition in the general election, she thanked the voters for their "expression of esteem" for her late husband. She then turned to family matters, which included another trip to Dallas to see her ailing Aunt Ellen and making arrangements to enroll Albert in the Gulf Coast Military Academy at Gulfport.[43]

Ellen Woodward became the third woman elected to the Mississippi legislature. Belle Kearney, a former suffragist and temperance leader and the first woman state senator, was only a passing acquaintance. The other, Nellie Nugent Somerville, had been the Washington County representative in the House since 1924 and had encouraged an ambivalent Ellen Woodward to make the race, promising to help Ellen should she be elected. Respected for her integrity, forceful character, and intellect and known as a woman who "did not suffer fools gladly," as one admirer wrote, Nellie Somerville was an effective legislator. It was to Woodward's advantage that the Mississippi press and her legislative colleagues promptly identified Ellen as a protégé of the "lady from Washington County." The *New Orleans Times-Picayune* described the interesting new woman in Mississippi as "a woman of simple and charming manner, a winning smile, a cordiality that immediately puts the visitor at ease . . . of slender build, medium height, blue eyes [actually they were green] and auburn hair."[44]

Although Nellie Somerville was best known throughout the state as the former president of the Mississippi Woman's Suffrage Association, she, like Woodward, was a ranking member of the Mississippi Federation of Women's Clubs. During the first week of the legislative session, the two MFWC leaders issued a public appeal to all women's organizations in the state to follow legislative deliberations, discuss them, and forward responses to their representatives.[45] Nellie Somerville's chairing of the Committee on Eleemosynary Institutions and Woodward's committee assignments—State Library, University and Colleges, Liquor Traffic, and Eleemosynary Institutions—offered ample opportunity to advance programs long on the MFWC's agenda. "It means so much to have such capable women in the Legislature," the MFWC *Bulletin* commented. Both Somerville and Woodward supported efforts to have the legislature establish a normal school at Cleveland, and Woodward was a member of a committee that made a site visit to the town.[46]

Political prognosticators, including Lieutenant-Governor Dennis Murphree, predicted before the legislature convened that the 1926 session would be brief and harmonious. As expected, the 5 January message of conservative Governor Whitfield called for fiscal responsibility. In the following ten weeks, the legislature fell in line and made few appropriations, a stance that cost Ellen three of the four "local" road bills she promoted for Winston County.[47] She drew the most satisfaction from the legislature's adoption of a bill drafted by Mississippi Library Association leaders to create a Mississippi state library commission. She chaired the State Library Committee in the House and championed the MLA's goal to establish a free library in every county. While the legislature did not fund the new State Library Commission, Woodward drew plaudits that it had at least been authorized, thus making all eighty-two counties eligible for that portion of federal funds that had hitherto gone to other states because Mississippi had no state agency to supervise library extension work.[48]

More controversial was Ellen's bill prohibiting the sale of Jamaica ginger, juniper extracts, and similar alcohol-laced "juices" widely sold over the counter as medicine. Supported by federal and state prohibition officers, the "Jake" bill drew the opposition of druggists and merchants who profited from brisk sales of the liquor substitutes. Similar bills had failed to pass, including one Albert Woodward had sponsored. When House Speaker Thomas L. Bailey and powerful veteran lawmakers Walter Sillers, Jr., of Rosedale, and Luther Kennedy, of Natchez, endorsed the bill, it passed with only five dissenting votes soon after Woodward's "short, terse, and pointed" maiden speech. Five weeks later, after House and Senate conferees compromised their differences, the liquor ban passed the House with only one opposing vote.[49]

Inexplicably, Woodward was "absent" when the House voted to prohibit the teaching of evolution in the schools following a protracted debate. If she chose to dodge the issue, she may have done so on the advice of her mentors in the House. Twenty-six members were recorded as "absent" at the time of the vote, including Speaker Bailey.[50] She did, however, vote for repeal of the ban on Greek-letter fraternities in the state's public universities. Originally enacted at the request of former (and now discredited) Governor Bilbo, the controversial measure precipitated a showdown between political and social factions in the legislature, with the anti-Bilbo legislators voting to permit reinstatement of the Greek societies.[51]

By concluding that "Madame arrives in politics" most often through "wifely devotion and the solidarity of the home," a writer for the *North American Review* unknowingly commented aptly on Ellen Woodward's brief career in elective office. Even more applicable was the observation of the *Albany* (New York) *News* the year Albert Woodward died: "The 'widow in politics' is becoming a somewhat familiar phrase." Ellen Woodward held her seat in the legislature primarily as a surrogate for her deceased husband, and his stature among his peers added to her own. "Mrs. Woodward does not come to the capital as a stranger," the *Jackson Daily News* had said at the opening of the session. Acquainted with her since she was a teenager in Oxford, the "Big Four" in the House (the speaker and the chairmen of the three most powerful committees) contributed greatly to her success. They had seen to it that she got choice committee assignments. They cosponsored her bills, schooled her in procedure, and at adjournment escorted her to the speaker's stand for an ovation and a bouquet of roses. Back home in Winston County, she found that her constituents judged her performance in Jackson an unqualified success.[52] She accounted for her stewardship there to civic groups,

Ellen Sullivan Woodward (probably in the mid 1920s) had a lifelong reputation for a flair for fashion (Courtesy Albert Y. Woodward, Jr.)

including the Rotary and Fortnightly Clubs and the Good Roads Association.[53]

Woodward's term would not end officially until January 1928; so she continued to maintain an office in Louisville. There was time to spend with family in the summer and fall of 1926—another long visit with Bessie in Miami that concluded just before the hurricane struck in September, a trip to Ohio to enroll Belle's daughter Dorothy in the Cincinnati Conservatory of Music, and a sad trip to Dallas in October for the funeral of Aunt Ellen. Fortnightly Club programs continued, as did her duties as district vice president of the Mississippi Federation of Women's Clubs (there were now thirty-seven clubs in her district).

She was among the group of Louisville women engaged in chartering a local Business and Professional Women's Club open to any woman "who through personal efforts, supports or partially supports herself." Trips to Jackson and Memphis—"looking after business interests," as the *Journal* put it—consumed much of her time.[54] "Business interests" in Florida were diminished by the September hurricane that dealt a final blow to the Florida land boom.

At age thirty-nine, Ellen Woodward was still undecided about her future. She still had to face the question of yet another new direction to take. The Mississippi legislature was merely a "citizen" assembly from the standpoint of remuneration. Having no ambition for political office, she had made it clear that she could serve only the remainder of her husband's term which meant attendance at only one session. In spite of this renouncement, there was a public appeal in 1927 that she run for reelection.[55] By that time, she had already begun a new job in Jackson, serving a new constituency and absorbed in work that would bring her in contact with politicians and public administrators from outside Mississippi. Aunt Ellen had written when the legislature adjourned in 1926, "I am glad that you enjoyed your political experience. But, if you take my advice you will decline to participate further in politics. It is a thankless game, and a little rough for the delicate nerves of a woman."[56] It was advice that her namesake chose to decline. Although she would not again seek an elective office, politics and public service would be her life for nearly thirty more years.

Events during Woodward's nineteen years of married life and community activism in two small Mississippi towns provided no significant glimpses into what would transpire in the next ten years of her life. She had not been involved in the woman's suffrage movement, and, other than her friendship with Nellie Nugent Somerville, had had no brush with advanced feminist thought. Her reformism and public spirit seemed grounded in a conviction that progress was synonymous with a community's growth and economic well-being. Through her own experiences, she had seen that organized women's groups were vital both for the personal growth of their own members and for the advancement of civic welfare. Suddenly left a widow in need of a way to support herself and her son, it seemed only natural that she convert her voluntary, community-based initiatives into a salaried professional position from which she could expand her endeavors throughout the state.

CHAPTER 2

Are We Sold on Mississippi?:
1926–1932

E llen Woodward's club and civic work during the two decades of domestic life in Louisville won her considerable recognition beyond the confines of her little hometown. A short stint in the Mississippi legislature had heightened her presence among men and women whose opinions counted in Mississippi. After joining the staff of the Mississippi State Board of Development late in 1926, she moved to the center of attempts to expand the state's industry, diversify its agriculture, market its products, and, in general, "sell the South." She calculated that, by the end of the 1920s, she had "spoken in every one room schoolhouse in the state on some civic matter." "All the women and almost all the men know me" was not just an idle boast.[1] Both her knowledge of conditions throughout Mississippi and her growing reputation as a new-style "public woman" placed Woodward at the center of action when, in 1932, relief appropriations began to trickle into the state. And finally, her involvement in Democratic politics and the presidential campaign of 1932 set in motion events that would change the direction of her life.

The Board of Development was formed in 1925 by merging the state Chamber of Commerce and a development program that had functioned since 1921. Subscribing members of the new MSBD were prominent farmers, merchants, bankers, and manufacturers who professed "undaunted faith" in the state's future. From the outset, the Board's general manager, Luther Folse, ran the MSBD offices in Jackson, Hattiesburg, and Tupelo. The earliest Board president, H. S. Wilson, was succeeded by Lucius Olan Crosby, a prosperous lumberman from south Mississippi. Not an official arm of the state, as was the later Balance Agriculture With Industry agency, the MSBD received no state funds and offered no subsidies to entice new plants and firms. It was substantially a private-sector organization intended to boost the perceived advantages of doing business in Mississippi and with Mississippians.[2]

18

On 10 December 1926, the MSBD sponsored a widely publicized conference on industrial development at Amory, a railroad town in northeast Mississippi, whose local leaders hoped to draw attention to the town's potential as a trade center. Congressmen from four states and a large number of Mississippi officials heard speeches on taxation, conservation of natural resources, and industrial development. As an enthusiast of the Good Roads Association, Woodward had good reason to be in Amory: both the host town and Louisville stood to benefit from completion of a proposed state highway that would link the two communities and terminate in Jackson.[3] Her appointment to the MSBD committee on resolutions at the Amory meeting was the first hint that she was to become affiliated with the Board. Shortly afterward, Board officials announced that she would be named director of a new woman's department.[4]

Beginning with the January 1927 issue of *The Mississippi Builder*, the official organ of the Board that styled itself "The Voice of the New South," Ellen wrote a monthly article entitled "Women Builders." She solicited from Mississippi clubwomen and community leaders ideas about homes, highways, or any public improvement they wished to advocate. "The work of upbuilding the New South is by no means confined to southern men," she wrote. "Women are real builders—builders of ideals, builders of progressive thought, builders of homes, communities, and cultural sentiment . . . builders of highways, schools, social centers, and welfare institutions."[5] Her articles in the journal throughout 1927 served as a clearinghouse for publicizing the activities of women's clubs and voluntary associations. She advertised the patriotic work of the American Legion Auxiliary and the historic preservation projects of the Daughters of the American Revolution, the charitable impulses of the King's Daughters, and the thrusts of the Women's Christian Temperance Union under president Nellie Nugent Somerville in the enforcement of the Eighteenth Amendment. No organizations, however, were more caught up in the New South spirit of the MSBD than were the federated women's clubs.[6]

That same year, the MSBD launched a "use more cotton" crusade. Intended to help reduce the surplus cotton that glutted the market that year, clubwomen throughout the state pledged to buy at least twenty yards of the fabric for making clothes and renovating houses. Those most responsible for the club's commitment to buy cotton were the federation president, Susie V. Powell and Blanche Montgomery Ralston, a former educational chairman of the MSBD and now the press chairman of the Mississippi Federation of Women's Clubs.[7] Reporting on the annual convention of the MFWC in 1927, Ellen printed the message of president Powell. In answer to her own query, "What are the Mississippi Club Women up to?" Powell elaborated on the "practical work" of her organization: disaster relief for victims of the 1927 Mississippi River flood, promotion of a modern system of municipal, county, and state parks, and a call for enactment of a law establishing kindergartens. The Club advocated the appointment of a woman state factory inspector and pushed for adequate funding for the new State Library and Forestry commissions. Some satisfaction in this respect came when the governor appointed Mrs. H. G. Reeves, the MFWC state conservation chairman, to the Forestry Commission.[8]

Writing for the *Manufacturers' Record* late in 1927, Ellen boasted that the women's clubs in Mississippi had "enlisted" in the work of the Board of Development. They had proven their grasp of the "more material undertakings" in industry, railroad construction, public works, and agriculture of the contemporary South. Clubwomen were diligent in the tick-eradication campaign, which would enable live-stock production to thrive, agricultural diversification be speeded up, and farmers to be liberated from their "one-crop folly." Clean milk meant not only improved health and nutrition, but would also encour-age major milk producers and cheese manufacturers to locate in the South.[9] The campaign paid off when several cheese plants and creameries began operation in Mississippi, and Ellen had the pleasure of throwing the switch at the opening of the new Kraft cheese plant in Louisville.[10]

Woodward's public relations work with the MSBD expanded as she grew in the job. For all practical purposes, the position was what she chose to make it. Thus she conferred with Dr. Felix Underwood, the state's chief health officer, about how public health care could be extended to those counties with no full-time health department. She accompanied Laura Wilson Wiseman, a pioneer home economist in Union County, employed by the Gulf, Mobile & Northern Railroad, into areas where the railroad conducted home-demonstration work. The railroad's president, Isaac B. Tigrett, boasted that where Wiseman "spent her time in homes along the road . . . their home life improved . . . [and] savings increased." The only woman in the nation doing such work for a railroad, Wiseman rode the train the length of its Mississippi line, stopping off in towns to conduct club work with girls and women. Her assistance to rural women was precisely what Ellen Woodward advocated in her *Mississippi Builder* series when she wrote, "The emancipation of the farm woman from the country home drudgery is noted not alone in the house and yard of each individual, but its effect is felt even further in the increased interest on her part in civic matters." Emanating from their rural homes, a "civic awakening" would "lead to the enlargement of the horizon of feminine interest" among country women. Viewing her primary duty as that of encouraging clubwomen to mesh their goals with those of the MSBD, Ellen toured the state, attending local club meetings and district conventions of the MFWC and BPW, whose Louisville chapter elected her president in 1927. Still a resident of the town, she urged the editor of the *Memphis Commercial Appeal* to print more news of her hometown. "Louisville has more building activity than perhaps any small town in north Mississippi . . . a live Rotary Club, wide awake women's clubs, enterprising citizens, many new industries and worthwhile interests."[11] Clearly, Louisville's goals were those all Mississippi towns should adopt.

In March 1927, the MSBD reconstituted the Woman's Department as the Division of Civic Welfare and Community Development, with renewed emphasis on the potential of women for "creating educational progress, social betterment [and] every form of human uplift close to the heart of every Mississippi woman." The Division's first attempt to achieve such a lofty goal was the revival of the Mississippi Products Campaign, first launched in 1921. Woodward coordinated exhibits at the state federated women's clubs convention in 1928, which featured more than a hundred products manufactured by some thirty Mississippi firms. "Are We Sold on Mississippi?" she asked clubwomen at their district convention in Louisville in November. She described the products campaign not as "a narrow, 'border bound' campaign" that would jeopardize potential markets outside the state, but rather as an educational foray to effect a better distribution of products and increase payrolls and taxable wealth.[12] Her message hit its mark, at least with the MFWC, for Blanche Ralston echoed Woodward in an article for the *Mississippi Builder*, "Mississippi women [will] do their part." Subsequently, the General Federation's 1928–1929 "Made in Mississippi" products campaign was the most comprehensive project it had ever undertaken.[13] Convinced that "women are the purchasing agents of America," making 85 percent of all consumer purchases, Ellen kept the products campaign alive during the remainder of her tenure with the development office. She remained cautious, however, about promoting a "too intensive trade-at-home consciousness" that could perpetuate interstate retaliation and trade discord.[14]

Another MSBD perennial for advertising Mississippi's economy and promoting its image was the Know Mississippi Better Train, a brainchild of Lieutenant Governor Murphree. The train made its first run in 1925, and in the summer of 1927, Ellen joined the two hundred "progressive Mississippians" in crossing six thousand miles of the West. Sweeping along, the rolling showcase carried exhibits designed to demonstrate the diversity of Mississippi's industrial and agricultural output, as well as enthusiastic passengers whose mission Ellen described as "telling the Facts about Mississippi." Alert to other possibilities for promoting Mississippi's interests, that summer she arranged for Mississippi manufacturers and distributors of playground equipment to exhibit their products at the National Recreation Congress in Memphis. "Recreation plays such a big part in the efficiency of all business," she wrote an NRC official, "and I am eager to see the day when Mississippi will stress this matter even more."[15]

Soon after taking over civic and community development for the MSBD, Ellen brought Mississippi towns into the annual Better Homes in America competition. She also kept the state involved in the contests throughout her tenure on the Board. After the 1920 census showed a decline in home ownership, Secretary of Commerce Herbert Hoover began the Better Homes endeavors in 1922 with the aid of Marie Mattingly Meloney of New York. Over the next decade, Hoover lent his prestige to raise funds for maintaining Better Homes as a voluntary association to implement his idea that home ownership was "a physical expression of individualism, of enterprise, of independence, and of freedom of spirit."[16]

Ellen fairly rhapsodized over the advantages that would accrue to those communities that participated. "Home ownership facilitates thrift . . . makes for self respect and wholesome living . . . fosters cooperative activity on the part of all members of the family [and] gives the family an incentive for sacrifice," she wrote. Most important, "the home owner puts down roots in the community." Adapting the aims of the Washington-based Better Homes in America headquarters to the small towns and rural communities of Mississippi, Ellen had her county chairwomen circulate and provide demonstration models for both the construction of new dwellings and the renovation of older structures. These women were also to emphasize property improvements, especially in sanitation, to all homedwellers whether or not they were owners.[17]

For Ellen, there was a close kinship between the BHA campaigns and the projects of her City Beautiful Association in Louisville. Sponsored by the PTA, by women's clubs and various civic organizations, the Better Homes movement was a success in Mississippi. The number of local chairwomen grew from 36 in 1924 to 633 in 1930. In 1931, Mississippi counties repeated their earlier successes, with the city of Jackson and Hinds County placing second in the "city-county class." Sixty-four agencies had cooperated to build demonstration homes in three Hinds County communities, conduct farm and home surveys, stage programs and exhibitions, and engage students from black homes in furniture-renovation projects. Governor Bilbo's selection of Ellen Woodward to head the state's delegation to President Hoover's White House Conference on Housing and Home Ownership, which convened in November 1931, was recognition of her work.[18]

As the Depression deepened and new-home construction and renovation were no longer realistic objectives, the Better Homes campaign was scaled down, becoming little more than cleaning up around homes and in public areas. As early as 1927, Ellen had advised that "cleaning up a city has much to do with bettering business conditions"; once the New Deal was underway, she saw new, if merely symbolic, possibilities for Better Homes chairwomen. "Let us further the feeling of optimism and well-being that the New Deal is bringing by cleaning up our homes and properties," she wrote her chairwomen. There were even modest opportunities for housewives to turn the annual BHA efforts toward economic recovery. In Louisville, each housewife was asked to sign a card pledging to hire an unemployed worker to do a small job around the home or yard. Ellen's office managed to keep the state Better Homes of America movement alive; in the last campaign before she left the Development Board, Mississippi communities and leaders again won national honors.[19]

Ellen's 1928 report makes credible the boast of a Development Board publicist that Ellen Woodward had "at her fingertips control over more development programs than some hardy males ever achieve in a long and eventful life." In addition to the Mississippi Products and Better Homes campaigns, she had facilitated electric power company demonstrations before women's groups, collaborated with the State Department of Education in drafting legislation for additional appropriations for vocational schools under the federal Smith-Hughes Act, and appeared before county boards of supervisors to promote interest in public health units. In addition, she promoted construction of parks, playgrounds, and libraries. While on the speaker's circuit she forwarded innumerable items of interest to Mississippi newspapers around the state. "Weighing the tangible, and sensing the intangible," she was encouraged to believe that 1928 had been a "banner year" for the Civic Welfare and Community Development office of the MSBD.[20] Her workload had grown so much that she had found it necessary to sell her Louisville home and move into an apartment in Jackson.[21]

In June 1929, when MSBD officials decided to solicit increased donor support to maintain their level of work, they asked Ellen to handle the drive.[22] At the same time, the Board hoped that restructuring would improve the relationship between the business and political factions represented on the MSBD and a scandal-ridden Bilbo administration viewed as antagonistic to the "better element" in Mississippi's public affairs. As a result, Lucius Crosby resigned as president and was succeeded by Robert B. Clark, a Tupelo banker. When Luther Folse resigned as general manager, Ellen was named executive director of the MSBD.[23] Until his death in 1948, Crosby, whose friends within the powerful lumbermen's association in Mississippi did not support Bilbo, remained Woodward's friend and financial adviser. That Ellen Woodward could survive the crossfire during the second Bilbo administration (1928–1932) is a testament to her charm and political savoir faire.[24]

Ellen's new job entailed all the duties and feverish pace of her first three years with the MSBD; as the Board shifted gears, however, new responsibilities emerged. There was renewed emphasis on establishing a traffic bureau to serve the needs of Mississippi shippers and receivers and to realign freight rates, the old bugaboo of Southern tradesmen. Also, she became an emissary of the Board to communities where new plants opened, even while others were closing for lack of business. In 1932, Ellen announced a major development. The American Tung Oil Products Corporation of New York had purchased ten thousand acres of cutover pine lands in several south Mississippi counties, with the intention of establishing a huge tung oil tree farm. Ellen inaugurated a weekly broadcast over station WJDX, in Jackson, promoting "Counties That Count in Mississippi's Progression of Progress." The state was "one great big frontier," she told the women's committee of the Mississippi Power & Light Company, "with a multitude of virgin opportunities awaiting development."[25]

Despite her optimism about Mississippi's potential for economic growth, the MSBD accomplished little between 1929 and 1933. First, there was a disastrous $4.5 million shortfall in revenue over the four-year period. The state debt in 1932 was about $50 million, and state bonds could not be sold. Between 1928 and 1932, property tax assessments dropped by $80 million. A headline in the May 1932 issue of *Literary Digest*—"One Fourth of a State Sold for Taxes"—is a staple of the Great Depression. By 1932, the unemployment rate was the highest in the state's history. How much worse matters would have been were there no State Board of Development must remain problematical. There is a larger, but also unanswerable, question of what credit is due Ellen Woodward for the optimism among economic planners at the time when Mississippi was, in the view of one historian, "engulfed in negativism—negative thinking, negative feeling, and negative action."[26] She was hardly naive; rather, she was endowed with a perpetual spirit of hope. Her hearty sense of well-being and confidence that all would work out served her well, not only in the personal crises she faced but also in the discouragement she often confronted in her jobs.

Seeking a way out of the morass that had enveloped the state, the Mississippi legislature enacted a bill drafted by the MSBD, creating a research commission. "The supreme need of Mississippi today is accurate information pertaining to economic and governmental affairs," Robert Clark, the MSBD president who would now double as chairman of the Commission, proclaimed in August 1930, when the new study began.[27] Legislative leaders took care to balance the twenty-five-member commission with Bilbo's supporters and detractors from among the state's business, banking, and farming constituencies.[28] To Ellen, the women appointees offered special promise; all three knew of her work over the past decade. Lucy Howorth had been a senior law student at the University of Mississippi when her mother Nellie Nugent Somerville was Woodward's associate in Greenville club and civic work. Now married to Joseph M. Howorth, with whom she practiced law, Lucy was a young woman with an established position among state officials. She had also chaired the State Board of Law Examiners. Mrs. Paul Gamble had been a tea-table companion of Woodward in social and club affairs in Greenville. The third member, Rosabel Foresman of Meridian, was the current state president of the Mississippi Federation of Women's Clubs and had known Woodward as early as the "Woman Builder" days of the MSBD.[29]

Ellen's casual acquaintance with Lucy Howorth, her junior by some fifteen years, blossomed into permanent friendship through a gesture on Howorth's part. When a man ambitious to become secretary of the Research Commission approached Howorth, she made no commitment to him, but instead contacted Ellen and advised her to apply.[30] Others saw the same logic in replicating the dual function of MSBD executive director and Research Commission secretary, which dictated that Clark be the chief executive officer of both the Board and the Commission. Woodward's appointment as executive secretary of the Research Commission was gratifying to women's organizations which had for years championed her as one of their own. Earlene White, an established businesswoman and former publisher of *The Woman Voter*, wrote Clark that "women of the state are behind [Woodward]."[31]

The Research Commission engaged the Institute for Governmental Research, of the Brookings Institution, which already had similar state studies underway, to conduct the comprehensive analysis of Mississippi's fiscal policies and governmental operations mandated by the legislature.[32] The corps of experts who took up residence in Jackson to direct fieldwork throughout the state included Frank Bane, whose easy working relationship with Ellen Woodward was to have significant consequences. Bane, then commissioner of public welfare in Virginia, was a man of great personal charm who possessed a true expert's knowledge of the administration of public welfare. A former associate of Louis Brownlow in reorganizing the municipal government of Knoxville, Tennessee, Bane had conducted a survey of North Carolina's welfare system similar to the one he was making of all of Mississippi's public welfare agencies and charity institutions.[33]

Bane's fieldwork included visits to the state charity hospitals, including Matty Hersee. Among the social service agency directors he interviewed was Dr. John L. Sutton, director of the Mississippi Children's Home, in Jackson. In 1928, Ellen joined the board of the Children's Home. Members of the board, which consisted of about thirty people whose service was often more honorific than actual, attended meetings as their business and public duties permitted. Although she had no professional degree or preparation in social welfare, Woodward was a keen student of the practical and political considerations that affected the delivery of social services in Mississippi. Her role as a facilitator proved beneficial to social agencies which often were meagerly supported or which needed a "friend at court." Her orientation of Frank Bane to social welfare in Mississippi made his work much easier, and his recommendations in the final report transmitted to the legislature by Robert Clark and Ellen Woodward in June 1932 had considerable bearing on Ellen's evolving awareness of the human dimensions of public welfare administration.

In the fall of 1930, shortly after the Mississippi legislature authorized the Research Commission, Ellen was one of five delegates from Mississippi to the White House Conference on Child Health and

Protection. The conference agenda was threefold: protection and stimulation of the normal child, aid to the handicapped child, and problems of the delinquent child. Penciled notes on Woodward's personal copy of the reports and program suggest that she concentrated on the Committee on Youth Outside of Home and School.[34] Whether she attended the White House conference as a representative of the Children's Home, or as executive director of the MSBD, is not clear. Whatever the case, the conference afforded another opportunity to expand her knowledge of public questions related to social welfare. Her fellow Mississippi delegates were all men with whom she would continue to work in the area of public health and welfare: Francis S. Harmon, general secretary of the national YMCA; Dr. Nathaniel B. Bond, a sociologist and dean of the University of Mississippi Graduate School; Dr. Felix Underwood, of the state health department; and Dr. Sutton, of the Children's Home. Acting in the liaison role she customarily assumed, Ellen reported her impressions of the conference to the Children's Home Society, just as she would later keep the Society apprised of Frank Bane's observations, as well as writing up the proceedings of the Mississippi Conference of Social Welfare. In addition, she was a prime mover and principal speaker on "Education and Training" at the Mississippi Follow-Up White House Conference on Child Health and Protection, held in Jackson in June 1931.[35]

Late to organize, Mississippi became the tenth southern state to form a state welfare conference. From 1928 to 1930, Woodward added to her secretaryships that of recording officer of the MCSW. Attendance at board meetings and conferences brought her in contact with top social welfare professionals. She was regularly a program participant speaking from a lay leader's perspective, as she did in her response to Frank Bane's address at the meeting of the Mississippi Conference, in 1931, held at Mississippi State College for Women. Addressing the topic, "A Pattern for State Welfare Administrators," Bane essentially outlined the recommendations that would appear in his forthcoming report to the Research Commission.[36] During a period of declining revenue resources for social services in Mississippi, Ellen retained the optimism of a "business progressive," believing that the private sector could turn around the economy of the ailing state. Her sense of reality, however, did not leave her oblivious to the unemployment and human misery that wracked Mississippi in 1930 and 1931, a consequence of the dual calamities of drought and a collapsing cotton market.[37]

Just as the state's economy began its nosedive, Ellen was drafted to handle yet another task, this one under the auspices of the MSBD. However reluctant he may have been, President Hoover finally responded to incessant demands from the states that he do something about unemployment. In October 1930, he created the President's Emergency Committee for Employment, a citizen agency charged with developing work opportunities for the jobless through the cooperative voluntarism of state and local agencies already in existence. In the opinion of one historian of the Hoover administration, PECE was little more than "a huge correspondence mill [and] a gigantic clearing house."[38] From the start, the organization, which included Frank Bane as the regional adviser for nine southern states, met with frustration. Essentially, designation of the MSBD as the agency to oversee PECE in Mississippi meant that Ellen Woodward would be the person through whom the state would clear its work.[39]

Like the earlier wartime Committee on National Defense, the President's Emergency Committee on Employment had its women's division, chaired by Alice M. Dickson with the assistance of Dr. Lillian Gilbreth, an industrial efficiency engineer and home management expert. PECE women's activities meshed well with the ongoing programs Ellen had already devised in her promotional work with women's groups in Mississippi. Dickson and Gilbreth steadily exchanged correspondence with Ellen Woodward and with Rosabel Foresman, president of the 8,000-member Mississippi federated clubs, about how to involve the MFWC, BPW, and YWCA in the voluntary creation of jobs. Foresman, however, did not know that Dickson's committee had named her to the Mississippi women's committee for PECE until she read it in the newspaper. Once matters were clarified, both Foresman and Woodward began to receive notices of nationwide radio broadcasts by women's organizations, urging clubwomen to maintain employment levels by retaining their household help or to stimulate employment by whatever methods they could think of. Pamphlets on such topics as "Care and Repair of the Home" were tailor-made for distribution to local leaders of the Better Homes campaign, then at its peak operating level in the state.[40]

General dissatisfaction with Hoover's views on relief, as well as the voluntary character of PECE, led to resignations among the top echelon in Washington and reconstitution of the committee as the President's Organization on Unemployment Relief.[41] Ellen remained on the Mississippi POUR committee until January 1932, when POUR virtually expired in Mississippi and Governor Bilbo left office. As of

May, the new governor, Martin S. (Mike) Conner, had taken no action to continue the committee. Ellen's final report to Washington, dated June 1932, closed the chapter on POUR in Mississippi; but, as secretary to the MSBD, she volunteered "to render any further assistance" that could be useful.[42]

It is difficult to ascertain what relief the PECE/POUR operation in Mississippi actually extended to those who were jobless and needy. As they were almost everywhere else, PECE and POUR were little more than paper administrations in Mississippi. One outcome is apparent, though: Ellen Woodward gained a practical lesson in the potential of made-work projects for coping with unemployment. POUR had encouraged no central direction from Washington, and the meager results of its reliance on local practices to stimulate recovery could not have gone unnoticed by anyone who participated in the administration of Hoover-style relief. Pamphlets such as *Diversified Community Employment Programs*, *Home Gardens for Employment and Food*, and *Five 'Made Work' Programs* crossed Ellen's desk on their way to the women's clubs and Better Homes leaders. She also had access to material describing local relief efforts elsewhere in the nation such as the short-term work unit during the winter of 1930–1931, which paid a hundred women in Wilmington, Delaware, thirty-five cents an hour to manufacture supplies for area hospitals. Operated for only a week, the program nevertheless provided income to a few beneficiaries that helped them stave off a sheriff's sale.[43] Apparently no funds were available in Mississippi for women's relief work, but it was during the course of PECE/POUR that Ellen recommended to her BHA chairwomen that housewives create temporary jobs for the unemployed in home renovation and landscape improvement.

Thad Holt, Frank Bane's successor as Southern regional adviser for PECE, informed his Washington chiefs in February 1931 that conditions in Mississippi were worse than at any time since the Civil War.[44] As the Depression decade began, Mississippi alone accounted for one-tenth of all the nation's farm tenancy; cotton prices slumped to six cents a pound in 1931, bottoming at four cents in 1932. With a state government in bankruptcy, Mississippi welcomed the federal funds that finally began to trickle down in 1932.[45]

Before POUR could be reinstated in the state, it had ended at the national level for all practical purposes and its duties had been subsumed by the Reconstruction Finance Corporation, which had been allotted $300 million under the Emergency Relief and Construction Act of 1932 for loans to states for relief and public works projects.

Prior to any attempt to obtain funds through the new source, Governor Conner, in August 1932, appointed a twenty-six-member advisory committee to study Mississippi's needs. Not unexpectedly, among the private citizens and public officials comprising the board were Ellen Woodward and Rosabel Foresman. Charged with the task of surveying needs in all eighty-two counties for direct relief and employment, the committee forwarded to Governor Conner a report that became the basis of his request for funds to see Mississippi through the year. When told that $892,000 would be forthcoming only on condition that he name an emergency relief committee whose work would be subject to review by the Reconstruction Finance Corporation, Conner, in November 1932, created Mississippi's first State Board of Public Welfare. To no one's surprise, Ellen Woodward was the lone female member of the Board. Ironically, on the same day Conner appointed the Board, the Federated Women's Clubs adopted a resolution asking the legislature to create a welfare board such as that recommended in the Brookings Institution report (by 1927, every Southern state except Mississippi had established some kind of state welfare system).[46]

There was yet another proviso that Conner had to accept before additional federal money would flow to his state. RFC officials insisted that the State Board of Public Welfare accept an administrator from outside the state to supervise establishment of an emergency relief organization. That person turned out to be Aubrey Willis Williams, a dedicated Alabamian already familiar to local officials from his management of Red Cross relief activities in Mississippi during the 1931–1932 drought. Williams arrived in Jackson in November 1932 to become temporary head of the Emergency Relief Administration (ERA). When he left the next month, Mississippi had an efficient setup functioning under his successor, George B. Power, a former clerk of the Mississippi House of Representatives. It was on Frank Bane's recommendation that Williams had been named a consultant to the RFC Relief Loans Division. Thus matters related to relief and welfare placed both Bane and Williams in Ellen Woodward's office at the Development Board during 1931 and 1932.[47]

Again, Ellen's duties with the new State Board of Public Welfare brought her in frequent conferences with Dr. Underwood and Dr. Sutton, as well as State Superintendent of Education Willard F. Bond, R. E. Kennington, a Jackson merchant, Mississippi American Federation of Labor leader Holt Ross, and Lamont Rowlands, a Picayune lumberman, state YMCA president, and the person widely believed to be Hoover's Republican representative in the state. This mix of people represented diverse interests that came to be recognized in the allocation of relief funds and the creation of work projects. The Board drew up contracts with municipal and county relief administrators designed to control the distribution of scant funds which, in the end, assisted about a third of all families in the state.[48] Between November 1932 and June 1933, the State Board of Public Welfare disbursed $3.6 million; by comparison, Alabama received less than $3 million and Louisiana just over $7.6 million. The Board's difficulties in countermanding the time-honored, yet cumbersome, local control of relief made evident the necessity of state-directed relief efforts.[49] Ellen Woodward's function in recording the minutes of the State Board of Public Welfare probably left her with a better grasp than anyone else of what had transpired and served to clarify for her relief administration problems and procedures.

"Politics as usual" absorbed Woodward's attention from 1928 to 1932. Precluded by her employment with the MSBD from playing a visible role in the Mississippi Democratic party's factional disputes, and too astute to do so anyway, Ellen was not proscribed from presidential politics. Ever since she had come to Jackson in 1924, she had moved among the state's power elite. In a state where a political woman was a rarity, Ellen Woodward was trusted by the clique that ran the state. Not personally involved in an election since her own in 1925, she still managed to win a spot as a delegate-at-large to the national convention in 1928, casting her vote for Mississippi's Senator Pat Harrison on the contested first ballot.[50]

Ellen supported the nominee, New York Governor Alfred E. Smith, in Mississippi (unlike Belle Kearney, vice president of the National Women's Democratic Law Enforcement League, who left Houston vowing to go home and organize Mississippi women against Smith). She did not, however, make the all-out effort needed to rally the state's women for Smith that she would later make for Franklin D. Roosevelt—probably because she respected the opposition among women's groups to a "wet" candidate (and probably because she was sensitive to Smith's Catholicism, a subject she discreetly left alone). Moreover, she was acutely aware of the popular appeal among Southern churchwomen of the Republican party's stand on prohibition and the stability of the home. Two contemporary analysts of the campaign wrote that it "seemed hopeless to expect any general feminine support for the Democratic candidate."[51]

Observers of the 1928 presidential conventions, particularly women in the press corps, were more effusive about the participation of women in the deliberations than later historians have found justifiable.[52] Glenda Morrison has concluded that women had little impact at the Houston convention, but she does acknowledge that those newspapermen who gave little attention to the role of women delegates failed to note those "who were slowing earning the right to be considered party leaders."[53] Some progress was made in Houston, however, where women comprised 14 percent of the delegates and won more convention committee assignments than at any prior quadrennial party gathering. Ellen Woodward's modest assignment was to the committee to "notify" Arkansas Senator Joseph T. Robinson of his nomination as vice president. Even though the trip to Hot Springs for the official ceremony was perfunctory, it did give Ellen her first opportunity to associate with Democratic women from outside her home state. Among the women she met in Houston was Nellie Tayloe Ross, a former Wyoming governor and director of women's activities within the Democratic party, whose own name had been placed in nomination for the vice presidency. From August 1928 to February 1934, Ross, a vice chairman of the Democratic National Committee, organized the women of the party for most of their day-to-day activities.[54]

When New York Governor Franklin Roosevelt wrote party leaders after the Democratic debacle of 1928, Ellen Woodward was among those he contacted. Once the Roosevelt boom was underway, Mary W. (Molly) Dewson, director of national campaigns for the Women's Division of the Democratic party, designated Ellen as organizer of Mississippi women for Roosevelt. When Dewson asked Woodward's opinion about particular issues that might interest a women's political club in Mississippi, apart from those that drew the attention of men, Ellen advised her that better results would flow from clubs composed of both sexes. Once women had acquired organizing skills, she added, they could "go out and form separate clubs."[55]

When a team of fundraisers for Roosevelt (unauthorized by his managers, however) appeared in Jackson, Ellen warned Senator Harrison that these free-lancers were "such types that would drive people away." She described an ill-planned dinner at the Edwards Hotel as "the poorest arranged affair I ever attended." She told Senator Harrison, "I am so eager to see Governor Roosevelt nominated on the first ballot." In March, she wrote Roosevelt of her advocacy of his nomination and of her contact with Elizabeth Smith Edwards, chairman of the National Committee of One Thousand Progressive and Democratic Women. She had expressed herself "very freely" to both Mississippi senators, she wrote Roosevelt, who replied that he welcomed her "observations and comments" about his Mississippi prospects. In the interim, as she proposed to Daisy McLaurin Stevens, Mississippi's Democratic national committeewoman, a woman from each locality should be enlisted to "increase and crystalize" sentiment for Roosevelt, and Woodward recommended that the "psychological moment to talk about Roosevelt" was just before the county conventions met in April. After Ellen confided to Dewson that the Mississippi women Dewson thought could be assembled for a preconvention conference were "luke warm" and "not inclined to be very active," she consulted other Roosevelt supporters, who concurred that the best strategy was that all of them write pro-Roosevelt letters to their friends in each county.[56]

When Daisy Stevens declined to seek reelection as committeewoman, state convention delegates named Ellen as her successor.[57] She attended the national convention in Chicago as an observer, along with the new committeeman, Louis Jiggitts. Convention activities gave her an opportunity to become acquainted with other Democratic women, including Molly Dewson; and she was among the women for Roosevelt who spoke over a national radio network from Chicago. Ellen also gained visibility as a vice president-at-large of the Southern Women's National Democratic Organization.[58]

Between convention and election, Ellen threw herself into Roosevelt's presidential campaign. The state Democratic executive committee that met in July vested management of the national campaign in Mississippi in the state chairman, committeeman, and committeewoman.[59] In August, Ellen met with Senator Harrison and the state Democratic committee to map strategy. To Dewson, they reported "harmony and unanimity," as well as a lack of funds. Ellen recruited as many women leaders as she could to be county chairwomen of the Mississippi women's campaign, and drew up plans for a statewide rally of the women, to be held on 11 October. The first gathering of its kind in the state, the rally resulted in the organization of women in each county down to the precinct level. Ellen enlisted the legislative wives she knew well, among them Lena Sillers and Nell Massey Bailey. She also drafted her sister, Belle Fair, and Mrs. John A. Clark in Kemper County (one day Ellen's successor as state committeewoman). Lucy Howorth, now representing Hinds County in the legislature, became chairwoman of the women speaker's bureau, while her husband, Joseph, headed the Young Democrats in Mississippi.[60]

In appointing women county leaders, Woodward invoked the name of Mrs. Franklin D. Roosevelt to drive home the importance of the "Stay-at-Home" women's vote. "I repeat," she wrote, "the woman vote will be a large factor in electing a Democrat president. Mississippi women must not fail." The women she directed for Roosevelt distributed literature, helped raise county quotas toward financial pledges, assisted Young Democrats in improving their organizations, and formed motor pools to take voters to the polls. Ellen wrote Molly Dewson of her tactic to involve churchwomen as county leaders in order to deflect the opposition to Roosevelt of "some of the preachers and WCTU's [who] are doing all they can to block the vote." She was now corresponding with Eleanor Roosevelt, who wanted particularly to target women in areas with a record of opposing Roosevelt.[61]

As soon as Roosevelt's victory was certain, rumors were rife that jobs were to be had in Mississippi—not only in federal courthouses and post offices and as customs collectors, but also in the myriad agencies of Washington. The day after the election, Ellen and Louis Jiggitts conferred, later cautioning members of Mississippi's congressional delegation not to promise jobs before consulting party leaders. She chided Senator Hubert D. Stephens that some of the very people who boasted of having the senator's endorsement for a post in the Democratic administration had done "nothing toward the campaign, either state or national."[62]

The Hoover interregnum was a feverish time. Ellen's post-election responsibilities swelled when James A. Farley, Roosevelt's campaign manager, asked her to be the party's director of finance for Mississippi, a dubious honor since it entailed raising $15,000 (the state's quota toward paying off the Democratic party's deficit). To achieve this goal, Ellen had to apportion the sum among numerous federal officeholders, including members of Congress. She consented to do the job but confided to the chairman of the Democratic executive committee in Mississippi that the assignment might "kill me politically in Mississippi but I will at least have helped the Party."[63] To the contrary, the work furnished Jim Farley and Molly Dewson with yet another reason to remember the name Ellen Woodward.

In the seven years between her arrival in Jackson to inaugurate a new women's program for the Mississippi State Board of Development and her campaign among Mississippi women in 1932, Ellen Woodward had demonstrated a growing ease and expertise in working with professionals in the field of social services. There were signs, too, that she had the makings of a first-rate public administrator. At the same time, she had become aware of the social and economic problems that

Belle Sullivan Fair (about 1932) was Ellen's oldest sister and her successor in the leadership of Better Homes in America and Democratic women's work in Winston County, Mississippi (Courtesy Davis L. Fair, Jr.)

burdened Mississippi; by 1932, she was convinced that the solutions to the problems lay not with the states but with the federal government. Until 1932, Ellen had performed her work with the MSBD and the clubwomen of the state with virtually no contact with women in neighboring states who were doing similar work or who shared her concerns. Later she would meet Southern women who had risen from "pedestal to politics." Anne Firor Scott has described their motivation as "complex," but believes they were driven by two desires, "to assert themselves as individual human beings . . . and to improve the world in which they lived."[64]

There is no indication, however, that Ellen had any exchanges with other men or women of the South outside Mississippi. Whatever isolation she may have sensed ended when the Brookings team arrived in Mississippi in 1931 and federal relief officials came in 1932. Of equal significance for Ellen's future was her introduction in 1932 to national leaders of the Democratic party, including Franklin Roosevelt.

The political scientist Herman C. Nixon pointed out in 1931 that, while the political philosophy of the business class of the New South was broad enough to promote progress in highways, education, and health, it embraced no "comprehensive challenge to laissez faire ideas in the sphere of relationship between capital and labor."[65] There is scant evidence that Ellen Woodward and the clubwomen of Mississippi adopted a stand for industrial reform that would benefit working women other than the federated club's faint call for a factory inspector. At some point, Ellen Woodward became a member of the National Consumers' League; but no correspondence remains in her papers to indicate that NCL leaders ever attempted to recruit her in their crusade for the better wages and more humane hours advocated by the Consumers' League and its allies in the Women's Bureau and the Women's Trade Union League. In a study of women in Mississippi, the Bureau found that white working women averaged $8.60 in weekly wages at jobs where sanitation standards also lagged.[66] When Lucy Randolph Mason, general secretary of the YMCA, surveyed women workers in the South for the NCL in 1931, she noted that Mississippi's Bureau of Industrial Hygiene and Factory Inspection employed only two persons and operated on an annual appropriation of $6,000. Only Florida ranked lower among the fourteen Southern states. She cited Mississippi as having no law prohibiting night work and found so many exemptions to the sixty-hour ceiling to a woman's workweek that enforcement of the limitation was difficult.[67]

Yet, according to the 1930 census, there were only 7,371 women in Mississippi industries, a figure that included those in cafes, bakeries, and department stores. Among the fourteen states (Mason included West Virginia, Oklahoma, and Kentucky), only Arkansas had fewer women in industry than Mississippi due to the fact that textile production was not extensive in either state.[68] Woodward was well aware that the preponderance of working women in Mississippi worked in agriculture and lived in grinding poverty. From her base in Winston County, she had more extensive contact with farm women than with factory women and knew of their deprivations. That knowledge accounts for the fact that she later weighed a federal work program heavily toward jobs suitable for unskilled women. After Lucy Randolph Mason became general secretary of the National Consumers' League, she invited Woodward to serve on a Southern committee of the NCL.[69] That nothing seems to have come of that affiliation is probably because Ellen left Mississippi for Washington in August 1933.

CHAPTER 3

This New Federal Relief: 1933–1935

The Mississippi State Board of Development warmly greeted Roosevelt's New Deal. Six months into the new administration, Ellen Woodward left Mississippi for a job with the mammoth relief administration authorized in May 1933. A virtual stranger to the Washington of the 1930s, she nevertheless established her credentials with both administration figures and the circle of women who looked to Eleanor Roosevelt for counsel and collaboration. By mid-1935, Woodward had constructed a jobs program for women in two successive works agencies, the Federal Emergency Relief Administration and the Civil Works Administration. Despite the frustrations in maintaining work relief for women on an equitable basis with that for men, the staff she assembled and the projects they devised during the formative stages of federal relief would be in place when the more ambitious Works Progress Administration was inaugurated in July 1935.

Woodward rode the special train to Washington that carried two hundred Mississippians to Roosevelt's inaugural on 4 March 1933. The Washington ceremonies aside, she went on to New York City, where Bessie and Hamilton Dutcher had moved. While in the city, Woodward made a radio broadcast touting investment opportunities in Mississippi.[1] She was soon selling New Deal agricultural and industrial solutions to Mississippi cotton farmers and small businessmen. Through a flyer heralding "Cotton Contract Week," she notified chambers of commerce and civic clubs that Mississippi growers must sign agreements to reduce the crop for 1933 by 1,209,000 acres. "The 'New Deal' is on now for Mississippi and it is wholly up to us whether we want it or not," she told the state's business leaders. Next, Woodward turned her attention to merchants, to whom she issued a round of letters urging use of the "Blue Eagle" as a symbol of compliance with the codes of the National Recovery Administration. Should they fail to abide voluntarily by the business practices detailed in NRA codes, she warned, women consumers of the state would stage boycotts.[2]

The threat never materialized. Most of the state's producers and retailers fell in line. But the proposed buyers' strike had the potential to do merchants harm because clubwomen heartily responded to Woodward's call for cooperation. The Jackson chapter of the BPW resolved "to assist loyally and patriotically" in the NRA crusade; the "Blue Eagle" won the endorsement also of the PTA, the Jackson garden clubs, the Altrusas, the Junior Auxiliary, and even the United Daughters of the Confederacy and the various church missionary societies.[3] The state president of the Mississippi federated clubs boasted that her hometown of Jackson had been among the first cities in the nation to place "the Blue Eagle in the homes of the city." One of Woodward's last functions while at the helm of the Mississippi State Board of Development was to organize a statewide NRA rally. At the rally, she assured the president of the federated clubs that the MSBD was "bending every effort to build strong public sentiment for . . . your great recovery program."[4]

Thanks to having been at the 1928 and 1932 Democratic conventions and to her newly acquired stature as state committeewoman, for the first time she was drawn into the circle of Northeastern and Midwestern Democratic women who formed the leadership core of the Women's Division. Election year 1932 was a propitious time for sharing confidences on a strategy to win for women the federal jobs from which they had long been excluded. During election week, Nellie Tayloe Ross, who probably had an eye on an important post for herself, invited Woodward to join a movement to "[crystallize] into permanent organization the new woman leadership." After the November victory, she began to hear from women promoting Ross and Frances Perkins, New York state's industrial commissioner, to head the Cabinet Interior and Labor departments, respectively; Woodward assured each petitioner that she endorsed both women.[5]

As it turned out, Perkins got the appointment to Labor, but Ross had to be content with the directorship of the U.S. Mint. Closer to home, Woodward approached the Mississippi congressional delegation to have women loyal to Roosevelt appointed to federal jobs in the state. She was following the heed of Mary Williams Dewson, whose first two initials, the journalist Bess Furman joked, stood for "More Women." Dewson did not need to remind Woodward of the obvious, that it would enhance the position of committeewomen to "have a certain amount of patronage go through [their] hands." The day after the election, Woodward and Louis Jiggitts discussed ways to accomplish this objective. Woodward told Molly Dewson that she found Senator Harrison amenable to women appointees. By mid-June, however, despite her recommendations, only one woman who had assisted in the campaign had been given a job in Mississippi—and that as a postmistress. Convinced that "women raised most of the money during the campaign and did the larger part of the work," she hoped Dewson would use her influence to help place twenty-three women whose names had been compiled by Woodward and her friend, Lucy Howorth.[6]

Whether Woodward knew that she was ranked on Molly Dewson's patronage list in the "Class C" category ("Very desirable recognition") and that Dewson had determined that she be given "some executive position" simply cannot be known through extant records. In late July, Dewson reminded Postmaster General James A. Farley that Woodward was among the women whom she had been "keeping [his] eye on since inauguration."[7]

Soon after creation of the Federal Emergency Relief Administration, Harry L. Hopkins arrived in Washington to take charge of the giant relief operation. Encouraged by Eleanor Roosevelt, Hopkins, soon dubbed the "Czar of Relief," conceded that FERA should have a women's program as soon as a suitable division head could be found. Even without prompting from the First Lady, Hopkins knew that women were being pushed aside by state relief officials. Soon after Hopkins left for Washington, a sympathetic FERA director in New York City had written that it was "just plain fierce the way [women] are being passed around in this town." Having agreed to add a top-level assistant, Hopkins was nevertheless nervous about the appointment and sought advice from his old friend, Frank Bane, by then director of the American Public Welfare Administration. Hopkins told Bane that he did not want a social worker to head the women's division; instead, he wanted a woman "who was a good organizer and operator," one who could deal with the congressional and business critics certain to contest federal relief.[8]

Bane immediately replied that he knew a woman in Mississippi who met all Hopkins's criteria. She was politically astute and a competent administrator, and she had humane and progressive ideas regarding social betterment, he told Hopkins. Hopkins asked Bane to have Woodward come to Washington as soon as possible to discuss the work. But there were other conditions to be met—senatorial courtesy, for instance, not to mention Molly Dewson's approval. Senator Harrison's consent came quickly. "Mrs. Woodward excellent material. I have discussed [the] matter with her," he telegraphed Hopkins. Dewson was not won over as easily. Fearing that Ellen Woodward was a "bit of southern fluff," she had in mind a lesser position for Woodward. The "executive" position she had in mind for Woodward was not one so important as the FERA post. Finally convinced by Woodward supporters that Woodward was capable of doing the work, Dewson gave in. Crucial to this capitulation were the arguments of Sue Shelton White in a late-night conference with Dewson. A Tennessee suffragist and Nellie Tayloe Ross's assistant in Democratic women's work, White was the ablest of all the women who served with Dewson in the campaign of 1932. She punctuated her defense of Ellen Woodward with the argument that it was essential for Southern women to be given a share of Democratic patronage.[9]

Certainly important was the backing Woodward received from women leaders in the Democratic National Committee. Both political journalists and critics of the administration attributed Woodward's appointment to the political pull of her mentor, Senator Harrison. But Lucy Howorth, privy to the circumstances of the Woodward appointment, believed that the job went to Woodward because "Frank Bane liked the way Ellen Woodward got things done." As a Southerner, Woodward may have had added appeal to Hopkins, who, according to one student of New Deal relief, had "a remarkable understanding for the special needs of this neglected region."[10] Hopkins probably consulted Aubrey Williams, now his chief assistant administrator at FERA, about the latter's impressions of Woodward based on his association with her in Mississippi relief work in late 1932. On 26 August 1933, Williams accompanied Hopkins to Jackson to pay what was reported as a routine visit to the state relief headquarters. It was then that Hopkins announced that Ellen Woodward would become director of the new Women's Division of the FERA. Publicity about the appointment gave no hint that Hopkins had already contacted MSBD executive Robert Clark and negotiated a six-month leave of absence for Woodward because of her initial reluctance to leave Mississippi. Two days after the Hopkins visit to Jackson, Woodward left the state to assume her duties. She never again worked or lived in Mississippi, although she always maintained her identity with the state, once chiding a writer who referred to her as a "former Mississippian": "I want to assure you first that I am a Mississippian and not a former Mississippian."[11]

Woodward assessed the early days of the women's work program as starting "from scratch." She began work with only a secretary and two desks in an office shared with the director of the FERA transient program. Hopkins's office was no better. ("Good Lord, it's terrible," the journalist Ernie Pyle wrote.)[12] Woodward devoted her early weeks to orienting herself to other federal agencies and bureaus directed by women and committed to their welfare. She conferred with Katharine Lenroot, of the Children's Bureau; Louise Stanley, of the Agriculture Department's Bureau of Home Economics; and Mary Anderson of the Women's Bureau in the Department of Labor. Her friend, May Thompson Evans, recalled that Woodward had conferred with Frances Perkins "as no one had every done so thoroughly." Workdays that extended long into the night were devoted to studying the complex machinery of FERA and assembling a staff of assistants and technical consultants. When Harry Hopkins officially notified each state relief head on 10 October of the new Women's Division, he instructed each to appoint a qualified woman who was to devote full time to a women's program. They were to be persons knowledgeable about social and civic agencies, employment services, and the status of current relief programs. Moreover, there were unwritten pragmatic considerations. For example, the appointees must be loyal to the purposes of the New Deal (this caution did not necessarily exclude Republican women, however). Both Eleanor Roosevelt and Molly Dewson submitted names to a grateful Woodward. Dewson added this note to one of her suggestions: "I see that I am going to get great pleasure [out] of our association."[13]

It would be difficult to overstate Eleanor Roosevelt's role in Ellen Woodward's administration of women's work relief. Throughout the five years that Woodward ran the Women's Division, the First Lady was adviser, first sponsor, first critic, and first official friend to her. In the first of Mrs. Roosevelt's monthly series for the *Woman's Home Companion*, she invited women to tell her "about the particular problems which puzzle or sadden you." Thousands of letters—more than 300,000 by the end of 1933—flooded her desk creating a ground-swell that confirmed the need for a comprehensive work program for women.[14] The pleas came from single women unable to support themselves or their dependents, from married women who were the only able-bodied breadwinners in their families, from widows and from mothers whose children were ill or disabled. The letters bore the names of women who until 1933 had been lost in the numerous surveys of unemployed or underemployed women. The Women's Bureau, the source of most of these surveys, had determined in

January 1931 that 2 million women were unemployed, or 18.9 percent of all women once gainfully employed.[15]

Woodward, too had a special feeling for another class of women, those "who at one time had money and gave unstintingly to every worthy cause." "We have many people like that in Mississippi," she told the state director there. Writing to Eleanor Roosevelt about the development of work for whitecollar women in the District of Columbia, Woodward said: "I think there are many cultured, refined, educated women here in the District who are actually destitute, but whose pride makes them reluctant to ask for the bare necessities of life." The middle- to upperclass women whose incomes had vanished and whose savings were depleted, she pointed out, had no preparation for placement in one of the projects intended for professionals; yet they could not accommodate themselves to the training programs for unskilled bluecollar occupations. When Woodward transmitted to a local caseworker a moving letter to Eleanor Roosevelt from an elderly woman, she asked that the woman's problems be held confidential because "her pride must not be hurt."[16]

Woodward read the grim studies that issued from the Women's Bureau, as well as a sizable portion of Eleanor Roosevelt's mail forwarded to the Women's Division. In October 1933, she wrestled with the daunting task of coordinating into national projects the often slipshod, local projects and neglected women's work activities administered by state offices of the Emergency Relief Administration that had only 50,000 women at work when her division began. Another task consisted of devising expansive and innovative new projects. To accommodate these tasks, Eleanor Roosevelt's office conceived the idea of a "White House Conference on the Emergency Needs of Women," which would focus the attention of leaders of women's organizations and social agencies on the Women's Division and invite their cooperation.[17]

Woodward—working through Edith Helm, Eleanor Roosevelt's secretary—and her new assistant, Dr. Chloe Owings, sent telegrams to national club presidents, executive directors of private charities, heads of government bureaus whose functions affected women, and every congresswoman. Quickly planned and executed, the conference on 20 November 1933 proved to be a stimulating forum where some forty participants exchanged information on the difficulties women faced in finding work in the private sector. Hopkins estimated that 300,000 to 400,000 women, many of them homeless, required immediate assistance and basic "decent attention." More important, they needed to be put to work in imaginative, practical, and socially constructive jobs that would be acceptable to the community. With his characteristic "do it quickly" optimism, Hopkins told the conference that within twenty-five days up to 400,000 women could be put to work.[18] Woodward pointed to the gravity of the problem and to the constraints that architects of a women's work-relief program faced. Women could not be employed on construction projects that had the potential for creating work for thousands of men. Nor could they work on projects that competed with the private sector. Eleanor Roosevelt added another caveat. Unlike men, women could not be expected to leave their families and dependents to accept employment; they would have to work in their own communities. Although it would be much more difficult to create a half-million jobs for women than 4 million jobs for men, she insisted that relief administrators be told to allocate jobs and funds to women.[19]

An experienced hand at moderating such forums, Ellen Woodward was able to guide the audience in proposing several activities for women. Rose Schneiderman, head of the Women's Trade Union League, suggested farm camps for women in the sewing trades who had been idled. Julia Wright Merrill, of the American Library Association, inquired about work for librarians; and Geline Bowman, national president of the BPW, recommended institutional service projects for women. Mary La Dame, of the Department of Labor, offered the idea of providing housekeeping services for public buildings; while Frances Zuill, of the American Home Economics Association, proposed that dietitians be employed in public institutions.[20] And so the ideas ran. If the conference produced no truly novel ideas, it did reenforce the "acquired convictions" that leaders of organized women's groups shared regarding responsibilities for the welfare of their sex. That the White House was the setting for their dialogue was significant. In her closing remarks, Woodward conveyed a spirit of optimism: "We have never had a greater opportunity for women to do something for women."[21]

Woodward labeled her own files on the conference, "Where the Women's Division was born." An immediate result of this birth was Woodward's suggestion to hold similar conferences in fifteen states, where women leaders suggested projects, created advisory committees, and devised methods of monitoring the level of women's work activities in the male-dominated ERAs. Clearly, women hit their mark in Mississippi, for George Power complained to an FERA field representative that clubwomen were "bombarding his office with silly reports." When the Massachusetts ERA chief told the ombundswomen that there were insufficient funds for a women's program, Eleanor Roosevelt intervened and promptly got results. The day after Mrs. Roosevelt advised her to issue a specific work order, Woodward was able to report to the White House that her field representative in Boston now found no "confusion" over the eligibility of women for work assignments.[22]

The urgency of the Conference was intensified by a new direction taken by the Roosevelt administration, which threatened the women's program almost before Woodward's work began. By an executive order issued on 8 November 1933, FDR created the Civil Works Administration. Over the coming winter, the CWA would provide 4 million jobs intended for workers employed on large-scale public works and related activities. Meeting with other FERA administrators at the old Powhatan Hotel over a weekend in early November and in Hopkins's unheated office to thrash out the CWA program, Woodward could see that the emphasis on civil works might well jeopardize her fledgling division.[23]

Only one communication under the imprimatur of FERA had gone from Woodward to her state directors before bulletins from the Women's Division began carrying the heading of the CWA. "W-l," the first of sixty-seven procedural memos that flowed from Woodward's office under the FERA and CWA was dated 14 November 1933. It delineated twenty-three work activities for registered nurses alone and twenty-eight for unemployed librarians and detailed a plethora of programs already in operation for other professional women. The directives advised that it was imperative to utilize the volunteer services of national women's organizations "to mobilize women's inherent capacities for community housekeeping." Based on her past experience, Woodward counted upon volunteers to assist in securing places and equipment for the sewing rooms, nursery schools, canning centers, and other work. Speaking from Warm Springs, Georgia, a month later, Eleanor Roosevelt, another veteran of the club movement, congratulated organized women for their demonstrated cooperation.[24]

The Women's Division needed all the help it could muster to focus attention upon the needs of jobless women. There were structural biases against the women's program inherent in the CWA setup that state ERA heads, now deputized as CWA directors, were quick to grasp. Wages for the Civil Works Service (CWS) component of the CWA, created to care for women and whitecollar workers, were to be financed entirely from remaining relief funds granted to states under the FERA and disbursed almost entirely at the discretion of the state CWA administrators. On the other hand, CWA projects would draw on the $400 million appropriated to that agency.[25]

Thus, CWS workers (mostly women) were subjected to the "means test" that had been required of job applicants under the FERA to show proof of need and be drawn only from the rolls of relief applicants certified as needy by local relief interviewers. Woodward received numerous reports, such as the one from Gertrude Martinez, Nevada's women's work director, that highly trained women were willing to do menial work at low wages, but that they "beg us daily not to ask them to register on direct relief."[26] There was an equally insidious and discriminatory angle in the wage structure: CWA workers drew pay protected by minimum scales, amounting to $1 an hour, while CWS workers were paid the prevailing wage in each locality, provided it did not fall below the FERA minimum wage of 30 cents an hour.[27] Because of the double standards of CWA and CWS regulations, Woodward's women's program was both hampered and misunderstood. Since CWA money, siphoned as it was from appropriations for the Public Works Administration, could be used only for public works and federal projects, it took considerable ingenuity and aggressiveness on the part of the Women's Division to create jobs for women on CWA construction projects so they could draw the higher CWA wages. Woodward managed to have assigned to CWA projects some clerical workers, statisticians, auxiliary personnel (such as nurses), and even unskilled day laborers. She also sought out women engineers for the CWA, but the pool from which to draw was low.[28]

Complaints flowed in to Washington regardless of how well intentioned the Women's Division was to see that women received decent wages. Because CWA public-works jobs paid more than CWS projects or were open to them where service projects were not available, many women were willing to join road and school construction crews as "landscapers," go into the woods to chop trees, or hew fence posts. Rebutting charges that such jobs were unsuitable for women, Woodward regretted that "a calamitous state of affairs" existed but declared that there were "women who will work wherever work is [and] who will search out jobs and even create them." Criticism arose from varying perceptions about what "woman's work" properly should be. A women's project leader from North Carolina, who knew women who had spent "weary days at such back-breaking work as plowing, chopping wood, scrubbing floors, dragging babies around, or bending over a wash tub for hours on end," was surprised to learn that CWA men directors thought furniture-making activities too strenuous for women. One county supervisor in Mississippi complained to Woodward that the state CWA chief had determined that beautification projects which called for raking were "too hard for women," that he would approve only projects "where the work is light, such as washing windows, and scrubbing floors and walls" and for which, he could have added, the CWS security wage was lower.[29]

Because pay scales were pegged to the source of funds (that is, PWA for CWA workers and FERA residual funds for CWS employees), women who performed similar tasks were often paid at varying rates. Nurses were perplexed when those who cared for CWA construction workers received more than those assigned to CWS county health departments. Similarly, the income of a cook depended on whether she prepared meals for construction workers (CWA) or for school lunchrooms and nurseries (CWS). Helen Hill Weed, of the National Woman's Party and one of the sharpest critics of the CWA, wondered why women with dependents received only 30 cents an hour while unmarried men received 50 cents an hour for the same kind of work.[30] Woodward never managed to win from Hopkins concessions that would protect women by setting separate quotas for their employment under the CWA; as a result, CWA administrators often barred women from payrolls.

In most states, the consequent bureaucracy of regulations resulted in harsh discrimination against women, as well as mitigating against the development of meaningful CWA-CWS programs for women. Harry Hopkins may well have been earnest in asserting that as many as 400,000 women would soon be at work, but his prediction proved false. When, in November 1933, Woodward convinced him that women were being shortchanged, Hopkins instructed state directors to "pay particular attention that women are employed wherever possible." At the same time that Woodward was pressing CWA associates in Washington for the exact amount of funds she could count on to run her division, her White House ally was urging Hopkins to reclassify CWA jobs by skills without regard to sex. When the First Lady brought Woodward to her weekly press conference, to focus their attention on the women's program, Mrs. Roosevelt took the stage to question pay scales and wage classifications that allowed the extremes of 30 cents an hour for women and $1 for men.[31]

Woodward did not have to inform Eleanor Roosevelt (although she did) that opportunities for women were curtailed under the CWA. Women from all over the country wrote letters to the White House.

"I should like to know why it is that men can be placed so easily and not women," wrote one. Another said: "I understand that the CWA cannot help unemployed girls." An Indiana woman asked: "Is there a place for us anywhere in America?" In addition, state directors of CWA-CWS projects complained about the delay of state offices in initiating projects for women and of the short shrift they received in requesting space. Mary Jean Simpson in Vermont went to work in a "small cloakroom in the capitol with one battered typewriter and a mountain of FERA directives." A Mississippi county director protested that for three weeks her desk had consisted only of "a big manilla envelope carried under her arm." She had been given no office space because, she supposed, it "was thought dangerous for a woman to be [found] around the CWA headquarters."[32]

The pattern of complaints from most states ran in the same vein. Aware that the Civil Works Administration was intended for public works, directors of state and county work relief were determined to procure every possible public improvement. At the same time, local civic groups wanted to build schools, roads, airports, and sewer lines. Most important, these groups were willing to "sponsor" such projects. Sponsorship stipulations, which had begun under the FERA and remained central to all subsequent federal work relief, hampered the women's program more than any other regulation. Federal appropriations were only for wages and designated construction materials; project costs such as rent, utilities, and furnishings had to be met through appropriations from state or local governmental units or public agencies, or by contributions from private groups such as civic organizations or women's clubs. Hence, it was far more common for states, counties, and cities to spend revenue to sponsor construction projects than it was to support the nonconstruction social or community services performed by women workers. Civic apathy among women in any one town or county could mean that federal work relief for members of their sex would be minimal or nonexistent.[33]

Despite the odds against them and the regulations neither Woodward nor Eleanor Roosevelt could revoke, the office of the Women's Division worked "day and night to get [the] program across." Working for Harry Hopkins meant total commitment. On a normal day administrators and staffers arrived at eight o'clock, ate lunch at their desks (unless they joined someone for a "working lunch"), went to supper in groups between 8:00 and 10:00 p.m., and returned to work that might last until midnight. "The pressure is tremendous," Woodward wrote a friend, "and seems almost as bad as war times . . . and this goes for

Sundays, too." The number of letters ran into the thousands each month. Eventually they were answered by a correspondence pool, which, by summer 1934, numbered more than a hundred. At her bedside, Woodward kept a pad and pencil. She would get up at intervals to jot down ideas.[34]

Woodward continued to live at the Wardman-Park Hotel. Home to many congressmen and government officials, the hotel was an exciting place to be; but, after ten months of hotel living, she found herself hoping that Bessie and Hamilton would move down from New York City. "The strain is telling on her and she looks tired," Earlene White told Lucy Howorth.[35] But plans to live with the Dutchers never materialized, and Woodward remained at the Wardman for three years.

The positive aspects of Woodward's work far outweighed the negative aspects; working with Hopkins topped the list. Then, too, there were bright spots in women's work relief. Lorena Hickok, Hopkins's roving troubleshooter, reported from the field that many women registering for work were being placed. She added, however, that in small communities the outlook was not optimistic: "your average businessmen just won't believe there are any women who are absolutely self-supporting." By the end of 1933, out of a total of 2,610,451 workers on FERA and CWA rolls, 100,000 women were at work. The number escalated rapidly, so that by mid-January 1934, Woodward could boast of 300,000 professional and unskilled women on "this new federal relief." She appeared optimistic that a "new order" had been created, one in which women would no longer be discriminated against. Further, assignments had evened out, with figures showing that, nationwide, 53 percent of men and women certified for work relief had been assigned to projects. This figure, however, masked the fact that it was much easier for men to be certified for work relief—for the very reason Hickok had discovered: local "intake" (certification) officials remained unconvinced that women were heads of households and would not place them on the rolls from which work relief recipients were drawn.[36] By the time the CWA ended on schedule in March 1934, women had worked intensely either on FERA-initiated projects or under the CWA-CWS rubric.[37]

Women who worked in fields represented by strong professional associations held distinct—and sometimes undue—advantage in getting relief-work assignments. Even before the White House Conference in 1933, Woodward was in contact with Ethel Swope, who ran the national office of the American Nursing Association and was well aware that, by 1932–1933, 60 percent of all nurses were unemployed. Swope became almost an adjunct to the Women's Division, designing most of the projects for unemployed nurses intended to expand public health care and education into communities where nursing services had been curtailed or were nonexistent. CWA-CWS nurses augmented understaffed hospitals and clinics and enabled public health departments to add programs in, for example, immunization and dental care. By the time the Civil Works Administration ceased operation, Woodward estimated that more than 10,000 nurses had been employed, many proving so indispensable that their relief jobs were converted to nonrelief permanent work.[38] As a result of the close working relationship between Swope and Woodward, nurses constituted 19 percent of all professional women at work under the CWA.[39]

The priority given nursing projects reflected the interest in public health Woodward had developed in her association with Dr. Underwood in Mississippi and the results she had seen in her home state, where even minimal improvements in public health services brought remarkable results. Similarly, Woodward's commitment as a clubwoman and a state legislator to library expansion and education accounted in large measure for her interest in the projects her division developed for librarians and teachers under the FERA and CWA.[40] Julia Wright Merrill, chief of the American Library Association's Public Library Division, hit it off as well with Woodward as had Ethel Swope; she worked so closely with the relief administrations that one historian of these programs has concluded that ALA and work-relief proposals meshed so closely that it is difficult to determine their origin. Relief librarians provided a boon to beleaguered communities that had shut down libraries or curbed services as the Depression wore on and for locales that had never even had a library. Women doing made work in 1933 and 1934 led book discussion groups, kept libraries open longer, prepared bibliographic and union lists, renovated card catalogues, and performed tasks in large municipal libraries that had gone begging for years.[41]

CWA librarians, like those of FERA and the later Works Progress Administration, delivered their books by packhorse in the Kentucky mountains, by flatboat in the Mississippi Delta, by snowshoe in northern states. Relief workers created libraries in log cabins, community houses, filling stations, country stores, barber shops, and houseboats. With donations of money, books, and magazines from women's clubs, services were expanded greatly. By the end of the FERA/CWA phase of relief work, approximately a thousand library projects had been established.[42]

When Chloe Owings assessed the record for women in March 1934, she calculated that approximately 8 percent of the CWA work opportunities for women had gone to those who could be classified as professionals.[43] The predominant number of women on relief were semi-skilled or unskilled individuals employed in the "goods production" program (mostly sewing and canning) that had formed the nucleus of the early FERA and that remained in place through the brief life of the CWA. Further confusion awaits anyone who tries to keep straight the administration of federal relief programs; after termination of the CWA, all projects reverted to the states under the "Emergency Work Relief Program." The EWRP lasted until summer 1935, when all work programs were brought under the Works Progress Administration.

Workers now had to play by the rules of the new EWRP—in essence, the old FERA. As a result, all work relief projects had to be "public," in the sense that they must provide economic and social benefit to the general populace, a stipulation that caused Woodward little concern, since she had always insisted that her division comply with this stipulation. But the return to other FERA rulings created hardships for women. Unlike applicants for CWA jobs, all FERA (or, now, EWRP) workers were drawn from the rolls of the "needy" who had applied for relief; that is, they had to submit to a means test.[44] Once again, the concept of prevailing wages was in force, and thus workers were paid the hourly rate common in the community.[45] While those stipulations were not new to women who had worked on CWS projects over the winter of 1933-1934, they were distressing to women who now had to be uprooted from their more remunerative CWA work and placed on former FERA projects.

Mary Gillette Moon, the women's director in Illinois, reported to Woodward that the "first effect of the new program is to put nearly all of our women's work out of existence." The goods production workshops could survive uninterrupted because workers there could be certified for relief; but those projects that required professional supervision and professional workers, such as nursing and recreation, would cease to function since many of the personnel could not meet the new, stiffer "needs" test. Some state relief chiefs seized the moment to release their women's work directors. The danger was sufficiently widespread for Harry Hopkins to issue a directive stating that dismissed women were to be reinstated. "We expect," he advised "that women will receive their full share of the jobs."[46]

Determined to reinstate discontinued projects, Woodward succeeded in doing so. In some locales where construction work prevailed under the CWA, women's work had its real beginning under the now better-organized FERA. Time and experience had helped. The summer drought of 1934 caused shortages in some areas while surpluses mounted elsewhere. The Women's Division responded to both conditions, expanding mattress and bedding projects that used 250,000 bales of surplus cotton purchased earlier and enlarging beef and food canning programs to supply winter needs. Through food production, FERA workers may have helped fill empty and gnawing stomachs; but, as mid-term elections approached in 1934, the protests from commercial canners and meat packers about unfair competition escalated. Woodward asked Eleanor Roosevelt to help monitor the projects. "Will you criticize very frankly my work and plans and give me those suggestions that have come from your first-hand contacts during the summer?" she wrote after the First Lady furnished her itinerary so that Woodward could recommend projects to be visited. After Mrs. Roosevelt reported that "the need for clothing everywhere seems to be becoming very much greater," the Women's Division stepped up sewing and clothing repair projects.[47]

The home economics and goods production work of the FERA developed rapidly in 1934 and 1935, partly because of Woodward's engagement as consultants of Claribel Nye, from Oregon State University, and Dorothy Bird Nyswander, former Utah director of women's work. More and more, the Women's Division was turning to programs that met the dual goals of providing community service and training individuals for practical work. "The FERA is committed not only to a policy of work relief, but to a policy of rehabilitation," Woodward told delegates to a Social Service Institute in her home state in August 1934.[48]

The Women's Division made a special effort to publicize those areas where its projects were community-coordinated. Chatham County, Georgia, furnished an example. There, nineteen Community Service Centers were set up in abandoned school buildings, churches, and vacant houses.[49] In 1935, when the *Democratic Digest* once more showcased relief work in a single county, it turned to a poverty pocket in West Virginia, where the FERA director for Randolph County maintained a community-based program that included a mattress and bedding factory, a day nursery for working mothers, a lending library, and a handicraft shop that sold toys, counterpanes, and rugs made by mountain women. FERA women were "doing more than meeting an emergency," said the writer. "Lives are being saved, health guarded, thrift inculcated, and the spirit of cooperation and neighborliness are growing steadily." It was "only another name for democracy." Even hard-boiled Lorena Hickok wrote Harry Hopkins after visiting sewing rooms in Florida, "I don't think you have any idea of what they have done to women themselves. . . . They come in sullen, dejected, half starved. Working in pleasant surroundings, having some money and food have done wonders to restore their health and morale."[50]

The FERA statistical division did not tally results as impressionistically as did Hickok and Woodward's public relations writers. FERA accounted for its stewardship in hard figures which nevertheless pointed to a great volume of activity on the part of the Women's Division. From April 1934 until the final FERA grants of December 1935, the 26,665 "Goods" projects (of which 5,530 were sewing rooms and 4,720 were canning centers) incurred 10 percent of the cost of emergency work.[51] Considering the federal government's outlay for wages and local sponsors for nonlabor costs, women's work under the EWRP phase of the FERA (1 April 1934 to 1 July 1935) boasted enormous productivity. The sewing centers, which had employed one-half to two-thirds of all women in relief jobs, had produced more than 16 million garments. Relief workers who made household goods produced 1,320,000 mattresses (enough to provide one mattress for one-third of all families on relief in any single month) and 16,400,000 towels in addition to bed linens, rugs, and assorted clothing articles.[52]

Production and social service projects developed for women under FERA and CWA became staples of the subsequent Works Progress Administration. So did those for women statisticians, clerks, and research scientists. For all its problems, the CWA had shown the way for the Women's Division to gain entree to fields that had long resisted women. Ellen Woodward was proud of the achievements of her division under the CWA and FERA. She was not blind to the limitations of the majority of unskilled and untrained women for whom her staff sought to create work, nor was she deaf to the criticisms that professionals and elitists would level at their work. Those problems would remain and demand much of her attention after 1935, when all relief work was accelerated and took on new dimensions under a huge new umbrella.

CHAPTER 4

Women's Right to Work Relief: 1935–1936

T
he three years 1935–1938 were the glory years for Ellen Woodward. Her association with Harry Hopkins and his "active program," she later reflected, was the "most challenging and satisfying experience" of her life.[1]

Like all New Deal organizations, the Women's Division went about its work with an increased awareness of the political ramifications of relief work in a presidential election year in which constituents were also certain to debate with their congressional representatives the merits of the WPA operation. As one of the most prominent women in the Roosevelt administration, Woodward took her message about relief work for women to regional conferences of the women's wing of the Democratic party.

Fueled by an appropriation of $1.4 billion initially the WPA was a mammoth undertaking, aimed at ending the federal "dole" by returning to the states the responsibility of direct relief for "unemployables" (those certified as too old, disabled, or incompetent to work), while putting about 3.5 million "employable" men and women to work on projects of public and social value. Although the administrative setup and daily procedures of the WPA were similar to those of earlier work-relief experiments, the new program was vastly larger; in addition, it was often inexplicably complex, perplexing, frustrating, and unintelligible.[2]

When questioned about who would be his assistants in the WPA, Hopkins replied that he had "made up his mind to keep the [FERA] people," adding that he could not "hire any better." His appointment of Ellen Woodward on 19 June 1935, as an assistant administrator of the WPA caught the attention of the press and threw a spotlight on the Women's Division. The *Literary Digest* described her as "personable [and] radiant with southern charm"; she was a "jealous votary of women's rights." While the *New York Times* noted that Washington feminists hailed Woodward's plans to put a half-million women to work, it commented that this figure represented only about 15 percent of the total 3.5 million for whom the WPA boasted it would provide jobs. In view of the fact that, in 1930, gainfully employed women comprised 22 percent of employed workers, the assignment of a half-million women to work relief appeared woefully inadequate. Thus, the *Times* suggested, "feminists might pause a moment . . . to reflect that unemployment among women needs separate handling precisely because women who work are far from being on an equal status with men." For her part, Woodward pointed to the employment of women already on innovative projects that constituted a "sphere of action . . . far more inclusive" for women than that of twenty years earlier. Typifying the confidence the women's press held in Woodward's ability to reach her goal, *Equal Rights*, the voice of a splinter group of the National Woman's Party, editorialized that, if women should not be given their fair share of jobs, Ellen Woodward "will do something about it." "Women are going to get a square deal," Woodward declared in the *Democratic Digest*.[3]

Conversion from FERA to WPA meant filling additional positions in the Washington office, reappointing all women directors in the state offices, and resubmission to Washington for reapproval of all ongoing projects, not to mention designing new programs for which funding was now available. In the midst of the transition, Woodward was called to the bedside of her sister, Belle, who had been seriously injured in a near-fatal automobile accident. Back at her desk a week later, Woodward returned to her schedule of fifteen- to eighteen-hour workdays, giving up her plans to return to Mississippi for the Christmas holidays.

The physical trappings of Woodward's division were as inauspicious as those of the old FERA: scarred walls, old unmatched furniture, cramped quarters (described by an assistant as a "rabbit warren") formed the setting for the new women's program.[4] She lived at the Wardman Hotel, eating most meals on the run, until Fall 1936, when she rented an apartment at the Westchester.

Woodward's position in the new WPA was more prestigious than it had been in the FERA or CWA. Her expanded role was the result of a victory over Jacob Baker, fellow administrative assistant. Baker, one of Hopkins's right-hand men, had been FERA director of Work Relief and Special Projects and Hopkins's assistant in overseeing the Civil Works Service arm of the CWA. In the summer of 1934, as remnants of the CWA were reabsorbed into FERA, Woodward lost control of many of the programs she had developed for nurses, teachers, librarians, and other professional women. The projects had passed to Arthur

Publicity photograph of Woodward while she was director of the Women's and Professional Division, Works Progress Administration, 1936 (Courtesy Albert Y. Woodward, Jr.)

Goldschmidt, whom Baker had put in charge of the new Division of Professional and Non-Manual Projects, an action that left state components of women's work technically responsible to both Goldschmidt and Woodward.

With 20 to 25 percent of all women on work relief assigned to professional projects, Woodward was not content to have her jurisdiction curtailed. Now a tenacious administrator, she moved quickly to have her loyal state directors initiate professional projects for both men and women. Unlike the national office, there were no separate administrative units in the states for professional projects. Thus the units tended to come under the aegis of the Women's Division, inasmuch as most whitecollar workers were female. Competition between the two administrators in Washington resulted from an imprecise line of command. As state leaders of the Women's Division initiated more and more projects for professionals, Woodward gained a grassroots advantage over Baker and Goldschmidt. She marshaled her core staff and presented a strong case to Hopkins for combining the Women's Division and the Professional Projects Division in the Washington office. This was done in July 1935, just as the new WPA took shape. Woodward was given a new title: director of Women's and Professional Projects. In the first of two victories she would win over Baker, Woodward recaptured control of the programs for women professionals.[5]

Baker bore no apparent ill will toward Woodward. Although he considered her appointment in 1933 a nod to the power of Pat Harrison, chairman of the Senate Committee on Finance, Baker told an interviewer years later that Woodward was a competent administrator. He had seen her prove herself during the days of the old FERA and CWA. Woodward failed, however, to gain jurisdiction of the bulk of the educational projects from Dr. Louis R. Alderman. She found Alderman unsympathetic to her argument that there were women as well educated as the men who dominated the WPA Emergency Education Division that Alderman held on to. Nor were all recreational projects absorbed by the WPP, for Eduard Lindemann retained control over a separate Division of Recreation. Neither man, however, held the title of WPA Assistant Administrator, as Woodward did.[6]

New consultants joined Woodward's staff. Five (later six) regional supervisors were placed in the offices of WPA field representatives, and 312 district supervisors went to work under the direction of the 48 state directors. Regional supervisors announced in August 1935 were Lula Martin Scott, of North Carolina (the Northeast); Izetta Jewel Miller, of West Virginia (Middle Atlantic and "Old Northwest"); Blanche Ralston, of Mississippi (the South Atlantic and Southeast); Florence S. Kerr, of Iowa (the Midwest); and Dorothy B. Nyswander, of Utah (the Far West).[7]

Regional leaders were on the road almost constantly, keeping projects moving and maintaining tranquility and efficiency in the many locales and state offices where problems arose. Fortified with material prepared by Woodward's office, regional representatives filled endless speaking engagements to help put across the new woman's program. Without exception, the women were loyal to Woodward, and she quickly announced her pleasure with their work. "Mr. Hopkins and

Colonel [Lawrence] Westbrook are delighted that our women are getting out and 'doing their stuff' so well already," Woodward wrote Lula Scott six months after the WPA began. For the most part, there was satisfaction, too, at the grassroots level. Louise Armstrong, a local relief official in Michigan, spoke of her superiors as "women so intelligent and . . . sympathetic to every suggestion for the betterment of the women's work." Writing years later, Chloe Owings stated that she had never "encountered a higher sense of personal responsibility for and interest in work to be done" than among the personnel in the field. Whatever problems arose "never came from [lack of] ability."[8]

Although each state director had an impressive background, some were better prepared than others for the job with the WPP.[9] Ella Graham Agnew, of Virginia, after years as an educational missionary in South Africa and as a YWCA worker in North Carolina and Ohio, had returned to her native state and become a pioneer in rural education.[10] Elizabeth Denny Vann, of the New Jersey office, after assisting her husband at a Methodist mission in Brazil, had settled in New Jersey, launched into liberal politics, and organized the first Democratic Woman's Club in her area.[11] Ethel Payne had worked with the national board of the YMCA in New York City and with the Italian Relief Agency in Chicago, and had held various posts with the Red Cross before returning to Mississippi as a pioneer in social welfare.[12]

Once the principal of a teacher's college in Baghdad, Iraq, Alma Kerr had been employed as a county ERA worker in her home state of Minnesota.[13] Jane Van De Vrede, a native of Wisconsin and a professional nurse who had settled in Georgia, became executive secretary of the Georgia State Nurses Association after a ten-year stint as a Red Cross nurse when she, too, had known Harry Hopkins.[14] Mary Gillette Moon, the director in Illinois, was a former director of the Chicago Women's Service Bureau. In New York City, which had a woman's program of its own, the WPA head named his executive secretary, Mary Tinney, a former social worker with the Brooklyn Bureau of Charities. Jane Ridder of Arizona was a graduate engineer in that state and one of two women to have become a member of the American Society of Engineers.[15] The fact that many of the state women leaders had known the ubiquitous Hopkins in Red Cross operations strengthened the bonds of loyalty and dedication to the purposes of the WPA, although Hopkins seems not to have taken part in hiring them.

Many of the state WPP heads had come from FERA and CWA

Head table at the Mayflower Hotel WPA conference for state and regional directors, 5 May 1936, l. to r. Florence Kerr, regional director, Midwestern states, WPA administrator Harry L. Hopkins, Eleanor Roosevelt, and WPA Assistant Administrator Woodward (National Archives 69-N-5858)

settings; others held fresh appointments. Because the Women's and *Professional* (emphasis added) Division, was a new wrinkle on the state operations scene, some WPA state directors seemed determined to appoint men to head the WPP sections. To correct these tendencies, Hopkins in December 1935, fired a bulletin to all state offices: "The Directors of the Division of Women's and Professional Projects in all states and districts shall be a woman." In the opinion of a team of public administrators who later chronicled work relief history, this move was "unquestionably 'political' in the broadest sense of the word." It represented an administrative recognition of the place that women would have in the dispensation of work relief.[16]

Problems also emanated from power struggles and personality clashes among women leaders. From the outset, in 1933, Woodward had never insisted that only Democratic women hold jobs in her division. Mrs. Charles Sabin, a prominent clubwoman and Republican women's leader, had for a time chaired the advisory committee for CWA women's work in New York state and been well received. Even as zealous a Democrat as Molly Dewson agreed with Woodward that it would be wise to place liberal Republicans in positions to which they were suited, especially in the case of a New Hampshire woman who was a Republican "but one like Governor [John] Winant," i.e., a friend of the New Deal.[17]

To the consternation of the state's powerful Democrats, Harry Hopkins had appointed Lois Rantoul, a longtime activist in the Women's Trade Union, to direct the state CWA's Women's Division. Rantoul had, however, resigned due to political fire. One of the messiest problems Woodward had to mediate was a protracted skirmish in Pennsylvania, where prickly but competent Democratic committeewoman, Emma Guffey Miller fought to remove Gertrude Ely, director of WPP work in the state. Convinced that Ely was a capable and impartial administrator, Woodward would not permit her to be sacrificed to Miller's partisan pique over Ely's refusal to permit a Democratic woman to run for office while holding a WPA job. Woodward who defined loyalty as devotion to the goals of the New Deal, did not find Ely wanting on this score. She wrote Izetta Miller that, "regardless of her imperfections [Ely] was in the program to stay." Pledging to support her 100 percent, Woodward expected others to rally to Ely's side. Weary of the slings and arrows of fortune, however, Ely resigned in July 1937. On her birthday greeting to Woodward that summer, Ely wrote, "Many thanks for what you have done for me." Similarly, when Sylvia Mariner was under fire during her women's directorship in Oklahoma, Woodward urged her to hang on.[18]

Loyalty was also an issue in Ohio, a state so plagued by patronage that its relief program was taken away from state officials and federalized in 1934. Woodward reiterated to her women's work director there that WPP appointees must be "people whose loyalty is unquestioned in this thing," adding that "you have got to have people you can trust on all fronts."[19] She pointed to another essential for women administrators: they had to be women "who will leave home." Woodward had been disappointed to see some women take a position in a state or district office, to be too constrained by family responsibilities to do the job. Personality and compatibility were other requirements for state directors. When Charley Tidd Cole antagonized coworkers in Missouri, Woodward told the regional supervisor, Florence Kerr, to "tell her that no matter how competent she is, unless she can get along with people, we will have to make other arrangements." But Cole's antipathy toward the Missouri WPA administrator, an appointee of state political boss Tom Pendergast, was well founded. One of the most capable of state directors, Cole was brought to Washington, where she performed superlatively as director of public information in the office of the Women's and Professional Projects. Woodward also summoned to Washington Mary Jean Simpson, Vermont's efficient director, to be the staff consultant on sewing when political attacks became unbearable for Simpson in Vermont.[20]

In New York, the first state director proved to be a woman of questionable ability and so indiscreet politically that she caused discord among subordinates and even project workers. Woodward involved Eleanor Roosevelt in the decision to remove the woman "as tactfully as possible," in view of the support she had from the New York congressional delegation.[21] In 1937, the First Lady was a party to an arrangement in New Mexico, where the congressional bloc split over a woman who had Mrs. Roosevelt's blessings. After the contender favored by the two senators got the job, Woodward worked with Aubrey W. Williams to find a position for Eleanor Roosevelt's candidate.[22] Balancing personal and professional considerations in recruiting and retaining women in key state positions was a constant headache for Woodward, especially in states where elected officials routinely played WPA politics.

Job demands affected the staffing of the Washington office as well. Clerical assistants and consultants (most of the latter came on leave from academe) could not maintain the rigorous schedule demanded by the job. Assisting Woodward, Agnes Cronin (who replaced Chloe Owings), and Charley Cole to turn out the work they thought essential to keep current on all division operations demanded innumerable overtime hours. When Woodward remained until late at night, so did others, to assist with whatever was pressing. Woodward was "a demon for work," Cronin recalled, but her "wonderful sense of humor" and spontaneous laughter served to ease tempers and tensions. Grace Allen, Woodward's longtime and devoted secretary, joined her boss many nights for a hasty supper, returning to the office for more dictation. The turnover did, however, cause slippages in efficiency.[23] Julia Merrill lamented to the Mississippi library project director that the frequent changes in WPP staff meant "a new approach each time."[24]

Problems that had vexed FERA women's work persisted under the WPA. The general public still had to be disabused of the idea that women did not need work relief. In her Michigan county, relief administrator Louise Armstrong was appalled that even some women held stereotypical views about relief recipients of their own sex. She related a dialogue that took place as she conducted two Chicago teachers through the local sewing room. When one remarked, "Why, none of these women look like relief cases," Armstrong countered: "Would you mind telling me just what you think relief cases look like?"[25]

Woodward's division could never dispel the widespread bias against married women working. Mary K. Taylor reported from Texas about WPA officials who insisted that husbands "earn the livelihood for the family." The refrain was common. Even when a woman was not the primary wage earner in her home, relief chiefs seemed not to understand that a family could require her income just to live at a subsistence level.[26] A study of women relief workers in Missouri in 1936 revealed that more than half had no husband at home because of death, divorce, separation, or desertion; of those husbands who were present, only 8.5 percent were able to work. Woodward knew that the statistics translated into pathos and conflict within the home. She received numerous letters like the one sent to Mrs. Roosevelt from a humiliated Connecticut man, certified as unemployable himself, whose wife held a WPA work assignment. "I'm called a kept man," the husband and father wrote. In Fergus Falls, Minnesota, a local sewing-room supervisor was heartsick to learn that a needy worker did not receive a notice of reemployment after a layoff because her husband destroyed the work-notification slip. "When she got [her] check he felt subordinate to her." Such tales were fairly common. In 1938, even after five years of program operation, Woodward was still trying to convince critics that many women worked out of necessity and not for "pin money."[27]

The dimensions of the married-woman-relief-worker question were not made easier by the fact that many states had passed laws that had the effect of driving married women from the labor force, particularly those employed in state agencies. Under Section 213 of the National Economy Act of 1932, even federal government jobs were closed to women married to men in government service. How much more difficult could it be, then, to convince local authorities that married women should have relief jobs?[28] In light of their narrow perception of what women could do outside the home, Woodward's advanced notions about the occupations open to women and those for which they could be trained seemed downright revolutionary. In a long memorandum prepared for Congresswoman Mary T. Norton in 1936, Woodward elaborated upon her ideas: "Under the Works Program the work week is not excessively long. A woman with home cares need not neglect her home. The self-respect engendered by her work responsibilities and her security wages will make her a happier, more energetic, and enthusiastic homemaker than if she were obliged to try to make both ends meet for herself and her family on a dole based on her budget deficiency." When the Boston Edison Company barred married women from employment in 1938, Woodward told the press, "I feel sincerely that a woman should not be denied the right to work or the right to self-expression through remunerative employment simply because she is married."[29]

Compounding the hostility to married women was the added debate over working mothers with minor children. Antipathy surfaced even within the Department of Labor, where Secretary Frances Perkins was unsympathetic to the idea; so, too, were administrators within the Children's Bureau. Grace Abbott, once director of the Bureau, wrote in her summary history of relief and Social Security, "To give work relief outside their own home to mothers of young children was a mistake." Mindful of the housekeeping aides and nursery centers, she said that "the WPA paid women to take care of other women's children; it would have been much more useful to pay them to take care of their own children."[30] Thus it would appear that Woodward achieved a breakthrough when an administrative order from Hopkins, dated 3 October 1935, directed that women were to be certified for work whether or not they appeared to be needed at home to care for minor children.[31]

From the onset of their collaboration in planning work relief for women, Ellen Woodward and Eleanor Roosevelt held grave concerns about single women such as those the settlement worker Mary Simkovich described as "just discards" and whom she found "huddled together in small apartments, three or four of them living on the earnings of one." It shocked Lorena Hickok to learn that case workers in Houston, Texas, in dealing out direct relief, had been ordered to cut weekly food allowances for single women to 39 cents. The nonfamily woman, Amy Maher wrote from Toledo, "seems to have been more 'forgotten' than the 'forgotten man.' "[32] The difficulty single women encountered in finding relief-work placement struck a responsive chord in Eleanor Roosevelt: "They say they can't place me as I do not have a family. What are we single girls going to do?" a Kansas City woman wrote the President.[33] In this woman's case, personal attention from Woodward and Mary Anderson, of the Women's Bureau, led to a job. Woodward's knowledge that innumerable, nameless single women were shunted aside prompted her to make sure that "unattached" women were not discriminated against.[34]

From its inception, the Women's Division served as an intermediary for several private charities and social agencies that appealed to the White House when their resources were exhausted. For example, investigation proved that the District of Columbia Little Sisters of the Poor genuinely needed the commodities they had requested for care of the aged. On the other hand, a women's service center in St. Louis was denied assistance after a probe indicated it had grossly exaggerated its statement of need and that its past performance had been inefficient.[35] Complaints about insensitive actions by local relief authorities drew prompt and thorough inquiries. In one case, the Women's Division found that the tattered underwear distributed to an Alabama child and then sent to Eleanor Roosevelt along with a bitter letter was the "charity" of a church group and not the doing of the FERA. Eleanor Roosevelt heard from a Missouri woman whose pregnancy was criticized by a relief official to whom she applied for aid. The woman eventually received an apology after the Missouri Women's Division identified the official.[36] Both Eleanor Roosevelt and Ellen Woodward were aware that they were sometimes victimized by fraudulent complaints and schemes. Even their attempts to prevent deception, however, led complainants to reproach their benefactors for betraying their confidences. Others who lodged protests feared recrimination from local relief authorities who resented "snooping" from Washington. "No matter how carefully we try to guard the handling of relationships with certain kinds of persons," Woodward wrote her White House ally, "there are heartaches."[37]

In late 1936, Woodward informed Harry Hopkins that more than 400 letters came to her each month from the White House. Analysis of referrals of White House mail in the spring of 1936 showed an increase, not only in the volume but also in the variety of problems described. Women wrote of delays in their assignment to WPA work, of their ineligibility for work because of age or disability, of the barriers that confronted mothers of small children when they sought work relief. Many letters demonstrated that the security wage paid by the WPA was too low to support a family. Single women vented their resentment that married women, whose husbands had jobs, were given work in the private sector, a circumstance beyond the purview of the WPP but one that, nonetheless, informed Woodward of what women faced during the Depression.[38] As the letters of supplication continued to come from the White House, the WPP staff, under the direction of Catherine Nonamaker, handled them with dispatch. There was a pragmatic reason for giving careful attention to White House referrals and informing regional directors of the cases and their disposal; it would help, Woodward wrote Izetta Miller, "make many friends for the Administration."[39]

Decisions about personnel and procedures, though important in Woodward's administration, were not as important as the moves she would make in the spring of 1935, when she knew that her women's program would have to begin anew under the WPA. She would have to fight for allocations and quotas for her women. Molly Dewson wrote Mrs. Roosevelt of her "shiver of apprehension" for women under the new works administration, given its expected rules and regulations. Woodward turned to Eleanor Roosevelt: "Won't you please ask the President to emphasize in his talk [announcing the WPA] . . . that employable women on relief will receive their fair proportion of jobs. . . . You are always on the alert to safeguard the welfare of needy women." For her part, the First Lady turned a press conference on 20 May 1935 into an open forum where Woodward could state her case and outline the extent of the FERA projects she hoped to keep alive.[40]

When state administrators were brought to Washington for briefings on the WPA in June 1935, Woodward assured them that there would be no significant changes in women's work. It would be the obligation of state WPA chiefs to see "that a fair proportion of the jobs are made available to women." Women directors were "to put their oars in for the welfare of women wherever it is necessary."[41] Her statements, however, proved to be more rhetoric than reality in the early months of women's work under the WPA. Woodward was not the only WPA division head who was up in the air; when Hopkins returned to Washington in October from a Caribbean cruise with the President, he found his entire staff agitated about filling the promised 3.5 million jobs by 1 December.[42] Much of the lag in the women's program during the first six months of the WPA can be ascribed to general policies mitigating against retaining many FERA projects. The WPA ruling that at least 90 percent of all persons on project work had to be assigned from public relief rolls affected the small units that had operated for professional and semiskilled workers under noncertified-that is, nonrelief, supervisors. In cases where untrained workers had been placed over projects because supervisory personnel with appropriate work experience could not be certified for relief-work jobs, efficiency and quality decreased while public criticism soared. Hence, sponsors became discouraged and dropped out. Woodward complained to Eleanor Roosevelt in October 1935 that her projects had suffered "a definite setback." Many of the well-integrated programs designed to utilize a wide range of women's skills in the 250 occupational categories the division had delineated had been declared ineligible in the rush "to put men to work first," a decision in which she had been told both the President and Hopkins concurred.[43]

It distressed Woodward to learn that only sewing rooms and recreation projects were now eligible activities for women. Where they operated in large urban centers, they were compatible with the concept of mass employment that dominated the thinking of the professional engineers who dominated WPA planning. "I should feel a pang of regret if our Federal government were to seem to follow the lead of less progressive nations in restricting the field of women's work," she added. To Hopkins, Woodward insisted that women be well cared for in the WPA, "in the interest in fostering public sentiment in a country where more than fifty percent of the population consists of women."[44]

Knowledge that additional funds appropriated for work relief under the act of 1935 could permit her to broaden her program left Woodward restive when she saw the edge that new regulations gave the Operations (construction) Division over her WPP. When in December 1935, the idea was conceived to reorganize state offices so as to place the forty-eight women directors under the state Operations Division, Woodward moved to thwart the transfer of the directors to a subordinate role. Her friend in the White House concurred, saying that it was "very hard to make [the engineers] see anything but the construction side," and thus, "inevitably, the proper insight and understanding of the women's problems will be lacking." Together Eleanor Roosevelt and Ellen Woodward were able to preserve the autonomy of the Women's and Professional Projects. At the close of 1935, Woodward reported to Harry Hopkins that 275,000 women were on assignments, although she regretted that the number represented only 57.3 percent of the number her division was obligated to put to work.[45]

With this crisis behind, others appeared imminent as a result of regulations more stringent under the WPA than in prior work programs. New WPA rules, which required sponsors to donate a larger portion of the nonlabor costs of projects, made it more difficult to continue many women's projects whose sponsorship had been subsidized by contributions from women's organizations to public social agencies with severely strained sources of revenue. Between July 1935 and August 1937, out of all WPA projects, 80.5 percent were sponsored by local governments and 15.5 by the states.[46] Such a level of dependency on local funding to pay for all but labor, equipment, and supervision meshed with local decisions to sponsor construction work for men rather than service projects for women. In view of sponsorship strictures, Woodward devoted an inordinate amount of time appealing to women's organizations to "visit the projects, study the work, talk to the sponsors," and, by implication, increase their moral support and financial assistance.[47]

The hardships inflicted upon women's work by the sponsorship ruling were exacerbated by the assumption some sponsors held that they should have a hand in operating the projects. Friction resulted when sponsors held standards inferior to those established by the WPA. For example, some tradition-bound communities balked at sponsoring projects that would hire mothers with children under the age of sixteen, and they questioned the cost effectiveness of supplying needy families and institutions with garments, food, and household furnishings produced by the women's projects. In one case, a woman's political club in Massachusetts pressured Washington to remove the state director for her "foolish projects." In another case, the state director commented in his report on Idaho's WPA: "We always found that sponsors of the projects were normally very free with advice and very chary of money."[48]

Central to Woodward's defense of women's right to relief jobs was her stand on equitable wages. Early in 1936, she wrote Frances Perkins that "women receiving equal pay with men" would have permanent results for nonrelief labor and boasted that the WPA's application of the principle was the first time in history that a government agency recognized the principle of equal pay for equal work. The WPA had "done much to break down the economic barrier which stood so long as a bulwark of the inequality of the sexes," she told her colleagues in the Federation of Women's Clubs.[49]

Only in the strictest sense, however, was there a policy of equal pay. Men and women who performed similar tasks were paid the same wages, but the WPA used so many gradations and criteria in classifying jobs that seldom were the jobs women held in nonconstruction truly comparable to those men performed on construction sites. The concept of "security wages" initially adopted by the WPA was tied so closely to local wage standards that great inequities resulted. As a result, Southern (and rural) workers received much less than non-Southern (and urban) workers. Even in the Northeast, however, factory wages remained so low that Frank March, a project supervisor on Woodward's staff, told the WPA head in Massachusetts that "we would not be justified in asking WPA women to take jobs at less than a living wage."[50] "This division should be constantly alert to see that women are given equal consideration with men," Woodward reminded the regional representatives.[51] Her division reported that, at the end of 1936, men who received 83 percent of the WPA's total wage payments averaged 52.4 cents an hour, while women earned 45.7 cents hourly.[52]

Political maneuvering complicated other administrative decisions, among them procurement of materials. The senators from Mississippi, Harrison and Bilbo, both backed efforts by the manager of Alponaug Manufacturing Company plants operating in Mississippi to have the WPA adopt specifications that would permit purchase of cloth manufactured by Alponaug. Because the Mississippi plants did not produce the weight of fabric called for by Women's Division specialists, Woodward had to withstand intercession from almost the entire Mississippi congressional delegation. When she learned that corporate directors in Jackson had approached WPA directors in states outside Mississippi and offered gifts of material to help them win textile bids, Woodward wrote a letter sharply criticizing the manager.[53] Ruth Chalmers, the specialist who handled most of the complaints, had to placate suppliers as to the weight and patterns of the fabrics as well as ride herd on manufacturers who supplied substandard goods.[54]

Woodward's experience in Mississippi had convinced her that taxpayers were more easily won over to public undertakings when they understood their purpose and were kept abreast of events. Well aware that government relief work was the target of widespread opposition and ridicule, Woodward wrote Molly Dewson: "I know our program is a 'hot spot,' " and so she moved early to build an effective public information section within her division. Before the WPA was actually in operation, she wrote a lengthy memorandum to Harry Hopkins, pointing to the need for press releases that deemphasized the amount of money to be spent and instead described projects and highlighted their benefits to individuals and localities. In 1936, Woodward told the project director in Pennsylvania (always a troublesome state for the Roosevelt administration), "You know the opponents of the New Deal are banging us every way." She recommended newspaper publicity and exhibits that would showcase the return offered by work relief allocations. "I think it is the proper business of the WPA to let people know what tax money is going for," Woodward told Anna Lebengood in Pennsylvania. While in Philadelphia for a WPA exhibit in 1938, she openly contradicted the state WPA administrator, Edward N. Jones, who was wary of telling the public how the taxpayer's money was being spent. When Woodward insisted that "the facts need to be spread among the people," the embattled Jones retorted, "she isn't from around here."[55]

In January 1936, the Women's Division set up an information service under the direction of Charley Tidd Cole and Esther Franklin. The purpose of the Division was to furnish material to national, regional, and state staffs; plan special exhibits for the Washington area and "project days" for the states; write newspaper releases; draft Ellen Woodward's speeches; and compose the magazine and journal articles published in her name. As Cole began her work, Woodward told Harry Hopkins that women "as a group [were] not yet clearly aware" of what the Roosevelt administration had done to help women in need, nor did women appreciate the "fine and lasting benefits" of the work projects to their communities. "Bally-hoo and sob-stuff" were to be "taboo," she told Hopkins, in the "dignified *educational* program" through which her Division would inform the public of the "fundamentally constructive work being done for women and children everywhere." The key phrase of the public information program she envisioned would be Women at Work. "I think it is a grand idea," Eleanor Roosevelt wrote after Woodward described the Division's plan for "good material, well written and attractively illustrated . . . in the hands of great numbers of people." Typical of the outpouring of publicity was the glowing description of the women's program, "This Woman Put 600,000 To Work," which appeared in *Mid-Week Pictorial* for December 1936.[56]

For Woodward's presentation, Cole's department engaged a group of competent, socially sensitive writers to emphasize the social values of the WPA. The writers added that the work program presented an opportunity to develop President Roosevelt's concepts of "the good neighbor" and a community's responsibility for the individual. Virginia Price, Cole's special assistant, was the principal writer for the Division, but Helen Greenblatt, Bryn Griffiths, Eleanor Carroll, Lucile Furman, and Roscoe Wright drafted many of the articles and speeches which told the story of "women at work" and bore the subtle message of permanent social reform and equality for women. Cole estimated that during June 1936 through March 1937, twenty-five articles released from her office reached some three and a half million readers.[57]

Finally, in an effort to present the aims, achievements, and problems of the women's work program to public-spirited women, Woodward made contact with those officers of national women's organizations she knew personally, especially those in the League of Women Voters and Business and Professional Women's clubs. [58]

No group was more accessible to Woodward than the Democratic women mobilized for the 1932 presidential campaign by Molly Dewson, who now formed the vital Women's Division of the party. Woodward was a regular at functions of the Women's National Democratic Club, which brought together the women of the New Deal. Included in this group was another Mississippian, Lucy Howorth, Woodward's longtime friend whom she had recommended to Dewson for a job in Washington. "I like your little Lucy Howorth. I knew I should," Dewson wrote Woodward, adding, "I was prejudiced in her favor" after Howorth arrived in 1934 to become one of the members of the United States Veterans' Board of Appeal. [59] The two women remained friends and were leaders in professional women's circles in Washington for two decades.

Among the other Democratic women activists Woodward met before coming to Washington were Lucile Foster McMillin of Tennessee, a Civil Service commissioner; Emily Newell Blair, from Missouri, now a member of the Consumers' Advisory Board of the National Recovery Administration; Nellie Tayloe Ross, director of the United States Mint; and Sue Shelton White, the Tennessean whose boost had helped make a place for Woodward on Molly Dewson's "team." Once on the job in Washington, Woodward came into contact with other prominent Democratic women, such as Mary La Dame, associate director of the United States Employment Service; Katharine Lenroot, chief of the Children's Bureau; and Marion Glass Bannister, assistant treasurer of the United States. The coterie also included Congresswomen Mary T. Norton of New Jersey, and Caroline O'Day, of New York, as well as the two women who followed Dewson as director of the Women's Division, Carolyn Wolfe (1934–1936) and Dorothy McAllister (1936–1940). Given the ease with which she made friends, Woodward was soon a well-known and sought-after member of the government women's network. After one social event at the New Hampshire clubhouse in 1936, Wolfe wrote a friend, "No new gossip here, but I have not yet seen Ellen Woodward. She always has more news than anyone else I know." [60]

But, then, with the exception of Secretary of Labor Frances Perkins, no other New Deal woman was as likely to be as close to administrative movers and shakers on a daily basis as was Ellen Woodward. Wolfe later reminisced: "She was quite a remarkable person . . . she knew

all the people down at Congress [and] had so many contacts through
the United States and all over in that emergency work." Woodward
could work with her new colleagues in government behind the scenes
to achieve some of her own goals for the WPA, as she did in the
summer of 1935 when she enlisted Caroline O'Day to recommend to
Harry Hopkins that two women be among the seven persons he would
appoint to a lay advisory board for the new WPA. "If we do not put
. . . women on Boards we are going to regret it," she told O'Day,
adding, "I don't think that the men quite realize what women can
contribute." Also, when she could, Woodward attended the luncheon
meetings of women in government which Mary Anderson of the
Women's Bureau reinstated in January 1936.[61]

Early in 1934, Molly Dewson had announced a plan to broaden
understanding of the New Deal among women at the grass-roots level.
Known as the "Reporter Plan," the strategy called for the appointment
of women by every county Democratic women's organization who
would then become resident experts in each federal agency. These
women were expected to disseminate information, speak to local civic
groups, and, in short, "become real forces in helping shape the trend
of government."[62] Obviously, the women were also expected to put
the best possible face on all the agencies and approaches comprising
the New Deal. Although the "Reporter" nomenclature was novel, the
idea was similar to Woodward's earlier attempts to organize clubwomen of her hometown to monitor public affairs and report to their
club members. Woodward endorsed the Reporter Plan concept and
very likely, Dewson thought, was behind the attendance of the state
director of the Mississippi Reporter Plan at the regional conference of
Democratic women held in Little Rock, Arkansas, in May 1935.[63]
Woodward shared Dewson's concern that the plan did not catch on in
the Deep South as well as they would have liked. "[W]e must do
something more in order to reach the large groups a little further
down the line," Woodward suggested to Dewson in the fall of 1935,
shortly after discussing her new WPA Women's Division on a Reporter
Plan educational radio broadcast.[64]

Woodward was a featured speaker at numerous regional confer-
ences, beginning with the gathering of Atlantic Coast women at
Richmond in March 1935, the same month the Women's Democratic
Club held a banquet in honor of its New Deal "stars." There, Frances
Perkins spoke on the nascent Social Security program and Harriet
Elliott, on leave from her post as dean of the Woman's College of the
University of North Carolina to run the Reporter program, explained

its workings. Attentive to Woodward's softly modulated but enthusiastic message at Richmond, Democratic women tended to view the federal government's work relief program for women as the most novel of the administration's Depression remedies. Dewson backed Woodward; the programs were proof that "plans have been made for a more abundant life for all, and women will have a share in it." The first of eight successive regional conferences, the Richmond meeting was to Dewson "a milestone in woman's evolution." Two weeks later, Woodward joined Josephine Roche, a successful Colorado coal mine owner who had become the assistant secretary of the Treasury, to take the message of "the more abundant life" to Democratic women at the Great Lakes regional meeting in Detroit.[65]

It was incumbent upon Woodward, she wrote James Farley, that she relinquish her post as a state committeewoman when she became a federal official, in order to "avoid any possible criticism of the Democratic administration." In fact, Eleanor Roosevelt arranged for her to discuss the matter with the President himself before submitting her resignation in March 1934. Hers was among a virtual avalanche of withdrawals from the DNC by new figures within the official family. The Mississippi Democratic state executive committee initially refused to accept the resignation on grounds that the work of the national committee in Mississippi was limited to presidential election years. After the committee tabled the resignation at its July meeting, Woodward resubmitted her statement in September 1934, when the committee finally acceded to what was mandatory from the President's standpoint.[66]

Thus, Woodward could hardly join the campaign for Roosevelt in 1936; but she could do her part behind the scenes. Anticipating a spirited contest, Eleanor Roosevelt gathered select groups for some judicious planning. "Miss Dewson and I think it would be a good idea to have a discussion about various things of political interest," she wrote in a dinner invitation to Woodward in October 1935, shortly before Woodward left to make contact with the directors of women's work in nearly a dozen western states. "I do hope all your regional women are playing politics from the woman's angle," Dewson wrote Woodward, adding that "all Democratic women [should] cooperate with whatever woman is in office." Dewson also worked through Woodward to get across to Harry Hopkins the ideas that her Women's Division publicists and *Democratic Digest* writers had for promoting the New Deal. "Our Mary Chamberlain . . . thinks Harry Hopkins' publicity boys are too dumb for words," she confided to Woodward while suggesting that she assist in seeing that Chamberlain's "A number 1" ideas become the property of "the brightest fellow" Hopkins had on his staff. Little is recorded of the confidential sessions she may have had with Hopkins as the summer of 1936 approached, but she did suggest that her old friend Francis Harmon, now a national YMCA executive, be brought into discreet political service. Harmon, "perhaps the most socially minded and the most progressive man" she had known in Mississippi, could "disseminate facts about our work in places where I believe such facts would be helpful."[67]

Woodward and her own writers took a cogent line in the speeches they developed for Democratic women, particularly those in the South where faith in Franklin D. Roosevelt sometimes wavered. She told the women assembled in Tampa in March 1936,

> The Administration is not willing to accept the implication that millions of American workers have suddenly lost all virility, all backbone and all capacity. . . . It assumes that in practically all cases the unemployed are victims of conditions over which the individual has no control.

She returned to the South in May, this time to Tennessee and then to her home state, for a two-day regional conference in Jackson, which Dewson concluded, Woodward "probably ran." Her standing among Mississippi women was such that their campaign to have her named as a delegate-at-large to the forthcoming Democratic national convention in Philadelphia culminated in her endorsement at the state convention of the BPW. After Molly Dewson prompted, "Go ahead, Ellen, it wouldn't be a convention without you," she attended, serving as one of eight Mississippi delegates-at-large and becoming one of seventeen women named as alternates on the Platform and Resolutions Committee through a scheme devised by Dewson and lobbied by the cadre of WD faithfuls.[68]

Once Roosevelt's campaign for reelection in 1936 was underway, Dewson and Carolyn Wolfe deliberated with Woodward the wisdom of having women on relief speak publicly about what work employment had meant to them. Woodward cautioned that such was not advisable. Discarded also, this time by Dewson, was the suggestion that publicity releases from the WPP Division be provided to "reporters" of the WD-DNC. The most effective approach to the already converted Democratic women was the extensive coverage given to all phases of the women's and professional projects in the June 1936 issue of *Democratic Digest*. Its timely account of women's work was an impressive document.[69]

But powerful congressional leaders were also engaged in heated races in 1936. Politics for women's work relief, as for the entire WPA, encompassed relations with a Congress often more receptive to constituents' complaints and demands than was the President. Most of Woodward's tactful, serene responses to congressional supplications regarded cutbacks that led to the release or reassignment of workers, attempts of elected officials to intercede for manufacturers eager to supply material to projects, and patronage prerogatives in the appointment of personnel.[70] Mollifying lawmakers whose votes were needed for relief appropriations was imperative, but so was protecting the women directors and relief clients subject to raids by ambitious politicians in both political parties. Always confident of the efficacy of a good education program aimed at potential detractors, Woodward told Aubrey Williams that she intended to prepare for congressmen a "simple, legible, easily understood" booklet on her Division's accomplishments. After all, "we get about 90% of the heat on something over 10% of the projects."[71] To Southern congressmen, who increasingly perceived the WPA as a vast giveaway to the urban poor, Woodward's concerns for rural southerners in distress and her close monitoring of projects in the South may have defused some of the hostility that Southern conservatives harbored toward relief spending.

Woodward continually faced a nasty situation in her home state, where Senators Bilbo and Harrison vied for control of the state's Democrats; both actively sought to build a following through the use of relief rolls. Partial to Harrison, Woodward was able to keep tabs on what transpired all over the state through Ethel Payne and such mutual friends as Walter Sillers, Jr., her ally in the Delta counties and a kingmaker in the Mississippi legislature. Most major political figures in the state knew Harry Hopkins and Aubrey Williams, since both had worked for a time in the state before the New Deal.

Aware of Woodward's position in the inner circle, both Mississippi senators and the state governors sought to win through Woodward the political affection of Hopkins and construction project awards. Certainly, Senator Harrison sought an electoral windfall; he was in the reelection fight of his life the summer of 1936. The state WPA administrator telephoned Woodward before the August primary to report that former governor Mike Conner, Harrison's opponent, claimed that the WPA was "trying to swing all the women towards Senator Harrison"; Woodward denied the allegation. Her defense was substantiated by the fact that few of the complaints that field representative Malcolm J. Miller investigated for Hopkins in Mississippi stemmed from the women's projects. The absence of scandal and political machinations did not mask the fact that Woodward was Harrison's ally. "Our Pat has beaten Conner and Bilbo by more than two to one," she telegraphed President Roosevelt from Mississippi, where she had gone to vote in the primary.[72]

Both Harrison and Bilbo, Harrison's junior colleague after 1934, supported Roosevelt, but there were states where anti-Roosevelt Democrats were bent on scuttling New Deal operations they could not control. Woodward warned Molly Dewson of a situation in Washington State where "the very crowd that elected Roosevelt are getting the hot end of this thing." Difficulties there stemmed from the efforts of Senator Lewis Schwellenbach to remove the director of women's work on the grounds that she "didn't amount to anything." ("That is no news," Dewson retorted. "They say that about all women.") Like almost all contests that pitted Woodward and Hopkins against powerful senators, the imbroglio in Washington issued from the determination of the solons to retain supervisory personnel whose record in putting women to work did not measure up to expectations. After Woodward went to "the Hill" for a personal meeting with Schwellenbach that did not go well, she disclosed to Dorothy Nyswander, "He is the only Senator I have ever seen who talked to me in that way." In the end, Hopkins backed the removal of Schwellenbach's candidate in favor of the woman Woodward thought could do a better job.[73] In a case involving a male WPA official in Oklahoma, Woodward told Wesley E. Disney, "It's against our policy, Mr. Congressman, to take a person out of a job when he's made good just because someone else wants the job."[74]

Neither political party was guiltless in playing politics with the women's division of the WPA. Florence Kerr reported repeated pressure from Democrats in Iowa who demanded jobs "as a right" and who were as persistent as the Republicans she had "deprecated" elsewhere. In the heavily populated states of New Jersey and New York, where unemployment among women was extremely serious, setbacks were a constant fact. Officials in New Jersey resisted caring for relief clients and were slow to forward to Washington project proposals for approval that would put women to work. "It is a bad situation altogether," Woodward told the regional supervisor, Izetta Miller. The foot-dragging there came in the wake of political frays in New York where Republicans exploited difficulties in finding an imaginative and competent state director in their campaign against Representative Caroline O'Day in 1936. "My appreciation of all the assistance you gave us in the Women's Division," O'Day extended to Woodward after her victory in November. Nearby, in Pennsylvania, Emma Guffey Miller, the Democratic state committeewoman, continued to snipe at Gertrude Ely precisely because she was too conscientious to play politics. Miller taunted Ely, "You ought to have a big list [of Democrats] who were turned down by the WPA for Anti-Roosevelt Republicans."[75] Holding Miller in check was ticklish for Woodward, since Miller worked in tandem with her brother, Joseph F. Guffey, senior senator, state boss of Pennsylvania, and chief beneficiary of WPA patronage in his state.[76]

Woodward deflected efforts to build up a Republican machine for Governor William Langer in North Dakota, where Florence Kerr reported "non-partisan . . . means a Republican out of power," and in Wisconsin, where the Progressive party attempted to make inroads at the expense of Democrats. Kerr even wrote of how she had put an end to a training school for housemaids in Wisconsin, where each session opened with a singing of the Communist "Internationale." Mercifully, she added, "no publicity escaped."[77] Democratic governors could be just as troublesome. Through Senator Richard Russell of Georgia, Woodward could verify reports of Governor Eugene Talmadge's attempts to control WPA operations. "I tell you things are not in good shape in Georgia," she lamented to one of Hopkins's assistants in 1936.[78] Northwest or Southeast, there was no section of the country where political considerations did not exist. While Woodward managed to steer the women's projects clear of the notoriety incurred by other WPA divisions, she was always mindful of latent difficulties. When a ticklish situation developed in New Mexico, she told an associate, "Our girl out there is feeling very chesty about our clean bill of health. I told her to quit bragging—we are all under fire."[79]

Woodward's sensitivity to pragmatic angles of the WPA, her strivings to keep its women's work in the spotlight, and her insistence on the complete loyalty of her staff to the aims of President Roosevelt led to the resignation of Chloe Owings in July 1936. Owings had a rich and varied background of academic achievement (her Ph.D. in sociology was from the University of Paris). She had engaged in a variety of social services, including the prewar secretaryship of the Associated Charities of Poughkeepsie, extensive war relief work in France, and the direction of the Social Hygiene Bureau of the University of Minnesota from 1926 to 1932.[80] Dedicated, adept, and extremely conscientious, she was more responsible than anyone else for getting the women's projects underway. Supervising their day-to-day operation was her job, and she worked miracles in initiating many of the work activities. Nonetheless, she resented the intrusion of others whom Woodward brought in as consultants, and she was especially piqued when Agnes Cronin arrived to direct training and placement work.

The gradual estrangement between Owings and Woodward erupted when Owings wrote a long accusatory memorandum to her superior in May 1936. That one document forms the only basis by which to judge the discord. In a stream-of-consciousness flow, Owings faulted Woodward for "over emphasis on political implications." The memo contained a veiled reference to Woodward's "maneuvering for place and position." Owings's grievances may have stemmed from a belief that she had not been given the credit she deserved. "You well know I built ELLEN S. WOODWARD as a *personality* into the nationwide program," she reminded her superior. Her critique closed with suggestions of new assignments for herself that Woodward could make to improve the projects. Woodward's response was just as brusque. "Your emphatic and final statements indicate clearly that there is no longer a common basis for a working relationship." And so she asked that Owings's resignation be effective June 30.[81]

In her unpublished autobiography, Owings left a more moderate view of Woodward, describing her as "a Southern lady of charm who, later I learned was a person of trained political acumen, a quality essential in one in her position." When Woodward asked her point-blank at the time of her interview in 1933, "Are you a Democrat?" and "Do you approve of the President's program?" Owings had answered affirmatively. By 1936, when she was spending more time in the Washington office and less in the field, she became "aware of political aspects coming sharply into focus for the re-election of the president." Troubled also by a conviction that President Roosevelt's personal power had increased to "overwhelming proportions," she was alarmed when Hopkins at a weekly staff conference early in 1936 spoke in "hushed, awed tones" that to accomplish the Roosevelt program "one must take from 'the Haves and give to the Have nots,' or words to that effect." When he further suggested that no one belonged on the executive team who did not share that belief, Owings concluded that she must leave the WPA. In her own story, she makes no mention of a confrontation with Woodward.[82] Her leavetaking would have been a disastrous loss to the WPP had not her successor, Agnes (Anne) Cronin matched her ability and excelled in working relationships with regional and state staffs.

For Ellen Woodward, the summer and fall of 1936 was probably the most gratifying period in her twenty-year tenure in service to two Democratic presidents. While there were numerous problems as yet unresolved (some never would be), her Division of Women's and Professional Projects was set in place. As she traveled throughout the country inspecting state operations and attending Democratic regional conferences, aggregations of clubwomen greeted her with warmth and affection; none was greater than the accolade that hailed her in Mississippi where she returned to vote in the November general election. Two days after Roosevelt's reelection, she told the Mississippi federated clubwomen that, since the launching of New Deal work relief, "greater advances have been made toward the goals of our clubs and all progressive people than were made in the preceding fifty years." Women should, she insisted, "maintain the confidence and courage of President Roosevelt until America's 'rendezvous with destiny' has been kept."[83]

CHAPTER 5

Women at Work: The WPA Women's Projects

W omen's work relief hit its stride in February 1936, when the Women's Division reached a peak employment of 450,000 women. An exhibit in Washington in May showcased the goods and services flowing from the women's program. It coincided with a national conference of state and regional directors convened to deal with questions that continued to trouble Ellen Woodward's staff as it strove to keep older projects going and develop new ways to meet the needs of minorities and unskilled women.

The Mayflower Hotel conference brought together state administrators for a working conference and an opportunity to meet the staff of the national office, hold individual conferences with Woodward, and visit the White House for tea with Mrs. Roosevelt and a brief interlude with the President. Coming after ten months of work relief under the WPA, the conference afforded an opportunity for the WPP Division to evaluate its accomplishments. Booths featured the handicrafts of WPA artisans and the work of public health nurses and medical researchers; Braille transcribers; nursery schools; and hot school lunch, museum, clerical, and survey projects. Widely publicized and lauded in a speech by Senator Joseph F. Guffey, the exhibits served as a model for future regional and state exhibits. In a dinner address, Woodward told the state directors that the exhibits were a significant means of "interpreting to the people of one class the lives of another." She told them that an important task they must assume was to convince "unthinking people that the unemployed are not a strange race." They were, Woodward said, "what we would be if we had not had a fortunate chance at life."[1]

This gathering of WPP leaders reflected Woodward's administrative style: frequent conferences, exchange of ideas, creation of feelings of mutual support, nurture of a sense of belonging to the organization, stimulation of morale, and facilitation of objective-setting and evaluation of work accomplished or of goals not yet achieved.

Project designers in the Division of Women's and Professional Projects were beleaguered by recurring problems inherent in devising effective projects for the large number of unskilled or semiskilled women estimated to comprise 79.5 percent of all women on relief in 1935.[2] Sewing projects proved to be the most feasible. Among the first activities developed under FERA, the Sewing Project could operate year-round. Most women heads of families among the unemployed could sew; and those who could not perform needlework might be trained to do simple tasks and even to operate power machines. Because teaching new skills was one rationale for the women's division as a whole, and because the garment industry was the second-largest industry in the country employing women, the Sewing Project appeared to be an appropriate undertaking.

Sewing production rooms varied from those in which all work was done by hand to those in which only one type of garment was made, using power machines. Project size ranged from as few as ten clients on small rural projects, where all women certified for employment in the area could be placed in one sewing room, to units employing 1,500 in large cities. For example, an eventual 12,000 to 14,000 women drew wages from New York City Sewing Projects; among them were 2,000 trained well enough to leave for jobs in industry.[3] Nationwide, in February 1936, there were 294,532 women employed on 9,000 sewing units at an average wage of 40.5 cents an hour.[4] Sewing rooms remained the backbone of the Women's Division as long as it existed. The projects called for fewer supervisors than did the professional projects, and sewing room supervisors were available from the lists of certified employables. Moreover, the procurement of textiles had a salutary effect on the depressed cotton industry. Between October 1935 and January 1937, the WPA Central Purchasing Division bought approximately 217 million yards of cloth.[5]

Among the nonconstruction projects, sewing produced visible and calculable outcomes that helped the women's programs compete with WPA construction projects that boasted a quantifiable result. By October 1937, women on the projects had made 122 million articles for free distribution through public agencies to certified relief families and charitable institutions. When tornadoes struck in April 1936, supplies from various projects were rushed to towns in Georgia and Mississippi. Ethel Payne told her Mississippi WPA boss that the WPA clothing room at Tupelo "looks like Sears Roebuck." When the Mississippi and Ohio rivers flooded in 1937, victims received clothing, bedding, and food that came from Sewing and Canning projects.

Sandbags made by women in New England units were used to hold back floodwaters. Then, when floods caused widespread destruction in Pennsylvania, the "entire [WPA] machinery went into action on a twenty-four hour schedule" to feed, clothe, and nurse victims.[6]

In Midwestern states, WPA workers converted surplus wool into material from which to make coats, trousers, blankets, and rugs. Hides processed from cattle lost to drought were distributed to WPA sewing rooms in Western states, to be made into coats and jackets. In Southern states, particularly Florida, women taught to make hats, bags, rugs, and other articles from native materials left WPA employment to market similar goods among tourists and winter visitors. Virginia women carded, spun, and wove flax into garments; American-Indian women crafted copperware in Arizona; women in Southwestern border states produced Mexican drawn work. And so it went.[7]

Through her own involvement with handicrafts and furniture, Eleanor Roosevelt encouraged the Women's and Professional Division to divert projects from sewing to crafts where skilled women were available or unskilled women could be taught. Older women were employed in weaving projects to teach these vanishing skills to younger women. Knitting projects drew older work clients and women too disabled to operate sewing machines on units that turned out sweaters, caps, mittens, and scarves. Toy-making projects utilized scrap material to provide cloth dolls and other toys for needy children, particularly during the pre-Christmas months. Woodward took special pride in the ingenuity of local directors, who devised work activities in which cheap, locally available materials were converted into useful articles.[8]

Women's work relief administrators—aware that many unskilled workers could not be employed on any other project—defended sewing and related activities against detractors who scorned them as "female ditch-digging." Woodward told Harry Hopkins that "the only alternative seems to be their return to direct relief . . . the disheartening condition from which they were rescued when they were given work relief on the WPA." Contingent upon congressional funding that was perennially uncertain, projects were initiated, terminated, and perhaps begun again, always provoking outcries from project supervisors and relief recipients. The files on sewing workers offer poignant studies of despair during the Depression. Some women who lost positions in sewing units were transferred to Social Security rolls late in 1936, but many were reluctant to leave the projects simply because public assistance was less generous than sewing-room wages.[9]

As an interlude before permanent employment in the needle trades or in garment plants, the Sewing Projects offered more in theory than in practice. Some contemporary social workers and labor economists condemned the sewing room as an "expensive and unfruitful blind alley" that misled project workers into thinking that legitimate employment lay ahead or that marketable skills were being learned. Most male WPA state heads did not like the projects any more than did a North Carolina Works Division chief who commented, "Frankly our hearts don't palpitate over sewing rooms."[10] Surveys of women on projects in garment trade centers show that many preferred to work in the sewing rooms rather than return to plants where the stress was greater, the hours longer, and the pay lower than both the minimum-wage levels set by the defunct National Recovery Administration and the WPA security wage. Although the WPA was not required to retain workers who refused private employment, Woodward backed project directors reluctant to dismiss relief workers who balked at private pay scales that were less than their WPA wages.[11] She knew that sewing units were often justifiably criticized for permitting women to use outmoded methods of hand sewing that reduced the cost efficiency of goods production.[12] Woodward believed that being able to work with their hands was a source of pride for many women who could do nothing else. Efforts made to raise production by installing modern machines and equipment were met by protests from representatives of organized labor. Woodward defended the training aspects of urban projects to William L. Green of the American Federation of Labor: "We consider rehabilitation of our workers part of our responsibility."[13]

At the outset of the WPA, Woodward admitted to Eleanor Roosevelt that a "multiplicity of sewing rooms may offer a conspicuous target for the opposition press and for the antagonistic sewing trades." Each publicity release of new WPA textile purchases provoked vehement letters from housedress manufacturers to her, to the President, and to Harry Hopkins. A New York representative of the industry charged that "the ultimate goal of the WPA is to remove private enterprise entirely," while an Iowa merchant implored Woodward "not to flood our trading area with free merchandise." When she advised Hopkins that challengers be given a hearing and submitted her diplomatic responses for his approval, he told her that he did not want to see the men or the letters, as she "was entirely responsible for this particular project." Woodward maintained to both manufacturers and merchants that the garments were distributed only to public charges with no purchasing power. Moreover, the wages of women working in the sewing rooms made them potential customers of commercially made garments. Indeed, between 1936 and 1938, the payroll of WPA sewers in Memphis, Tennessee, amounted to $200,000 annually. Yet, Woodward never mollified her critics.[14]

Two other projects for unskilled and semiskilled women—mattress-making and bookbinding—drew sharp criticism from private enterprise. The columnist Drew Pearson doubtless exaggerated Woodward's powers in dealing with irate mattress manufacturers when he wrote, "They are sent to Mrs. Woodward. She stands behind her desk in a tailored blue serge with a cream colored shirtwaist and a polka-dot scarf at her neck. Then she steps out from behind her desk, extends her hand, and smiles. After that the mattress makers go home." But it was not Woodward's charm that dispatched the complainants as much as her assurances that mattress production was coming to an end. Before the mattress "factories" were finally shut down, the WPA had distributed more than 2 million mattresses to the poor—mattresses so well made, one WPA defender wrote, that manufacturers complained they would not wear out as fast as their own products.[15]

From the onset of bookbinding and repair activities under the FERA Library Projects until the liquidation of the WPA projects in 1942, commercial binders protested that competition from WPA projects, especially those engaged in textbook repair, caused heavy losses, shutdowns, and bankruptcy.[16] Woodward never conceded that WPA book-repair projects competed with private industry; she maintained, instead, that the school boards and public libraries which submitted books to be salvaged had no funds with which to contract professional binderies for repairs and that, in most cases, they had never engaged commercial binderies to mend their books. Harry Hopkins concurred in Woodward's defense of the projects. Nevertheless, Florence Kerr wrote from her regional office in Chicago to Woodward, urging that she be discreet if she attended the annual bookbinders' convention. While Kerr's suggestion was that Woodward "admit defects," her best advice was "don't go," and Woodward did not.[17]

The multidimensional work of the WPA Library Projects replicated activities begun under FERA. The availability of WPA labor meant that libraries could spend more of their meager budgets on materials and books, remain open longer, and inaugurate new services, particularly to isolated areas. Woodward was proud of the fact that in 1938, 2,300 new libraries had been established, 3,400 reading rooms had been created in existing libraries, and 5,800 traveling libraries were reaching into sparsely settled areas. In one year alone, WPA Packhorse libraries circulated 100,000 books in the remote areas of twenty counties in Kentucky.[18] Urban libraries benefitted, too, as WPA workers made permanent contributions by reworking card catalogues, compiling union lists, indexing urban newspapers, initiating special collections, and expanding services to hospitals and shut-ins. Many WPA librarians found their work as rewarding as did those in Hancock County, Mississippi, who were told by a grateful patron that, at the end of a hard workday, "me and my old man pulls the tables up on either side of the bed, lights the lamps and reads and reads." "Them books you brought us," she added, "has saved our lives."[19]

Early in 1938, the myriad library projects that existed throughout the country were brought under the supervision of Edward A. Chapman, formerly of the Indiana State Library, who was added to Woodward's staff as the national library consultant. In appointing a man, Woodward explained to Julia Wright Merrill, of the American Library Association: "It is a mistake for the Women's Division to have a personnel that is exclusively feminine." The addition of Chapman and his field assistants, Agnes D. Crawford and Nellie L. Glass, gave the WPA projects the character of a genuinely national program, and they remained in existence until the demise of the WPA in 1943.[20] Furthermore, due to enhancements of the WPA program, women librarians made progress in the 1930s.[21]

Braille Transcription Projects that employed the blind comprised a small adjunct of the library program. Woodward had been impressed by the work done in Mississippi, where Addie W. McBryde, through the blind commission, pioneered FERA activities for the sightless. Braille projects and allied work activities for training the blind to produce marketable goods became favorites of Woodward, and she promoted them throughout the country. By the middle of 1936, Braille projects were operating in twenty-three states, some in cooperation with private institutions such as the Perkins Institute in Boston. Encouraged by the American Foundation for the Blind, project workers in New York City built talking-book machines that were loaned through the Library of Congress to state commissions for the blind, to schools and community centers. Relief maps for children in Massachusetts prompted one schoolgirl to exclaim, "Now for the first time I know what my country looks like."[22]

Contrary to the remark of a *Commonweal* writer, that the WPA projects for the blind "certainly cannot arouse controversy," they did.

Skeptics questioned the practical value and authenticity of the work, as well as its duplication by other agencies. Eventually the WPA dropped the Braille projects.[23]

Although sewing absorbed more women than did any other WPA endeavor, other projects were necessary to provide relief wages for women whose only work experience was in the home. Probably the best supported of all WPA activities for women were the School Lunch and Canning Projects; they ranked second to sewing in terms of total relief employment. Adopted by Parent-Teacher associations in the early 1930s, school lunches for undernourished and needy children were provided and expanded under federal work relief. Project operations ranged from large-scale preparation of lunches in New York City to small kitchens in rural schools, which not only prepared lunches but also helped establish community standards in regard to water supplies and food handling.[24]

The School Lunch Project, operating in every state, found willing sponsors in either the state department of public welfare or health. The Project was generously subsidized by civic clubs, women's organizations, and PTAs. Food, milk, and meat were issued from the federal government's store of surplus commodities, but other sources were the canned food and meat produced by relief canners. Meat canning was a large operation in Texas, where 286 community plants processed the beef purchased by the government in drought-stricken areas. Over an eighteen-month period in 1936-1937, 12,000 relief workers served approximately 80 million hot meals.[25]

Some states ran a summer program in which the children of needy families were fed in churches, parks, and child-care centers. While women employed on School Lunch Projects were assigned to Gardening or Canning Projects where it was seasonally appropriate, others were able to can food and meat almost year round. The New England novelist and public affairs activist Dorothy Canfield Fisher wrote: "Any American would have been ashamed to oppose [school lunches]," but there was scattered criticism like that which appeared in a letter to *Parents' Magazine* expressing the fear that "the children of those now in the classroom will expect yet more from the schools." In replying to that fear, and to the companion fear that the school lunch was "educating a great part of the nation to socialism," Woodward wrote: "[without strong children], the bill for ill health and low morale . . . will be of such a nature and size that our country can ill afford to pay for it."[26]

When the WPA national home economics consultants, Margaret

Batjer and Ruth Chalmers, filed their program history in 1943, they concluded that the School Lunch Project had remained the most popular of all programs within their jurisdiction. Although many communities were unable to continue the food programs when federal funding ceased, others could and did. Like most of the women's projects, the School Lunch, Gardening, and Canning projects produced consumable goods and services that have long since vanished. Probably more than any other service project, the WPA school lunchroom contributed to bringing about public acceptance of the idea that free or inexpensive school lunches are neither emergency nor relief measures, but instead are an essential element in child and youth development. Linking school lunches to nutrition and defense after 1941 sustained their popularity, and in 1946 the National School Lunch Act institutionalized the program.[27]

The Women's and Professional Division worked to maintain the rapport with professional nurses it had established during FERA and CWA days and to maintain the favor of Pearl McIlver, public health consultant for the United States Public Health Service. Numbering about 7,500 in 1936, WPA nurses performed numerous duties. McIlver lauded the WPA projects for introducing recent graduates of nursing schools to the field of public health, while Woodward continued to advocate the extension of public health services to rural areas. Writing about WPA home care in 1937, she said: "Nowhere are the services of these nurses more welcome than in isolated homes of poverty stricken country folk who never before have had anyone on whom they could call for help when stricken by illness."[28]

WPA nurses who staffed health clinics in mill towns and among rural blacks expanded their access to immunization, physical examinations, and a variety of health-care procedures. As noncontroversial as the work might appear, Woodward's office received numerous letters from women proposing that WPA nurses provide birth-control information to mothers who applied to WPA offices and clinics for assistance. Aware of the explosive nature of the matter, Woodward could only reply that all WPA projects relied on local sponsors (state health departments, for the most part), whose policies must be respected. There were letters, however, that opposed birth control or argued that dissemination of birth control information was an inappropriate function for the WPA.[29] Before the debate had run its course, Woodward and Hopkins were no longer WPA administrators; but they left behind a service project in nursing that had just completed the most far-reaching inventory ever made of the nation's health.[30]

From the standpoint of health and general welfare, the WPA Housekeeping Aides Project rivaled the school lunch program in meeting a genuine need. Visiting housekeepers proved to be one of the most useful FERA and CWA ventures in creating work for domestics whose jobs had been terminated, as well as for women who had never worked outside their homes. WPA housekeeping aides went into the homes of relief clients to provide temporary help where there were ill, aged, or bedridden individuals or blind or handicapped persons who needed special care. During the 1937 floods, for instance, they helped the Red Cross distribute commodities, cleared debris from flooded homes, assisted in bedside nursing, and established soup kitchens. By the spring of 1937, more than 12,000 women were working through 480 housekeeping aides projects, ministering to over 300,000 needy families.[31]

Woodward considered WPA housekeepers valuable to communities because they saved local governments the cost of institutional care for stricken individuals. In addition, many of the aides—who received pre-assignment training in household maintenance, nutrition, bedside care, and related fields—subsequently found employment in private homes and public institutions. She described the program as a "practical, tangible, and clearly defined" type of assistance that met a need for which no other program had yet been devised. Even after Social Security benefits began to trickle down to the chronically ill and aged during the late 1930s, care of preschool children and homebound, aged, or ill persons remained a grave problem for families.[32] Still, the Housekeeping Aides Project presented problems. It was difficult to supervise scattered workers and adhere to standard WPA regulations. Woodward spent an inordinate amount of time responding to officials of the American Nursing Association, who questioned the competence of WPA housekeepers to nurse or care for sick clients. The problem stemmed from practices at the local level, where aides were called "community visiting nurses" or "practical nurses." The ANA wanted assurance that nursing professionals were adequately supervising WPA aides in caring for the sick. Seeking "to warrant the confidence and trust of the professional groups," Woodward asked for the cooperation of officials of the United States Public Health Service in preparing manuals of instruction for the training of housekeepers. Writing from a later perspective, both Phyllis Palmer and Winifred Wandersee have issued indictments of the WPA aides while at the same time acknowledging the good work they did. Housekeeping "kept women firmly on the periphery of the job market and clear of traditional men's work," Palmer writes; while Wandersee points out that the skills developed were not transferable to other aspects of the labor market. Too, there were the same implied statements about racial stereotyping attributed to projects designed to assist domestic workers and develop training programs for women with virtually no skills.[33]

Clarifying project goals for unskilled workers, long a problem, was never so prominent as it was at the Mayflower Conference in 1936. Would it not be better to absorb the unskilled into service projects, such as school lunchrooms, that were intended to raise community standards than to train the unskilled for entry or reentry into nonexistent jobs? How could project directors prevent exploitation of relief labor by private employers when jobs did materialize? And how far should WPA officials go in forcing women into private employment?[34] Harry Hopkins and Aubrey Williams thought the last option potentially disastrous. Both of them knew that state officials, particularly those in the South, had attempted to subvert CWA and WPA training programs to benefit new factories attracted by the prospect of hiring relief workers who might cost employers nothing during the training period and very little during subsequent employment. Mississippi was "especially susceptible," the historian George Brown Tindall has concluded, and "contrived some bizarre innovations" whereby towns contrived to have the WPA construct factories billed as "industrial training schools."[35] Based on information relayed by Molly Dewson and from Ethel Payne, Woodward was able to keep abreast of predators in the garment industry anxious to set up shop using labor trained in the sewing rooms. When she arrived in Washington fresh from her "business progressivism" promotional activities for Mississippi industry, backers of a plant in Columbus, Mississippi, which intended to "train" 1,000 girls in the garment trades, misled her into recommending to Hopkins the construction of the factory as a CWA endeavor. Subsequently, her superiors in the FERA-CWA offices informed her of the practices of the "fake schools" in Mississippi on which Hopkins maintained a thick file. Hence, she cautioned Ethel Payne not to say anything about vocational training schools in her own program planning.[36]

Nevertheless, Woodward was sold on the idea of women's programs emphasizing training. She had first met leaders in workers' education at a planning conference convened by Frances Perkins in February 1934. Representing the FERA Women's Division, Woodward quickly saw the opportunities that workers' education offered for unemployed teachers and recreation leaders.[37] Subsequently, she presided over a

White House meeting planned by Hilda Worthington Smith to discuss resident camps for workers and unemployed women.[38]

Later that year, Harry Hopkins tapped Smith to direct FERA camps for women workers; but the program suffered from administrative confusion at the state level. In about a third of the states, Woodward's women's work directors were in charge of the camps, but she believed that vigorous pursuit by her office of the queries would have led her division into Smith's arena. One study of New Deal camps and resident centers for women workers concludes that Woodward "showed little enthusiasm for Smith's program" and that neither Woodward nor Hopkins conveyed a sense of commitment to the camps.[39] Another views Woodward as "a Smith ally and close colleague . . . in the New Deal sisterhood of social feminists." Hilda Smith wrote Woodward after the New Deal ended of her debt "for your consistent support all through the FERA-WPA period."[40]

"The major tragedy of it all," Woodward reiterated in most of her public statements, was that 80 percent of unemployed women on relief rolls were unskilled and inexperienced in any kind of work. As early as 1935, Alfred Edgar Smith, a native Arkansan who became an adviser and investigator on black affairs for Hopkins, wrote in his annual report, "Adequate work opportunities for untrained Negro women is a problem for which Federal, State, and local administrative officials frankly admit having no solution." Only a portion of untrained domestics could perform even the simplest of tasks on the sewing projects. It was a dilemma that led Woodward to conclude that training projects should be the chief function of the Women's Division and one that would make its work program distinct from that for men.[41] In July 1935, she added Agnes Cronin to her staff. Cronin, a graduate of Radcliffe College who also held an M.Ed. degree from Harvard University, was at the time of her appointment the director of training for Gimbel's Department Store in New York City. When Cronin replaced Chloe Owings as Woodward's administrative assistant a year later, Celia R. Case became director of a training program that not only taught job skills to workers but general instruction in health, hygiene, and budgeting as well. Woodward pointed out to Eleanor Roosevelt, "the women in our program, because of their dual function of mothers and homemakers as well as breadwinner . . . must be given training on projects." After all, they could hardly be expected to attend evening adult classes while also performing their relief-work duties and tending to their homes.[42]

While a major goal of nearly all the projects was to provide workers with a marketable skill, Woodward was enthusiastic about the one program set up for the sole purpose of training: the Household Workers' Training Project. During discussions in late 1935 with Hilda Worthington Smith and Louis Alderman (director of the WPA's Education Division), she worked out a design for nonresident household demonstration centers that would not compete with the resident centers operated by Smith and Alderman. The Women's Division's operation was to provide courses lasting ten to twelve weeks that would prepare female heads of families for domestic service in private homes and public institutions. [43]

As the occupational option most open to women, particularly unskilled minority women, domestic service was both unorganized and unprotected by legislation. Because of the absence of a group to speak for this occupation, there had been no National Recovery Administration code for domestic workers. It was a field in which the largest number of women certified for FERA and WPA assistance showed a work history. The low status of the occupation—with attendant low wages, uncertain hours, and poorly defined duties, together with the chaos in domestic employment practices—had long troubled Eleanor Roosevelt, who since 1928 had been honorary chair of the National Committee on Household Employment. Writing in the *Woman's Home Companion* in 1935, Mrs. Roosevelt wrote that one solution to the dilemma in domestic service was to consider the work as "a business and train for it exactly as you prepare for any other work." When she read one of Woodward's memoranda on the subject of training household workers, she answered, "I was very much interested . . . Let me know how you come out."[44] Thus, the First Lady endorsed Woodward's project to elevate domestic employment to the level of a skilled profession.

The Household Workers' Training Program began in 1935 when Harry Hopkins released $500,000 to set up centers in seventeen states and the District of Columbia to educate women aged eighteen to twenty-five in household skills. Expanded under the WPA the next year, by 1938, the project included about 15,000 young women. Despite the conscientious work of Anna Marie Driscoll, the Women's Division Home Economics consultant, the three successive household workers' projects never accomplished what Woodward intended. Both workers and project directors complained that the projects were a dumping ground for women removed from other projects when their quotas were cut.[45] Final reports revealed that the trainees who completed the courses (and many did not) could not find employment at the wages and under working conditions they were told to expect. The final report from South Dakota stated the paramount obstacle succinctly. The unit there closed because there were too few women "who desired . . . to learn an industry which rated least in their desires."[46]

Woodward's and Roosevelt's rationale for and approach to Household Workers' Training showed that they shared a certain naiveté regarding domestic work. A latter-day critic of the WPA domestic projects has written: "The program trained women who did not need such training; it trained them in employment areas severely contracted by the Depression; and it trained them in an occupation that had been losing occupational status and prestige for over a century!" Even where the projects succeeded, there were drawbacks. Lorena Hickok found that after the project saturated the Houghton, Michigan, area with trained maids, the surplus "graduates" were directed to Detroit and Chicago, where a WPA investigator found them making $10 a month. "Oh God damn this women's work anyway," she wrote Eleanor Roosevelt, adding that she had a mind to "tell that damned fool woman down in Lansing [the state director] a few of the facts of life."[47]

When Woodward had outlined to Harry Hopkins what she hoped to accomplish under the WPA, she stated as one goal that of developing state and local advisory committees "to make communities actually aware of their responsibility for seeking some solution to their own unemployment problems." Given the difficulty in measuring accurately what real influence the laity may have had, it is still safe to conclude that the WPA's reliance on lay advisory committees and citizen advice, a practice that could be traced to President Roosevelt's wish to counter accusations of regimentation, too often resulted in projects that had little chance of effecting true social change.[48] The lay committee for Household Workers' Training in Tucson, Arizona, was typical. There the group consisted of members of four women's clubs (the PEO, Junior Women's Club, Junior League, and Democratic Women's Club), a member of the YWCA Employment Service, and a representative of the United States Employment Service.[49] No one advocated the point of view of the domestic workers themselves, an omission explained by the absence of an organization to represent them.

For the most part, placing women who enjoyed professional and social status—the "ladies bountiful"—in an advisory capacity for Household Workers' Training was patronizing of minorities. It also placed in juxtaposition two groups with dissimilar motivations. Phyllis

Palmer, who has written at length on the history of domestic service, calculates that Woodward's altruism in designing household training for the unskilled was tempered by her sense that, politically, it was a smart move to help domestics learn better how to do work that would not offend whites who both supported and criticized the New Deal.[50]

The disproportionate involvement of black women in the projects for household and sewing workers points to aspects of discrimination that marred New Deal efforts to relieve unemployment, as well as the difficulties stemming from policies that left decision-making to the local level. There is abundant evidence that black women were hit harder by the Depression than were whites. More black women were the sole supporters of their families. Nationwide, in 1936, a female was the head of 14.3 percent of all families, whereas in thirteen Southern states and the District of Columbia, women were the heads of 41.7 percent of all black families. Julia Kirk Blackwelder has chronicled the "quiet suffering" of Atlanta women who lost their work as domestics and for whom no other jobs opened.[51] And yet, when deprived of jobs, black women could expect little help from relatives and had few resources to fall back on and thereby postpone application for relief.[52]

For both women and men, FERA and WPA programs were intended to be nondiscriminatory; but, in reality, widespread, institutionalized prejudice and unjust practices thwarted the rule. A black woman, who could not readily obtain information about the man who was legally the head of her family but who was absent so often that he provided no assistance, faced a delay in being certified for work until some resolution was made about his absence. The ruling that only the head of a household could obtain a relief job disadvantaged black families where, before the Depression, both husband and wife had to work just to eke out an existence. In addition, the seasonal nature of WPA programs for men inflicted unfair hardship on black families; during winter months, when outdoor work was not available for men, wives could not be certified as household heads. Finally, many certification clerks expected a black family to demonstrate a greater degree of destitution than a white family.[53]

The biggest single factor in the inequitable employment of black women was their underrepresentation on sewing projects. Workers and their advocates continually reported to Ellen Woodward and Harry Hopkins the pitiless treatment of black women by local authorities or supervisors. In the South, where there was fear that cheap agricultural labor would vanish if relief work were provided for blacks, work clients lodged complaints that sewing rooms closed at cotton-harvest time. Those workers able to retain WPA employment were then dispersed to projects, often outdoors and at reduced wages, that entailed hard physical labor on "landscaping" projects. The manual-labor projects prompted a great deal of investigation by Alfred Edgar Smith, who concluded that projects involving light labor were satisfactory when "skillfully devised and tactfully administered." Smith condemned, as did the black press, instances where women were transported in open trucks and worked in bad weather. Critics also targeted gardening projects to which black women were assigned when no sponsors could be found for sewing projects.[54]

When sewing and mattress-making were curtailed following outbursts from commercial producers, manual-labor projects for black women increased in inverse ratio to the decline in the number of sewing rooms. There were reports that white women were assigned to work with lighter-weight fabrics for making dresses or infant layettes while blacks were given materials to produce men's work clothes.[55] Whenever sewing rooms were integrated in the North or the South (the latter case was rare), black workers customarily filed complaints that they were assigned to menial chores not expected of whites.[56]

Woodward monitored the treatment of black women in the sewing rooms and routinely investigated complaints which often dead-ended in reports that contradicted the workers' charges. Even before Lawrence Pinckney, a South Carolina WPA administrator, reported to Smith that the only evidence of an arduous work requirement for women was "one woman's chopping down a small shrub with an axe," it was clear to Smith that state WPA officials were not "anxious to confess discrimination."[57]

Most cases of neglect and unjust treatment of black women could be traced to complications in FERA and WPA sponsorship. WPA project designers found it difficult to negotiate with sponsors for black women's projects where local prejudice held sway and where communities wished to retain women in domestic or agricultural work. In Georgia, WPA administrator Gay Shepperson attempted to assist blacks but was forced to back down when her efforts antagonized sponsors who threatened to cancel projects.[58] The problem worsened when the Women's Division was forced to close sewing rooms whenever congressional funds were near depletion and deficiency appropriations were still pending, leaving project directors no choice but to call for an increase in sponsor contributions to keep projects alive.

Such was the case in 1937, when WPA administrative entanglements escalated as an assertive Congress cracked the appropriations whip in the wake of hostility toward the agency which surfaced in the special Senate Committee on Relief created in January. Congress cut its allotment to the WPA by $1.5 billion, a figure that reflected the President's desire to retrench spending. Further reduction by executive order in the summer of 1937 not only led to layoffs of workers but also forced Woodward to reduce her administrative staff by forty. "I haven't been able to put one single person on," she explained when Congresswoman Virginia Jenckes, of Indiana, sought a job for a constituent.[59] The cuts placed mothers with dependent children in a double bind. These mothers lost the WPA jobs but were not yet eligible for aid under the new Social Security program in states that had failed to make funds available. As always, those who suffered most were the large number of needy and unskilled at sewing and in allied home-economics activities.

Blacks predominated in enrolling in visiting-housekeeper projects.[60] The Housekeeping Aide Project could be maintained only by adhering to local social patterns. Alfred Smith received complaints from black women sent to "well-to-do white houses" when there was a greater need for assistance in black homes. Black women were sent into the homes of both black and white families, but few white women were willing to care for black families. In Texas, Anglo women complained that their work as housekeeping aides was "dirty and exhausting." There were problems based on class as well; many workers, both black and white, resented having to provide domestic service for women as poor as themselves.[61] Black leaders justifiably complained that the Housekeeping Aides Project perpetuated the notion that black women were subservient to whites.

Woodward knew that FERA and WPA home-economics projects for the unskilled were being criticized for perpetuating the domestic status of women regardless of race or ethnicity. Nonetheless, she and her regional and state directors faced the fact that 90 percent of the black women certified for relief work lacked skills beyond those of rudimentary homemaking, and that many women did not perform even these tasks well. The approach of Woodward and her directors was no different from that of the New Jersey Urban League, which conducted training programs for housekeepers, cooks, and laundry workers; or the New York and Brooklyn Urban Leagues, which had initiated a successful Visiting Housekeeper's Project under the CWA that was taken over by the WPA. In the summer of 1937, Mary McLeod Bethune, now head of minority affairs in the National Youth

Administration, inquired about the progress of a large household training project in Harlem. "I am very anxious," she said, "to put more emphasis on this home training work for negro girls through the southern states"—emphasizing, "I want to have that done." One writer suggests that black advocates promoted WPA housekeeping aides and household training because "[these projects] implied federal recognition for traditionally black and despised work."[62]

At first, household-worker projects offered promise. Smith reported that the WPA Household Training Project "worked veritable wonders in raising a comparatively few Negro domestic workers to a level enabling them to command what is in this occupation unsmilingly called a living wage." Thomas C. Walker, a black consultant in the state relief office, described the success of projects that operated in four Virginia cities improving personal standards of participants as well as the circumstances of their employment.[63] There was severe criticism, however, that the projects were only dummy organizations whose ultimate purpose was to remove blacks from relief rolls at substandard wages.

The program undoubtedly had serious shortcomings, which helped perpetuate racial segregation. Some Southern states had longstanding laws prohibiting whites from teaching blacks. There was never a WPA policy deliberately to segregate workers, yet sewing rooms were segregated on a de facto basis, allegedly because their location made them accessible to workers. Where attempts *were* made to integrate projects, sponsors gave in to public animosity and threatened to abandon their support. In Georgia, for instance, the Women's Democratic Club complained to Gay Shepperson that both black women and white women were working together in sewing rooms. The club wanted the practice stopped.[64] Like the disenchanted household trainees in South Dakota, black women did not embrace preparation for household work. Jane Van de Vrede told Lorena Hickok, "The only trouble is that [they] won't go for it. They don't want to learn how to be servants."[65] The reluctance of women to take up housework as a "profession" matched the lack of enthusiasm among women's organizations, which refused to sponsor projects because they were not interested in endeavors aimed at increasing domestic wages. Hickok wrote to Hopkins from Baltimore, "My own feeling was that what the good housewives ... really want is a block of Negro mammies who will work for their room and board."[66]

Similar prejudices and problems beset WPA programs for black professional women. In July 1935, Woodward sent a memo to her field staff, saying, "It is our desire to do everything within our power to see that Negro White Collar Workers are given a fair chance." Where communities and sponsors would not sanction "proper representation" of blacks in the "regular run" of white-collar projects, special programs were to be designed for black professionals.[67] Acting in response to Robert C. Weaver's reports of discrimination against black professionals in Chicago, Agnes Cronin contacted Florence Kerr and asked her to create projects for them. At the same time, Woodward pressed the New York City administrator about the distress among white-collar workers there. In 1938, T. Arnold Hill, on leave from the Urban League, joined the WPP to help devise projects for black professionals who found assignment difficult to secure on other than all-black projects or in menial work. Anticipating that she could add a black woman to her staff, Woodward asked Smith for recommendations; but, in 1938, she was forced by budget deficits to make drastic cuts in her staff.[68]

Disgruntled by the small number of blacks in administrative positions in the New Deal and by the failure of federal programs to serve the black community at levels anywhere near approximating those at which it served whites, black leaders held a series of conferences in Washington between 1935 and 1937.[69] In February 1938, Bethune and Woodward set in motion plans for a White House conference which Eleanor Roosevelt had discussed with Bethune earlier. Woodward herself processed the invitations that went out under Roosevelt's name, and she worked with Bethune to determine who among the invited delegates should have their travel costs paid out of Woodward's office budget. At a conference held on April 4, fifty-two representatives of constituent organizations within the National Council of Negro Women joined women administrators of government agencies and bureaus whose social welfare services extended beyond the WPA work activities. Bethune wished only that the government women listen to her NCNW associates. Behind-the-scenes steps were taken to avoid disquiet among both groups. Woodward told Mrs. Roosevelt in a confidential memorandum that Richard Brown, of the National Youth Administration, "had counseled Mrs. Bethune to see to it that her group makes an objective and unemotional presentation." Meanwhile, Agnes Cronin advised Woodward that it would be wise to take Bethune "at her word and to do a great deal of listening and very little talking."[70]

As it turned out, the conference presented no problems. If anything, everyone was overly polite and restrained. Resolutions adopted by the

Mary McLeod Bethune, speaking to the Council of Negro Women attending the White House Conference on the Participation of Negro Women and Children in Federal Programs, April 1938 (National Archives 69-N-13843)

NCNW delegates at the morning session called for the appointment of black women advisers in federal agencies so that black women and children might participate in federal welfare programs proportionate to their need. (In the end, the resolution proved merely perfunctory.) At the afternoon session, Mrs. Roosevelt conceded that minority consultants were important but told the audience that their real job was "getting this thing into localities." She recommended that biracial (and intrinsically nonthreatening) women's committees work together in each community to focus the attention of officials and sympathetic citizens on the needs of all people.[71]

In discussions prior to the conference, Woodward had concurred with Bethune that "Negro women have not gotten their share of jobs, but that the disparity resulted from the fact that the Washington office had no jurisdiction over certification for work relief.[72] Applicants must be declared "employable" by local relief officials who often defined the term to fit local notions of what was acceptable employment for minorities. She recognized that black women were the victims of local reluctance to pay a WPA security wage to persons with no recognized occupational status. It was for that reason, she maintained, that WPA assistance in training the unskilled had resulted ˙in tangible progress for black women.[73]

In a preconference briefing, Woodward reminded Mrs. Roosevelt that the main thrust of the parley would be the employment of black representatives in the central administration of the WPP. Her office also received requests from Mexican-Americans and Native-American leaders, but, because of budget restrictions, she could not add special representatives for each group. Thus, she thought it best to work "unobtrusively" for blacks, "since the whole matter is so highly controversial," adding that "too much publicity" concerning efforts for one minority group "is bound to prove a boomerang."[74] Minority representatives were not added to the Washington office, though Woodward did ask for an extension of Hill's assignment, due to expire in September 1938.[75]

Requests by other minorities for representation on the WPP staff suggest the neglect and discrimination Mexican American and Native American women experienced in their treatment by work relief authorities. Julia Blackwelder's sensitive study of an area of high density of minority women, San Antonio—from 1929 to 1939—describes the failure of the WPA women's program to make any permanent change in the lives of black and Hispanic women. The account is a litany of unfortunate aspects of the WPP operation. White women received a disproportionate number of work relief openings and worked on projects segregated from those in areas that served Mexican-Americans and blacks. No minority women were prominent in administrative positions; not even household trainees worked under supervisors who were members of their own ethnic group. The reluctance of Texas WPA officials to place women in nontraditional work only reinforced occupational segregation. This was particularly true for minorities. "Programs for black women functioned," Blackwelder found, "on the assumption that the destiny of the black woman was domestic work." Ironically, in an area where women on relief were considered only temporarily "in the work place," it was only black women in household training who were viewed as permanent workers.[76]

The difficulties in San Antonio were similar to those elsewhere in the country. The secretary of the Tampa Urban League had "no luck" in acquiring equipment or locales for sewing and mattress projects for black women, because Tampa relief administrators claimed they lacked authority. Advocacy groups such as the National Association for the

Advancement of Colored People received petitions from other groups, including the American Committee for the Protection of the Foreign Born.[77] Irish-American women complained about the sanctimoniousness of Anglo-Saxon Protestants who supervised many of the Boston projects.[78] Finally, Woodward's office found it difficult to deal with the conflicts that grew out of divergent religious beliefs or lifestyles.

The WPP faced setbacks, too, in its attempts to institute projects for Native-American women. Administrative logjams developed when Woodward—working with E. Reeseman Fryer, general superintendent of Indian Affairs in Arizona, and with officials in the Office of Indian Affairs—attempted to start sewing projects on the Navajo Reservation in Arizona. Project approval in Washington impinged on certification by the United States Employment Service of the women as needy. At the time, however, USES quotas permitted no additional certifications. Thus, Native-Indian women faced problems similar to those of blacks and Mexican Americans where local decisions on certification blocked opportunities for placement on relief rolls. Nothing developed in rug-weaving for Navajo women. "We were less enlightened in those days, I'm sorry to admit," Fryer recalled nearly fifty years later. In Florida, Seminole women who produced clothing for needy members of the tribe learned some useful sewing skills, but those who hoped to sell quilts found that there was no local market in a tropical climate, and they had no means of developing sales beyond their own area.[79] Even more than Anglo males, some Native-American men were adamant that women not work outside the home. Such ingrained convictions restricted women on work relief to such traditional tasks as adobe-plastering, rug weaving, and basketry.[80]

Hispanic women in New Mexico faced gender and class discrimination from both the state WPA head, a man who believed that "women should not earn as much as men," and women state administrators who considered work projects better suited for women clerical workers in Anglo-American communities than for Hispanic villagers. As was the case with black women in the South, a Hispanic woman who had an unemployable or absent husband was often denied work because she was not the legal household head. Nonetheless, sympathetic local supervisors reported great success, both in the production of useful goods and the lifting of morale for those Hispanic women who secured placement in sewing or mattress production.[81]

Suzanne Forrest, now director of the Albuquerque Museum, has described traditions that restricted Hispanic women to the age-old tasks of preparing food and producing men's work clothes and chil-

dren's garments. She found that Ellen Woodward contested the practice of the WPP New Mexico women's director in paying Hispanic
women with no work experience lower wages than the security wage
paid to men, but Woodward could not countermand decisions made
by the wage division in Washington. On the other hand, Forrest found
many positive aspects to the "cultural agenda" of the WPA to expand
the Hispanic heritage in crafts, music, art, folklore, and drama through
projects that all employed some women.[82]

Lorena Hickok observed racial tensions growing out of New Deal
agency stipulations for pay scales that preserved prevailing standards
in the South and Southwest, where blacks and Mexican-Americans
were relegated to lower wages than whites or Anglos.[83] In a conference
in Woodward's office on 14 January 1937, where her regional directors
discussed their difficulties with regional wage scales, Southeast director Blanche Ralston reported widespread criticism that unskilled black
women on sewing projects were paid $35 a month even when they
had not learned to sew. Woodward responded that the South's long
neglect in providing educational training for blacks was "responsible
for the bad condition there and [was] one of the direct causes of the
economic condition in the South today." When Ralston pleaded that
funds were inadequate to meet the first priority of educating whites,
Woodward countered: "We shouldn't wait until we get something for
the white people before doing something for the Negroes." "The
Government isn't justified in paying people starvation wages because
they only got that much before," she continued, further admonishing
the directors: "If the Government gives them a living wage we should
be glad and not do something to tear it down."[84]

Woodward cared a great deal about the neglect and discrimination
that were the lot of minorities in WPA work relief. Her correspondence and memoranda to southern relief officials reveal the dilemmas
encountered by Washington and local project directors. She knew the
WPA would unrelentingly hold to its principles of channeling relief
through public and not private agencies, and that the states must share
the financial relief burden. Hence, there was the insistence that state
agencies, ultimately subject to voters, sponsor nonlabor costs. To
maintain this obligation, it became a major tenet of the WPA that
states be given a measure of control and that lay advisory committees
be involved in decision-making. "The responsibility for 'Jim Crowism'
in the WPA," Ruth Durant, a writer for *Survey Midmonthly*, stated,
"must rest with the local welfare agencies and the sponsors."[85] Writing
to a Mississippian, Woodward summed up the major impediment the

WPA confronted in dealing with discrimination and inequities: "It is not believed that a problem of this magnitude can be solved in one generation, especially through the efforts of a government organization not designed to cope with such a problem."[86] In short, the WPA, plain and simple, was in the business of relief, not reform.

Other New Dealers made similar choices in pulling back from reform that might result in abolition of their agencies. One of them did not want to jeopardize his operation: "To undertake to tie up the solution to a deep-seated social problem with the Agricultural Adjustment problem would probably make it impossible to carry out these emergency programs successfully."[87] The entire relief structure was subject to public scrutiny and censure. Congressional appropriations were never enough to permit the WPA to assume the total cost of relief work and thus be in a position to demand compliance with the agency's standards. Thus the reforms such WPA liberals as Harry Hopkins, Aubrey Williams, and Ellen Woodward advanced were not achievable in the administration of work relief.

There are instances when Woodward's racial views surprised people who expected her views to be typically "Southern." A breezy column in a Washington newspaper feature described a party in 1938, where "guests held their breaths and fearfully watched" as Woodward met several black writers—this at a time when a bitter debate raged on Capitol Hill over an antilynching bill (Senator Bilbo railed before the Senate that "the flower of Mississippi womanhood" had been defiled by attending a mixed-race social gathering).[88] But, reported the column, "nothing happened."

In July 1938, Woodward attended a meeting of the National Emergency Council. She was there at the invitation of Lowell Mellet, executive director of the NEC, whose report would define the South as the nation's "No 1 Economic Problem."[89] Later that summer, Woodward went home to the South, in both a physical and thematic sense. Whether she had been sent to help pave the way for acceptance of President Roosevelt's controversial focus on the region's problems is problematic; but both she and Harry Hopkins were in Memphis that August for a conference with WPA directors in the South. "I've always been particularly interested in women of the South because people have the idea they should sit at home," she told her audience. "I've found that when Southern women get firsthand knowledge of conditions, they'll do something about them. . . . They've always been leaders in welfare movements." A month before the Southern Conference for Human Welfare convened in November 1938, Woodward and May Thompson Evans were in Birmingham for a conference of Democratic women, where they urged the delegates to keep alive the liberal policies of Franklin Roosevelt. The only ones who opposed the President were those "too prejudiced or too disinterested to seek the truth," Woodward asserted.[90] She instructed her Southern state directors to send exhibits of their activities to Birmingham for a meeting of the Southern Conference for Human Welfare.[91] Although the reaction of many Southerners to the SCHW ranged from wariness to open hostility, Woodward wrote to Judge Louise O. Charlton that she considered it a "definite step forward."[92]

Along with Evans, Woodward followed the hearings in 1940 on a congressional measure to abolish the poll tax. Later, during World War II, she expressed her hope to the Georgia-born president of the National Broadcasting Company that "when this war is over we should no longer be content to be known as 'Economic Problem No. 1.' "[93] To her fellow Southerner and close contact, Francis Harmon, former editor of the *Hattiesburg-American*, Woodward mused: "You know that few people here think that anyone from the South can be liberal in his thinking so that is a little problem that will take time also." Wilbur Cohen, who came to know Woodward when she joined the Social Security Board in 1938, told an interviewer that for the first time in his life, he knew "a liberal from Mississippi who was interested in social reform."[94]

Woodward once had a pipe dream that somehow Whitworth College, a small Methodist-supported college in Brookhaven, Mississippi, always precariously financed, could become an experimental school to train young people from all Southern states for positions in social service. "Wouldn't it be grand to put some new ideas into effect in the deep South," she wrote Eleanor Roosevelt. Always open to new ideas about educational innovations and opportunities for the young, she corresponded with the educator Mary Ritter Beard. "Dear Ellen, honored Ellen," Beard addressed her in one of several long letters she wrote expounding her own views.[95]

By the end of 1937, Woodward's rank among Washington's women leaders was secure. She gave every indication of having the resilience and tenacity that were the hallmarks of successful New Deal officials. The columnist Emma Perley Lincoln observed that when Ellen Woodward had first come to Washington, "a good many people who didn't know her thought she was just a pretty woman with an attractive southern voice [who] wouldn't last long in the hardboiled job." She had fooled the skeptics. Woodward thought it remarkable that, in spite of "all the desires on the part of the Administrators to turn [the WPA] into a road building, airport building program, we have come out pretty well."[96]

Circumstances had also improved for Woodward personally. Her living arrangements became more stable with the arrival from Louisville of Mona Johnson, a gifted young black woman whom Woodward had known earlier. It was Belle's urging that her sister employ a full time housekeeper. In 1938, Mona married Otis Harden and continued to live in the District, remaining in Woodward's employ for more than thirty years.[97] A superb cook and gracious hostess, she did much to enhance Woodward's reputation for delightful parties and impressive receptions. In addition to her own skills, she was adept at managing caterers. More important, she did much to make the apartment at the Westchester a comfortable place when Woodward returned exhausted from work assignments or travels. Both increased greatly when Harry Hopkins lodged within her division the cultural programs of the WPA.

CHAPTER 6

Women's Work and the Four Arts: 1937–1938

F rom its inception, funding for the WPA ebbed and flowed; but the perennial battle of the ledger with Congress, the President, and a straitjacketed Bureau of the Budget was heightened in 1937 and 1938 as President Roosevelt and Congress debated whether the economic emergency declared when Roosevelt took office had ended. Across-the-board cuts in New Deal programs took a heavy toll on the WPA during the recession that arrived in 1937 in the wake of retrenchment. The ensuing hardships meant that Ellen Woodward had a double task: keeping viable the institutional and community-service activities that employed unskilled and professional women in whitecollar and "white apron" jobs while also defending the cultural WPA that came under her jurisdiction in 1936. The latter became the special victim of congressional harpies during the resurgence of hostility toward the WPA in 1938. Thus, to understand Woodward's administration of the WPP, especially during her last two years at the helm, requires that we keep track of shifting regulations that endangered both aspects of her division.

As we have seen, the original Women's Division of FERA and CWA became the Women's and Professional Division at the onset of the WPA; that was the time when Woodward bested Jacob Baker to have professional work projects performed by women returned to her after a temporary loss to him at the demise of the CWA in 1934. She scored an even greater victory over Baker when she gained control of Federal One, a group of projects developed by Baker for writers, musicians, artists, actors (the "Four Arts") and other highly skilled workers among whom were many women. Gaining Federal One meant that Woodward was now the chief administrative head of programs employing about 750,000 men and women. She pledged to "continue steadfast in her purpose of safeguarding the rights of women workers under the WPA."[1]

Woodward's continuing priorities lay with the women's projects developed by early 1936, when the direction of women's work relief had been defined. It was these projects that stood to lose ground to the Four Arts whose workers were both vocal and well organized.

Many of the predominantly women's projects were threatened with curtailment and even liquidation. Many were "institutional" activities that provided work to clients who performed services for local governments in hospitals, schools, "poor" homes, parks and related social agencies. Woodward used a number of tactics to protect the projects. A reporter described "the missionary zeal" with which she addressed a conference of Quota International, one of the women's groups on which she had always relied for support. Her schedule was brimming with such appeals. As she told Harry Hopkins, "securing sponsorship for the projects which result in improved services rather than the construction of tangible assets still requires a good deal of educational and missionary work."[2]

It distressed Woodward that the proportion of women on WPA assignments declined from 17.7 percent in October 1937 to 13.7 percent in March 1938. She was well aware that the bind was disadvantageous to the South, where a fifth of all WPA workers were women.[3] The President's reservations about the institutional projects impelled Woodward to make a hasty trip to Val Kill in July 1938 to air her frustrations to Eleanor Roosevelt about pending restrictions on service projects. A month later, the Hyde Park hostess received Woodward and WPP regional directors at the cottage for lunch with the President. A subsequent "My Day" column praised the projects. Woodward's boast, "I got the Institutional projects matter satisfactorily settled," seemed confirmed when President Roosevelt forwarded her memorandum on the projects to Hopkins, requesting of him: "When you come to Hyde Park will you speak to me about this?" Summer 1938 passed with no other serious fiscal threats to the nonconstruction projects.[4]

Woodward maintained her pace of publications and public speaking. At year's end, Virginia Price, her chief "ghost writer," estimated that her boss had averaged at least two magazine articles a month for a period of two years and had often made two or three major speeches a day.[5] Typical were her remarks to Democratic women in a Birmingham speech a week before the November congressional elections that homed in on the lasting value of the WPP's "intangible services."[6]

Woodward's Alabama address was a positive message that merely hinted at the division's problems. Any assessment of the WPA women's programs should go beyond tallying percentages of women on work relief or indicting WPA policies as discriminatory against women.

Writing of the division's activities, Charley Cole said that they were "so interwoven with the life of individuals and communities that one can only guess as to their far-reaching effect on the life and culture of the American people."[7] The community services of the Women's and Professional Projects were institutionalized. Federal, state, and local governments continued hot school lunches, nursery schools for low-income groups, library extension, historic preservation, and delivery systems for social services. "We are concerned," Woodward once said, "with the fundamental issue of whether our government is responsible for its citizens."[8]

Deeply committed to economic equality and social progress, Ellen Woodward deserves recognition as an effective human engineer of the New Deal. For social services reinstated under the New Frontier of John F. Kennedy and the Great Society of Lyndon B. Johnson, there are historic antecedents in the work of the Women's and Professional Projects initiated under Woodward. She was speaking prophetically when she told Harry Hopkins that the services of her WPP were fields in which "the WPA is really building new frontiers."[9]

Woodward's capture of the Four Arts requires explanation. When the WPA began in June 1935, Jacob Baker became assistant administrator of the Division of Professional and Service Projects, which included Federal One. At the state and district levels, however, Woodward's and Baker's divisions were combined and placed under the director of women's work in each state. The two functions remained separate in Washington until July 1936, when Hopkins combined and placed them under Woodward. Approximately 300,000 additional workers were now under her division.[10] Jake Baker was eased (or thrown) out, depending on one's reading of Hopkins's actions. The fact that Chloe Owings, Woodward's assistant, was offended by office politics suggests that it was Woodward who maneuvered Baker out. Records attest to frenzied memoranda pouring from both Woodward's and Baker's offices to Hopkins as they vied in presenting reorganization plans that would expand the authority of each by encroaching on that of the other.[11]

No one, then or since, has questioned Baker's ability, intellect, or administrative skills. In 1937, a writer for *Fortune* attributed the presence of the Four Arts directors in Washington as "pretty largely owing to [Baker's] good sense and courage." Described by the magazine as "a bald thickset, amiable engineer of forty whose casual manner conceals a vigorously theoretical and inventive turn of mind," Baker had been a rural high school teacher, ranch and mine supervisor, personnel whiz in the steel industry, and founder of a publishing company. His driving force may have been his greatest liability, however. Treated as almost sacrosanct, the Four Arts raised the hackles of state WPA administrators who had little say in their operation. The tone and content of Baker's directives aroused their ire and led to demands that Federal One be reorganized. Woodward confided to Florence Kerr that she would not discuss her difficulties with Baker unless he were present. "I want to face it with him and Mr. Hopkins," she told Kerr.[12]

Matters came to a head in June 1936, when Hopkins moved to oust Baker. A drama involving ideology was being played out. Always interested in large-scale social experiments and increasingly drawn to European affairs, Baker let his erratic behavior begin to reflect his political bias. For example, he once attended a White House social event wearing a black shirt, to express his belief that the New Deal had not moved far enough to the left. By contrast, Woodward was "a respectable southerner" whose personal and political style was not likely to offend anyone.[13] Baker was not actually fired, but since he no longer had Hopkins's ear and his jurisdiction had been greatly curtailed, he resigned from the WPA. Other circumstances lay behind Hopkins's replacement of Baker. When Baker moved to decentralize the arts projects, the four directors rebelled. Hallie Flanagan (the Federal Theatre), Holger Cahill (the Art Project), Henry Alsberg, (the Writers' Project), and Nicolai Sokoloff (the Music Project) insisted to Hopkins that they maintain firm control from Washington. When Hopkins consulted Eleanor Roosevelt, she remarked, "Have you ever thought the difficulty might be with Mr. Baker?"[14] Hopkins soon saw the wisdom of turning the projects over to the more evenly tempered Mrs. Woodward. Also, it seemed wise to appease certain powerful figures on Capitol Hill, particularly the Senate Finance Committee chairman, Pat Harrison, who had been lukewarm to the WPA's brand of culture. No fan of Baker, Cahill, who witnessed Woodward's challenge, figured that she "beat him" because she was Harrison's "protege."[15] As William McDonald observed in his account of the Four Arts administration, if the political ties established by Woodward's appointment "did not in the end save Federal One [they] were not inconsequential in prolonging its life."[16]

Woodward's women friends congratulated her warmly on the victory over Baker. "Swell!" wrote Carolyn Wolfe, of the Democratic Women's Division. After Woodward wrote Molly Dewson of her busyness in "merging Jake Baker's Division and mine," Dewson wrote back:

"You are doing a truly remarkable job. Gradually it is seeping in on the men."[17] Woodward was keenly aware of the opportunities Federal One offered women on relief. In January 1936, she learned that more than a fourth of the Four Arts workers were women. "As a woman," she said in her first public statement about the new WPP, she was gratified that helping preserve professional skills and talents was to be her task.[18]

The moment Woodward gained control of Federal One, the projects faced one of the periodic crunches that afflicted the entire WPA. Since the beginning, Federal One directors had been granted an exemption to the WPA ruling that no more than 10 percent of project workers could hold nonrelief status (that is, they need not be certified as needy). Dependent upon supervisors with professional skills, the Four Arts enjoyed a 25 percent nonrelief exemption. Extended only through the summer of 1936, the exemption fell to 10 percent, leaving Federal One directors aghast that, to remain as employees, some of their best talent would be subject to the means test. Woodward warned Hopkins: "We will have to keep close watch on Federal One to safeguard it during coming weeks."[19] She was correct. An administrative order further reduced the nonrelief exemption to 5 percent. Not only were the Four Arts required to stay within a nonrelief labor bind, they also experienced several quota reductions from fall 1936 through summer 1937, which meant no new employees could be added. Woodward spent more than six months pleading with Hopkins that employment on Federal #1 through #6 be stabilized, coordinating her defense of the projects with her regional supervisors and state directors, and deluging Hopkins with favorable media publicity of the Four Arts.[20]

In substantial ways, Federal One funding differed from that for other WPA work. Although the WPA survived only on congressional appropriations, and though most projects were dependent on local sponsorship, in large measure the Four Arts flourished or withered at the discretion of the President and his Bureau of the Budget. As William McDonald aptly put it, both held "a nice regard for the attitude of Congress." With Franklin Roosevelt insistent that Federal One be a relief program employing only the needy and not an employment program—that is, a program for hiring noncertified workers—Woodward on several occasions pleaded the cause of the cultural WPA with him.[21]

Federal One's funds were near depletion when Woodward took over the project in 1936. The first layoffs were ill-timed, however, coming as they did after a presidential campaign in which Roosevelt boasted of his work program for the unemployed. Since Hopkins thought the state WPA heads were "too hostile" to the federal projects to give the Four Arts "a fair break," it fell to Woodward to administer the cuts. "I need not point out to you," she cautioned her regional supervisors, "how important it is to stir up as little commotion as possible in connection with this." She fully expected there to be "delegations of disgruntled workers . . . especially the City Projects Council of New York City with its avowed standard of 'no dismissals.'"[22] As Woodward had feared, a clash between FAP pickets and police in New York City precipitated a riot that led to arrests and suspended sentences for more than two hundred workers. That rumble was only the beginning of almost incessant conflict, verbal and physical, between New York artists and their supervisors.

Only one desk removed from her superiors, Harry Hopkins and his alter ego, Aubrey Williams, Ellen Woodward was the buffer throughout numerous controversies swirling around Federal One. In his study of New Deal artists, Richard McKinzie placed her at the nexus of the

Aubrey Williams, Assistant Administrator (WPA), Eleanor Roosevelt, and Woodward with a doll display in Woodward's office at the Walker-Johnson building (1938) (National Archives 69-N-14091)

Four Arts operation: "Mrs. McMahon [New York City FAP director] shielded Cahill; Cahill shielded Mrs. Woodward and Hopkins; and Mrs. Woodward and Hopkins shielded the President and Congress." Woodward said as much to New York Congresswoman Caroline O'Day during a stormy outburst among federal writers, "We've been trying to save Mr. Hopkins as much as possible—taking it all ourselves."[23]

Only by short-term fiscal reprieves were the projects funded until January 1937, when Congress appropriated additional funds for the entire WPA. The President, however, was unwilling to allocate fresh money for Federal One projects, and thus they operated on a hand-to-mouth basis. In the spring of 1937, Congress reduced WPA funds by 25 percent, which resulted in the eventual release of 11,000 Federal One workers, and in New York City, confrontations with federal artists and actors. Inseparable from the budgetary crises were Woodward's difficulties with Colonel Brehon B. Somervell, New York City's WPA chief, and the director of Federal One, Harold Stein. An army engineer with General Pershing in the expedition against Pancho Villa in 1916, the colonel displayed an administrative style typically military.[24] Although Woodward did not share Somervell's view that leftists permeated the projects in New York City, she did hope that he could restrain the projects. Presuming that they stood on common ground, the colonel boasted to her, "They just don't know the persons they are dealing with," adding, "You're a red head, aren't you?" "[W]e are not going through a lot of scenes," she lectured the colonel.[25] She was mistaken about this, for the summer of 1937 was a fiery time of trial for Federal One directors and workers in New York City.

A showdown was reached when *The Cradle Will Rock* was cancelled on the eve of its opening. *Cradle* has been described by the FTP historian Jane De Hart Mathews as a riveting opera "complete with bloated capitalists, sadistic cops, heroic union organizers, and the proverbial prostitute with the heart of gold." The opera went into production soon after laborers and a management group known as "Little Steel" clashed over unionization and after General Motors had given in to the demands of sitdown strikers. The clash was enough to draw a prepaid audience of 14,000 before *Cradle's* scheduled opening on June 16.[26]

The brouhaha over *Cradle* came just as Congress prepared to pick up the pursestrings of the WPA. On 10 June, Washington ordered a 30 percent cut in the New York FTP, which affected 1,700 workers. With funds near depletion, Ellen Woodward and Aubrey Williams thought it wise to allow no new shows to open until after the beginning

of the new fiscal year, 1 July. A day after Woodward informed Hallie
Flanagan that *Cradle* was not to open, the FTP actor-director Orson
Welles and Archibald MacLeish, his assistant, flew to Washington for
a conference with Woodward and David Niles. The conference turned
into a heated confrontation. According to Agnes Cronin, Woodward
"gave Orson Welles a real skinning." John Houseman, Welles' pro-
ducer, later described the scene with Niles as so "sharp" that it
made "peace no longer possible between us and the WPA."[27] On a
memorable night in American theater history, Welles' and Houseman's
new Mercury Theater staged a production of *Cradle* in another locale
as a non-FTP production.[28]

Acting through Woodward, Harry Hopkins named Harold Stein as
chief officer for all arts projects in the city. After dissident workers,
angry over dismissals, barricaded Stein in his office, Woodward notified Aubrey Williams that a delegation was demanding that either
Hopkins or President Roosevelt rescind the cuts made in New York
City. Williams became point man because Hopkins was out of town;
neither he nor Woodward had any intention of involving the President.[29] The standoff ended a day later, when New York City administrators Stein, McMahon, and others hastily assembled in Stein's office
and conceded that the dismissals should be postponed until a review
process could be instituted. Williams, however, cancelled the concessions for lack of funds. In assessing the problem for Charles Ryan,
personnel director of the FTP in New York, Woodward said: "They
seem to think we are cold blooded, but they are simply beside
themselves." Federal One workers, she added, would have to remem-
ber that it had only been through previous exemptions that Federal
One had originated.[30]

Disturbances continued in New York City. Woodward sent Agnes
Cronin to New York to confer with Federal District Attorney Lamar
Hardy, an old Mississippi friend, to explore what recourse to federal
action the WPA might have. Hardy boasted, "I'm right in the midst of
the thing up here with Colonel Somervell"; privately, he viewed the
strikers as "a radical crowd." He told Woodward that it was highly
problematic that federal protective measures were applicable. After
Cronin told Woodward that the workers intended to make her "the
goat" in the matter of dismissals without appeals, the WPP head was
even more anxious to put the New York City disorder behind her.[31]

It was Williams who spoke more sharply to the workers than any
other Washington official, telling union representatives: "A few more
things like that and you might as well kiss WPA out the window."

While delegations continued to descend on Washington, Williams and Woodward maneuvered to contain the demonstrations to New York, hoping that Stein would master the problem. "We don't want anything to get to Mr. Hopkins, and unless he [Stein] handles it out there, it's going to keep on coming closer and closer," Woodward advised Niles.[32] Stein was transferred to Washington, losing his position to Paul Edwards, a finance officer on the Washington WPA staff, who was expected to hold a firmer rein on the recalcitrant workers.

Brooks Atkinson, dean of theater critics, attributed the FTP's loss of vigor in New York to the "eminently businesslike fashion" in which Edwards ran Federal One as relief projects rather than treating them as bonafide professional endeavors. Edwards was, of course doing exactly what the WPA was created to do; that the WPA was, first of all, a relief program was made abundantly clear to Woodward by no one less than President Roosevelt himself. Woodward defended Edwards to Winifred Mallon, a writer for the *New York Times*. "Mr. Edwards is doing a grand first class job and they are making it difficult for him," Woodward told her. Like Niles, she chafed under criticism that appeared—too often, in her estimation—in New York newspapers of Washington's centrality in the administration of the arts. She did not like writers to base their articles on surmise rather than fact, or to extract conjectures from someone in her office. She told J. Howard Miller, who took William Farnsworth's place as Flanagan's deputy in Washington, "I am going to have to stop anybody handling any publicity except myself." Philip Barber, who ran the New York City FTP from 1935 to 1938, recalled years later that Washington was "very disturbed" at unfavorable publicity and that Woodward called him on several occasions to ask if he could prevent the *New York Times* from running stories critical of the WPA.[33]

Another blow came in July 1937, when Roosevelt approved only one-third of the amount requested to carry Federal One through June 1938. "These last few weeks have been the most trying [since] I have been on Mr. Hopkins's staff," Woodward told a Los Angeles woman who had called to complain of cuts that affected a contentious California Federal One.[34] It was then that she sought out President Roosevelt and the budget director, Daniel Bell. The President rescinded his cutback so that the arts project might live on, although on far less money than the directors had requested. Recounting her conference with the President and Bell to David Niles, the WPA's information chief, Woodward reported: "We are not going to be washed up." After Roosevelt directed Bell to provide the less-than-desired operating funds for the projects, Woodward nevertheless was "[h]appy because he didn't wipe it all out"; but she still feared that the budget director would disburse the funds too slowly. "You know now nasty Bell has been," she reminded Niles. She was gratified that Roosevelt had a "fine interest" in the WPA arts. "I told him that I couldn't claim credit for initiating all this work but that I had tried my best . . . and he said that I had done a good job," she told Niles.[35]

One bright spot in the grim summer of 1937 was a successful workshop at Vassar for FTP personnel. An in-house magazine report on the "first Federal Summer Theater" (which also proved to be the last) featured a photograph of a smiling Ellen Woodward greeting members of the workshop on the day of her visit, July 25. After seeing a special run-through of a living newspaper in production, entitled *One-Third of a Nation*, she acclaimed the Poughkeepsie-based workshop as "the finest thing that has happened to this whole project." Soon after she returned to Washington, she talked with President Roosevelt. She found him upbeat about the Theatre, although he wanted the "ham actors and flunky musicians" who had "no chance in the world" to be absorbed into the private theater off the rolls. "We won a lot of points today," she told Hallie Flanagan as they discussed some way of dealing with the President's wish to see FTP companies go on tour. Both knew that the cost was prohibitive. As Woodward reminded the FTP director, however, "the President has to know something is underway or he'll get right on us."[36]

The summer of 1937 finally came to an end. Despite the difficulties of the Federal Theatre Project, there had been major triumphs. Even as she remained anxious about the continuing criticism of several productions, Woodward gloried in their success. In the hinterlands, productions were lively, audiences were growing, and the FTP was truly enriching dull and drab days for countless Americans hungry for inexpensive entertainment.

In the fall, however, the President again reduced funding for the arts, with a resultant "tragic rise" in unemployment, which Woodward detailed to Hopkins. The paucity in funding stirred her to gather the Federal One directors for another session with Eleanor Roosevelt. Early in 1938, a congressional appropriation of $250 million improved circumstances for the WPA in general, but it brought only a modest improvement for the Four Arts. Thus, funding was virtually on hold.[37]

Meanwhile, yet another emergency struck Federal One. The President and his budget advisers objected that man-year costs (the amount of money expended for one year's employment of a worker), at $1,200 per employee, ran higher for the cultural projects than for the rest of the WPA. After man-year costs were ordered in June 1938 to be held at $1,000, Woodward's division pleaded for continuation of the preferential treatment the arts had enjoyed since the beginning of the arts projects in 1935. She did not think it "unreasonable" that slightly more than two-thirds of Federal One personnel were classified as "professional." "[W]e are either operating professional art programs or we are operating no art program worthy of the name," she remonstrated to Aubrey Williams. To Hopkins, Woodward expressed her concern about reducing wages for workers in urban areas where they were "the best organized and most militant on the program"—this in a congressional election year. Aside from the disruption the cuts were certain to provoke, she was troubled that disturbances would come "just when we have reached the most efficient operating status in our history."[38]

She kept up the pressure. "Mrs. Woodward calls at least once a day . . . she pleads with you and asks that you take it up again," a member

Alfred Edgar Smith, minority affairs adviser for the Works Progress Administration (Courtesy Special Collections, University of Arkansas Libraries, Fayetteville)

of James Roosevelt's staff penciled on a memorandum from the WPP director, reminding the President of the pledge he had made to Federal One. She tried other strategems to capitalize on the First Lady's high regard for the arts. Anticipating that Mrs. Roosevelt could play a role, Woodward made sure the Roosevelts' home county in New York State was the site of an FAP art center; but the President forbade his wife's participation. Eleanor Roosevelt did, however, accept Woodward's invitation to join a select group of Washingtonians to hear the four directors make reports on the highlights of their programs.[39]

Woodward was only one member of the vigorous WPA administrative team for the arts during the crisis of 1937-1938. Lawrence Morris, her assistant for Federal One, described by an FWP principal as a "man of superb finesse," drafted many of her statements. Williams and Hopkins were equally intent, but the latter devoted much of his time to his ailing wife, Barbara, who died of cancer in October 1937. Hopkins, himself suffering from a stomach ailment, was developing a case of Potomac fever. By spring 1938, he was increasingly drawn into the President's strategy for purging conservative congressmen in the upcoming Democratic primaries.[40] After a downturn in the economy returned unemployment levels to its highest level since 1933, the President agreed to release additional funds for the WPA, which benefited Federal One. Between June and November 1938, employment in Federal One grew from some 29,000 to 40,000 persons as the WPA lumbered toward its peak enrollment of 3,335,000 the week before the November elections. There is little doubt that the election had much to do with the new well-being that the Four Arts enjoyed.[41]

The funding reprieve did not account entirely for the augmented relief rolls, however. Faced with the mandate to reduce labor costs, Woodward recommended hiring thousands of additional workers on Federal One projects, particularly for the Historical Records Survey, at less than "professional" status (and hence at less than $1,200 man-year rates), in order to reduce the average labor cost to specified limits. Hopkins forwarded her requests, which became part of the final solution. As Elsie L. George has observed, Woodward "had become a superlative bureaucrat, expanding her program while reducing it."[42]

In January 1938, a new production that opened to a rousing reception was hailed as the greatest of the "Living Newspapers." *One-Third of a Nation* is an epic of the quest by New York slumdwellers for decent housing. Broadsides for the production attracted considerable attention at an impressive exhibit of the WPP that ran at the Smithsonian from 10 to 31 January 1938. Molly Dewson was so taken with *One-Third* that she inquired about the possibility of the DNC assuming the costs of sending the props and cast to agricultural fairs around New York State. Woodward rejected the idea. Other Democrats, including powerful U.S. senators, were irate over the way the show portrayed their callousness toward the New Deal's public housing policy.[43]

As the FTP took on new life, Woodward and Hopkins, the latter now recovering in Florida, encouraged the Federal Theatre to tour the nation's nonurban regions. Meanwhile, FDR renewed his insistence that the FTP reach out to more communities. But the idea was never feasible. By late summer, the hard realities of funding, together with the resistance of WPA state administrators to the idea of touring companies, caused Woodward to have second thoughts. By the time plans for the tours were abandoned in the early fall, the Federal Theatre had become a target of the House Un-American Activities Committee. Woodward, with whom the final decision lay, was fearful about bringing even a play about Abraham Lincoln to Washington.[44]

In other ways, the FTP expanded to reach audiences outside the major cities. Among the pageants and spectacles produced in the South and Southwest, none was more successful or long-lived than *The Lost Colony,* Paul Green's romance of North Carolina's ill-fated Roanoke settlement.[45] Woodward used a performance in 1938 as an occasion to pay a visit to Dare County projects where, according to a local reporter, she "left a half-hundred State women executives pop-eyed and breathless." Coming at the end of a nerve-wracking summer in Washington, the visit was a welcome respite. For one thing, it gave Woodward a chance to confer with May Campbell, director of North Carolina's women's relief work, who proclaimed the visit "one of the most pleasant things that has happened to the Women's Division in North Carolina."[46]

Happily, a few Federal One projects were not difficult to administer. By a stroke of luck, the Federal Music Project fell under the direction of Nicolai Sokoloff. A musician who commanded wide respect in the music world, Sokoloff insisted on a high level of artistry in the Federal Music Project.[47] Sokoloff's competence, the public's warm reception of WPA musicians, and involvement in virtually no activities that could be deemed propagandistic combined to make the Federal Music Project the one unit of Federal One that was almost entirely free of controversy. Woodward did not have to devote the time to it demanded by the other art projects. It was not until a 25 percent reduction precipitated the crisis in June and July 1937 that Sokoloff became unhappy with Woodward. "I can't help feeling a terrific mental jar," he told her during a conference of the four directors in September. "There is just so much confusion—our hands and feet are tied." Sokoloff could not dismiss lightly recent demonstrations in New York City, where WPA musicians had participated in a one-day work stoppage on all projects and angry musicians had conducted an all-night sitdown strike at a concert hall.[48]

Sokoloff knew that Woodward wanted him to spend more time in Washington than in New York. Uneasy because Hopkins was absent so often, she was more comfortable in having the directors close at hand when so many unexpected problems were cropping up daily. William Mayforth, Sokoloff's assistant, professed not to "know the reason" for Woodward's "unwillingness" to accede to Sokoloff's wishes to direct the FMP primarily away from Washington.[49] The fact that some FMP staff directors thought Woodward impervious to the demands of Sokoloff's schedule probably accounts for the sharp criticism that came from Harry Hewes, head of the FMP music analysis unit, when Florence Kerr inherited the WPP in late 1938. "Before that," Hewes scoffed, "we had a woman with a distinguished Confederate ancestry who knew nothing at all about art."[50]

The Historical Records Survey, free of controversy, held special appeal for cultural conservatives. Harry Hopkins had created the HRS as a federal project to inventory and codify the records that lay decaying or lying in disarray in federal, state, and local archives. Initially it functioned as an administrative wing of Henry Alsberg's Writers' Project under the supervision of Dr. Luther H. Evans.[51] Convinced that Alsberg misdirected historical records personnel to do work that would reflect greater glory on the beleaguered FWP, Evans urged Woodward in the summer of 1936 to make the HRS independent of Alsberg and give it status equal to that of the Four Arts. Sharp differences in temperament and style made working with Alsberg exasperating for Evans, whose letter set off a dispute that Woodward had to settle. Even after she separated the two functions and made the Survey a distinct entity within Federal One, Evans continued to believe that she was partial to Writers' Project personnel. He also continued to detect in Alsberg "a strong desire to chisel on the Survey for the benefit of the Writers' Project."[52] In view of the backing Woodward gave the HRS, Evans' pique hardly seems justified.

Of the Four Arts directors, Holger Cahill, of the Federal Art Project, seemed the most partial to Woodward. Although he expressed no opinion about her knowledge of art, Cahill was positive about

Woodward as an administrator. "You have gone to bat for us on so many things," he remarked during a conference at the end of the summer of 1937.[53] Like its companions, however, the FAP did not escape the economies that threatened all the arts. Smaller than its sister projects, the FAP was still very productive.[54] Community art centers, drawing many aspirants, reflected its social orientation.[55] While Woodward personally had nothing to do with programming FAP art classes, she did have to fend off unremitting protests from private art teachers in Florida, a state with more pre-Depression art activity than most others. Following her investigation of charges made by art teachers that the WPA classes were unfairly uncompetitive, a new policy was promulgated that required all children to pass a means test in order to receive WPA instruction.[56]

Molly Dewson and Harriet Elliott view an exhibit of pottery made on a WPA project in North Dakota at the great WPA exhibit of the Women's and Professional Projects at the National Museum of the Smithsonian, January 1938 (National Archives)

"Social themes abound," a *New York Times* writer said in reporting on FAP gallery exhibitions in the autumn of 1937. Although Congress and a vigilant press did not accuse the FAP of foisting foreign ideologies on Americans as they claimed other Federal One workers did, neither did it escape controversy. Cahill, embarrassed that pictures of Marx, Lenin, and Stalin were hung in the lobby of a federal theater, asked for their removal. When news of the offending art reached Washington, Woodward—speaking "in her sweet Southern voice," Cahill remembered—told him that Aubrey Williams had summoned her to his office twice and "stamped [her] face right into the floor." Even though Cahill conferred with his superiors, they did not broach the subject again. "Apparently," he concluded, "Ellen went in to Aubrey Williams and just knocked his head off."[57] This relatively minor incident typified Woodward's role as an intermediary in an ambiguous chain of command.

From the start, Congress and the Federal Theatre were on a collision course. The first of the "Living Newspapers," a new form of drama intended to address contemporary issues, indicated the dynamics Flanagan wished to bring to the new FTP. *Triple A Plowed Under* and *Injunction Granted*, both presented in 1936, represented new departures in the experimental theater, Flanagan's forte. *Triple A* praised the New Deal's agricultural acreage control policy; but it was *Injunction Granted*, through its pro-worker bias in depicting labor's battle for unions before antagonistic tribunals of law, that foreshadowed trouble for the Federal Theatre Project. Within a few weeks, talk that *Injunction Granted* was a political bombshell was circulating within Roosevelt's official circle. Woodward told Molly Dewson that William Hassett, a White House staffer, had called to complain that the play was "very communistic and anti-Catholic" and that it should be stopped. As a liberal, Dewson was "tickled" with the production. She believed it "used nothing except what was in the press." Still, she advised that its engagement be permitted to "peter out" and that it not be revived until after the presidential election of 1936. Confessing to Hassett her displeasure with the production's slant toward John L. Lewis and against "the other labor groups," Woodward told Hassett that she had stopped the sale of *New Masses* and the *Daily Worker* which leftist groups were hawking in the lobby of the Biltmore Theater, an activity Flanagan found appalling.[58] "We are going to come to grief about this thing yet," Woodward told William Farnsworth, Flanagan's deputy. "It ought to be cleaned up or closed up, one of the

Charley Tidd Cole, head of the Office of Information of the Women's and Professional Projects, with wool blankets from a Missouri project at the Smithsonian exhibit of the WPP, January 1938 (National Archives 69-N-12836)

two," she advised, adding: "I don't want to put my oar in and be the whole boss."[59]

Before *Injunction Granted* closed, however, other FTP productions had tongues wagging. Newark's actors staged *John Henry*, a play which, according to WPP regional supervisor Izetta Jewel Miller, bore "political implications." Categorized by Flanagan as a "Negro drama," the play was withdrawn from Newark and sent to Los Angeles. Explaining the switch to Miller, Woodward said, "We are not interested in censorship, but we know there are times when it is better to put on some plays and also when it is not advisable."[60]

Even before *John Henry* completed its two-week run on the West Coast, there was a flare-up in Chicago over *Hymn to the Rising Sun*, a one-act play by Paul Green. Neither Chicago mayor Ed Kelly nor the

Woodward and Blanche Montgomery Ralston of Mississippi, Regional Director of the Southeastern states under the WPP, at the Smithsonian exhibit of the Women's and Professional Projects, January 1938 (National Archives 69-N-12805)

state WPA head, Robert Dunham, wanted the show to go on, and it did not. Before the play was to have opened, David Niles advised Woodward and Lawrence Morris not to do "anything within the next two or three weeks that would get Mayor Kelly sore at us." Advance publicity scored the play for its strong language and portrayal of excessive cruelty. They knew also that Kelly was wary of the presentation in his city of a play based on "a negro situation."[61] In fact, Dunham flatly instructed Woodward, "The thing you don't get is our local political situation."[62] When Woodward conferred with Hopkins over *Hymn*, he admitted that the play's "sexual angle" posed a risk, although he was not "afraid of criticism on the grounds of radicalism." FTP administrators were already nervous over the forthcoming simultaneous opening in seventeen cities of the FTP's version of Sinclair Lewis's explosive novel about America's susceptibility to fascism. Farnsworth predicted that "our main fight . . . is going to be *It Can't Happen Here.*" Like Hopkins, he preferred not to "waste any shots" with Mayor Kelly over *Hymn.* The problem in Chicago had arisen in part from Hallie Flanagan's failure to read the play at a time when her schedule was too full to permit even a hasty perusal. Woodward told Howard Hunter, whose WPA regional supervision encompassed Chicago, "[I]f Flanagan is going to have authority to do these things, she is going to have to accept the responsibility of looking over the script." To Niles, she said, "Nearly every play which we had trouble with were the ones she hadn't read."[63]

Flanagan hoped that the multiproduction scheduling of *It Can't Happen Here* would garner greater laurels for her program. Early in September 1936, she told Woodward that, from a political standpoint, "it was the best blow we could strike for the administration." Molly Dewson, less certain, advised Woodward: "Why not wait until the election is over to put on [the play]?" Talking with William Hassett, Woodward admitted, "I have almost gotten to the point that I don't know what is a help," explaining, "Mr. Hopkins gave these arts people a pretty free hand" and that the programs had come to her division only recently.[64] After all, it had been only two months since the July 1936 reorganization and Baker's exit.

It Can't Happen Here was certain to be no sleeper. Despite Woodward's visceral feeling that it would be prudent to delay opening the play until after the first week in November, it opened on 17 October 1936, at the Adelphi Theater in New York City.[65] Flanagan understood the ramifications that Hopkins, Williams, and Woodward had explored in a conference on October 13. As Woodward pointed out, there was "danger of losing the whole business" if the FTP did not "lighten up on this, because the President can't continue to stand the pressure coming to him from all sources." Moreover, when Congress convened in January, "We are going to be in a bad position."[66] David Niles— more jaundiced than his colleagues, since he had to handle publicity for the entire WPA—proclaimed the play "lousy" and predicted its "natural death."[67] Both the critics and the public were more receptive. The production established the FTP as a national theater that appealed to many who had never seen live theater.

By the end of the second season of the FTP, Roosevelt was into his second term. Although cost-cutting had begun to take its toll on the Four Arts, and administering them seemed more difficult by the day, Woodward was enthusiastic about the Federal Theatre. For the moment, she could relax and enjoy productions that boldly presented social messages she privately endorsed without worrying how they might affect presidential politics. Like other administrative figures, she had no reason to think the President would seek a third term. She believed that his new political security freed him to "run this program [the WPA] right, the way it should be run."[68] When the New York unit produced *Power*, which glorified the Tennessee Valley Authority, she and Hopkins wanted the play brought to Washington. Woodward likely was attracted to the theme because northeast Mississippi towns were among the first to contract for the reduced rates that TVA guaranteed. She did not see the play; her enthusiasm was based on the generally warm reception it received despite such reviews as that by Brooks Atkinson, who pronounced it "the most indignant and militant proletarian drama of the season."[69]

California WPA officials were unenthusiastic about the Federal Theatre. The state, which nearly matched New York for FTP administrative snarling, presented in the early winter of 1938 one of the most blatant cases of censorship and general disruption by a state WPA administrator that could be found anywhere. Lieutenant Colonel Donald Connolly (army men were always intractable) demanded approval of all aspects of the Federal Theatre even down to the kilowattage of lightbulbs. As Woodward prepared to include an inspection of Connolly-related problems during a western trip over Christmas 1937, the FTP's new deputy director, J. Howard Miller, predicted, "[S]he will not meet any persons . . . who she cannot be perfectly frank with." Always candid, Connolly made a convincing case that he should call the shots in California. Upon her return in January, Woodward informed the stunned Four Arts directors that Connolly was to be the final arbiter in matters of personnel and even in play selection. Thus, Connolly's decision stood to cancel two scheduled productions, *Stevedore* (about race and union conflicts) and Elmer Rice's polemic against fascism, *Judgment Day*.[70]

The capitulation to Connolly flabbergasted Flanagan. Without question, however, Woodward's crackdown originated at a level higher than her own. Under pressure herself, she told a Los Angeles WPA official, "It is warm up there [Congress] insofar as Federal Projects in Southern California are concerned."[71] She was aware also that the views of David Niles represented those of Hopkins. Whatever agreements Woodward and Connolly made were tenuous at best. Woodward managed to have some key personnel reinstated, but Connolly's actions continued to anger theater figures in the state, including well-known Hollywood members of the Screen Writers' Guild and Actor's Equity, who championed a censorship-free Federal Theatre. Their threats to resign from WPA audition boards worried Woodward who was kept busy trying to maintain her own authority over Colonel Connolly. She never completely succeeded, for Connolly kept to his ways until he resigned from the WPA in 1939.[72]

Woodward's style often displeased Writers' Project head, Henry Alsberg, to whom her bent toward content analysis spelled censorship. Her insistence that the directors present a united and consistent front, not only to workers but also to congressmen and the press, stemmed from her own precepts of what constituted good administrative policy. Monty Penknower, a historian of the Writers' Project, has suggested that one source of the difficulties Woodward had with Alsberg was his antipathy toward her "southern emphasis on tribal loyalty."[73]

Brought into the WPA by Jacob Baker, Alsberg had had a peripatetic career as a lawyer, foreign correspondent, and erstwhile playwright. Both philosophically and administratively he was something of an anarchist. Kathleen O'Connor McKinzie, the first scholar to narrate the history of the Writers' Project, describes Alsberg's conduct as "quixotic." His coworkers tolerated—some even appreciated—his often careless and casual work style far more than did Ellen Woodward and Aubrey Williams.[74] Too often, Alsberg handed out jobs in his division without first clearing them with Washington. "I am wondering if you told Henry Alsberg that no appointment should be made without my approval," Woodward asked Cronin after he named a new state FWP head for Virginia. Her concern about state directors ran deep, given the experience of the national office in some states, where project directors were slow to act or simply failed to use common sense. Even Alsberg recognized this concern in Kansas, where the assistant FWP director wrote a book in 1936 on Alfred Landon, Roosevelt's Republican opponent. Alsberg asked him to resign. "There is a lot of politics there," Woodward remarked to Alsberg.[75]

In 1937, politicians and press alike were in turmoil over the lack of WPA regulations preventing those with leftwing sympathies from receiving work assignments as federal writers. The spotlight that turned on projects in Chicago, California, and New York forced the Washington office to face up to the need for project discipline in at least some form. Appointing an acceptable director for the Chicago project became imperative in the summer of 1937, just when Williams and Woodward were trying to placate President Roosevelt and his tightfisted budget director. Calling for "careful handling," Woodward told Reed Harris, the assistant FWP director, "You know, Reed, one more big newspaper splurge out there is going to make the President send us another memorandum." Despite Washington's perception of problems in Chicago, a number of talented writers worked there— among them Richard Wright, a native of Natchez, Mississippi, who won first prize in a competition for FWP writers sponsored by *Story* magazine. "Being a Mississippian myself," Woodward said, "I was particularly proud."[76]

Matters came to a head with the release of a guide to Massachusetts whose content provoked gubernatorial epithets so caustic that "they almost peeled the gilt off the dome of the State House," according to one wag.[77] Woodward long regretted, FWP memorialist Jerre Mangione surmised, that she was center stage when the Bay State guide was presented to Governor Charles F. Hurley on the Capitol steps in Boston. Through Reed Harris, Alsberg had conveyed an invitation to Woodward to make the presentation. "It would be a nice spot of publicity," Alsberg told her, in that "a lot of Republicans are going to be there." If she could "wrangle the time . . . it would mean so much."[78] In her brief remarks, Woodward showered praise on a federal government that, after years of supporting the development of natural resources, had now "given a helping hand to the development of our cultural resources."[79]

Hurley's pleasure over this first guide to a New England state (he had not read it) turned to outrage within a day when the *Boston Traveler* informed him and like-minded patriots nationwide that "Sacco-Vanzetti Permeates New WPA Guide." The accompanying article ticked off thirty-one lines devoted to the passionate Sacco-Vanzetti trials of 1921 and 1927, while allocating only fourteen to the Boston Tea Party and five to the Boston Massacre.[80] Blair Bolles, writing for *Saturday Review* a year later, described the incident's effect on Woodward: "Nothing makes this Mississippi widow feel more heavily her responsibility as the ultimate apologist for the actions of her heterogeneous group of authors than the frequent accusation that the Project leans well to the Left and slips into its volumes expressions of communistic discontent." When the Washington, D.C., guide weighed in at 1,600 pages and candidly described such disreputable aspects of the nation's capital as its slums, Senator Harrison advised Woodward that it would be unwise to place a copy with each member of Congress "at this time." Hopkins agreed that the only recourse was to present a copy to any member upon request. Bolles surmised that it was Hopkins who counseled Woodward to engage an editorial assistant in her office to read all manuscripts that came in for "politically dangerous remarks."[81]

When Eleanor Roosevelt met Louise Lazell in 1934, she asked both Woodward and Rexford Tugwell, then undersecretary of agriculture, if they needed "a woman of this kind." Attractive, versatile, and competent, Lazell impressed the First Lady. She worked temporarily for Woodward as a speechwriter, which prompted Mrs. Roosevelt to write, "You are an angel to do so much for Mrs. Lazell."[82] When it seemed judicious that Woodward employ a "policy editor," Lazell was hired. Sharp-eyed but careful to a fault, Lazell substituted words and phrases and recommended deletions that probably saved the Washington office a number of repetitions of the Massachusetts fiasco.

Actually, the Four Arts had friends in Congress who held advanced notions about government patronage of the humanities. As the year 1938 began, a battery of hearings on Capitol Hill, conducted by partisans of the Four Arts, became a forum for Woodward and the proud directors of the Four Arts. Before a meeting of the House Appropriations Committee in January, she pleaded eloquently for sustaining funds while describing the new democratic culture and "fresh current" which the Four Arts had injected into American life. She was back three weeks later, again in the company of the directors and Larry Morris, this time before the House Committee on Patents to discuss a joint resolution establishing a permanent cabinet-level Department of Science, Art, and Literature.[83] Lavish in his praise of Woodward's organization, New York representative William Sirovich deemed her testimony the "finest" he had heard in his fourteen years in Congress.[84] Although his bill never made it to the floor of the House, the congressmen tried again to bring to a vote a joint resolution to create a "Bureau of Fine Arts," this time in the Department of Interior. Colleagues tabled his bill after opponents had ridiculed the WPA arts program to a degree of levity that stunned Sirovich.[85]

Woodward repeated the remarks she had made to the Patents Committee when she appeared before a subcommittee of the Committee on Labor and Education, chaired by Florida's Senator Claude Pepper, who introduced in January 1938 a bill creating a permanent Bureau of Fine Arts. Pepper requested Woodward to estimate the cost of supporting WPA art programs under a new Bureau of Fine Arts if they were to provide wages equal to those demanded by labor unions in the private sector. Woodward submitted to the committee a week later a calculated cost of almost $77.5 million to provide full employment to the 28,176 workers whose projects currently cost over $33 million annually. The sum was more than double because, first, to stay within budget, WPA artists were limited in the number of hours they were permitted to work; and, second, sponsors met many nonlabor costs. Woodward was careful not to take a position on the proposed legislation.[86] She knew that the national arts projects directors shared the fears of professional artists, writers, and actors that artistic integrity would be compromised if a national arts program were compelled to employ artists solely on the basis of need. Hallie Flanagan's opposition to the Coffee-Pepper bill was generally known. She later described both the patronage bills as "more benign than practical."[87]

Despite the fact that Congress never gave serious consideration to any bill that would disseminate culture on a scale far grander and more permanent than the WPA, the measures piqued interest among critics and cultural arbiters. Debate spilled over onto editorial pages, and WPA enemies in Congress seized the opportunity to lambast WPA "boondoggling." Woodward and her WPA administrative colleagues sensed that Federal One was in jeopardy with Congress. Hence, in the winter and spring of 1938, she defended the WPA arts before a number of arts patrons and was, indeed, prophetic in predicting that "the final judgment will come years from now when the full effects of this program are known and the history of our times is written."[88]

Whatever goodwill Woodward's pep talks generated, they could not dispel persistent rumors that New Jersey Representative J. Parnell Thomas intended to cite the Federal Writers' and Theatre projects as subversive and summon their directors before the House Un-American Activities Committee. The committee had been created in May 1938, just when champions of the WPA were beginning their drive for fresh funds and as opponents sought material with which to enliven congressional campaigns later that year. The committee chairman, Martin J. Dies, of Texas, was unequivocal that "practically every play . . . is sheer propaganda for Communism or the New Deal." Dies, self-styled "President of the House Demagogues Club," represented Texas voters who, Kathleen McKinzie has written, "liked their patriotism undiluted, their ideas of American society untinged by concern with Negroes or immigrants, their participation in free enterprise unfiltered by labor unions, and their rural values uncorrupted by big cities."[89]

HUAC commenced its investigation on August 12, by turning attention to witnesses who testified on the Communist party's alleged capture of the Theatre and Writers' projects. Early accusations came from Hazel Huffman, an ex-WPA mail clerk who had opened Hallie

Flanagan's mail and found it to be "revolutionary."[90] Huffman's unconfirmed charges comprised only part of infuriating and damaging testimony that spilled out of the committee room to become the topic of
conversation by night in Washington and newspaper headlines by
day. During the first month of its hearings, HUAC demonstrated its
enormous capacity to mount a detrimental case against the Federal
Theatre, the Achilles' heel of Federal One.

By mid-September, Woodward and her staff were chafing over the
lack of opportunity to refute the injurious testimony. Finally, the day
after the committee turned the spotlight from the Theatre Project to
the federal writers, Woodward wrote an open letter to Dies, excoriat-
ing the committee's failure to summon any responsible WPA official.
In failing to respect the WPA's "right of a hearing," she said, the
Committee stood to "forfeit the right to any confidence" by the
American people in its proceedings.[91] Dies made no response until
October 6, when he informed Flanagan that she could be heard,
although he set no date for her appearance. When the hearings began,
the administration—all the way up to the President himself—
downplayed the investigation as just another ill-conceived attack on
the New Deal. Woodward wrote Molly Dewson, "there is entirely too
much 'loose talk about Communism,' " adding, "if they are hungry we
will feed them just as we would anybody else."[92] As she later reminded
the Dies Committee, it was Congress itself that stipulated no one was
to be denied a relief job on the basis of political convictions.

Throughout October, HUAC heard from a parade of witnesses who
recounted a range of subversive activities which they perceived within
the WPA operation. As congressional elections grew nearer, Roosevelt's cavalier air turned to one of concern, and WPA officials began to
prepare refutations to the charges. While the WPA defense team
explored its options, the committee continued to call witnesses who
were sometimes heard only in closed sessions. In November an
exuberant Dies released to the press especially damaging statements
made by employees of the Writers' Project including a puzzling
account by Louise Lazell.[93] Woodward knew Lazell was slated to
appear. The columnists Drew Pearson and Robert S. Allen wrote that
she sent Lazell before the committee to defuse charges that the project
was lax regarding communist activities. What Woodward learned too
late was that Lazell "was a double agent" primed by Dies to "under-
mine the whole project, including Mrs. Woodward herself." So
thought Harold Coy, chief editor of the Washington FWP and one of
Lazell's targets.[94]

It surprised Flanagan and Alsberg to learn that Ellen Woodward, and not they, would present the case for their projects, a decision actually made by Harry Hopkins, which neither the press nor HUAC members knew.[95] It is difficult to explain why Hopkins sent Woodward before HUAC, and not the two project heads. Elsie George concluded that Woodward would be less threatening: "A gentlewoman of the old school from Mississippi, speaking in a pleasant voice with a southern accent . . . does not conjure up visions of Communists and wild-eyed liberals."[96] Hopkins likely calculated that his assistant would not know the precise answer to the tough questions the committee was certain to ask, whereas Flanagan and Alsberg would be much more vulnerable and less able to convey innocence.

Whatever the case, Woodward's Southernness had no salutary effect on the demeanor of the two Southerners on the committee, Dies of Texas and Joseph Starnes of Alabama. In the grilling by the committee on 5 and 6 December, as Henry Alsberg later told the committee, Woodward was given "quite a lot of rough handling."[97] She entered the committee room expecting to read from a carefully prepared brief; but, from the outset, Dies, Thomas, and Starnes virtually monopolized the hearing, questioning whether Woodward was the "proper party to refute the charges." It was evident they were lying in wait for others.[98]

It was also evident that the inquisitors did not intend to hear Woodward's prepared statement, for they interrupted her each time she attempted to return to the script. "Would you kindly listen for just a minute?" she demanded at one point. The committee was attentive, however, to her denouncement of Hazel Huffman's qualifications as a drama critic, but it remained more impressed with Huffman's testimony than with Woodward's attempt to diminish it. Woodward also attempted to dismantle the testimony of witnesses who had attacked a Writers' Project anthology, *American Stuff*. She tried to discredit the most effective witness before the committee, former FWP employee George Banta, as a "sick man" (so was "Mr. Hopkins," Starnes shot back). The upshot of the exchange was that Woodward could not deny the committee's assertion that there were "confessed" Communists on a project.[99]

Near midmorning, Woodward took the committee to task for its methods. "I must express my deep concern and my disappointment over the very un-American way in which the committee has handled charges made against this project under my jurisdiction," she stated. Newspaper accounts praised her challenge to the committee, but that only served to make her adversaries even less amenable to her.[100]

Increasingly, the committee members pressed her for details about various FTP or FWP scripts and galleys which they found questionable. Repeatedly, Woodward either had to confess that she could not answer or responded so obliquely that it was evident she knew more than she was willing to say. The morning session of 5 December ended with the committee concluding that Woodward lacked firsthand knowledge of the material within her brief.[101]

The afternoon session went no better for Woodward. Pressed by Thomas, Starnes, and Dies, she had to admit that she had neither read the scripts nor seen some of the offending plays. The fact that *Power* had, on the whole, drawn favorable reviews from the nation's foremost drama critics failed to impress the committee. Nor did *Power* set well with John E. Rankin, a Mississippi congressman who, Starnes pointed out to Woodward, was one of the characters portrayed. Exasperated by her heavy reliance on reviews to defend the Federal Theatre, Dies lectured her that a drama review was not an adequate response to Huffman's assertion that a play was "prounion or . . . communistic, propagandistic, or anything else." Woodward's choice of words in arguing that the "capitalistic" press would surely have made an issue of anti-Americanism within the FTP if it had found such cost her dearly. "That is a communistic term," Dies countered.[102] Thus the Committee continued its heckling and disregard of Woodward's defense of the plays for their artistic value.[103]

Hallie Flanagan and Henry Alsberg accompanied her when Woodward returned the next morning for further questioning—to the obvious pleasure of the Committee. The sparring continued. At one point Woodward chastised Dies: "Be just a little careful how you state what I said." By its reception of "unqualified, irresponsible, and misinformed" witnesses, the Committee had, she charged, "jeopardized . . . the jobs and daily bread of thousands of these needy good American men and women." Starnes rebuked her when she tried to ask a question herself: "You are here to answer questions." When she announced that she was ending her testimony so that Flanagan and Alsberg could speak, Dies assured her, "You are perfectly at liberty to sit right here all day long."[104]

In general, newspaper writers and contemporaries in the WPA agreed that Woodward had done as well as possible before HUAC. "Mrs. Woodward Clashes With Dies on Reds," the *Washington Post* headlined a story describing "a tumultuous hearing." TELLS DIES INQUIRY IT IS UNAMERICAN, the *New York Times* headed its account of Woodward's "long wrangle" with the disputatious congressmen. Kathleen Sexton, a columnist for the *Jackson Daily News* "Mississippians at the Capital," reported that Woodward "was in there battling to the end," while the indignant congressmen waved cigars, shoved books around, leaned over their imposing table, and pointed "accusing fingers" at her. Sexton noted that, while Mrs. Woodward was not wearing the ubiquitous orchid, when she gathered her papers to leave at the end of the second day, someone had placed a large red rose on them.[105]

Friends wrote encouragingly of her effort. "I see you and Hallie Flanagan are being pestered by Dies," Molly Dewson wrote, adding, "I thought you both did good." May Thompson Evans recalled that Woodward's "courage was terrific."[106] Hallie Flanagan described her superiors' efforts as "gallant." Holger Cahill, whose Federal Art Project had escaped the grilling, called Woodward "a real fighter"; but Philip Barber, at one time the FTP administrator in New York City, faulted her because "she really didn't know the job," although he conceded that "the congressmen weren't willing to listen at that

Woodward and Holger Cahill, Director of the WPA Art Project, at the WPA Artists' Index Exhibit at the Smithsonian exhibit of the WPP, January 1938 (National Archives 69-N-363)

point." Irwin Rhodes, an FTP official looking back at the demise of the Federal Theatre, concluded that Woodward was "afraid of being too forceful and antagonizing too many people" but added that, without Woodward, "maybe it [the FTP] would have ended sooner." Francis Bosworth evaluated the resilience demonstrated by Woodward and Charley Tidd Cole, with whom he worked in preparing WPA exhibits. Bosworth recalled, "All through the thing—we had some tough maggies . . . . I mean these women were tough."[107]

Woodward was neither as uninformed nor as naive as she chose to appear. She was aware, however, that all was not well. In a long memorandum to Harry Hopkins, she recommended that the WPA continue to investigate the charges "already known" and take "appropriate action." She called for a fresh look at procedures, to make certain they prohibited all illegal activities. She had already taken steps to review with David Niles the most prudent way for Flanagan and Alsberg to deal with members of the press throughout the hearings. Woodward questioned Morris about how a teacher's *Guide to Soviet Russia* cited by Congressman Thomas as a product of the Writers' Project had been published without having been "read for policy" by either Louise Lazell or herself.[108] Ultimately, no remedies could compensate for the lack of time her schedule permitted for review of all the productions of the FTP and publications of the FWP, nor her administrative decision to permit the directors virtual autonomy over their projects.

Extant records do not reveal the moment when Woodward learned that Harry Hopkins was leaving the WPA to become Roosevelt's new Secretary of Commerce. An outline submitted by Charley Tidd Cole to Woodward at the end of November 1938, projecting an ambitious expansion of the Women's and Professional Projects suggests that the two women presumed their division would happily continue uninterrupted by drastic change.[109] Presumably in private conversation, Woodward and Hopkins discussed her future, and she weighed her options. By mid-December, rumors of a shakeup were rife. At a press conference on 20 December, the President announced that Woodward would join the Social Security Board. When Hopkins formally resigned to take the Cabinet post three days later, the columnist Ernest Lindley speculated that the new WPA chief, Colonel Francis C. Harrington, would likely not have retained Woodward. Like other newspapers, the *Washington Herald* predicted "a general house-cleaning" of the WPA that would sweep well below the top level of administration. That Harrington, a West Point-trained Army engineer, and not Aubrey Williams, succeeded Hopkins portended a new departure for the WPA. Williams was shunted back to the National Youth Administration. Work relief would be revised, Lindley predicted, to meet the standards of a man "who has learned a great deal about the needy unemployed, but who never forgets that he is an Army engineer."[110]

Departing Federal One officials sensed the loss of direction and inspiration that former administrators had provided. Julius Davidson, the finance officer for the Four Arts, thought Woodward was "a very dedicated person [who] . . . worked herself to the bone," and bore no ill will that she characteristically called "people up around midnight and kept them on the phone for two or three hours." While cleaning out his desk on the last day in the life of the Federal Theatre, its deputy director, J. Howard Miller, paused to write Woodward, "The Professional and Service Division, of this Administration is stamped with your imagination and initiative." Representative of the letters that arrived from state offices to express the affection of women with whom Woodward had worked for more than five years, Mary Isham, the western states WPP supervisor, wrote of Woodward's "kindness and consideration" in dealing with subordinates. Reluctant to see her go, Isham nonetheless recognized that the new appointment "is a great triumph for our division and for all women."[111]

Woodward had arrived in Washington in 1933 to a one-room office, one stenographer, and one desk. She left a division of 300 persons directly under her jurisdiction.[112] In an affectionate handwritten letter to Hopkins, she reflected upon five years in which "new worlds [had] been opened." "I consider myself the luckiest woman in the world," she concluded.[113] The new post with the Social Security Board would prove a challenge, as did all Woodward's positions in a public service career that spanned nearly thirty years. But never again would she have the influence, status, and following she had as the director of the WPA's Women's and Professional Projects.

CHAPTER 7

Security for the Home
and Family: 1939–1946

I n seven years as a member of the Social Security Board, Ellen Woodward found new opportunities to advocate greater economic security for American women and their families. As a "political appointee" to the Board, she found her role circumscribed by lack of technical expertise in social insurance but compensated for her limitations by adopting a role as an emissary of the Board to housewives and working women for whom the message of Social Security was vital. Her continuing rapport with Eleanor Roosevelt proved beneficial in creating a public forum for women whose Social Security benefits were negligible or who remained uncovered under the original act of 1935 and its 1939 amendments.

While the records are virtually silent regarding the exigencies of Woodward's resignation from the Works Progress Administration, they reveal the flurry that preceded her appointment to the Social Security Board. The same good friends who were party to her appointment to the FERA collaborated in her transfer to the SSB. This time, however, Molly Dewson played a larger role because, as a retiring Board member, she was very much an insider within Social Security circles. Even before the three-member SSB was created under the Social Security Act, signed by Roosevelt on 14 August 1935, Dewson was eager to have a woman included on the Board, and the president made it clear that he wanted a Southerner among the three. Federal law required a bipartisan board but said nothing about gender. Hence, under the Roosevelt administration, the Board could be expected to consist of two Democrats and one Republican. Shortly before the bill became law, Arthur J. Altmeyer, the Labor Department official who prepared the executive order creating the President's Committee on Economic Security and destined himself for a long career as a Board member and its chairman, wrote Dewson that the Board should have a woman member.[1]

Despite the names Dewson and Altmeyer bandied about, the initial Board had no woman member. Instead, it consisted of John Gilbert

Winant, a liberal Republican and former governor of New Hampshire, who became the first chairman, and two Democrats, Altmeyer and Vincent Miles of Arkansas, the latter widely viewed as the political legatee of Senate majority leader Joseph Robinson. When Winant resigned in 1937, Altmeyer became chairman, and the Republican slot went to George E. Bigge, an economics professor at Brown University who had the backing of Rhode Island Senator Theodore Green.[2] Then, when Miles resigned the same year, the President named Dewson herself to the Board, but she soon became weary of the routine. She confessed that she found the job to be "a bundle of chores," the material she had to peruse uninspiring, and the position one in which a Board member became simply "anonymous." After nine months of service, she ended her Social Security duties, citing failing health. In late December 1938, her letter to the President was made public: "I no longer have the endurance for a great Federal post."[3]

Meanwhile, Dewson had been pressing Roosevelt—to the point of

Swearing-in ceremony for Woodward as a member of the Social Security Board, December 1938, l. to r., Arthur Altmeyer, Chairman, Social Security Board; Chief Clerk George E. Scott of the SSB; Woodward; Senator Pat Harrison of Mississippi; Eleanor Roosevelt (Courtesy Mississippi Department of Archives and History)

being "pestiferous"—she feared, to name Ellen Woodward as her successor. She thought the Mississippian would be "a perfect team mate for Arthur Altmeyer." Altmeyer agreed. Woodward was their "pick out of—not Heaven—but available humans," she told Clara Beyer, another New Deal woman officeholder. Woodward was "no lazy southerner," Dewson assured Beyer, characterizing the Mississippi woman as "another hurricane," like herself. Very likely, Woodward's mentor in public welfare, Frank Bane, the first executive director of the Social Security Board, was a party to the decision. Still, Woodward attributed her new job to Dewson. "Thank you a million, Molly," she wrote after Roosevelt announced her appointment on the afternoon of 20 December 1938. "I shall do my dead level best to follow in your footsteps."[4]

There was another major player in the Woodward appointment. Her closeness to Pat Harrison, the powerful chairman of the Senate Finance Committee, was so evident that Dewson had made it part of her argument with Roosevelt, reminding him that "since WPA was folding up, Harrison would expect [Woodward] to be found another position." "I'll think it over," the President told her. Harrison had skillfully guided the Social Security Act through his committee, and it would be Harrison to whom the administration would look for passage of liberalizing amendments in 1939. The ever acerbic Drew Pearson prattled that, "with a woman behind him" Harrison had "pulled down a juicy piece of patronage," thereby provoking "bedlam" among Roosevelt partisans who knew that the Mississippi Democrat had broken with "the Chief" in 1937. Other observers were quick to counter that it was precisely because the President needed the favor of the Finance Committee chairman that Woodward's appointment was timely.[5]

Woodward promised President Roosevelt that she would "measure up to the high standards set by our beloved Molly Dewson. . . . It was grand of you to appoint me . . . and to give me this broader opportunity to serve you."[6] Generally, the press treated her appointment as the occasion for yet another feature article that typically ranked achievements by women in public affairs only slightly ahead of their domestic skills. "Woman Is Named to Security Post," trumpeted one headline, followed by "Mrs. Woodward Competent in Kitchen," with the added assurance that the new Social Security official "can make cheese omelets or wear orchids with equal grace." Women journalists were quick to rush into print stories heralding Woodward's "having gone through life holding a good many jobs that no woman ever held before" (thus overlooking the fact that her predecessor on the Board had been a woman). "Her own administrative ability has put her where she is," a writer for *Pathfinder* bragged, adding that at her new salary of $10,000 a year, Woodward had become one of only three women in the executive branch ever to earn that sum.[7] The *Washington Times* editorialized that, in view of the new Board member's credentials, "the President can't be accused of playing politics over ability." Even so, the writer could not refrain from adding, "Besides, she is a very charming woman."[8]

The Senate would vote when it returned in January; meanwhile, plans were made for the oath-taking ceremony. Rumors were rife that the President's conservative opposition would raise objections.[9] With the date for the swearing-in set for 30 December, Woodward forwarded to Altmeyer a list of friends she wished to be present. Her special guests were, of course, Senator Harrison and Eleanor

Woodward as a member of the Social Security Board, about 1940 (Courtesy Albert Y. Woodward, Jr.)

Roosevelt. She also requested that Mona Harden be invited. To Mrs. Roosevelt she wrote, "[Y]ou have been my inspiration and guiding hand ever since I came to Washington." The First Lady was indeed present and became the first of the well-wishers to congratulate the new Board member. Her "My Day" column the next day praised Woodward as a woman of "executive ability, tact, and the ability to give in and see the other person's point of view." She could, the White House columnist added, "be adamant when it is necessary."[10]

The SSB's public information office drafted for Woodward a public statement reflecting current Board concern that programs to assist dependent children not be shunted aside in public discussion of old-age pension plans. "My appointment . . . means to me an opportunity for service where my deepest interests lie—security for the home and family," Woodward said upon taking her oath, adding: "we should also do more for the children . . . they are our first responsibility." Citing a million and a half needy dependent children in the nation, she called for an extension to them of aid in those states not yet participating in the program. As benign as her remarks might appear, they drew objections from interest groups eager to extend benefits to the aged. The sharpest rebuke appeared in a public letter from the General Welfare Federation of America, which outlined its own program for a more adequate old-age pension than the program provided by the Social Security Act.[11] A Southern black man (and a Writers' Project staffer in Washington) responded that Woodward's "sympathetic understanding" of the large number of workers in agriculture and domestic service not covered by the Social Security Act augured well for "an expanded social welfare program."[12]

Rumors of mounting resistance in the Senate to Roosevelt's appointment of Woodward, based in the still fresh animus toward the "communist-dominated" Federal Theatre and Writers' Projects, proved to be just that—rumors. After the Senate Finance Committee approved the appointment without a hearing, on 12 January the Senate confirmed the new SSB member, the only opposing vote coming from Utah's crusty Senator William H. King, whose hostility to Pat Harrison was well known.[13]

Woodward's move from the WPA to the Social Security Board was appropriate in view of the close kinship of the two agencies. Framers of the Social Security Act intended that it replace emergency relief with a permanent program of economic security. Initially, they recommended that several of the new grant programs be placed within the

Federal Emergency Relief Administration, still in existence when the Committee submitted its report in January 1935.[14]

Woodward did not arrive at the Social Security Board uninformed about how the Social Security Act affected women and children. Inequities in the WPA stemming from constraints within congressional laws troubled both Woodward and Eleanor Roosevelt, and they took on new dimensions under the Social Security Act. Because public assistance payments in many states were actually lower than the WPA wages women had been earning, many work relief clients questioned why they were expected to give up their WPA jobs to accept Aid to Dependent Children. The injustices, Woodward pointed out to President Roosevelt, resulted from the premise of the Social Security Act that individual states provide the primary assistance to be given mothers through enactment of supportive legislation and appropriation of adequate funds.[15] Serious questions of federal policy were involved. If the WPA were to continue to employ needy mothers, it would delay the assumption by states of their responsibility under the public assistance features of the Social Security Act. As a result, women and their children were whipsawed between two programs, both dependent on a federal-state sharing of responsibility that was never fully developed.

Under the Social Security Act, the Board was to administer functions defined in the titles of the new law: a national system of contributory old-age annuities (commonly known as "Social Security"), a state-administered but federally supervised unemployment compensation system, and federally subsidized public assistance programs to categories of needy persons, including the aged, the blind, and dependent children. The system was also to select the personnel who would administer the provisions of the Social Security program; but, prior to Woodward's appointment, the Board had already named the eight bureau chiefs.[16]

Few if any could equal SSB chairman Arthur Altmeyer in mastering the details and understanding the ramifications of social insurance; nor was it likely anyone else could suffer tedium as he could. A Wisconsin native, Altmeyer was an apt student of the pioneer labor economist John R. Commons at the University of Wisconsin. While head of the Wisconsin Industrial Commission, he was called to Washington in 1933 by President Roosevelt to become director of the NRA's Labor Compliance Division. A year later, Frances Perkins made him an Assistant Secretary of Labor; he was almost immediately named to serve as chairman of the technical board of the President's Committee on Economic Security. With all his experience and technical knowledge of social insurance, Altmeyer was tolerant of Board members whose expertise was considerably less. He permitted them the latitude to perform in areas where their discrete contributions lay, and he was astute enough politically to recognize the rationale behind the appointments of SSB colleagues. Nor did Altmeyer press for a decision until the two other members had studied an issue and could make an informed decision.[17] Nevertheless, both Bigge and Woodward were reactive, not proactive, regarding the work of the constituent bureaus that performed the workaday functions of the larger Social Security Board. Of the two, Woodward was the more liberal; clearly, she was under the influence of Jane Hoey, whose Bureau of Public Assistance dealt with the vast number of clients for whom Woodward's WPA division had provided an array of social services.[18]

Beginning in the late 1930s, Ellen Woodward suffered an annual bout with respiratory problems and a lingering sore throat. To escape Washington winters, she customarily took vacation leave in January to spend two weeks at Miami Beach, where she owned property or, during World War II, in the Los Angeles area, where her son lived. Immediately after her confirmation to the SSB, in January 1939, she left for Florida. By the time she returned to Washington to attend her first Board meeting, Congress was at work on crucial amendments to the Social Security Act, which would convert the federal old-age insurance program into a family-protection plan by providing payments to surviving widows and young children of workers covered by the earlier program. New provisions to pay small monthly benefits to the wife of a retired worker meant that what had in 1935 been protection for an individual worker would expand to include protection of a couple after each had reached age sixty-five. The amendments found favor among congressmen still under the spell of radical schemes for an extravagant "revolving" old-age pension plan or the "share-the-wealth" panaceas that had hastened passage of the Social Security Act in 1935. There were, on the other hand, a sufficient number of harsh critics of the 1939 amendments to warrant concern on the part of the SSB; it was not until June that the House passed a bill, albeit by a sizable margin.[19]

At the hearings, few congressmen understood the technical presentations of Altmeyer and others; so, as the Social Security scholar Edward Berkowitz puts it, the lawmakers "translated what the actuaries told them into the cost-benefit ratio of politics." As a new member of the SSB, Woodward had only minimal understanding of the fiscal niceties of the Social Security program. There can be little doubt that her first article, which appeared in the February 1939 issue of *Democratic Digest*, was written in Max Stern's Office of Informational Service.[20]

Although there is no documentation of Woodward's sessions with Senate Finance Committee chairman Pat Harrison and other Southern senators during the two weeks in June that the House-approved amendments were before the Senate Finance Committee, contemporary colleagues spoke of her assistance in winning over Senate skeptics intent on adding crippling provisions to the House measure. "Sweet old Ellen, I am so glad you have won out in this cantankerous Congress," Molly Dewson wrote from Maine. Years later, Altmeyer recalled, "I am sure that if it had not been for Senator Harrison's confidence in her, we would not have received his support which was absolutely vital." Wilbur Cohen, Altmeyer's assistant, was also convinced of the salutary role Harrison played in producing a bill that both Roosevelt and the Social Security Board could live with.[21] As a result, the measure signed by the President on 10 August 1939, took its place as one of the "three founding pieces" of legislation for Social Security.[22]

Meanwhile, Woodward left Washington for a tour of six Southern states. After Attorney-General Frank Murphy assured her that the Hatch Act did not preclude her speaking to "groups of political women"—that is, Women's Division gatherings—she took to the hustings to talk about further revisions needed to cast a larger security net for American workers.[23] More significantly, on the day the President signed the bill, Woodward engaged in a radio dialogue with Eleanor Roosevelt to advertise the new supplementary benefits for aged wives and dependent children of annuitants and the benefits for surviving widows and for children of workers who had contributed to the system.[24]

After nearly a year on the Social Security Board, Woodward appeared to have found her niche. She could be an effective liaison with Congress and at the same time oversee the implementation of the new welfare services in her home state. She could advocate equity for women in personnel matters and press for extension of social insurance to women at work in uncovered jobs, as well as for greater public assistance to dependent children. Her most effective task, she believed, was to oversee the Board's public information program, to make certain that women received the gospel of Social Security. Woodward would devote a preponderance of her time as an emissary to women's organizations and to her beloved South. Still, the SSB post was not as demanding as her WPA job had been, and she had more time to "network" with Washington women beset by new anxieties after the advent of World War II. (This involvement, as well as the international dimensions that the war had added to her work, took Woodward away from her office and into other areas of economic security for women. But that is a topic best described in a separate chapter.)

Just as Woodward had closely monitored Mississippi politicians hostile to WPA regulations, she kept a vigilant eye on the administration of public welfare in her home state now that social services under the Social Security Act had added new functions to the State Department of Public Welfare.[25] The greatest difficulty confronting Willard Bond, Mississippi's new public welfare commissioner, arose from the patronage demands that caught him in crossfire between manipulative politicians and a Social Security Board determined that states comply with the 1939 amendment mandating a merit system in each state participating in the new public assistance programs. Elected officeholders found within the new county welfare departments the same opportunity to refuel political machines that had existed under the WPA, and county welfare agents were subjected to inordinate pressure. Although, in 1940, the Mississippi legislature established a merit system for personnel, state officials hedged in complying, and a nasty situation ensued that was the subject of much discussion by the SSB in its biweekly sessions.[26] Though always involved sub rosa, Woodward managed to keep her distance from the factionalism that marked Mississippi state politics.

Just as President Roosevelt was conferring for the last time with congressional leaders on the 1939 amendments, two arch rivals faced off in Mississippi in a gubernatorial race in which the stakes were high for the two United States senators as well. Paul B. Johnson, with the backing of Senator Bilbo, entered the second primary with Mike Conner, whose final rally of the campaign featured as platform guests Ellen Woodward and Senator Harrison. Woodward stated publicly that she would remain in Louisville until election day so she could vote for Conner, whose earlier gubernatorial administration she credited for "the first relief programs . . . to meet human needs in our state." Her fear that Johnson would win (which he did) prompted her to ask Roosevelt to urge House leaders to accede to the Senate's inclusion of a merit system among the Social Security amendments, then in a House-Senate conference committee.[27] At an SSB meeting in September 1939, in which the Mississippi situation was the topic of considerable discussion, Woodward spoke of the merit system as a vehicle to "save our program."[28] Woodward's confidant on Mississippi politics was Walter Sillers, Jr., an old friend from her days in the state legislature. His suspicions that Governor Johnson would place in county welfare offices workers loyal to himself seemed confirmed when fifteen county welfare agents were fired, dismissals that "would never have been made without Bilbo's knowledge and consent," Sillers informed Senator Harrison.[29] Alarmed by the political hardball being played in her state, the SSB member told Jane Hoey emphatically that the Board must take steps to reinstate the agents and "hold up submission of Mississippi's [public assistance] grant until we know what the real situation is." As a result, throughout July and August 1940, the SSB provided grants to Mississippi on a one-month-only basis until Commissioner Bond and Governor Johnson could agree on merit considerations. When Bond appealed to Woodward, she advised him to insist to Governor Johnson that he "establish a worthwhile department there . . . and take the higher ground."[30]

By summer 1940, another major race was underway in Mississippi— the Senate race between Bilbo and former governor Hugh L. White, an old ally of Woodward and Harrison. Privately, neither Sillers nor Woodward was optimistic about White's chances. "The whole damn affair is [a] typical Bilbo-Johnson factional political mess," Sillers complained to Woodward, adding that "You have a BIG STICK in your hands." Withholding further grants from Mississippi altogether, rather than merely delaying them, was the strongest medicine; but Woodward advised caution, telling Altmeyer "since they do need the money we do not want the people to suffer."[31] In mid-August, when Bond made a command appearance in Washington before SSB officials, Woodward absented herself from the cross-examination; but she was well aware of what transpired. She insisted that the SSB "tell Bond that we would not put up with a lot of 'shenanigans' " in Mississippi. She was pleased that the dismissed agents were reinstated without a punitive denial of funds to needy grantees.[32] A year later, however as welfare districts were redrawn, county workers in Mississippi were again in jeopardy. Sillers complained that "the supposed merit system which the Federal authorities stressed so much is a farce." Mississippi was not the only Deep South state where the governor played politics with welfare. Georgia posed a similar problem, prompting Woodward to remark in an SSB meeting, "I think we must take positive action in all these southern states or the merit system will amount to nothing at all."[33]

Woodward was immune to serious retaliation in Mississippi for her role in the electoral brawls in 1939 and 1940, although Sillers informed her that Governor Johnson "is mighty mad at you for interfering with his Welfare Agents." Drew Pearson, whose distaste for Mississippi's arcane politics was undisguised, predicted that "red-headed Mrs. Ellen Woodward . . . is headed for plenty of trouble from the irate Bilbo." In Pearson's opinion, the fact that "she [had] quietly slipped down to her home state and pulled campaign wires for Harrison and Conner" was a violation of the Hatch Act. On the contrary, Woodward looked upon her participation in the 1939 election as an act of loyalty to Roosevelt, who wanted a Mississippi delegation to the 1940 Democratic convention committed to his third term. As a special election approached to select a senator to replace Pat Harrison after his death in June 1941, Woodward quietly informed the President that he need not "bother" about the Mississippi race; either candidate would give him full support.[34]

Woodward found Governor Johnson cooperative in expanding social services to Mississippians. While in Jackson in November 1939, she urged that Mississippi, one of only eight states not then taking part in the state-federal matching grant ADC program, enact legislation and appropriate funds to bring the state into the system. She left the state with Johnson's pledge to recommend such legislation to the Mississippi legislature, and in April 1940, the lawmakers approved an act that would provide funds for ADC grants.[35] However, monthly grants, which began in March 1941, remained low, and the future of categorical assistance in Mississippi, as in all Southern states, was not promising.[36]

Woodward supported Hoey whenever the BPA pressed the Board to sanction policies permitting more generous grants for women and children. Woodward's concern about children's welfare had developed long before she attended the 1940 White House Conference on Children in a Democracy; but the discussions at the conference reenforced convictions she expressed upon joining the Board. Acquiring facts to become an effective advocate, she devoted considerable time to memoranda generated by experts on ADC.[37] She knew that Congress remained uninterested in Aid to Dependent Children and that grants were woefully parsimonious in state plans for public assistance submitted to Washington. With what Wilbur Cohen described as "a mother's concern," she made ADC expansion a focus of her public appeals for an expanded Social Security program, pleading for increased aid to children and youth, not only through more generous ADC grants but also by paying greater attention to standards of health and decency under other public assistance titles. In SSB meetings she explored methods of forcing fathers to assume greater financial responsibility for the care of children under ADC, but the problem was too thorny for immediate solutions.[38]

Most of the regional staff for the Social Security organization were employed by the time Woodward joined the SSB. Both Dewson and Woodward urged that women be employed whenever the opportunity arose. In 1939, Woodward recommended Loula Dunn as the regional director for the Southeast, just as Dewson had earlier supported Gay Shepperson for the same office. Woodward confronted the fact that "some people [state administrators] say they don't want a woman." Both Dunn, a former regional supervisor for the FERA and, in 1939, the commissioner of public welfare in Alabama, and Shepperson, the former state WPA head in Georgia, eventually declined the position, and Region VII went to a man. Later, when Region V sought a new administrator, Woodward spoke up: "I really think we ought to take into consideration every woman who has the qualifications." But she lost out again.[39] When Lavinia Engle at first declined promotion to a field division office during World War II because she wished to remain in the Washington office, Woodward told her, "When a woman is in line for a promotion . . . she should take it." Advising Engle that "you should demonstrate that a woman can do the administrative job in the field," Woodward persuaded the Marylander to accept the offer and go to the Baltimore office. "It was a very interesting experience," Engle later concluded.[40]

Woodward defended women employees in Social Security offices on other occasions. During Board discussion of an Alabama woman's unsatisfactory performance, she suggested that the woman had not been given adequate supervision. As a result, the employee was not terminated but was given examinations for two other positions.[41] When the Board was informed that in Connecticut male clerks were paid more than female clerks, Woodward asked that the Board reaffirm its principle of equal pay for equal work. She encouraged women to seek employment, not only in Social Security offices, but also on the unpaid advisory councils. To that end, she succeeded in having a Business and Professional Women's Club colleague, Margaret Hickey, named to an advisory committee on merit system administration, a move that represented the BPW's strong endorsement of the merit system wherever it existed because it extended protection to women against traditional practices to avoid the hiring of women.[42]

More than other government agencies, the Social Security Board made "every effort . . . to make sure women were given the same chances men were," Ida C. Merriam, an economist who joined the Board in 1936, stated to interviewers from the Schlesinger Library at Radcliffe College in 1987.[43] Whether the presence of Molly Dewson and Ellen Woodward on the panel made a difference in maintaining an inviting climate for women is problematical. Men such as Frank Bane and Arthur Altmeyer, who held the higher executive offices in Social Security administration, were from social welfare backgrounds or liberal university environments where women in the profession had long been active, effective, and respected. Wilbur Cohen was also one of this group. Early on, he became important in Woodward's education on Social Security issues. Fresh from the University of Wisconsin, Cohen had gone to Washington at the age of twenty-one to be a research assistant for the Committee on Economic Security.[44] With an office adjacent to those of the SSB members, Cohen was only two doors away from Woodward, who soon came to rely on him to answer her questions, either approve the contents of her memoranda and correspondence or prepare them outright, and to help draft speeches and articles. It was not timidity alone that accounted for her caution; all Board personnel were careful not to misrepresent inordinately complicated materials in simplifying them for public consumption. "I count on you to know everything," she once wrote Cohen, whom she called "Chief of the Brain Trust."[45]

As early as 1936, Mary Anderson, head of the Women's Bureau, commended component programs of Social Security as beneficial to women "one way or another."[46] But it stretched the case to find much in the Social Security Act of 1935 for women other than for the relatively few women workers who contributed to their own accounts as covered employees.[47] With survivor's benefits added in 1939, there was more in the system for women; Woodward knew even then that there were limitations and discriminations remaining which left Social Security titles offering more to men than to women.[48] Pragmatic as she was, Woodward set herself the task of seeing that women got all the benefits due them.

Emily Blair, a Democratic party activist, wrote when Woodward joined the SSB that the post was "above all others in the Government, the one of greatest opportunity and usefulness for a woman." Within two months of Woodward's arrival, Robert Huse, an assistant in Max

Stern's office, prepared a list of conventions of women's organizations before whom she could appear.[49] The assignment included chapters of the National Federation of Business and Professional Women, local affiliates of the General Federation of Women's Clubs, and, as Blair had most in mind, regional conferences of women Democrats. When Lucy J. Dickinson, national GFWC president, called for "plain lay language" on Social Security benefits for women, she prescribed the approach Woodward would take.[50]

Woodward's itinerary for summer-fall 1939 began with appearances in Virginia and North Carolina, in which she set forth her dominant themes. To working women whose incomes were subject to old-age annuity deductions, Woodward explained the advantages and limitations of their coverage. By 1938, nearly 30 percent of the more than 45 million workers who had applied for Social Security accounts were women, whereas only slightly more than 20 percent of gainfully employed persons were women. The high turnover among women in the labor market accounted for the larger proportion of women applicants. Many would marry, stop working outside the home, and never draw benefits based on their own earnings. Furthermore, terms set forth in some states for unemployment compensation penalized married women. Woodward protested a New Mexico regulation that came before the Board because it penalized a woman who left her job to be with her husband in another state or who ceased work because of pregnancy. She did not think the SSB should give "aid and comfort" to legislatures that discriminated against married women.[51]

Woodward involved a willing Eleanor Roosevelt to enlighten the public about what Social Security could mean for women and to urge states to assume a larger financial responsibility for public assistance and unemployment compensation. They relied a great deal on Jane Hoey, and in January 1940 the three women conducted a conversation over CBS stations to publicize the expanded coverage of the 1939 amendment. "I am becoming increasingly conscious of the importance of the Act in the lives of a great many people," the First Lady wrote in a "My Day" column.[52] In 1939, she told readers that, at the urging of Ellen Woodward, she had for the first time gone to a regional Social Security office and begun to receive regional directors at the White House.[53]

Woodward's talks were intended primarily to inform women, as wives and mothers, of their stake in Social Security. The SSB was justifiably fearful that millions of housewives had no notion of the potential benefits due them from deductions in their husbands' paychecks. Speaking over the NBC network in July 1940, on the occasion of the signing of the fifty-millionth Social Security enrollment card, Woodward urged women to monitor the status of their husband's Social Security.[54] Four years later, the Board chose a thirty-three-year-old widow of an insured worker and the mother of two small children, Mrs. Mary Rex Thompson of Parma, Ohio, to represent the "Millionth Benefit." Even Altmeyer and Bigge worked on the statement Woodward made as she delivered the first survivors' check due the Thompson family. With publicity cameras snapping away, the ceremony presented yet another opportunity for the SSB in the person of Ellen Woodward to broadcast the family protection that Social Security offered, in the case of the Thompsons a monthly check of $60.[55]

Woodward's month-long trip to the Midwest and Pacific Coast in the fall of 1940 was related to the approaching elections, as probably was the overnight visit with Eleanor Roosevelt in September, for "a little talk" before leaving. In California, she met with labor leaders, the governor, staff in the office of the President's son, James, and state Democratic committee members, including the new national committeewoman and rising party luminary, Helen Gahagan Douglas. An opportunity to spend a little time with Albert Junior, then working in Los Angeles in petroleum marketing, relieved the tedium of incessant meetings.[56] Described by reporters as "a very amicable lady," she made a favorable impression as she met with one small group of women after another eager to meet a "star" from Washington.[57] A stop in Salt Lake City reunited her with Carolyn Wolfe, former chair of the Democratic National Committee Women's Division.[58]

Although the Committee on Economic Security recommended inclusion of domestic and agricultural workers in social insurance, Treasury officials had objected on the grounds that collecting the payroll taxes would be administratively impossible.[59] Again omitted in the 1939 amendments, black women, who were predominant among 23 million domestics in 1940, were victims of a faulty plan. Of the nearly 30 million contributors to an old-age insurance account in 1938, only about 6.7 percent were black, none of them in domestic service or farm production.[60] When Woodward asked Old Age and Survivors Insurance experts about the exclusion of domestics, she learned that problems included the small employing units (the individual housewife in most instances), the prevalence of wages paid "in kind," the high incidence of parttime work, and the unfamiliarity of housewives with bookkeeping methods. There were, on the other hand, valid reasons to extend coverage: low wages for domestics, lack of protection for domestics by workmen's compensation or private pension plans, and serious unemployment for domestics in times of depression. Aware that the census of 1930 revealed 90 percent of domestics to be women and 45 percent to be black, Woodward asked for material to use with groups likely to advocate coverage once they had the facts.[61] Of a particularly effective speech that hit hard at the problem, Altmeyer told her, "I hope it gets lots of circulation and that you will use it over and over again."[62]

In repeated appeals to organized women for a more inclusive Social Security program, Woodward underscored the large number of unprotected workers who were either self-employed or public employees who were engaged at work in nonprofit and educational institutions.[63] She urged teachers through their professional journals to seek Social Security.[64] She advocated coverage for registered nurses, but the same medical establishment that successfully denied health-care clauses in the Social Security Act fought provisions to benefit nurses.[65] Woodward and Mrs. Roosevelt were strangely silent on other inequities. They made no reference to the unfairness in OASI for a woman who was eligible for dual entitlement—that is, eligible for a spousal benefit of 50 percent of her retired husband's award and also due a pension as a retired worker herself—yet who was permitted to receive only the higher benefit of the two. Because SSB policymakers were not yet addressing the problem, neither did Woodward or Roosevelt.[66]

Woodward explored other biases against women. *Woman Worker*, published by the Women's Bureau, questioned the wide variance among states in interpreting unemployment compensation for a woman who left her job to relocate with her husband out of state. When Dorothy Crook, of the national BPW legislative service, wrote Woodward for a clarification, the latter replied that, while unemployment compensation was collected by the federal government through a payroll tax, states disbursed the money under their own laws. That arrangement was part of the initial federal-state compromise to ensure adoption by all states of some measure of unemployment insurance. To remedy the inequities, Woodward informed Crook, required a congressional amendment to the Social Security law, "to make unemployment compensation national." When interstate shifts of wartime workers exacerbated problems in collecting unemployment compensation for both men and women, Woodward stepped up appeals for a federalized unemployment system.[67]

Five years of complying with congressionally mandated WPA rules likely explains the position Woodward consistently took in Board discussions, spanning the years 1940 to 1944, on how to determine public assistance grants. Increased caseloads forced the SSB to come to grips with a basic decision to permit states to compute payments to eligible recipients, either by determining family budget needs or by making flat grants out of which grantees would budget their own expenses.[68] Throughout the protracted debate, Altmeyer remained the minority member in a two-one split with both Bigge and Woodward standing for flat grants (more precisely, "flat grants minus income").[69] They believed them to be truer to a literal interpretation of an imprecise law; and furthermore, they thought flat grants mitigated against the "snooping" that a social worker's investigation might engage.[70]

In a sense, the recipient would receive the grant more as a "right" than as a "welfare" payment subject to abuses of the degrading means test. Woodward's stand for flat grants put her less in league with social workers than with public officials who saw flat grants as easier to administer. Too, she likely equated an individual's right to an income through old age assistance with the right of work-relief recipients to an earned income without the services of a case worker to determine need. Whereas Woodward consistently advocated budget counseling for women on work relief, she had never believed they should have their wages pinned to budgetary needs that were ascertained by a social worker. She stood on common ground there with Harry Hopkins, but, as often as Jane Hoey influenced her on matters of public assistance, Woodward did not go along with Hoey's strong preference for family budgeting. In the end, flat grants were rejected; but Woodward's consistent stand for them suggests that she was in the corner of those who advocated what later became known as "welfare rights."

Roosevelt's reappointment of Woodward in June 1943 to another six-year term on the SSB was almost routine. Nonetheless, she rallied her DNC friends to make helpful contacts on Capitol Hill, and she was gratified when Leslie Biffle, the Secretary to the Majority, told her that Senate Finance Committee chairman Walter George would poll his committee to hasten confirmation. Anticipating that Bilbo would fight her reappointment, Woodward contacted a few Senate friends of the deceased Harrison and fortified Bilbo's new junior colleague, James O. Eastland, with her résumé, "in case some question should arise" before the confirmation vote. Senate confirmation came on 5 July, without a recorded vote. Woodward never established the rapport with Harrison's successor she had with "Senator Pat," and thus was now bereft of close friendship with either Mississippi senator.[71]

World War II presented concerns about women's economic security to Woodward and Eleanor Roosevelt that were reflected in the latter's White House mail. They discussed assistance for children of service men lost in the war for whom there were no Social Security provisions, a subject already before the Board, and expanded wartime social services that went beyond Social Security.[72] In November 1942, at Woodward's invitation, Mrs. Roosevelt reported at an SSB session on her recent trip to England. She described day nurseries for children of mothers engaged in war production as well as the mobilization of women in hospitals, factories, and auxiliary military services.[73] The inference was, of course, that the United States could profit from the British experience in policymaking to improve the lot of women.

When the SSB directed its focus toward the postwar implications for Social Security, Woodward spoke for the South, particularly its farm population, another major group excluded from OASI. Along with domestics, farm wage workers and self-employed operators qualified for no benefits other than the old age assistance that suffered the opprobrium of "welfare" throughout the South. Like domestics, farmers had lost out because Treasury officials had advised lawmakers that administering payroll deductions would not be feasible.[74]

"The war has changed the yardsticks by which we measure social values," Woodward wrote in 1945. "More of us are beginning to see we must reduce regional inequalities," she asserted in a long analysis of the inequities that a combination of economic limitations, congressional shortsightedness, and state-imposed restrictions had visited upon Southerners. Despite an expanding war economy, the per capita income in the South in 1943 was only $600 ($484 in Mississippi, up from $212 in 1936). Lagging behind other regions in income, health as measured by mortality and morbidity rates, and in educational opportunities, the South stood in desperate need of more federal funds. Even those who worked in covered occupations suffered penalties because of the discontinuity of their work as they shifted from covered to uncovered jobs. As a result, OASI benefits were lowest in the South where, even after World War II, most OASI recipients had need also of Old Age Assistance.[75] Hence, expanded Social Security programs were imperative as an avenue of uplift for Southerners, individually and collectively.

Like other Board members, Woodward did not contest the resistance of Southern states to funding public assistance for blacks. Fearful that WPA jobs would diminish the cheap labor supplied by tenants and sharecroppers, Southern planters also resented public assistance provisions of Social Security, particularly to the aged. Old-age assistance plans submitted to the SSB, and approved, included residence requirements for applicants that held in check the number of black recipients. Local autonomy and its accompanying discriminations had been the concession the Roosevelt administration made to Southern congressmen to obtain passage of the Social Security Act.[76] It was also the price the SSB paid to have programs at all in some states. Whether writing for labor union organs, trade magazines, or agricultural journals or speaking to her old associates of the Mississippi Conference of Social Welfare,[77] Woodward was often preaching to the choir, although there were conservative elements in each group that questioned program advancements.[78]

After 1942, the SSB strove to shape public opinion on the Wagner-Murray-Dingell bill introduced in Congress every two years from 1943 to 1947. The most ambitious of its broad-scale proposals was a comprehensive national health insurance program.[79] As early as 1940, Woodward's speeches reflected the SSB's advocacy of health insurance coverage although, when pressed by her listeners, she refrained from commenting on the reaction of the medical profession.[80] Despite the fact that organized labor came out for Wagner-Murray-Dingell in 1943, President Roosevelt held back from endorsing the bill. When Congress also appeared reluctant to adopt the bill, Woodward drafted letters for Eleanor Roosevelt's signature that called for health insurance. In their last exchange over Social Security matters before the President's death in 1945, the two women examined ongoing strategies to pass the bill.[81] Despite congressional opposition and the President's coolness, the SSB continued its efforts to woo the public. Woodward's homiletics continued to reflect the SSB's optimism that, under the impetus of the war, plans for the future would result in minimum peacetime protection for all American families as "a first line of defense."[82]

As a WPA administrator, Woodward valued a vigorous information program. She was no less convinced that developing public confidence in Social Security depended on a well-informed citizenry. "The general public is not enlightened regarding government activities," she wrote Eleanor Roosevelt shortly after joining the Board. After eighteen months of intermittent Board discussion on information dissemination, Woodward spoke of the need to "devise more ways to get right down to the grass roots."[83] She wrote a lengthy memorandum to Altmeyer, suggesting that the Board initiate an educational program at the local level to bring together "leading citizens" to inform their communities of issues and problems relating to Social Security.[84] She recommended that the SSB offer consultative services to college faculties in government and social work so they could develop instructional materials on Social Security and that the Board provide copy for high school "current events" publications.[85]

Woodward developed genuine antipathy toward Max Stern. She believed that Stern neglected important groups and relied too much "on his contacts with labor groups to keep himself in his job." Woodward wrote an old friend: "I personally do not think he could sell fur coats to Eskimos in mid-winter."[86] A heated exchange ensued between the two when Stern failed to meet a request of the GFWC in time to arrange a session on Social Security for its national convention in 1944. "I have been urging you to put forth every reasonable effort to obtain the interest and support of these groups," she admonished him.[87]

Stern resigned and was replaced by Robert Huse. In recalling the Woodward-Stern impasse, Cohen remarked that Woodward "was constantly second-guessing Max and riding him." In justifying her part in the matter, Woodward admitted to Frank Bane, "I am a bit 'hipped' on the . . . interpretation of the Social Security program." "How can we expect quick action by Congress," she asked, when "so few people know anything about the . . . program?"[88]

Woodward became piqued in 1943 over the unresponsiveness of the Federation of Business and Professional Women's Clubs to Social Security under the leadership of Dr. Minnie Maffett. Maffett, whose private practice was in Dallas, Texas, was cool to the health insurance provisions of the Wagner-Murray-Dingell bill and used her influence to block Woodward's efforts to have Social Security included in the BPW legislative program. Woodward was not reticent about her differences with Maffett, and in 1943 she refused the request of Louise Bache, the BPW's executive secretary, to intercede for Maffett with Mrs. Roosevelt to explain the circumstances of an embarrassing racial matter arising in the New York City clubs. Two local clubs disciplined by the State Federation for accepting black members threatened to bring suit, and Bache was afraid that Mrs. Roosevelt, who still retained membership in a New York club, would be offended. Woodward refused to intercede, believing that "Dr. Maffett would want to take the leadership of her Federation," not failing to add, "I don't understand why the Federation should ask me to do anything . . . they haven't taken any interest in my work; in fact, Social Security is not included in your legislation."[89] Two years later, Woodward succeeded in having Social Security included on the study agenda for the 1945–1946 biennium, and asked SSB publicists to prepare a course of study for local clubs that included material on social insurance for domestic workers.[90]

Woodward became more optimistic that the BPW would be receptive to Social Security under the new national president, Margaret Hickey, after Maffett had not been willing to have the subject even discussed.[91] Her resolution that the BPW go on record—at least as supporting the principle of "individual security, education, health, and well-being"—won the endorsement of the Legislative Recommendation Committee but was rejected at the national biennial meeting in Cleveland in July 1946.[92] BPW lassitude toward Social Security continued to frustrate Woodward.

On 15 July 1946, Woodward bade farewell to her coworkers in the Social Security Administration, following the abolition of the Board under executive reorganization and weeks of great anxiety about her own future (see chap. 9). She left believing that "no other person on the Board had the opportunity that [she] had to see and know what *insecurity* does to people."[93] In a final, emotional SSB meeting in which all three Board members spoke poignantly of their years together, Woodward thanked her associates for their contributions to her "understanding of each phase of this broad program."[94]

Woodward's impact on the SSB should be assessed in light of the role she was expected to assume. As a good bureaucrat, she was expected to advocate policies as they were and to refrain from discussing inherent weaknesses beyond what SSB policy strategists believed could be changed. Questioned long after he had left government service about the effectiveness of both Molly Dewson and Ellen Woodward, Arthur Altmeyer replied that both were women of "wide experience in social . . . and political action" and important in "informing the public of the character and purpose of the social security program." The ease with which the two women moved between the executive and legislative branches had made their role "indispensable."[95] Woodward's behind-the-scenes encounters on Capitol Hill went unrecorded, but her many speeches gained wide coverage; thus through her actions the "public" Board can be seen at work. She was an effective liaison with Eleanor Roosevelt, whose championing of Social Security reforms surpassed that of her husband.

Wilbur Cohen saw in Woodward a blend of a Southern woman's "ability to be polite, attractive, friendly" while pursuing an objective "like a steel trap." "Ellen was a very tough woman," he remarked. Maurine Mulliner, the technical assistant to the SSB who compiled the informal notes, found her more "complex than she appeared," her "intelligence and drive" underestimated by persons who never saw beyond "her beauty and that soft southern speech and manner."[96]

Ironically, Woodward was not always considerate of those women whose clerical or technical assistance she required. Just as she had been in the WPA, she was too often a "slavedriver," demanding of subordinates what she demanded of herself.[97] Not everyone appreciated her efforts. Chloe Owings had resented the acclaim and credit the public gave Woodward, a noncareer professional and outsider to social work, for the crucial work Owings did herself. Similarly, some associates on her staff in the SSB worked hard to prepare materials that enhanced Woodward's public *persona*.[98] Unaware (or unappreciative) of the position she occupied in women's affairs and political circles, some coworkers resented her frequent absences. But, as a public woman of whom much was expected by others, Woodward was often in demand, especially after 1939, when the women of the New Deal shifted their focus to charting new paths in time of war.

CHAPTER 8

A New Deal Woman in Wartime Washington: 1939–1945

S cholars who assess the permanent impact of the women New Dealers leave the impression that by 1940 their influence had diminished considerably.[1] Further studies will not likely dispute the conclusion that there were fewer opportunities for women to hold administrative level offices after "Dr. New Deal" capitulated to "Dr. Win-the-War." Nonetheless, women who worked in wartime Washington and, most particularly, those of the Democratic faith, maintained their cohesiveness. They formed new, often informal and ad hoc, alliances to advance the economic security of all women, to create a climate in government that would be favorable for the appointment of women to policymaking positions, and to chronicle the achievements of all women. Among the women whose names consistently appear in the columns written by Washington-based women journalists and the records of women's organizations was Ellen Woodward.

Woodward seemed happiest when she was "in the know" of the many circles that attracted public women in Washington. In the twilight years of peace, women leaders, proud of past gains, appeared anxious to press toward new goals and forge new links. Many goals proved to be transitory, but they reflected the sense of urgency that compelled feminists toward action. Whatever the reason—creeping frustration over lost ground as the decade of the 1930s ended, a sense of history as the centennial of the beginning of the women's movement approached, or a thickening masculine atmosphere as war appeared imminent—women in government in 1939 and 1940 coalesced to flex what remaining muscle they possessed.

The National Advisory Committee on Women's Participation in the New York World's Fair never seemed to have much result. Nevertheless, under Helen Astor in 1939 and Mary P. Lord in 1940, Ellen Woodward served as the Mississippi chair, with the responsibility of naming prominent clubwomen of the state to assist Grover Whalen, the Fair's president, in planning and executing the event to ensure inclusion of women's attainments in the state exhibits. As it turned out, Woodward had little time to devote to the Fair. She provided the names as requested and attended the opening of the Fair in April 1939, traveling on a special train engaged for Washington officials who went to hear President Roosevelt speak.[2]

Similarly, the Women's Centennial Congress, in November 1940, never developed as more than a media event. At the instigation of the octogenarian suffragist Carrie Chapman Catt, a consortium of women leaders staged a three-day gathering in New York City to commemorate a hundred years of feminine achievement.[3] Catt failed to get Eleanor Roosevelt to attend, but some three hundred women delegates converged on New York City to "review the history of the past century and make a program for the next."[4] The "Women's Congress," Catt's swan song, proved to have limited impact. The discussions of the day faded away, and no new feminist agenda emerged; but at least the occasion convened leaders from all the states, including five who represented Mississippi, among them Woodward and Lucy Howorth.[5]

It was on the eve of World War II that a project of the historian Mary Ritter Beard to establish a World Center for Women's Archives finally collapsed. The Center dated to a proposal made by Beard in 1935 to create both an archival depository for the records of women's activities and a research center for the study of women's history. Sometime in the winter of 1936, she took the initiative and met with Woodward to see if WPA funds could support the archives project. She was elated that in her meeting with Woodward and Luther Evans, head of the Historical Records Survey, discussion elevated Beard's project to the scale of a women's Smithsonian. Beard made much of Woodward's offer to provide copies of material on women in the files of the WPA's HRS, which presumably would include scripts of the radio series "Gallant American Women," a joint venture of the WCWA and the HRS. When Beard met with Washington-area women for the first time in February 1936, Woodward expressed interest in seeing a history of the FERA and WPA women's projects preserved in the proposed center.[6] In June, Beard addressed the White Sulphur Springs national convention of Chi Omega sorority, where Woodward was initiated as an honorary member.[7] Woodward contributed $100 to the project and was one of twenty Washington women who cohosted a luncheon for Beard at the Cosmos Club in March 1938.[8]

It was not until early 1939 that a District of Columbia branch of the

WCWA was formally organized, with Mrs. Emil Hurja as president and a board comprised of, among others, Woodward, Howorth, Emily Newell Blair, and Mary McLeod Bethune.[9] Bethune had been added to the committee on a motion made by Woodward. The celebrated educator and New Deal "Black Cabinet" member attended three or four committee sessions; but her admission into the group, and the inclusion of the records of black women became a contentious issue. Beard was distressed that a stubborn element within the white WCWA coterie did not wish to accept black women or their history, and she counted on Woodward to help resolve "the D. C. problem." "I came home blue . . . [because] our bylaws prevent discrimination," Beard wrote Woodward in the fall of 1939, after it appeared that a distressing number of the white conservatives would have no part of her compromise.[10]

In 1940, as Germany advanced into the Low Countries and racial tensions thickened within the Washington WCWA unit, the project lay in jeopardy. "I shall keep you informed about the progress—hoping I shall not have to inform you of the demise," Beard wrote.[11] Time ran out on the WCWA that summer of 1940. There were causes for failure other than difficulty in raising funds. Beard's correspondence with Woodward reveals the "strong chagrin" she felt that women leaders could not be made to see the necessity of preserving women's history. "Its defeat is grievous indeed," Beard sighed to Woodward, who hastened to assure the historian that "you have awakened women, and men too, to a new appreciation of the value of preserving an authentic history of the achievement of women."[12]

By 1944, after discussions with Radcliffe College officials, Beard's spirits lifted considerably. Radcliffe welcomed the files of "our extinct World Center for Women's Archives." Two years later, she was satisfied that "the archives movement is swinging along in the college world." "The main part of our lost WCWA . . . will be recovered in Cambridge," she wrote Woodward, suggesting that she offer any "material, books or documents." Upon learning that Woodward had made arrangements to deposit her papers in the new women's archives, Beard responded that "students will be stimulated by studying them."[13] Subsequently, the Schlesinger Library received portions of Woodward's papers, comprising primarily speeches made in 1946, 1953, and 1959. In a warm exchange of letters, the two friends explored ways to advance their view that women were not sufficiently educated to social problems. Beard heartily concurred when Woodward wrote in the fall of 1939, "We can't pound too hard on women's

Harriet Elliott, Dean of the Woman's College of the University of North Carolina, longtime activist among Democratic women, and Woodward's confidant from 1936 until Elliott's death in 1947 (Courtesy University Archives, Walter Clinton Jackson Library, University of North Carolina at Greensboro)

'right' to work—there is visible evidence all around that the ground is slipping out from under some of our sex." When Woodward asked for Beard's advice on how she might address the Virginia Federation of the BPW, the latter responded, "I wish you could help to stretch women's minds to sharper thought about the road ahead and security on a more permanent basis." Woodward's talk pleased Beard, who wrote: "It goes into our Women's Archive at once." Beard's antipathy toward the harsher aspects of a capitalist society brought no rebuke from Woodward, who was touched by the affection Beard extended. "Your warmth of friendship lights the way [of] woman's rough road," Beard wrote. In 1946, after Beard encouraged Woodward's "uphill battle" to have the BPW adopt Social Security as a legislative item, Woodward wrote of her own setbacks: "[I]t does not take much gift of prophecy to foretell the kind of a world we will have if women do not wake up to the fundamental problems which have plunged us into war at least once in every generation."[14]

Politics as usual absorbed the women Democrats during the presi-

Lucy Somerville Howorth, Woodward's friend for forty years and a member of the New Deal women's "network" as a member of the Board of Appeals of the Veterans' Bureau (Courtesy Mississippi Department of Archives and History)

dential elections of the 1940s. In May 1940, the Women's Division of the Democratic National Committee staged a political-education extravaganza in Washington, known as the National Institute of Government. The three-day affair was the first conference of its kind in the political history of women and was the culmination of an earlier series of regional institutes conducted about the country by Women's Division chief Dorothy McAllister and her assistant, May Thompson Evans. It evoked a tremendous response. "Dorothy planned for three hundred and five thousand came," wrote Bess Furman, a Washington-based journalist. Furman described the Institute as "superspectacular" campaign-year initiative which provided instruction about administration programs given by key administration figures. Fronted by Eleanor Roosevelt, the headliners included the women New Dealers who held office by presidential appointment. Woodward's role in the event was as a round-table discussant (with Arthur Altmeyer) on the topic, "Conservation of Our Human Resources."[15]

Woodward's comments reflected the thrust of the Institute as an issue-centered forum rather than a blatant display of Democratic feminism. Molly Dewson presided at a closing symposium which asked, "What Do Women Want in the 1940 Democratic Platform?" It was a timely question, since WD leaders expected delegates to the nominating convention, for the first time, to place a woman from each state on the Platform and Resolution Committee. The "50–50 Plan" of equal participation by women in the committee councils of the party had been a longtime goal of the Women's Division. Now, in 1940, as a number of Democratic women quietly pleaded their cause with men already named to the Platform Committee, Woodward met with her old friend, Pat Harrison, a committee perennial. "Thanks," Dorothy McAllister wrote after Woodward reported a warm reception from the senator.[16]

Woodward heeded the advice of presidential secretary Missy Le-Hand and sought a ruling from Attorney General Robert Jackson on whether she could participate in the Chicago convention in July without violating Hatch Act strictures on the political activities of government employees. Informing LeHand that Jackson advised that her position did not fall under the Act, Woodward added, "I am dying to be there."[17] Not only did she attend, but she was one of eight at-large delegates from Mississippi. After delegates decreed that women were to be admitted to the Platform Committee, Woodward became one of twenty-five named at hastily called state caucuses. Her recommendation for expanded Social Security benefits was only one of such endorsements discussed by the Platform Committee.[18]

With the convention over, Woodward prepared for an August field trip to the West Coast, representing the SSB. She left Washington with instructions from McAllister about how she might work most expeditiously for Democratic women. Upon her return she reported using her time "to good advantage" doing what she could "to bring the warring factions together in northern and southern California," as well as making useful contacts in Utah, Colorado, and Nebraska.[19] Woodward offered to provide the President with "a few comments" on the political picture in the west, although there is no evidence that he took note of her observations.[20]

The Women's Division celebrated Roosevelt's November victory over Wendell Willkie at an elaborate tea hosted by Woodward at the Women's National Democratic Club. Special honorees included Molly Dewson, who had come from her home in Maine to help Woodward greet a full turnout of the prominent women of the New Deal, as well as numerous Democratic Senate and Cabinet wives.[21] Dorothy

McAllister was leaving the Women's Division to a new leader. Helen Essary, writing in a Washington newspaper, reported that among the names bandied about as a successor to McAllister was that of Ellen Woodward. She described the Mississippian as "a good speaker . . . quite handsome [who] dresses well and is a clever politician in an agreeable Southern way."[22] There is nothing to substantiate such a rumor, but the post did go to a southerner, Gladys Tillett of North Carolina. Democratic fetes continued as the jubilant third-termers celebrated the victory. An omnipresent Woodward was particularly excited when, as one of the hostesses at the President's Birthday Ball during the inaugural month of January 1941, her escort was Hollywood star Glenn Ford.[23]

The largest social affair Woodward ever planned was a reception given by the Mississippi Society of Washington for Senator and Mrs. Harrison, in February 1941, marking the beginning of the senator's thirty-first year in Congress.[24] Less than five months later, Senator Harrison was dead, the victim of colon cancer. His death was doubly hard on Woodward, for he had been her valued personal friend and her mentor and political protector since she had entered public life.

Bess Furman has estimated that by 1941 the women's movement in the Democratic party had reached its peak.[25] A shift in focus of *Democratic Digest*, the official organ of the Women's Division, bears her out. One has only to scan successive issues of the *Digest* after January 1939 to see that it now directed readers toward foreign affairs and the threat of totalitarian governments in Europe and the Far East. Less and less appeared about New Deal agencies and the women standouts who had been the object of the Women's Division's political affection since 1933. Increasingly, the Women's Division turned toward imperatives for national defense. In the 1939 BPW speech that Mary Beard had liked so much, Ellen Woodward described "the larger world in which [women] also have a part."[26]

Wielding her influence as an SSB member, Woodward engineered the appointment of Bess Bloodworth, a sister BPW member, to the Federal Advisory Council for Employment Security, an arm of the United States Employment Service. Bloodworth was Woodward's pick because, as vice president of the Namm Store in Brooklyn, she was the first department store employer to back wholeheartedly minimum wage laws; she had also "shown intelligent interest in all social legislation." Woodward hoped Bloodworth could help prompt USES to make greater use of women workers, who were still a minority in the labor market just as they were on the Federal Advisory Council.

The efforts of women, Woodward knew, "will become even more important in industry as the defense program progresses."[27] The USES advisory council had little impact on the status of women workers in industry, but Bloodworth's appointment was the initial attempt to get women named to defense-related councils.

Through access to USES, Woodward became a contact for other women alarmed about the unpromising status of women in industry, including Lorena Hickok, now executive secretary of the DNC. Woodward learned that the limited number of positions for women "had been largely due . . . to prejudices and traditions not within the specific realm of Employment Service solution."[28] Her response to Hickok conveyed the haplessness of government agencies when faced with the problem of discrimination and neglect of women in war jobs.

Anxious to seize the dual opportunity to meet the need for national defense workers and protect nonconstruction WPA projects, Woodward discussed with Paul McNutt (her superior as head of the Federal Security Agency since 1939) utilizing Kerr's "whole 'set-up' as an important part in the defense program." She was, she told Eleanor Roosevelt, "so worried about what might happen to Florence Kerr's Division."[29] In January 1941, Harriet Elliott, a former study program director of the Women's Division and now a new member of the National Defense Advisory Committee of the Council of National Defense, tried to have the First Lady assume the chairmanship of a women's volunteer defense committee adjunct that Elliott envisioned for the CND. Simultaneously, Woodward wrote to declare, "You and you alone, Mrs. Roosevelt, can supply the leadership we need at this critical period." Nothing came of the strategy Elliott and Woodward explored to have "the splendid machinery" of Kerr's WPA staff become central to the CND's women's component, because Florence Kerr took steps on her own to convert women's work relief into civilian defense.[30]

Receptive to Kerr's plan that the WPA Community Service Division become the primary apparatus for training an anticipated multitude of women volunteers, Roosevelt summoned a number of federal officials to hear it in January 1941. Woodward was one of the group that included, among others, the First Lady, Secretary of Labor Frances Perkins, Interior Secretary Harold Ickes, and Federal Security Administrator Paul McNutt. So many questions were raised and alternate ideas presented that Kerr later told the President: "I seem to be treading upon all the agency toes in Washington." As a result, Kerr's grand design was stillborn, and on May 20, by executive order,

Roosevelt created the Office of Civilian Defense, in which neither women nor volunteers alone would be central, although each would play a part.[31] So would Eleanor Roosevelt, Kerr, and Woodward.

Soon after the President named New York mayor Fiorella H. La Guardia to head the OCD, it became clear that OCD policy planners were concerned primarily with protecting civilians in the event of an armed attack. With opportunities for women in the OCD diminishing by the day, Kerr vented her frustrations to Woodward, who, as was her habit, conveyed them to Eleanor Roosevelt. Kerr, she wrote, was a "bit discouraged." Woodward had thought of going to La Guardia to have "a frank talk" about his "definite plans" but had discarded the idea because she was "so afraid of muddying the water." The day after Woodward wrote Mrs. Roosevelt, Kerr resigned.[32] Ironically, the day Kerr left OCD, in July 1941, the President authorized La Guardia to appoint a nationwide Volunteer Participation Committee, whose function it was to advise OCD on proposals designed to sustain national morale and provide for constructive civilian participation in the defense effort. Five members were named in each of the nine Civilian Defense regions. Two of the members for the eight-state Southern Region Four were Ellen Woodward and Jonathan Daniels, editor of the Raleigh *News and Observer*. At a White House conference, Woodward met other women VPC members including Dorothy McAllister, the President's daughter Anna Roosevelt Boettiger, and Helen Gahagan Douglas.[33]

Convinced that "no more patriotic people can be found anywhere in our country than in the Southern states," Woodward threw herself into a program that turned out less vigorous than she hoped.[34] Within two weeks she was urging Eleanor Roosevelt to press La Guardia to appoint a woman assistant as Kerr's replacement. Already there were charges, such as those made by the GFWC, that there was discrimination against women in the civilian defense program. Woodward was willing to "find ways to work with [La Guardia] amicably," adding: "I always feel that it is up to me to learn how to work with anyone whom the President appoints." But she was unable to refrain from extolling the attributes of May Thompson Evans as a woman who could "organize right down to the grassroots."[35] The job went to Eloise Davison, the Home Institute director of the *New York Herald Tribune*, whom Woodward had known when Davison had worked for the Tennessee Valley Authority in Knoxville.

Meanwhile (in the late summer and fall of 1941), Woodward concentrated on civilian defense mobilization plans in her region. She sought from Governor Paul Johnson a report on the work of the Mississippi Civilian Defense Committee under its chairman, Colonel Lea Robinson. Woodward told Johnson she wanted information in order to "discuss intelligently" at an upcoming regional VPC meeting in Atlanta "the plans underway in the South." She left Washington for the gathering, convinced that "things are still pretty confused over at the Mayor's office."[36]

Finding herself the only woman among the fourteen participants in Atlanta, Woodward was disturbed by the military character of most of the activities discussed. It remains problematical whether she was effective in pointing to ways volunteers could function in community service programs. Colonel Irvine Belser, the regional deputy administrator, informed her: "I like women who have opinions and are able to express them so convincingly." "The light seemed to break through a few of them," Woodward wrote to Mrs. Roosevelt, but "we have made very little progress in this whole civilian defense program."[37] When Eleanor Roosevelt criticized the OCD's heedlessness of women at a press conference in August, events moved rapidly along to *her* appointment, on September 29, as La Guardia's assistant. She was resigned to accepting the beleaguered job. "I fear," she wrote Lorena Hickok, "he isn't interested in volunteer work or the women's end of it."[38]

Woodward remained active that fall returning to Atlanta for the second regional VPC conference. She involved Dale Carnegie, the popular success guru, in writing material for the regional speakers' bureau and prepared Colonel Robinson for the approaching visit to Mississippi by an OCD field representative, Mary E. Judy. Despite the fact that Judy initially felt "terribly blue" at the beginning of her week in Mississippi, she became reconciled to the lesser role assigned her rather than "the job [she] wanted to accomplish." It was clear that women leaders in the civilian defense in the state had been spurred to action by Woodward and not by Colonel Robinson.[39]

In November 1941, Woodward took her message on "Women's Part in Civilian Defense" to Georgia's women Democrats. "[T]he *what* and *why* and *how* of volunteer activity must begin with the realities of daily life," she insisted.[40] The talk scored well with an enthusiastic audience, received good press in the *Democratic Digest,* and brought Woodward compliments from the new Women's Division head, Gladys Tillett, who assured her that "the Georgia women were delighted." Tillett herself considered Woodward "always a wonderful friend to the Women's Division."[41] It is likely that Woodward wrangled her own appearance at a Southern governors' conference after advising Mayor La Guardia that the regional VPC should be represented. "I thought," she confided to a committee colleague, "it was a good idea to let the head knockers" know that the VPC should be in on such conferences. Again, she urged that volunteers in defense could best serve by "doing everyday jobs" rather than "something they never heard of before."[42]

While Woodward fretted over getting the Region Four office in Atlanta "speeded up a bit," Eleanor Roosevelt chafed about her own problems in La Guardia's office.[43] She found it difficult to hold discussions with La Guardia. As Woodward perceived in Region Four, Mrs. Roosevelt was dismayed that the mayor's outlook on civilian defense was too narrow to encompass morale-building. Some of her own appointments, particularly those in the fields of recreation and dance, were subject to congressional ridicule and provoked public antagonism. Consequently, Eleanor Roosevelt resigned in February 1942, as did many of her protégés. Criticism of its bungled enterprises was so biting that even La Guardia exited the OCD.[44] "No member of the Volunteer Participation Committee has yet discovered what his function is," Jonathan Daniels groused, concluding that most members considered themselves "mere surplusage." Obviously, Woodward took the appointment more seriously than did her compatriots. "In this Civilian Defense business you are the rock on which I take my stand," Daniels wrote her; "and, if that doesn't sound like a gallant thing to call a Southern lady, I add that it is one of the best rocks I know." Their task, whatever it was supposed to be, ended 15 April 1942, when OCD was reorganized. "I am no longer serving in any capacity in connection with Civilian Defense," Woodward wrote a Mississippi friend in the spring of 1942.[45]

Nonetheless, Woodward was still at the business of national defense, working with WD leader Gladys Tillett in a Treasury Department war-bond sales campaign. As was often the case, Woodward's role was that of adviser, in this instance, to provide Harriet Elliot with names for state directors. Elliott, on leave from her deanship at the Woman's College of the University of North Carolina was to coordinate the many bond-promotion campaigns launched by women's groups. A skillful organizer, Elliott soon had a division director in each state, and she brought them to Washington for a conference in September 1942. When she named six regional advisers, the number included for the South, Nancy Curry Robinson of Mississippi, one of Woodward's clubwomen associates from the early years in Jackson. Robinson did such a creditable job that Elliott ranked her "no. 1 among her woman leaders."[46]

Direction of a new sales crusade to promote peacetime savings passed to Nancy Robinson, who moved to Washington. Elliott, now back in Greensboro, retreated to a secondary role, and Woodward remained a member of the advisory committee, serving now under the honorary chairmanship of the new First Lady, Bess Truman. She remained active into the 1950s with the peacetime bond drives and chaired the Woman's National Advisory Committee, finally leaving in June 1951.[47] Woodward regretted that Harriet Elliott, who died in August 1947, had not lived to see the vigorous bond drives conducted under Robinson's leadership.[48]

However much federal policymaking slighted voluntary participation by women during World War II, production managers were eager to recruit women for jobs in defense industries. Opportunities for the emergence of a large female workforce elicited the interest of women long dedicated to issues of women's welfare and economic security. Southern states were bristling with defense plants and shipyard-operations all of which drew women into employment and Ellen Woodward onto the speaker's circuit. Eight months before Pearl Harbor, in a radio address on "Women's Place in National Defense," she categorized homefront prospects for women. Work in the auxiliary medical fields and government agencies would not be new ventures for women in wartime, nor would domestic economies in the home, where most women would "do their bit for democracy." It was the industrial front that presented a new challenge, one that women must seize.[49]

Back on the airwaves in August 1941, and under the auspices of the BPW, she touted training programs that assisted women who transferred into jobs once held by men, citing the nimble-fingered women needleworkers at a Pennsylvania arsenal who were making time fuses for torpedoes after male watchmakers had failed.[50] As the demand for war production mounted, she echoed the common complaint of women leaders that nearly two-thirds of defense jobs were not yet open to women despite the fact that they could perform 80 percent of the tasks essential for war production. In a well-publicized speech on the subject of "Womanpower," she cited the widespread usage of the word as evidence of its "*Special Place* in the struggle for victory."[51]

Woodward could apply SSB figures on the nationwide enlistment of women workers and rely on the Federal Advisory Council for Employment Security to formulate plans for complete registration of women whenever the USES determined it was necessary. Despite popular demand for registration which even Eleanor Roosevelt supported, the Advisory Council viewed an all-out registration of women for war work as "ill-considered." Soon after FSA administrator Paul McNutt, privy to the internal debate over the registration of women, left the FSA in May 1942 to head the new War Manpower Commission, he announced that there would be no registration.[52] Nowhere is it more evident that Woodward reflected President Roosevelt's views than in her outspoken opposition to a compulsory registration of women workers. There were, she pointed out, fifteen hundred local offices of the Employment Service that could channel womanpower as required into local communities. By summer 1942, with a million women registered with USES not yet placed in jobs, she argued that, if compulsory registration were conducted, thousands of women would register for whom work would not be available. To have patriotic women "all signed up and no place to go" would lower their morale.[53] It was more important, she told Democratic women in Boston, that women seeking war jobs learn the labor needs of their own communities. "Every woman who does an effective job, particularly in a new field, opens the door to many others of her sex."[54]

Opening new doors for women workers was the charge given the Women's Advisory Committee appended to the War Manpower Commission in August 1942 and chaired by Margaret Hickey, a national BPW officer.[55] The fourteen-member WAC soon learned that it had minimal effect on WMC operations. Indeed, Woodward complained to Eleanor Roosevelt that the War Manpower Commission was "very slow in appointing women to administration positions." She admitted that she had "no real authority in connection with that setup"; but "somebody has to keep the matter of the employment of able women right before the heads of these agencies." And so she plugged away at it. Her friend Bess Bloodworth, one of the WAC fourteen, finally concluded that the advisory committee was being used as "a mere palliative to women." Woodward probably got an insider's angle from another WAC member, Blanche Ralston, the former WPA regional supervisor for the South and her confidant since their years in the Mississippi federated women's clubs.[56] There were other disappointments. Even Social Security benefits that should have assisted women were narrow in scope, Woodward learned. She was reluctant to have the SSB Information Service distribute over her signature a bulletin on "Unemployment Insurance Rights of Women in Wartime Jobs" because "the rights are not that extensive."[57]

By early 1943, Democratic women were collaborating with Eleanor Roosevelt in pressing the chief executive to appoint women to organizations then being planned to maintain the anticipated peace and administer relief to postwar Europe. In January, the First Lady invited to the White House a group that included Gladys Tillett, Lorena Hickok, Harriet Elliott, and Woodward to discuss the role of Democratic women while male leaders were away at war. Hickok, who had been working with the DNC and living at the White House since 1942, was frequently in contact with the often absent Eleanor Roosevelt and with Tillett to push her own initiatives. She asked Woodward to send names to Mrs. Roosevelt to be forwarded to Herbert Lehman, newly appointed director of the Office of Foreign Relief and Rehabilitation Operations, who was expected to appoint a number of social service specialists. Harriet Elliott, however, advised Woodward privately not "to have her name connected with the Lehman appointment" at a time when the President would know nothing of the strategies of the Democratic women. "We must not permit Ellen to be placed in the position of trying to run things without the President's approval," Elliott advised Tillett. In the interim, Woodward and the First Lady held a frank telephone conversation on the subject.[58]

Quite firmly the First Lady advised, "[I]t is wiser for you to stay where you are . . . because that is a permanent thing." In turn, Woodward assured her mentor that she had no desire to leave the SSB just when it needed "people who have had experience in knowing how to talk to people on the 'Hill'." The two agreed that preparing a roster was the best way to nudge the President to appoint women to the international conferences that would take place as the United States extended relief to Europeans liberated by advancing American armies. Pressure on the president also came from women outside the Women's Division. In April 1943, "Hick" wrote the First Lady, "Well—all Hell seems to be breaking loose among the gals over this business of getting women on these post-war commissions."[59]

In October, Gladys Tillett submitted to the President a list of women who might be appointed to a forthcoming international conference on relief. Of Woodward, she wrote, "[She] has always worked closely with the Women's Division . . . [and] has enormous prestige among women because of her outstanding record in administering a very important section of the biggest emergency relief job that has ever been done in the world."[60] In November, the President directed that Woodward and Elizabeth Conkey, were to be among nine advisers to the U.S. delegation at the first conference of the United Nations

Relief and Rehabilitation Administration, scheduled to convene at Atlantic City on 10 November. Dean Acheson, Assistant Secretary of State, and Francis B. Sayre, special assistant to the Secretary of State, were to lead the delegation. Once the conference assembled, it was widely noted that, among delegations from forty-four nations, there were only three women, two from the United States and one from Greece.[61]

Because Woodward left for the conference on short notice, she sought Jane Hoey's guidance on principles and procedures appropriate to the emergency needs of displaced or stranded Europeans. Hoey recommended that mass care and group billeting be terminated so that family units might be preserved; that local personnel be used at all points of contact with people to be assisted; and that no discrimination should be made on the basis of political affiliation, race, creed, color, or nationality. Thus, at an early meeting of the United States delegates, Woodward advised Acheson that the United States take the lead in presenting a resolution against discrimination. It surprised her that he received her idea "in his usual polite manner," only to suggest that some other nation take the initiative. She justified to Mrs. Roosevelt the "Memorandum on the Administration of Relief Without Discrimination" that she subsequently forwarded to Acheson: "I felt very strongly that the USA should put itself on record at the very beginning of the conference on this important point."[62]

It disturbed Woodward that the conference recommended standing technical advisory committees in the UNRRA structure to study problems in agriculture, health, and industrial recovery, but none in welfare. The concept of progress in international councils, she soon surmised, was like that of Congress. The emphasis lay on economic development with a lesser commitment to social welfare. Therefore, her subcommittee on Welfare Services undertook to draft a statement outlining the functions of a standing technical committee on welfare. Woodward drafted the document herself, based on the guidelines Jane Hoey had proposed. She submitted the draft to Dean Acheson, hoping he would press for the creation of such a committee with other United States delegates. Woodward's document pointed especially to problems in child care after World War I, conditions expected to be far more complex after World War II. She pointed out that a substantial segment of public support for UNRRA in the United States and the United Kingdom came from people who believed that the agencies most concerned with the victims of war "are welfare agencies." One of the great contributions the United States had made to the "sum of human knowledge," she argued, "has been the development of social welfare programs."[63] She drew heavily on a hastily written memorandum by John J. Corson, of the SSB, which suggested that UNRRA quickly attempt to reestablish social insurance institutions that had long succored unemployment, sickness, physical disability, the death of a breadwinner, and old age "the same causes of distress that affect people everywhere in an industrial civilization."[64]

When Woodward became apprehensive that U.S. delegates were faltering in their support of a standing committee on welfare, she telephoned Eleanor Roosevelt, who had presidential adviser Samuel Rosenman forward her message to Undersecretary of State Edward R. Stettinius. "I agree with Ellen Woodward," the First Lady told Rosenman. In protracted discussions with Acheson, Woodward made the point that, if she were not to support the creation of a standing committee on welfare in her own subcommittee, the United States would be the only nation to dissent. Her case thus put, Acheson authorized her to vote for a technical committee on welfare. She rationalized to Mrs. Roosevelt, "[T]he representatives from countries whose people are starving and in desperate need, listened intently for an expression from the USA."[65]

What Woodward observed at the conference was similar to what she and Eleanor Roosevelt had seen in the OCD. There was "so little social thinking among the men on the USA delegation," she wrote Lucy Howorth. Although men were conversant on the subjects of finance, supplies, agriculture, and industrial rebuilding, with the exception of Dr. Thomas Parran, the U.S. surgeon-general who had been at the conference, they all appeared unfamiliar with social welfare problems. Also, they seemed unaware of how displaced persons were actually to be assisted on a daily basis. She expressed her feelings to Margaret Hickey about the resistance she had met. "I have had to quit being a diplomat on some occasions and have had to employ direct language and methods." Regarding the proposed standing technical committee on welfare, she said proudly, "if such a Committee is established, it will be almost entirely through my efforts."[66] In the end, the committee was established; and in January 1944 President Roosevelt asked Stettinius to forward names of women who could be appointed as alternates to Acheson to attend successive meetings of the new standing UNRRA committees. (It was a "fine list," Mrs. Roosevelt remarked.) Acheson then formally requested that Woodward accept appointment to the Standing Technical Committee on Welfare.[67]

Woodward's role at the conference may not have been as pivotal as she thought, since she was not alone in pressing for a policy of nondiscrimination and careful attention to social welfare principles. As complex and decentralized as this and subsequent conferences were, it is difficult to assess the influence of any one individual. However, much of the phraseology of the working papers and memoranda in her handwriting in her own files appears in the final printed proceedings of the first UNRRA conference resolution on relief distribution policies.[68]

Whatever the extent of her influence, Woodward worked long hours during the two weeks in Atlantic City and returned to Washington physically drained. She had developed a "terrible cold and bronchitis" that left her "limping around" her SSB office.[69] Nevertheless, she was soon carrying the message on UNRRA to the BPW and to social-welfare interest groups. It helped that her sister, Elizabeth Dutcher, was now living in Washington, working as an activities director for the War Department's Employee and Personnel Department.[70]

Woodward knew about the rumors that her appointment as an UNRRA delegate had been political. "I am sure the Children's Bureau crowd are still upset about Katharine's [Lenroot] not being selected," she confided to Lucy Howorth. Tongues wagged that Roosevelt should have sent Jane Hoey to Atlantic City. To Margaret Hickey, who had heard the bickering, Woodward wrote: "If women will only support women whole-heartedly when they do a constructive job, we would soon be able to break down the kind of resistance you and I know exists." Above all, Woodward's detailed letters to Eleanor Roosevelt from Atlantic City may have been a subtle way to dispel the criticisms which the president surely heard. "We all agree . . . that every woman who serves well opens the door a little wider to other women," she wrote.[71]

Woodward sensed that now, of all times, women would have to band together as they struggled to find a niche in the wartime and postwar Washington world. She wrote Hickey from the UNRRA conference: "I do not want to be trite but I want to say and with all due emphasis—this is still a man's world." Whether speaking from her own experience or from that described to her by others, in a candid moment she let her guard down to Eleanor Roosevelt. "I hope now that the State Department will stop appointing women to any international conference unless they are to be given an opportunity to make a constructive contribution." Even in the social world, Woodward faced barriers. She commiserated with Bess Bloodworth that they were told "in the year of Our Lord 1943" that they could not have a cocktail at the Statler Hotel in New York City unless accompanied by a male. She wryly referred to the incident as "one of my richest experiences."[72]

In May 1944, the First Lady hosted a luncheon where her guests talked of little else but a place at the peace table.[73] Good Democrats all, they were looking as well to the presidential election in November, an event likely to predate peace. Eleanor Roosevelt knew that Gladys Tillett had told the President outright that women could win the election for him, but that Tillett had warned him of their slackening interest in his policies because of "this lack of recognition, especially in agencies dealing with postwar planning," a neglect "now being widely discussed among women leaders."[74] Thus motivated, Eleanor Roosevelt offered the prestige of the White House for the conference on June 14 on "How Women May Share in Post-War Policy Making."[75] More than two hundred women representing seventy-five organizations heard keynoter Lucy Howorth point out that, unlike 1919, there would be no single peace conference at the end of World War II. As was already apparent, there would be numerous conferences to discuss technical matters, and, unless women were in policymaking positions, they would be "ineffective in this hour of destiny." Following the keynote address, six women who had attended international councils in 1943 and 1944 spoke briefly; but Ellen Woodward's remarks gave no hint of her frustrations at the conference in Atlantic City.[76] The delegates moved quickly to implement Howorth's pragmatic suggestion that women's organizations prepare a roster for the State Department of "able, intelligent, and personable women."[77] Woodward reported the deliberations to Herbert Lehman, who obligingly lauded the affair as "an important occasion," giving assurances that he would alert UNRRA's personnel division to the projected roster.[78]

Three months later, on 16 September 1944, Woodward was off to Montreal, site of the second UNRRA assembly. She was one of seven designated as an alternate adviser to the U.S. UNRRA Council member, Dean Acheson.[79] Before leaving she dashed off a note to Eleanor Roosevelt, telling her of the trip, although she was certain her friend knew of the assignment. "Most opportunities that come to me come through you," she wrote. The sessions were long and the discussions tedious. Woodward was fortunate to have the assistance of Savilla Millis Simons, whose knowledge of social welfare principles, expertise in welfare administration, and analytic ability would be invaluable resources for Woodward for years to come. Simons, a Phi

Beta Kappa graduate of the University of Chicago, also held a graduate degree from the School of Social Service Administration at the same institution. A social welfare administrator since 1923, she was with the Bureau of Public Assistance in 1944, when Jane Hoey released her on an indefinite basis as a technical adviser to Woodward.[80] Simons was, in Wilbur Cohen's words, Woodward's "brain trust when she did all that United Nations work."[81]

With the Allies moving across Europe, and expecting that peoples soon to be liberated would require vast resources, delegates at Montreal adopted standards for relief assistance for displaced persons.[82] As a result of the German counteroffensive in December 1944, and the mounting Japanese resistance, UNRRA operations planned at Montreal were delayed. The war was almost over by the time Woodward flew to London for the UNRRA council that convened on 7 August 1945. This time, the U.S. council member and delegation head was William L. Clayton, Assistant Secretary of State for Economic Affairs. Clayton, a native of Lee County, Mississippi, knew Woodward well.[83] So did John Winant, Clayton's alternate and the American ambassador to Great Britain, whose London staff now included Maurine Mulliner, on loan from the Social Security Board to join the American UNRRA delegation. Mulliner's presence added an air of collegiality to the month-long stay in London for Woodward, and the two spent some time together enjoying the London theater and ballet.[84]

Prior to her departure for London, Woodward had expressed her ongoing concern about welfare services for "multiplied thousands of displaced children" and other equally desperate population groups. "Men who do not know anything about social welfare seem to think that all that needs to be done is to buy supplies and see that they are shipped—that somehow or other everything else will 'just happen.' " She believed that reinstated leaders in many countries requested supplies only in order to create a political following, but that they did not welcome welfare services personnel. "One can see signs of countries growing more and more selfish . . . since liberation," she wrote Eleanor Roosevelt.[85] In pre-departure conferences with State Department officials she had stressed the need for a public campaign to educate Americans about UNRRA operations and the necessary role of welfare workers in its program. She thought that particular attention to the plight of women and children would prove advantageous in winning public support for the large commitment the United States had made to UNRRA.[86]

Woodward was worried about the children who comprised one-fifth of the populations in camps for repatriated individuals. As a consequence, when the conference ended, Clayton requested military clearance and transportation to dispatch her to Germany, where she visited six camps, each the temporary home of 5,500 to 8,000 displaced persons under UNRRA care. She reported to Clayton that housing, food, and clothing were all in limited supply. At Clayton's invitation, she attended in March, at Atlantic City a fourth session of the UNRRA Council, again as an adviser to Clayton, the U.S. member. "Your memorandum on the Displaced Persons problem was especially help-ful," his assistant informed her at the session's close.[87]

Woodward, who had greater confidence in her association with Clayton than with Dean Acheson, spoke frankly of her observations that the policy-making role of the United States in UNRRA was not commensurate with the moral and financial obligations the nation had assumed. Inasmuch as "UNRRA is identified in the eyes of Europeans with American generosity," she regretted that its support at home was not stronger.[88] Publicly, she appealed to the two groups she had consistently approached to support her concerns, the Women's Divi-sion of the Democratic party and the national BPW.[89]

Woodward saw her BPW work both as an adjunct to her advocacy role with the SSB and as volunteer public service. She accepted the program chairmanship of the District of Columbia chapter in 1943–1944 as "a war service [she] could perform."[90] Similar motives prompted her to accept Margaret Hickey's request to chair the na-tional Committee on Public Affairs under Hickey's BPW presidency, 1944–1946. Woodward was relieved that Minnie Maffett had not sought reelection, leaving the presidency open for Hickey; for she considered Maffett and her headquarters staff "quite reactionary . . . [and] against most of the liberal administration programs."[91] In a 1945 report, her first as a national committee head, Woodward lamented the fact that only 18 percent of the clubs nationwide had their own public affairs committees. "No one has the right to be a bystander," she admonished inactive clubs she hoped would investigate issues such as housing, the cost of living, and child care. When it became apparent that the war would end soon, she began to speak more about postwar extensions of social policies at home and the immense ramifications of international social problems that comprised the agenda of her UNRRA Technical Committee on Welfare.[92]

Woodward did not attend the July 1945 meeting of BPW national officers, electing to remain in Washington with Albert, on leave before going to duty in the Pacific. Since 1943, Albert had been an officer in the U.S. Army. He had served first in Washington as chief of the Fuels Division in the office of the Quartermaster General. In July 1943, he was married to Felicia de la O, a nurse he had met during hospitalization for pneumonia in 1942. Woodward described Felicia to friends as "a lovely girl." "I really like her very much," she added. She was gratified that Albert had "found real happiness at last." After the marriage, Felicia remained in Washington during Albert's absence and worked with the District of Columbia public health service. She occasionally accompanied her mother-in-law to public events and social functions, although she preferred to remain apart from Washington social life. Friends observed that an estrangement developed between the two women in later years because of the elder Mrs. Woodward's disappointment that her daughter-in-law chose not to become involved in Washington society and remained, instead, a very private person. In brief, the two women simply were not compatible and had few common interests other than in Albert.[93]

Margaret Hickey believed that Woodward's BPW agenda offered "a practical viewpoint" on timely endeavors ranging from political education to cooperation with the OPA's vigilance against the black market. Work plans for her Public Affairs Committee emphasized specific approaches women could take to ensure that reconversion from war to peace would "bring about the economic conditions which make it possible for women to hold the jobs they now have." For one thing, BPW clubs should examine local potential for new industries and study tax rates that might hinder business.[94]

In 1946, at the annual midyear (January) conference of national BPW officers in New York City, Woodward offered no new directions in public affairs, simply reiterating her appeal that women "open [their] eyes and minds to the community."[95] She had already alerted Margaret Culkin Banning, the legislative recommendations chairman, that "supply and demand—for goods and for workers" was an "evil" more "fundamental" than the barriers of discrimination confronting women in the business world. That is why she advocated a federal policy of full employment and continued to include the topic in her own Public Affairs agenda. After the President signed the Full Employment Act in February 1946, the subject dropped from her prepared materials.[96]

Woodward pressed the BPW to endorse President Truman's recommendation to Congress in January 1946, for federal aid to education and Social Security protection to uncovered workers. Motivated by her "affection of friendship," Mary Beard assured Woodward, "Fundamentally you seem so right in emphasizing the *society* aspect of economy."[97] Woodward pursued the same liberal social issues that earlier BPW leaders had been reluctant to endorse. She was "not at all surprised" when delegates at the biennial convention in July 1946 defeated her plank to liberalize Social Security coverage.

For the remainder of her stint as national Public Affairs chairman, Woodward returned to safe, nonpartisan stands. Pushing for more women in appointive and elective office continued to be a popularly accepted goal, although Woodward reported that state activity was "unexpectedly weak" among clubs nationwide. She attributed the apathy to the fact that 1946 was not a presidential election year.[98] But there was more to the retreat of women from their wartime gains in industry and government. The ambivalence of women themselves, singly or collectively, over the renewed debate in the 1940s about the Equal Rights Amendment certainly contributed to the general impression that women did not know what they wanted.

In spite of her forthrightness on many women's equity issues, Ellen Woodward opposed the ERA. She never pressed her opposition and discreetly wrote nothing to disparage the amendment or its partisans. Only by conjecture can the basis of her opposition be determined. She was certainly aware of Eleanor Roosevelt's antipathy to the amendment until the late 1940s, when the First Lady modified her stand only slightly.[99] Like other government officials, particularly Labor Secretary Frances Perkins and Women's Bureau director Mary Anderson, Woodward feared that the amendment would nullify protective legislation for women. It is probable that Social Security Board actuarial experts ran projections on the effect of the ERA on the entire range of social insurance benefits. In 1943, a Department of Labor position paper predicted "highly undesirable" changes in the Social Security system, should the ERA be effected.[100] Furthermore, Woodward presumably deferred to Dorothy McAllister, who in 1944 chaired the National Committee to Defeat the Unequal Rights Amendment, an umbrella for twenty-seven groups that opposed the ERA.[101]

Scattered memoranda in Woodward's papers provide clues to the reasons she resisted the ERA. One document, origin unknown, describes the ERA as a "deceptive as well as dangerous" amendment that would prohibit any additional legislation to safeguard women, while all "existing laws protecting the health of women workers would be unconstitutional." Moreover, discrimination against women under state laws was "not a Federal problem but a state one." Existing inequities against women should be eliminated by "enlightened public opinion"; finally, in view of the guarantees of the Fourteenth Amendment, the ERA was "unnecessary."[102]

Woodward's opposition within BPW circles is buried in the minutes of the executive council she occasionally attended. Not all BPW members adhered to the endorsement the BPW gave the ERA at its Atlantic City convention in 1937. First introduced in Congress in 1923, it had little support, dying on the Senate calendar for a second time in 1943, the year the BPW council reaffirmed its support of the ERA.[103] Not then a member of the council, Woodward was, however, present at the meeting in January 1946 when the council endorsed the ERA in another of its biennial decisions on its own legislative program. Woodward cast one of two dissenting votes, although in her written statement on the Legislative Support Program she had simply offered "no comment" on the ERA. She did write that she was "heartily" in favor of continuing the BPW plank that "the right to work for compensation shall not be abridged or denied by reason of race, religion, sex, economic, or marital status."[104] Apparently, she remained silent about the urging of the Mississippi BPW Federation that Congress adopt the ERA.[105]

Renewed BPW deliberations on the ERA coincided with a favorable Senate Judiciary Committee report in January 1946. Woodward was not at the July convention that came just as the Social Security Board was shutting down, but she asked Nina Horton Avery to preside over a preconvention Public Affairs Round Table that conducted a discussion on the ERA plank. She made the request in order to have "an objective presider" despite the fact that Avery, as a vocal member of the National Woman's Party (and said to be an NWP "plant" within the BPW) favored the ERA.[106] By the time the question of full equal rights for women came up again in the BPW, Woodward was no longer on the council. While she continued to attend meetings of the DC chapter, she was not a local or national officeholder in the organization. Thus it was not incumbent upon her to comment when Margaret Hickey's successor, Sally Butler, opened in 1947 in Washington a BPW legislative office fully understood to be a headquarters for promoting the ERA.[107]

Although the long battle over the ERA provoked personal enmity and name-calling within women's organizations, many friendships survived the fracas because adversaries understood each other's opposition. Marguerite Rawalt, a Washington lawyer, fervid champion of the ERA, and later BPW national president, recalled that members respected the opposition of women like Woodward. Nina Avery considered it "more than fair" that Woodward had asked her to preside at the BPW forum, and she appreciated Woodward's decision that "legislation which the Federation had supported over a period of years should not have any suggestion of prejudice against it."[108]

Elsie George, the first scholar to give serious attention to the women appointees of Presidents Roosevelt and Truman, has concluded that, as a group, the appointees were "not radical feminists." Rather than focus on "the rhetoric of woman's rights," they chose to become exemplary officeholders whose actions would prove woman's equality. Reflecting on Woodward's persona years after her death, a veteran observer of Washington women, Hope Ridings Miller, commented that Woodward was more inclined to "pay attention to doing her job [than to] getting her rights" because she knew she "would get her rights if she did her job."[109] Woodward had said as much to the Washington BPW in 1938 when she declared that women had to be "a bit better" than a man to hold a comparable position. "Every woman who makes good on a job brings the day nearer when there will be no thought of sex but only of fitness in choosing public officials."[110]

Above all, the death of President Roosevelt in April 1945 was an irreparable blow to the Women's Division; for he had always been aware of its goals and known its members. The grief Woodward and her associates experienced with the President's widow was accompanied by the stark reality of what her exit from the White House meant. On V-E Day, May 8, Woodward wrote, "Mrs. Roosevelt, I miss you so that sometimes I can hardly stand it," and in July she wrote, "I shall never be able to tell you how much I miss you. So often problems come up . . . and right away I think—I must phone Malvina and see if Mrs. Roosevelt will let me talk over this matter with her. Then suddenly I realize that those happy days are gone."[111]

For Democratic women, the Roosevelt theme of "Happy Days" had been a kind refrain. The disconsolate tone of Woodward's private letter to her departed White House ally replaced that of the confident spirit characteristic of the women who had held public office since 1933. Uncertain of the future, they possessed a drive that was not yet exhausted and that would serve them well as new challenges to their positions and leverage appeared in the Truman administration.

Woodward and a few New Deal women would survive in Washington until retirement. Never as vital as they once were as women in public affairs, their post-New Deal activism does demonstrate that there were clusters of women whose work helped bridge the gains of the Roosevelt-Truman years and those of feminists who would revitalize the quest for women's rights in the decades that followed.

CHAPTER 9

I Have Not Had an Easy Time: The FSA, 1946–1953

T
he year 1946 proved to be an anxious one for the
women of the Roosevelt administration, who were now
uncertain how the new president would treat their
quest for appointments. The same groups that had been energetic
during the war—the National Federation of Business and Professional
Women, the Women's Division of the Democratic National Committee, and less formal coteries of government women—continued to
champion women's causes but with less result. Woodward's gravest
concern in 1946 was the effect President Harry S. Truman's Reorganization Plan No. 2 had on her own job. Retaining for Ellen Woodward
a position tantamount in rank to those she had held since 1933 became
the focus of an intense campaign waged by her Democratic colleagues.
Their effort was successful, but the responsibilities of the new FSA
Office of International Relations that Woodward held for the remaining
seven and a half years of her federal career expanded while budgets
declined, creating for her a difficult situation. When she retired late
in 1953, she was exhausted.

Woodward's personal relationship with President Truman was like
that of almost all other Democratic women. She had known him only
casually. "I have had no chance to know Truman since Roosevelt
died," she told Harriet Elliott in describing the sparring among the
women affected by executive shuffling. As Susan Hartmann has
pointed out, the presence of public women in Truman's background
was negligible. The new First Lady differed from her predecessor as
well. Although Bess Truman was gracious, she made no overtures to
the political women who had encircled Eleanor Roosevelt. In only a
few instances did Ellen Woodward use Mrs. Truman as an intermediary to reach the President. In one case, to make certain that the chief
executive read her plea that the Social Security Administration have
its own building, she asked the First Lady to deliver her letter to
him personally. Bess Truman complied, but left no doors open for
future favors.[1]

Women in government and their friends met often to shore up past achievements and push for new goals. Both Lucy Howorth and Ellen Woodward were members of the Committee on Women in World Affairs, a coalition of women activists who represented their constituent organizations. Formed in 1942 by educators Mary Woolley and Emily Hickman, the CWWA first bore a highly goal-specific name, the Committee on the Participation of Women in Postwar Planning. It had been one of the groups behind the White House Conference in 1944. Active in roster-making and letter-writing campaigns, the CWWA expanded its focus from the appointment of women to international assemblies to their appointment as well to national offices, especially after 1946, when it appeared that women as policymakers were on the wane.[2] In the view of one sympathetic Washington columnist, the CWWA "worked assiduously" so that the U.S. government would not have "to stand before the world as a man-run Government which is the usual totalitarian pattern."[3]

Yet another group consisted only of Washington women. Sometimes referred to as the Committee of Ten, it met without fanfare whenever a need arose. Howorth and Woodward were members of the little band that remained alert to what was happening to women in Washington. Other members were May Thompson Evans and Jewel Swofford. As a Missourian, Swofford, a personal friend of the Trumans and a commissioner on the United States Employees Compensation Commission, had the ear of Bess Truman more than did any other woman. Certainly Howorth's and Woodward's little company needed whatever reserves they could muster, and Swofford did lobby the President through the new First Lady whenever the local Committee of Ten alerted her to a job opening.[4]

Nonetheless, President Truman was always circumspect about the role women would play in his administration. He had no reservations about Woodward, though, once writing to her, "I always have had a feeling that you and Mrs. Swofford were two good women I could absolutely count on politically." After the CWWA sent a list of women to the State Department in 1947, Woodward confided to a friend, "Frankly, I do not think that many women have been appointed— period." In his first three years as president, Truman named only three women to posts high enough to merit Senate confirmation.[5]

"I agree with you," Harriet Elliott wrote Woodward in June 1946. "[I]t makes my blood boil when I think about the control which men have in all public affairs." Events that summer were more disturbing than they had been at any time since the death of President Roosevelt.

Difficulties for women were apparent as soon as the details of the President's Reorganization Plan became known. Executive reorganization, the columnist Malvina Lindsay wrote, was "the old nemesis of career women."[6] Women Democrats coalesced for action. "We didn't call it 'sisterhood' then," Lucy Howorth remarked years later; but "we knew that we were all in the same boat." Whenever one of the presidential appointees was threatened, all others "threw in whatever political weight that [they] could."[7]

Actually, Woodward had no quarrel with executive reorganization. At least, that was the official position taken by the Social Security Board. Altmeyer had informed Board members and staff that "anyone who felt he should oppose the President's plan ought to resign, in fairness to the President." Truman's reorganization was a "second step," Federal Security Agency director Watson B. Miller declared, toward further coordination of kindred fields of social service first advanced when President Roosevelt created the FSA in 1939 to merge into one agency the Office of Education, the Public Health Service, and the new Social Security Board. Unlike 1946, in 1939, Woodward's job had not been affected. Now, under the new scheme, the Social Security Board was eliminated.[8]

Woodward spelled out her predicament to Harriet Elliott after returning from Florida and her annual siege of bronchitis. It had been a "shock" to her when Altmeyer had telephoned late on May 16 to tell her the reorganization plan actually included abolition of the Social Security Board. While Woodward had assurance of some kind of job in the revamped FSA, she did not want one that would be, in reality, a demotion. "Harriet," she wrote, "I have *not* had an easy time climbing the ladder and at this time in life, I just don't believe I could stand being demoted and just 'taken care of'."[9]

At one time, Woodward had been heralded as the second highest ranking-woman in the federal government, only one notch below Labor Secretary Frances Perkins. Perkins's exit after Roosevelt's death in 1945 hardly left Woodward at first rank, since the SSB post was not as prestigious as the former WPA office. Wherever Woodward was on the hierarchy of Washington women in 1946, she enjoyed the affection and respect of a number of men and women who were determined that she not be victimized by reorganization. Her women friends, in particular, feared that if she were eased out, no woman officeholder of rank would be safe. More was at stake, too, as Howorth reminded Harriet Elliott. Woodward had "served the progressive program of the party most valiantly."[10]

The campaign began in earnest in late May, when Howorth forwarded details to Emily Hickman just how women in government posts were endangered by the reorganization plan. She pointed to the abolition of the U.S. Employees Compensation Commission, chaired by Jewel Swofford since 1933 and an agency a majority of whose members were women, and to that of the SSB. Furthermore, Bess Goodykoontz would lose her job with the removal of the statutory office of Assistant Commissioner of Education. Finally, the increased control over the Children's Bureau given to the FSA head jeopardized the rank and authority of Katharine Lenroot. The only top-level post left to a woman was that of Civil Service Commissioner, and the woman presently in the post, Lucille McMillin, was seriously ill. "There should be a concentrated drive for reopening policy making positions to women," Howorth concluded.[11]

Gladys Tillett appealed to Democratic party chairman Robert E. Hannegan on behalf of all women affected by reorganization, whose pledge that Woodward would be "taken care of in a proper way" offered some relief. Specifically at Hannegan's request, Tillett drafted letters for his use in contacting both Watson Miller and President Truman about an administrative position for Woodward in the new FSA setup.[12] In another move, Lucy Howorth and May Thompson Evans alerted some twenty-five women Democratic officials, "Women will make a real mistake if they forget that President Truman and Mr. Hannegan do not know personally the thrilling role that women have played in public life these past dozen years." Stressing that Democratic women "lost a top spot" when Woodward's SSB post fell to reorganization, the appeal glowingly described the role the Mississippian had filled "with distinction" within the Democratic party, in the WPA, and on the Social Security Board.[13] With Eleanor Roosevelt's influence diminished, no one seems to have asked her to write a letter to hold the line for the women who stood to lose under reorganization. Woodward could not refrain from hinting to the former First Lady that she longed to be at the latter's Val-Kill retreat to tell "what [is] happening here."[14] But no invitation came for a visit to the cottage.

During the last week of June, letters rained on the White House and the office of Watson Miller.[15] By early July, it was apparent that the White House had accepted Miller's recommendations for new assistants in his agency, when he assured U.S. Circuit Judge Florence Allen that "Mrs. Woodward's valued services to this Agency in a responsible position will be continued."[16] On July 16, President Truman named former SSB chairman Altmeyer the new commissioner of

Social Security, and new directorships were created within the Federal Security Agency for each former Board member. Bigge was to head the Office of Federal-State Relations and Woodward was to be Director, Office of Inter-Agency and International Relations.[17]

Woodward confessed "a terrible strain . . . both mentally and physically" from the anxiety about where she would land after reorganization. She was "loath" to give up her Social Security duties even though she had "put in very long hours and hard licks."[18] To Eleanor Roosevelt, who had inquired, Woodward expressed reservations about what the transfer would mean personally. She was uncertain that she could be effective unless the duties of the office were better defined and adequate staff were provided. "I will not accept this or any other position where my responsibilities would be great and my *authority small*," she wrote.[19] To former colleagues in the Social Security Administration, however, she spoke positively of the opportunity to "pioneer" activities that would interpret and apply " 'security' as an integral part of world security."[20]

Less openly, Woodward set about exploring the possibility of succeeding Lucille McMillin as one of the three members of the Civil Service Commission. McMillin, who had been one of the loyal Democratic women invited to Washington in 1933, was rumored to be seeking retirement.[21] On 19 July, Woodward wrote Truman, asking that she be considered for the Civil Service Commission, using Bess Truman as a conduit for the request. From the President she received only a polite reply that he was "glad to know of her interest." Meanwhile, Gladys Tillett once more gathered forces and informed the President of "pressures from all sides" to move Woodward to the Commission.[22]

Jewel Swofford could be frank with her old friend from Missouri. Woodward, she explained, was "very grateful" for the President's instructions that she be given an adequate position. However, the new office in the FSA was one that "has to be developed from the very beginning." Thus it seemed "a pity" not to take better advantage of Woodward's wide acquaintanceship throughout the country by placing her in an office where she could be used to greater advantage for the administration and the Democratic party. May Evans added that at least one commissioner should be a woman since women then constituted 23 percent of all federal employees, a figure as high as 50 percent during the war.[23]

The entire Mississippi delegation in the House of Representatives wrote letters of support, as did Herbert Holmes, chair of the Mississippi Democratic Executive Committee. The support for Woodward of Verda W. Barnes, director of the women's division of the CIO Political Action Committee, signified the unspoken (by all but Jewel Swofford) political ramifications of the appointment.[24] Woodward's name did not appear in the press's speculation about who would succeed McMillin (who coupled her 9 August resignation with a pledge to the President that she would remain until he named a new commissioner). Among those mentioned were Frances Perkins, Colonel Mary Agnes Gordon of the Veterans Bureau, who won the endorsement of the BPW, and the former Woman's Army Corps commander, Oveta Culp Hobby. In early January 1947, Truman selected Perkins. It was not, however, the job she had hoped for upon leaving the Labor Department in 1945. She had wanted to go on to the Social Security Board, but an opening never occurred; and now the Board no longer existed for her or for Woodward.[25]

And so, Woodward remained in the Office of Inter-Agency and International Relations and set about developing its functions and a professional staff. Most immediately, during the late summer of 1946, she made plans to attend the fifth UNRRA conference. Held in Geneva, 8-16 August, its concerns revolved about fine-tuning the international-relief functions outlined at the earlier sessions she attended. Will Clayton was once again the U.S. delegate; Woodward was the sole woman among thirteen U.S. advisers.[26] The principal task at Geneva was to initiate plans to terminate UNRRA, slated to cease operations on 30 June 1947, and shift functions to permanent international agencies mostly within the United Nations. Woodward left Geneva very satisfied that she had played a major role in drafting the resolution regarding the transfer of UNRRA's social welfare functions to the UN.[27]

Woodward spent two weeks in the fall of 1946 in New York City, working on behalf of the newly created International Children's Fund, set up to assist children and adolescents in formerly enemy-occupied countries. In lobbying for the fund, she renewed contacts with Eleanor Roosevelt, now a member of the UN Human Rights Commission. The presence of former Social Security Administration colleagues removed some of the disappointment of having lost daily association with them. Working toward favorable action by the UN Economic and Social Council on the Geneva resolutions for welfare and children's services reunited her with Arthur Altmeyer, the new U.S. member of the UN Social Commission, and John Winant, who held a similar post on the

Savilla Millis Simons was Woodward's adviser in the Office of International Relations, Federal Security Agency, from 1944 to 1951 and the "ghost" writer of most of Woodward's OIR articles and speeches. (Courtesy Social Welfare History Archives, Walter Library, University of Minnesota)

UN Economic and Social Council. With Altmeyer and Winant she attended a session of ECOSOC in October 1946.[28]

By fall 1946, Woodward had begun to develop a realistic program. Watson Miller had specified the functions of the office in a grandiose FSA order dated 16 July 1946. As a practical matter, her office was to help avert duplication of the international functions of the Children's Bureau, the Social Security Administration, the Public Health Service, the Office of Education, and the Office of Vocational Rehabilitation. It was never intended that Woodward's office develop policy for any one FSA constituent bureau, nor was she to administer any of the domestic welfare services emanating from the FSA branches.[29] Further, Woodward was to serve as the FSA member on interdepartmental committees, whose other members represented the interests of federal departments outside the FSA in matters relating to health, education,

Mona Johnson Harden, a native of Louisville, who was Woodward's house-keeper, friend, and mainstay from 1938 to 1971 (Courtesy Otis L. Harden)

and allied areas of social welfare. This meant, in particular, the State Department, now that it had become a major player in international social welfare. She would also attend a series of interminable sessions of State Department committees.[30]

"[A]ctivities in the international field have been growing by leaps and bounds," Woodward stated in late 1946, as more and more FSA undertakings were lodged in her office, soon to be called the Office of International Relations. Overall planning for teams of foreign visitors, who were coming in a steady stream for observation and training within FSA branches, consumed much of the OIR's attention.[31] In January 1947, the Social Security Administration received an initial group of trainees from South America, and by the summer the SSA was developing procedures to handle UN fellows in the Children's Bureau, the Bureau of Public Assistance, and other divisions.[32] The OIR also coordinated the observation and study experiences of the UN fellows program established in 1946. Together, Savilla Simons and Dorothy Lally, the latter a specialist in the SSA for international social welfare, had programs underway by the summer of 1947 for in-service training and scientific and technical consultancies in the American republics and countries in Europe, the Near East, and the Far East.[33]

With Simons as her alternate, Woodward attended the fourth session of ECOSOC that met at Lake Success, New York, in February and March 1947. It was the first time two women delegates had taken a place at an ECOSOC conference table to give depositions for their country on social problems since the Council had first met fourteen months earlier.[34] It was exacting to absorb mounds of reports over a month-long span of workdays that ended at midnight. She did not think she had ever had "such an assignment in all [her] working years"[35]; but her reward was to see the growing assumption by the United Nations through ECOSOC of the international social welfare initiatives of UNRRA and earlier functions of the League of Nations.[36]

Woodward was present at the fifth session of ECOSOC in July 1947. It was another enervating conference, but at its conclusion she spent a weekend at Val-Kill, reporting on ECOSOC progress and speculating with Eleanor Roosevelt what changes might occur in the FSA as Watson Miller left in August to become commissioner of Immigration and Naturalization and Oscar Ewing assumed direction of the agency.[37]

Always a joiner, Woodward participated fitfully in the postwar reactivation of the International Conference of Social Work, first organized in 1923 as a forum for the exchange of information and experiences among social workers and agencies throughout the world.[38] As one of thirty-three members on the U.S. Committee, she attended a few meetings and attempted to use her contacts with women's organizations to solicit funds to support the ICSW and to pay the expenses of U.S. members who attended international conferences. In a move reminiscent of earlier years, Woodward prevailed on Eleanor Roosevelt to devote a "My Day" column to the ICSW. More important, she succeeded in having Roosevelt use her influence to persuade the U.S. State Department to place a social welfare attache in its Paris office. "You see what a visit from you does to the boys at State," Woodward joked to her longtime ally.[39]

International educational activities of the U.S. Office of Education fell within the scope of Woodward's office. Probably the most significant was the exchange of teachers between the United States and Britain, begun in 1946 and expanded to include Canada in 1947 and France in 1948.[40] As with the UN fellowship program, the FSA Office of International Relations performed duties of a protocol nature and arranged events for foreign teachers during their brief stay in Washington, including a session with President Truman.[41] Woodward was also expected to extend to the teachers the official greetings of the FSA and plan other amenities as a representative of the host nation.

However devoid of important policymaking the work of the OIR may have been, the workload and paper flow increased vastly as the State Department increasingly relied on the FSA to implement technical assistance under the Point 4 Program of Technical Cooperation outlined in Truman's 1949 inaugural address.[42] By the end of 1951, nearly a hundred Agency-sponsored experts were in the field as members of various U.S. missions, including a large number engaged in the development of community welfare services. Incoming visitors, far outnumbering American experts on foreign assignments and including the exchange teachers and UN fellows, all received their orientation through Woodward's office.[43] In 1953, Woodward's last year with the FSA, approximately a hundred UN and Point 4 fellows were in the country.[44] The office facilitated security clearance of employees working on international programs and developed and issued agency policy statements in consultation with FSA branches.[45]

Savilla Simons left her post in January 1951, to become director of community services in the Technical Cooperation Administration (the official name of the Point 4 program).[46] Her replacement, Gertrude Gates, had spent six years in the field of international social welfare as welfare adviser on the UNRRA Czechoslovakia mission, director of the UN program in social welfare fellowships, and finally budget director of the International Refugee Organization in Geneva.[47]

Once again, Woodward had at hand an experienced professional to bear the workload in her office. Gates's competence, like that of Simons, helped compensate for the budget deficiencies Woodward cited to confidants almost from the outset. She had a staff of seven. Arthur Altmeyer shared her concern about diminishing allocations for scientific and cultural cooperation that severely curtailed programs undertaken by the Social Security Administration in the Western hemisphere. Just as Woodward left in February 1950 to join the United States delegation at the tenth session of UNESCO, she was confronted by the perennial twin woes of a illness and budget crisis. "I do not see how I can keep going on feeling well unless I have more staff," she complained to Eleanor Roosevelt. She lay the blame on an FSA administration and budget division that "placed much higher priorities on domestic programs."[48]

Wilbur Cohen remarked years after Woodward's office was created that it was "a difficult assignment . . . important . . . but not on the main line of traffic." She had to "earn her own way," he added. At the time of reorganization, Woodward had told Harriet Elliott that she would have to "carve out her own job," and in the ensuing years the office projected itself into the busy thoroughfares of international cooperation.[49] During fiscal 1953, for instance, it coordinated the attendance of some 125 professional and technical personnel of the new Department of Health, Education and Welfare at 91 international meetings.[50] Furthermore, the technical assistance missions of Point 4 channeled their requests for personnel through Woodward's office. The paper flow became almost overwhelming, but Woodward's well-informed deputies, including, by 1953, Dorothy Lally, remained energetic in running the office. More important, the increasing assumption of foreign aid to underdeveloped countries by the President, Congress, and the State Department added new functions yearly to the international specialists in each FSA bureau and their umbrella office, that of Woodward and her assistants. Throughout, Lally remembered, Woodward was "very positive" and "a helpful influence" upon the office staff.[51]

Like her UNRRA committee work, many of Woodward's functions in the Office of International Relations were related to protocol. In her WPA post, she had presided over true lines of authority, and subordinates reported directly to her. She was in direct contact with field workers. She read their reports and knew when they obtained results. Even Social Security Board membership had placed her at an upper administrative level. It was not the same in the FSA. Changes occurring outside the office called for adjustments also. There was not the same intensity in relationships among the Washington women in public affairs that had made the New Deal days exhilarating. Many of the women had left Washington or taken jobs in a postwar bureaucracy that defied the old bonds of unity. According to a Women's Bureau study made in 1949, of the almost 1 million women added to federal civilian employment, three-fourths left after the war.[52] No new networks developed to sustain them, as had the Women's Division of the DNC during earlier years.

For a time, the WD continued to pay homage to the old stalwarts as it did when the *Democratic Digest* featured Woodward and Eleanor Roosevelt, along with Helen Gahagan Douglas and Esther Brunauer, as "Women of the Year" in the August 1946 issue. The journal found its heroines now in foreign affairs.[53] India Edwards, the new head of the Women's Division, was supportive of Woodward, writing to Watson Miller when she became alarmed at an oversight that omitted the Mississippian's name in the 1947 *United States Government Manual*. In 1948, Edwards included Woodward in the group invited to her home to hear the November election results that returned Truman to office (much to Woodward's relief). She had been "terribly sorry" about the "revolting Southerners," including Mississippi friends who abandoned the Democrats for the States Rights candidates. In a sense, the WD was too successful in its campaign for equality for women within the party; for, in 1953, the division was eliminated and the *Democratic Digest* ceased publication, leaving some disillusioned women to chafe that women were integrated out of the Democratic party structure.[54] Dissolving the WD must have given Woodward pause: the event marked the close of an era for her and coincided with her own retirement from office.

Woodward's link with women's groups that could have promoted large-scale involvement of women in community betterment had weakened. She no longer was active in BPW councils; nor from her FSA office could she lobby women's groups for Social Security and health-policy reform. Most of the few speeches she made in the postwar era were to younger women, especially those on college campuses.

It was probably the influence of Harriet Elliott, who had decided to devote her final years to the college classroom, that attracted Woodward to the college podium. In 1947, Elliott's school, the Woman's College of the University of North Carolina, awarded Woodward an honorary degree. The citation lauded her as a "fighting yet wise leader for public welfare in Mississippi, for social security in the United States, and for the organization of relief and peace in the world."[55]

In her postwar messages to young women, Woodward appeared to reflect the new public temper, one that dispatched women back to the home, and to deal with the reality of the immediate postwar rush of young women to marry. It was a turnaround for her to say, as she did to the Girls Nation assembly in Washington, "the first and greatest career for a woman is to be a wise, wonderful mother and homemaker," or to tell graduating seniors at Mississippi State College for Women, in 1945, that the first freedom granted to women by equality was "freedom to be themselves and to elect women's age-old career of homemaker." When she gave the first commencement address made by a woman at Winthrop College, in 1951, she expanded her concept of home and community as the basis for democracy by rather simplistically describing the United Nations as a family of nations whose charter was analogous to a "code of family life."[56] This speech apparently was her last major address.

Presidents who preceded Dwight D. Eisenhower had all made recommendations to reorganize federal welfare services. Soon after his election in 1952, it was certain that the Federal Security Agency would undergo reorganization. FSA division chiefs knew in November that

Oscar Ewing would be replaced by Oveta Culp Hobby, a Texas Republican and former head of the Women's Army Corps.[57] Whatever reservations Ellen Woodward may have had about the new administrator, she maintained a supportive stance among friends. In December 1952, she predicted that Hobby "will be a good Administrator," and she told her staff not to engage in criticism. To Stella Reading, a new British friend and correspondent, Woodward added, "I hope women will not begin to be critical of another woman—we should give her a chance." "Isn't it strange the way females act towards each other?" she mused. A few months after Hobby assumed the post, Woodward wrote again to Reading, this time to report, "Mrs. Hobby has made a fine start." She wrote in a similar vein to Eleanor Roosevelt, reporting that the new FSA head had "made a good impression on the personnel."[58]

When the new Department of Health, Education and Welfare became official in April 1953, Woodward's Office of International Relations was one of several retained at the department level to perform administrative functions for constituent agencies.[59] Woodward seemed assured that her work would continue. Despite the fact that her staff was small, they were "all very able professional people"; so, in January, she had confidently transmitted to Hobby a long memorandum describing her work plans for the next six months.[60]

On the other hand, there were ominous signals to FSA veterans that their jobs were not secure. Two weeks before HEW came into being, the top FSA jobs were taken out of Civil Service and designated in "schedules" of employment outside the merit system.[61] The shift meant that Hobby could more readily transfer FSA personnel or ease them out. In April 1953, associates were stunned that Altmeyer was forced out only three weeks before he would have completed twenty years of federal employment. Offered a demotion, Cohen resigned and left Washington, as did other men in the SSA.[62] Women divisional directors wondered if they, too, would become victims of the partisan shakeup. After Eleanor Roosevelt wrote in the summer of 1953 asking Woodward, "what is happening to you?" her protégé replied that after "difficult months" she did not know what "the score was." Nothing would be settled until the new HEW assistant secretary, under whom international relations fell, was appointed. Meanwhile, Woodward dared not take a summer vacation. In November, Hobby removed Jane Hoey as director of the Bureau of Public Assistance, a position she had held for eighteen years, after Hobby ruled that the post was a policymaking assignment, subject to administrative appointment, and Hoey refused to resign.[63]

For Woodward, circumstances were not as abrupt. She learned in October through discussions with Nelson A. Rockefeller, the new HEW undersecretary, that the Office of International Relations was to be abolished and its functions merged with the Foreign Operations Administration under Harold E. Stassen. She declined another position never made public, but it would have been, in any case, a demotion, as were the posts offered other Democrats. Woodward was grateful that almost all her small staff were given jobs in other HEW offices and that she could remain as a consultant on international affairs during the transition until her retirement could become effective 1 January 1954.[64] By mid-November, former SSB associates about the country knew of her decision to leave federal service after a career spanning two decades. In a long letter to Eleanor Roosevelt, she described what had transpired. There had been "no unpleasantness" with Hobby or Rockefeller; she simply could not endure another round of executive reorganization. She was, after all, now sixty-six years old and, as she wrote to Stella Reading, "fairly tired both physically and mentally and . . . looking forward to January 1."[65]

Woodward had once joked that at retirement she wanted "to buy a rocking chair and go back to Mississippi"; but, in 1953, she purchased her apartment at the Westchester, home to many of Washington's distinguished citizens. Mississippians could expect to see more of her, although not as a candidate for governor as the *Jackson Daily News* wistfully editorialized.[66] Trips home to join her two sisters were dearer as the family circle grew smaller. In 1941, Murray Sullivan, the younger of her two brothers, had died after a heart attack. In May 1952, Belle's husband, "like a father to [Woodward] for many years," died as did Bess's husband, Hamilton Dutcher, in July.[67] In 1957, the elder brother of the Woodward sisters, William Van Amberg Sullivan, died at the age of eighty-six. There were happier moments, however. Old ties with friends in Louisville were renewed when the Fortnightly Club presented her with a life membership in 1959.

There were economic interests as well in the home state. On the recommendation of Luther Folse, her colleague on the Mississippi State Board of Development in the mid-1920s, Woodward had invested in 320 acres of land in Pearl River County, where there was high potential to grow tung trees; by 1937 half the acreage had been planted.[68] Predicted as one of the leading industries of the South, tung-oil production attracted a group of Woodward's former businessmen friends, including Lucius Crosby, Jr., who served as vice president of the American Tung Oil Association while Woodward was an

ATOA director in 1953. At the Tung Oil Association meeting in 1955, members elected Woodward vice president and Washington representative.[69] The 1955 crop was a failure, and by 1969 production was dismal. At some point during the decline, Woodward sold her acreage to Crosby, gaining little on her investment.

Maintaining contact with the Washington network of women was important to Woodward. She retained her membership in the BPW and in the American Newspaper Women's Club on whose board of governors she served in 1952–1953. Her continuing affiliation with the Women's National Democratic Club was likely the most rewarding, for it brought her into contact with the newer echelon of leaders and rising figures in the party. In August 1956, she attended the Democratic convention in Chicago, where Adlai Stevenson was nominated for president, and in September she gave a reception for Jane Dick, a co-chair of the Volunteers for Stevenson and Estes Kefauver. She thought the Democratic candidate to be "so very able, experienced, dedicated [with] such feeling for the 'little man'." There was no common ideological ground between her and Mississippi Senator James Eastland, although she was cordial to him and did invite him to social functions at her apartment. In respect for Mona Harden's antipathy toward Eastland—she was active in the National Association for the Advancement of Colored People—Woodward accepted her request that she not assist at parties Eastland attended. On the other hand, Woodward admired John C. Stennis, the junior senator from Mississippi who had entered the Senate in 1947 at Bilbo's death, and she sought to establish ties with him.[70]

But it was her circle of women friends that meant the most in the early years of retirement. Lucy Howorth described to Molly Dewson the birthday party friends gave Woodward in July 1954. "She looks fine," Howorth wrote. Holidays prompted an exchange of greetings. "I am always thankful for your never failing friendship," Woodward wrote Dewson at Thanksgiving 1956.[71] Retirement had brought to an end the frequent requests from Eleanor Roosevelt for help in dealing with the many letters she received from supplicants for Social Security. Even after Woodward left the SSB, Roosevelt had continued to send requests about public assistance generated by her "My Day" column to Woodward who forwarded them to Jane Hoey. In fact, during her last week in office, Woodward informed Roosevelt that her most recent inquiry would go to Lavinia Engle now that Hoey was gone and Woodward herself would not be able "to follow up properly." She confessed that she would miss "checking on facts and replying to letters" as she had done for many years. They had been "good old days" when "*we made something happen*," she reflected, for people who "were not just names on a letter." Perhaps the last time that Woodward saw Eleanor Roosevelt was when they were both at the head table at a campaign conference for Democratic women in 1958. "I always love the glimpses I have of you," Woodward wrote afterwards. Extant records indicate no exchange between the two aging veterans for relief and security after that.[72] By the time Eleanor Roosevelt died in November 1962, only two weeks after Molly Dewson died, Woodward's own long debilitating decline in health had begun.

Woodward's problems were both physical and emotional, the two ailments interrelated. In January 1961, she wrote Lucy Howorth, who had retired to Mississippi, that she had been under her doctor's care for four months. His final report of "no malignancy" suggests that she may have been troubled by recurrences of the old lung problems. That January, she made what appears to have been her last trip to Mississippi to receive in Jackson the Foundation Award presented by the First Federal Savings and Loan Bank.[73] At some point in the early 1960s, she began to sink into a deep melancholy triggered, perhaps in part, by the loss to death and distance of the New Deal circle of friends. Even Molly Dewson had twinges of regret over her loss of intimate contact with the Roosevelts. According to Susan Ware, Dewson's biographer, the venerable old New Dealer "looked back on her days in the New Deal with increasing nostalgia but did not wallow in the past." Nevertheless, Lucy Howorth detected "a slump" in Dewson, alleviated by her "good sense to leave Washington."[74]

May Thompson Evans thought Woodward had simply "burned herself out." The "wear and tear on her mind" had taken its toll, and she seemed content to be alone, going out only to walk around the grounds of the Westchester. Had her physical strength been greater, she might have been able to throw herself into new activities to help alleviate the pain of the loss of friends and of the limelight that had once been her delight. For a few years she made an effort to be active in the Metropolitan Methodist Church, but the involvements there did not prove strong enough "to hold against the emotional conflict," Lucy Howorth surmised.[75] Woodward intended to write an autobiography and made a futile effort to organize her papers and memorabilia. After all, she had a great belief in her work and the accomplishments of her programs. "Write a book on all this," a BPW friend had urged her when she retired. She had known important people and reveled in their friendships and for two decades had been at or near the center of the Washington world. Lucy Howorth saw Woodward whenever she returned to Washington, as she did for the President's Commission on the Status of Women from 1961 to 1963. When the two friends were last together in 1963, Woodward was surrounded by her materials but seemingly confused by them. Howorth realized then that Woodward was "slipping badly," and when she attempted a telephone conversation in 1968, Woodward was incoherent. It was Howorth's last contact with her friend of forty years.[76]

Other associates detected a serious decline. Wilbur Cohen thought that by 1961, she was "more or less demobilized." When Arthur Altmeyer last saw Woodward in 1966, while he lived a block away from the Westchester during a two-year return sojourn in Washington, he found her to be "the same warmhearted and gracious lady," but he recognized that her memory was failing. There is no mention of her presence at the gala reunion of Social Security stalwarts in August 1968, to celebrate the thirty-third anniversary of the advent of the program.[77]

The 1960s were difficult years for Woodward, as she suffered deteriorating illnesses, and the decade remains opaque for a biographer. Few friends saw Woodward in her last years. May Evans dropped by occasionally, as did Grace Allen, Woodward's former secretary. The aging lady was reconciled to the fact that life had grown simpler, and that the biggest social outing might be a ride on a city bus with Mona Harden to the People's Drugstore at Friendship Circle for an ice cream soda. It was the presence of Harden as a round-the-clock housekeeper and attendant that permitted Woodward to remain in her apartment until the last. By all accounts from those who knew the demands on Harden to provide for Woodward's physical and emotional needs during the final years, "Mona was a jewel," a "life-saver." A mutual affection had been the hallmark of their relationship for almost four decades. In fact, the last item in Woodward's papers in her own handwriting is a 1963 Christmas card on which she inscribed "from my Sweet Mona." At the very last, Harden protected Woodward from visitors, answered telephone calls, and in other ways sought to mitigate the embarrassment Woodward suffered because of her disabilities.[78] Near the end, Woodward's memory was so impaired that she did not recognize Albert, Felicia, or Bess. At least her mental lapse may have spared her the anguish that would have come at Belle's death in 1970 at the age of eighty-five.

Woodward suffered no pain and died finally of a heart attack on 23 September 1971. The death certificate named "generalized arteriosclerosis" as the cause. After services at the United Methodist Church in Louisville, she was buried beside her husband in the Old Masonic Cemetery.[79] The final honor given her by Mississippians, who had long recognized her as one of their most distinguished citizens, was election in 1976 by the board of trustees of the Mississippi Department of Archives and History to the Mississippi Hall of Fame "honoring illustrious Mississippians of the past" and, especially, her innumerable contributions to "this nation's cultural patrimony." At the ceremonies at the Old Capitol where her portrait was hung, it was fitting that Lucy Somerville Howorth should give the eulogy.[80]

It was tragic that in Ellen Woodward's last years she was robbed of the capacity to enjoy post-retirement honors and continued contacts with her former associates. Friends who survived her had keen memories of how she had befriended them. Even so natural a leader as Margaret Hickey remembered the " 'network' Ellen established during the 1940s and 50s [and the] great momentum given to the careers of a number of women," including her own. Woodward had brought to the Washington scene a blend of gentility and hard-boiled determination that came foremost to the minds of those who remembered a special aura of unceasing cordiality about her. Elizabeth Wickenden, who watched Woodward establish the women's work relief program from her own office in other WPA functions, found it "impossible to think of Ellen Woodward without thinking of her as a southerner."[81] Like so many others, her initial reservations, based on the Mississippian's gentleness, femininity, and desire always to be agreeable, gave way to an awareness of her inner strength and administrative competence.

Woodward never lost faith that people of goodwill could be brought together to solve their common problems. What had worked for her in smalltown Mississippi could be made to work in the Washington bureaucracy or even in international councils dedicated to furthering human welfare. She brought to assignments spanning thirty years of public service a down-to-earth constructive wisdom that brought results. Her grassroots approach to the administration of programs to promote economic security and social betterment brought significant change to the lives of many women, not the least of whom were the "forgotten women" at home and abroad for whom she helped make the Roosevelt and Truman administrations accountable.

Essay on Sources

Manuscripts

There are 107 boxes of Ellen S. Woodward papers at the Mississippi Department of Archives and History containing voluminous correspondence, press releases, newspaper clippings and magazine articles, photographs, official records and agency publications, and many extremely informative transcripts of telephone conversations and conferences. Received and processed as they arrived three separate times, they bear accession numbers 1139, 1139.1, and 1139.2, the last being by far the fullest. Because each contains all types of archival material, it is necessary to cite laboriously the accession number in all footnotes. There is a small collection of Woodward's papers at the Arthur and Elizabeth Schlesinger Library at Radcliffe College.

Record Group 69 at the National Archives comprised of the agency records of the FERA, CWA, and WPA. I relied upon the General Subject Files, selected project files (e.g., home economics, library, clothing, feeding), and the state series. One must be aware that there are several series within RG 69; thus the citations may include references to a Women's and Professional Projects (WPP) group and Final State Reports.

The records of the Social Security Board and Administration (RG 47) were located at the National Archives in Washington and at Suitland, Maryland, when I used them. In addition to the Executive Director's Files, the Informal Minutes of Board Meetings, while baffling, indicate Woodward's presence. The Social Security library at Woodlawn, Maryland, holds a bound volume of Woodward's speeches, as does the library of the Department of Health and Human Services in Washington. RG 73, the records of POUR and PECE, in the National Archives contains a small amount of material on the women's programs.

The papers of Eleanor Roosevelt, Mary W. (Molly) Dewson, Harry L. Hopkins, and the Women's Division of the National Democratic

Party are at the Franklin D. Roosevelt Library in Hyde Park, New York, and are all essential to this study. The Woodward-Eleanor Roosevelt exchange in the microfilm edition is much abbreviated and should not be relied upon exclusively. The president's Official Files on the WPA and the President's Personal Files contain relevant material. The Harry S. Truman Library has very little on Woodward beyond the files on executive reorganization in 1946.

Extremely helpful material on Woodward's tenure on the Social Security Board may be found in the papers of Arthur J. Altmeyer and, to a lesser degree, those of Wilbur Cohen at the State Historical Society of Wisconsin (Madison). Savilla Millis Simons's papers in the Social Welfare History Archives (University of Minnesota) help fill in everyday details on international relief conducted by Woodward while she was with the SSB and the FSA. The Frank Bane papers at the University of Virginia are disappointing in their lack of personal exchanges with Woodward.

Two manuscript collections of Democratic women contain informative personal correspondence with Woodward. They are the papers of Gladys Tillett in the Southern Historical Collection at the University of North Carolina (Chapel Hill) and of Harriet Elliott at the University of North Carolina at Greensboro. Lucy Somerville Howorth's papers in the Schlesinger Library contain some revealing letters, but by far the most informative of Howorth's letters are those she has written me over a period of ten years. Chloe Owings's autobiography at the Schlesinger Library is highly useful, and her file at Knox College contains biographical information also. The papers of Margaret Hickey at the University of Missouri-St. Louis have nothing on Woodward. The papers of two of Woodward's political confidants in Mississippi, those of Pat Harrison (University of Mississippi Library) and of Walter Sillers, Jr., (Library, Delta State University, Cleveland) contain real nuggets on politics and personalities. The papers of Theodore G. Bilbo at the University of Southern Mississippi are disappointing. The Alfred Edgar Smith Papers (University of Arkansas) contain much material I did not see in RG 69 at the National Archives on work relief for minorities.

Interviews, Correspondence, and Oral History

Despite the lapse of more than twenty-five years since Ellen Woodward was among friends, family, and coworkers, many had keen memories of her and talked to me in person, revealing valuable facts and assessments: Lucy Somerville Howorth (Cleveland, Mississippi); Grace Allen, Ewan Clague, Marianne Cummings (Pat Harrison's daughter), May Thompson Evans, Otis Harden, Dorothy Lally, Maurine Mulliner, and Albert Woodward, Jr. (Washington); Mrs. Mitchell Robinson and Charlotte Capers (Jackson); Wilbur Cohen (Austin, Texas); and Dorothy Fair Brown and Davis L. Fair, Jr. (Louisville, Mississippi). Telephone interviews with others were productive: Frank Bane (Alexandria, Virginia), John Corson, Hope Rydings Miller, Marguerite Rawalt, and Roy Wynkoop (Washington); Elizabeth Wickenden (New York City); and Emily Earley (Madison, Wisconsin). Frank Bane, Margaret Hickey, Lucy Somerville Howorth, Helen Twombly McAleney, Maurine Mulliner, and William Parkes assisted by correspondence.

Within the Columbia Oral History Collection, I consulted with great profit the memoirs of Arthur J. Altmeyer, Holger Cahill, Oscar Ewing, Florence Kerr, and Maurine Mulliner. Highly personal comments about Woodward's role in the FTP are in the Federal Theatre Project oral histories of Philip Barber, Francis Bosworth, Agnes Cronin, Julius Davidson, and Irwin Rhodes at George Mason University. Through interlibrary loan I was able to read the oral interview with Holger Cahill in the Archives of American Art (Detroit).

Interviews of Abe Bortz with Social Security personnel (read in the SSA historian's office at Woodlawn, Maryland) were less productive because many of the individuals knew Woodward only casually. Blanche D. Coll's interview with Wilbur Cohen, in her possession, deals with important issues. Constance Ashton Myers' interview with Lucy Howorth (Southern Historical Collection, Chapel Hill) is informative about the New Deal women. An interview with Carolyn Wolfe in the Women in Politics Oral History Project at the Bancroft Library (University of California) gives a good description of the Democratic women's coalition.

Government Publications

For Woodward's brief legislative tenure two publications are necessary: *The Official and Statistical Register of the State of Mississippi, 1924–1928* (New York, n.d.) and the *Journal of the Mississippi House of Representatives* (1926). The official Brookings Institution report to the Research Commission, *Report on a Survey of the Organization and Administration of State and County Government in Mississippi* (Jackson, 1932), is useful for its description of welfare services in the state. Woodward's clubwoman work is described in *A History of the Mississippi Federation of Women's Clubs*, a typed WPA Historical Research Project in the MDAH.

For the New Deal agencies there are valuable final reports that sort out chronology, project starts and stops, and data on employment figures. On the FERA and EWRP, consult Doris Carothers, *Chronology of the Federal Emergency Relief Administration, May 12, 1933 to December 31, 1935* (Washington, 1937), *Emergency Work Relief Program of the Federal Emergency Relief Administration, April 1, 1934–July 1, 1935* (an offset publication in the Woodward Papers), and Theodore E. Whiting, *Final Statistical Report of the Federal Emergency Relief Administration* (Washington, 1942). For the WPA, see *Inventory: An Appraisal of the Results of the Works Progress Administration* (Washington, 1938) and the Federal Work Agency's *Final Report on the WPA Program, 1935–1943* (Washington, 1946). Extremely helpful on the WPA is Charley Tidd Cole and Esther Franklin, *REPORT: Division of Women's and Professional Projects, WPA, July 1, 1935 to January 1, 1937*, a bound volume in the Woodward Papers.

Several bulletins of the Women's Bureau provide essential background information on the status of unemployed women: *Employment Fluctuations and Unemployment of Women: Certain Indications from Various Sources* (1933), *Women Workers in the Third Year of the Depression* (1933), *Women Unemployed Seeking Relief in 1933* (1936), and *The Negro Woman Worker* (1938). Footnotes cite others.

Newspapers and Magazines

For Woodward's early years, I read the *Oxford Globe* (later *Eagle*) from 1889 to 1906, the *Winston County Journal* from 1906 to 1935, and the Greenville *Daily-Democrat Times* from 1919 to 1922. *Mississippi Builder* (Mississippi State Board of Development) carried Woodward's columns from 1927 to 1933.

In reading ten years of the *Washington Post*, the *Washington Evening Star*, and the *Jackson Daily News*, for an earlier study on Senator Pat Harrison, I prepared my own index on Woodward. Footnotes indicate the heavy reliance upon these newspapers. Vertical files on Woodward in Special Collections at Mississippi State University and numerous news service clippings within the Woodward papers (MDAH), as well as her own carefully preserved news items, account for many of the random references to newspapers.

The Woodward papers contain dozens of magazines and clipped articles either written by or about Woodward from her clubwoman years in Mississippi until her final retirement. Articles under her name most often appeared in the *Journal of Home Economics*, the *American Journal of Nursing*, and other official publications of professional associations. The *Social Security Bulletin* routinely published articles under her name but "ghostwritten" by technical assistants or the information service. It is necessary to read successive issues of the *Democratic Digest* (WD-DNC) and *Independent Woman* (NBPW) for their many news stories about Woodward. A run of *The Mississippi Woman's Magazine* of the MFWC is in the MDAH.

Primary and Secondary Sources

Footnotes point to many printed primary and secondary accounts that provide a larger context for Woodward's life and work that I do not describe in this essay.

For the Louisville years, I consulted Louis Thornton and Nancy L. Parkes, *Winston County and Its People: A Collection of Family Histories* (Louisville, 1980). For general Mississippi history, a ready reference is Richard A. McLemore, ed., *History of Mississippi*, II (Jackson, 1973). Among the general histories of the period I consistently turned to are William E. Leuchtenburg, *Franklin D. Roosevelt and the New Deal, 1932–1940* (New York, 1943), George B. Tindall, *The Emergence of the New South, 1913–1945* (Baton Rouge, 1967), and James T. Patterson, *The New Deal and the States: Federalism in Transition* (Princeton, 1969).

Books describing in general New Deal work relief written by contemporaries are: Nels Anderson, *The Right to Work* (New York, 1938), Louise Armstrong's touching and effective *We Too Are the People* (reprint, New York, 1971), Corrington Gill, *Wasted Manpower: The Challenge of Unemployment* (New York, 1939), Harry Hopkins, *Spending to Save: The Complete Story of Relief* (New York, 1936), Marie Dresden Lane and Francis Steegmuller, *America on Relief* (New York, 1938), Donald S. Howard, *The WPA and Federal Relief Policy* (New York, 1943), Arthur W. Macmahon, John D. Millett, and Gladys Ogden, *The Administration of Work Relief* (Chicago, 1941), and Edward A. Williams, *Federal Aid for Relief* (New York, 1939). More recently, Bonnie Fox Schwartz wrote *The Civil Works Administration, 1933–1934* (Princeton, 1984) with a chapter on "The Forgotten Woman" that I consider too harsh an indictment of the Women's

Division. Forrest A. Walker's *The Civil Works Administration: An Experiment in Federal Work Relief, 1933–1934* (New York, 1979) is informative but less interpretive. William R. Brock, *Welfare, Democracy, and the New Deal* (Cambridge, Eng., 1988) is a thorough study with sharp insights.

Five books that deal in part with aspects of women's work relief are: on the food programs, Janet Poppendieck, *Breadlines Knee-Deep in Wheat: Food Assistance in the Great Depression* (New Brunswick, 1986); on household training, Phyllis Palmer, *Domesticity and Dirt: Housewives and Domestic Servants in the United States, 1920–1945* (Philadelphia, 1989) and Donna L. Van Raaphorst, *Union Maids Not Wanted: Organizing Domestic Workers, 1987–1940* (New York, 1988); and on the library projects, Daniel F. Ring., ed., *Studies in Creative Partnership: Federal Aid to Public Libraries During the New Deal* (Metuchen, 1980) and Edward B. Stanford, *Library Extension Under the WPA: An Appraisal of an Experiment in Federal Aid* (Chicago, 1944).

I relied upon several descriptive and interpretive published works on the Four Arts supplementing them extensively with material in the Woodward papers. Hallie Flanagan's own *Arena: The Story of the Federal Theatre* (New York, 1940) is a gold mine of information. Also written by participants is Tony Buttita and Barry Witham's *Uncle Sam Presents: A Memoir of the Federal Theatre, 1935–1939* (Philadelphia, 1982). The standard work is Jane De Hart Mathews, *The Federal Theatre, 1935–1939: Plays, Relief, and Politics* (Princeton, 1967), but Malcolm Goldstein, *The Political Stage: American Drama and Theater of the Great Depression* (New York, 1974) provides another context, as does John O'Connor and Lorraine Brown, *The Federal Theatre: Free, Adult, and Uncensored* (London, 1986). The definitive study of the FAP is Richard A. McKinzie, *The New Deal for Artists* (Princeton, 1973). Participant Jerre Mangione wrote a valuable insider's account, *The Dream and the Deal: the Federal Writers' Project, 1935–1943* (New York, 1972) that can be compared with Monty Noam Penkower, *The Federal Writers' Project: A Study in Government Patronage of the Arts* (Urbana, 1977). Other reliable accounts of the Federal One are described under "Unpublished Studies."

William McDonald's interpretation of the origin of the Four Arts programs in his *Federal Relief Administration and the Arts* (Athens, 1969) displeased the directors, but his encyclopedic handling of facts, figures, and dates made the book indispensable to me. I also drew upon Charles C. Alexander, *Here the Country Lies: Nationalism and the Arts in Twentieth Century America* (Bloomington, 1980) and Grace Overmyer's *Government and the Arts* (New York, 1939) for assessment of the cultural WPA.

General studies of the depression's toll on individuals to which I turned are Anthony J. Badger, *The New Deal: The Depression Years, 1933–1940* (New York, 1989), and Edward Robb Ellis, *A Nation in Torment: The Great Depression* (New York, 1971). I found much appeal in John L. Robinson's *Living Hard: Southern Americans in the Great Depression* (Washington, 1981). For a basic understanding of the outcomes of depression and the early New Deal, nothing is better than Richard Lowitt and Maurine Beasley, eds., *One-Third of a Nation: Lorena Hickok Reports on the Great Depression* (Urbana, 1981).

A number of histories have been written on the New Deal at the regional, state, and city levels, all of them containing details on administrative difficulties of women's work relief. For the South, see Douglas L. Smith, *The New Deal in the Urban South* (Baton Rouge, 1988). Three very worthwhile municipal accounts are Roger Biles, *Memphis in the Great Depression* (Knoxville, 1985); Barbara Blumberg, *The New Deal and the Unemployed, The View from New York City* (Lewisburg, 1979); and Julia Kirk Blackwelder, *Women of the Depression: Caste and Culture in San Antonio, 1929–1939* (College Station, 1984). For Boston, see Charles H. Trout, *Boston: The Great Depression and the New Deal* (New York, 1977). Informative states studies include Carl Douglas Abrams, *Conservative Constraints: North Carolina and the New Deal* (Jackson, 1992); George T. Blakey, *Hard Times & New Deal in Kentucky, 1929–1939* (Lexington, 1986); Ronald L. Heineman, *Depression and New Deal in Virginia, The Enduring Dominion* (Charlottesville, 1983); Michael S. Holmes, *The New Deal in Georgia: An Administrative History* (Westport, 1975); Richard M. Judd, *The New Deal in Vermont: Its Impact and Aftermath* (New York, 1979); and John Dean Minton, *The New Deal in Tennessee, 1932–1938* (New York, 1979). Sandra Schackel includes splendid material in *Social Housekeepers: Women Shaping Public Policy in New Mexico, 1920–1940* (Albuquerque, 1992).

On Social Security, I have benefited greatly from a typescript copy of Blanche D. Coll's forthcoming *Safety Net: Welfare, 1929–1979* (New Brunswick). Arthur J. Altmeyer, *The Formative Years of Social Security* (Madison, 1968) and Edwin E. Witte, *The Development of the Social Security Act* (Madison, 1963) are essential for putting straight the early years, as is Charles McKinley and Robert W.

Frase, *Launching Social Security: A Capture-and-Record Account, 1935–1937* (Madison, 1970). Among the numerous books written in the last decade that analyze Social Security policies, and are generally critical of the system's leadership, I gave particular attention to Mimi Abramovitz, *Regulating the Lives of Women: Social Welfare Policy from Colonial Times to the Present* (Boston, 1988) and Jerry R. Cates, *Insuring Inequality: Administrative Leadership in Social Security, 1935–1954* (Ann Arbor, 1983). Helpful are the early chapters in Edward D. Berkowitz, *America's Welfare State from Roosevelt to Reagan* (Baltimore, 1991).

For Harry L. Hopkins and Aubrey W. Williams, I relied upon George McJimsey, *Harry Hopkins: Ally of the Poor and Defender of Democracy* (Cambridge, 1987) and to a lesser extent upon Robert Sherwood, *Roosevelt and Hopkins: An Intimate History* (New York, 1948). John A. Salmond's *A Southern Rebel: The Life and Times of Aubrey Willis Williams, 1890–1965* (Chapel Hill, 1983) is my model for this book on Woodward. There are yet no biographies of Arthur Altmeyer or Frank Bane. I have earlier explained how this book intersects at many points with my earlier book, *Pat Harrison: The New Deal Years* (Jackson, 1978).

There are several published accounts that are vital to understanding Woodward's position among women. Barbara F. Turoff cites the Woodward correspondence in *Mary Beard as Force in History* (Dayton, 1979). Footnotes demonstrate my reliance upon Susan Ware, *Partner and I: Molly Dewson, Feminism, and New Deal Politics* (New Haven, 1987). Of the many biographies of Eleanor Roosevelt, only Tamara Hareven, *Eleanor Roosevelt, An American Conscience* (Chicago, 1968) deals at length with the First Lady's involvement with women's work relief, although several of the essays in Joan Hoff-Wilson and Marjorie Lightman, *Without Precedent: The Life and Career of Eleanor Roosevelt* (Bloomington, 1984) have relevant material. On women's organizations, particularly the Democratic party's Women's Division, the premier account is Susan Ware, *Beyond Suffrage: Women in the New Deal* (Cambridge, 1981). Other useful books are Susan M. Hartmann, *The Home Front and Beyond: American Women in the 1940s* (Boston, 1982), while for the Truman years, one should read Cynthia Harrison, *On Account of Sex: The Politics of Women's Issues, 1945–1968* (Berkeley, 1988). A similar work, that contains material on Lucy Somerville Howorth, is Leila J. Rupp and Verta Taylor, *Survival in the Doldrums: The American Women's Rights Movement, 1945 to the 1960s* (New York, 1987). Two studies of women's issues that deal briefly with women's work relief are Lois Scharf, *To Work and to Wed: Female Employment, Feminism, and the Great Depression* (Westport, 1980) and Winifred Wandersee, *Women, Work, and Family Values, 1920–1940* (Cambridge, 1981).

Journal Articles

I hope my book indicates that I profited from Clarke A. Chambers's "Toward a Redefinition of Welfare History" *Journal of American History* (September 1986) and William W. Bremer, " 'Along the American Way': The New Deal's Work Relief Programs for the Unemployed" *Journal of American History* (December 1975).

Citations to numerous articles appear in the footnotes, but I should like to point to several that deal with Woodward. Two sprightly journalistic sketches are by Margaret Christie and Wellington Brink in the "Southern Personalities" series in *Holland's Magazine* (March 1936 and June 1944). Mrs. Raymond Clapper described Woodward as one of "Washington's Ten Most Influential Women" in *Look* (20 October 1945). Among the several articles I have written on my subject, I like best: "ER and Ellen Woodward: A Partnership for Women's Work Relief and Security" in *Without Precedent* (*op. cit*), " 'The Forgotten Woman': Ellen S. Woodward and Women's Relief in the New Deal" in *Prologue* (Winter 1983), and "A New Deal for Mississippi Women" in *Journal of Mississippi History* (August 1984).

On Federal One projects, I made use of two articles written by contemporaries: George Biddle, "Art Under Five Years of Federal Patronage" in *American Scholar* (July 1940) and Ray A. Billington, "Government and the Arts: The WPA Experience" in *American Quarterly* (Winter 1961). David L. Smiley described the HRS in "A Slice of Life in Depression America: The Records of the Historical Records Survey" (*Prologue*, Winter 1971). Blanche D. Coll writes with clarity on "Public Assistance: Reviving the Original Comprehensive Concept of Social Security" in Gerald D. Nash, Noel H. Pugach, and Richard F. Thomasson, eds., *Social Security: The First Half Century* (Albuquerque, 1988), while Edward Berkowitz presents an important explanation of the 1939 amendments in "The First Social Security Crisis," *Prologue* (Fall 1983).

Unpublished Studies

A number of graduate studies contain a wealth of information about subjects germane to Woodward's public career. Some have appeared in some published form since I used them. One good example of a specialized study is Janet Anne Hutchinson, "American Housing, Gender, and the Better Homes Movement, 1922–1935" (Ph.D. diss., University of Delaware, 1989). On women in public life, four studies served me well: Paul Taylor, "The Entrance of Women in Party Politics in the 1920s" (Ph.D. diss., Harvard University, 1966), Jean Azulay, "Female Networks for Social Change: Progressive Reform in the New Deal" (M.A. thesis, Sarah Lawrence, 1980), Elsie L. George, "The Women Appointees of the Roosevelt and Truman Administrations: A Study of Their Impact and Effectiveness" (Ph.D. diss., American University, 1972), and Eleanor F. Straub, "Government Policy Toward Civilian Women During World War II" (Ph.D. diss., Emory University, 1973).

The only full-length study on the Depression and New Deal in Mississippi is Roger D. Tate, Jr., "Easing the Burden: The Era of Depression and New Deal in Mississippi" (Ph.D. diss., University of Tennessee, 1978). John Joseph Wallis, "Work Relief and Unemployment in the 1930s" (Ph.D. diss., University of Washington) helped me understand some of the regulations and procedures of the agency.

For specific women's and professional programs I consulted Brenda Faye Clegg, "Black Female Domestics During the Great Depression in New York City, 1930–1940" (Ph.D. diss., University of Michigan, 1983), Lois Rita Hembold, "Making Choices, Making Do: Black and White Working Class Women's Lives and Work During the Great Depression" (Ph.D. diss., Stanford University, 1983), and Susan Wladaver-Morgan, "Young Women and the New Deal: Camps and Resident Centers, 1933–1943" (Ph.D. diss., University of Indiana, 1982), a study of the "she-she-she" that deals with some overlapping in training under the WPP. Only through a group of dissertations could I read comprehensive studies of some Federal One projects: Cornelius B. Canon, "The Federal Music Project of the Works Progress Administration: Music in a Democracy" (Ph.D. diss., University of Minnesota, 1963), Janelle Findlay-Warren, "Of Tears and Needs: The Federal Music Projects, 1935–1943" (Ph.D. diss., George Washington University, 1973), Edward F. Farrese, "The Historical Records Survey: A Nation Acts to Save Its Memory" (Ph.D. diss., George Washington University, 1980), and Wilton C. Corken, "Architects, Preservationists, and the New Deal: The Historic American Buildings Survey, 1933–1942" (Ph.D. diss., George Washington University, 1984). Indispensable on the FWP is Kathleen O'Connor McKinzie, "Writers on Relief, 1935–1942" (Ph.D. diss., Indiana University, 1970).

Notes

Notes to Preface

1. ESW to Mrs. Joe Henry Morris, 5 January 1939, ESW 1139.1, Box 6.

2. For example: Jacqueline Jones, *Labor of Love, Labor of Sorrow, Black Women, Work and the Family from Slavery to the Present* (New York: Basic Books, 1985); Lois Scharf, *To Work and to Wed: Female Employment, Feminism, and the Great Depression* (Westport, Conn.: Greenwood Press, 1980); Winifred Wandersee, *Women's Work and Family Values, 1920–1940* (Cambridge, Mass.: Harvard University Press, 1981); and Susan Ware, *Beyond Suffrage: Women in the New Deal* (Cambridge, Mass.: Harvard University Press, 1981).

3. Holger Cahill interview, Archives of American Art (Detroit).

4. Douglas Smith, *The New Deal in the Urban South* (Baton Rouge: Louisiana State University Press, 1988).

5. McAleney to the author, 1 June 1988; telephone interview, 10 July 1993.

6. ESW to ER, 30 June 1943, ER, Box 896.

Notes to Chapter 1

1. Elizabeth K. Read, "Advice to Wives," *Syracuse (N.Y.) Post Standard*, 17 April 1938.

2. Mrs. Raymond Clapper, "Washington's Ten Most Influential Women," *Look* 9 (30 October 1945): 74. The other women were Eleanor Roosevelt, Congresswomen Mary Norton, Edith Nourse Rogers, and Clare Boothe Luce; newspaperwomen Eleanor (Cissy) Patterson, Agnes Meyer, and Evalyn McLean; social activist Cornelia Pinchot; and League of Women Voters president Anna Lord Strauss. With Perkins no longer in the Cabinet, Betty Clapper concluded that Woodward's "present post places her at the top federal position."

3. Biographical Directory of the American Congress, 1774–1971 (Washington, D.C.: U.S. Government Printing Office, 1971), 492; James Barnett Adair, *Adair History and Genealogy* (Los Angeles: Boylan and Boylan, 1924), 70, 107–10, 118, 122.

4. Genealogy folders, ESW 1139.2, Box 59, Mississippi Department of

Archives and History (MDAH), Jackson. Hereinafter, unless otherwise indicated, all references to Woodward's papers will be to those in Jackson. James Patton Anderson, a brother of Nancy Belle Anderson Murray, lived in Hernando from 1838 and for a time practiced law there. He then had a distinguished career as a member of the Mississippi legislature (1850–1851), Washington Territorial Delegate to Congress (1855–1857), a member of the Florida secession convention in 1861, and a Confederate general. Margaret Uhler, "Major General James Patton Anderson: An Autobiography," *Florida Historical Quarterly* 55 (January 1987): 341–45.

5. Biographical sketches of Sullivan are found in *Biographical Directory of the American Congress, 1771–1971*, p. 1775; *National Cyclopedia of American Biography* 14 (New York: James T. White, 1962 reprint), 365; *Who's Who in America* 7 (Chicago: A.N. Marquis, 1912), 2038; and Dunbar Rowland, *Mississippi: The Heart of the South* 3 (Chicago-Jackson: S.J. Clarke, 1925): 784–85.

Of the four law students who enrolled when Vanderbilt advertised its new law school in 1874, "One advanced student completed the requirements and received a law degree in May, 1875," states the historian of Vanderbilt University. In 1900 that graduate, by then Senator Sullivan, returned to make the principal address at the University's twenty-fifth anniversary celebration. Paul K. Conkin, *Gone With the Ivy: A Biography of Vanderbilt University* (Knoxville: University of Tennessee Press, 1985), 55, 144–45.

6. Standard reference biographies of Ellen Sullivan Woodward are in: *Who Was Who* 5 (Chicago: A.N. Marquis, 1973): 797; Dunbar Rowland, *Official and Statistical Register of the State of Mississippi, 1924–1928* (New York: J.J. Little and Ives, n.d.), 290–91; Durward Howes, ed., *American Women* 3 (Los Angeles: Richard Blank, 1929), 1005; Martha H. Swain, "Ellen Woodward," *Notable American Women: The Modern Era* (Cambridge, Mass.: Harvard University Press, 1980), 747–49; Swain, "Ellen Woodward," *Historical Dictionary of the New Deal* (Westport, Conn.: Greenwood Press, 1985), 547–48; and Swain, "Ellen Woodward," *Biographical Dictionary of Social Welfare in America* (Westport, Conn.: Greenwood Press, 1986), 797–800.

7. *Mississippi: A Guide to the Magnolia State* (New York: Viking Press, 1938), 258.

8. Judge Julian B. Wilson to ESW, 1 January 1939; W. A. Henry to ESW, 5 January 1939, both in ESW 1139.1, Box 7. Both men wrote recollections of her father soon after Woodward was named to the Social Security Board. Ironically, there appeared in *Forum* magazine in 1896 the observations of a French traveler that the relationship of American fathers and daughters was surprisingly close and equal. "The intellectual life [which they share] makes them friends by choice." Quoted by Paul Taylor, "The Entrance of Women in Party Politics: The 1920s" (Ph.D. dissertation, Harvard University, 1966), 142–43.

9. *Oxford (Miss.) Globe*, 2 June 1898.

10. Albert Y. Woodward, Jr., to the author, 7 September 1986; Rowland, *Mississippi: Heart of the South* 2:428. Albert D. Kirwan has written that Sullivan later maintained that McLaurin had pledged to support him for the full term, then reneged when he claimed it for himself. *Revolt of the Rednecks: Mississippi Politics, 1876–1925* (Lexington: University of Kentucky Press, 1951), 105–106.

11. *Greenville (S.C.) News*, 19 September 1900; Lillian S. Kibler, *Benjamin F. Perry: South Carolina Unionist* (Durham, N.C.: Duke University Press, 1946), 499–500. Sans Souci "remains shrouded in the mists" of Greenville's local history, Marian E. Strobel of Furman University wrote to the author (29 January 1985). For a brief comment on her aunt's school, see Tallulah Bankhead, *Tallulah: My Autobiography* (New York: Harper, 1952), 54.

One of the teachers at the "Washington College for Girls" between 1891 and 1896 was Sarah Mattingly, daughter of a Mississippi planter who lived near Oxford. In all probability, she was the Mississippi connection that led Sullivan to send his daughter there.

12. *Syracuse (N.Y.) Post Standard*, 17 April 1938. Belle attended Blue Mountain Female College, a Baptist school in northeast Mississippi, during the 1898–1899 session and was listed in the *Twenty-Sixth Annual Catalogue* as an undergraduate, although she was only fourteen at the time.

13. ESW to Women's Division, Democratic National Committee, Sioux Falls, South Dakota, 20 May 1938, ESW 1139.2, Box 21.

14. Gabriella Bondurant to ESW, 20 June 1936, ESW Scrapbook 1139.2; George Morris in *Memphis Commercial Appeal*, 6 December 1936. Maurine Mulliner, longtime secretary of the Social Security Board, compared the Sullivan sisters of Oxford with the famous Langhorne sisters of Virginia, among whom were Irene Gibson and Nancy Astor. Mulliner Memoir, Columbia Oral History Collection (COHC), 154.

15. *Oxford (Miss.) Eagle*, 28 May 1903.

16. *Oxford (Miss.) Eagle*, 21 May, 30 July, 19, 26 November 1903; 21 January, 21 April, 23 June, 4 August 1904.

17. *Memphis Press-Scimitar*, 6 August 1938.

18. Louis Thornton and Nancy L. Parkes, *Winston County and Its People: A Collection of Family Histories* (Louisville, Miss., 1980); *Winston County Journal*, 29 June 1906.

19. Jennie Newsom Hoffman, *A History of Winston County* 3 (Works Progress Administration, Federal Writers' Project, 1938): 357, copy in Louisville Public Library.

20. *Winston County Journal*, 16 June 1911; 17 January, 25 May 1913; 30 November 1914. For a well-written assessment of the study club movement, see Theodore Penny Martin, *The Sound of Our Own Voices: Women's Study Clubs, 1860–1910* (Boston: Beacon Press, 1987), esp. chap. 5, "Study Club Programs." According to Martin, "Fortnightly" was a popular name for these groups.

21. *Memphis Commercial Appeal*, 23 October 1956. Remnants of a Fortnightly Club scrapbook are in the Louisville Public Library.

22. *Jackson Daily News*, special women's edition, 6 July 1916.

23. *Winston County Journal*, 18 February, 6 May 1910.

24. *Mississippi Federation of Women's Club Yearbook, 1915–1916*, p. 122 (copy in MDAH).

25. *Winston County Journal*, 5 November 1915, 30 June 1916. Boasting of its 1,500 citizens, paved sidewalks, electric utilities, and other improvements, Louisville launched a search for out-of-state investors in 1919. *Winston County Journal*, 24 October 1919.

26. *Winston County Journal*, 13 April 1917; Hoffman, *History of Winston County*, 551; Margaret Christie, "Southern Personalities," *Holland's Magazine* 55 (March 1936): 15.

27. *Winston County Journal*, 16 March 1917. Regarding the defeat, a Bilbo scholar has concluded, "Had there been a certificate, it must surely have listed the cause of death as Texas tick fever." Chester A. Morgan, *Redneck Liberal: Theodore G. Bilbo and the New Deal* (Baton Rouge: Louisiana State University Press, 1985), 39.

28. *Winston County Journal*, 13 July 1918; William J. Breen, *Uncle Sam at Home: Civilian Mobilization, Wartime Federalism, and the Council of National Defense, 1917–1919* (Westport, Conn.: Greenwood Press, 1984), 101, 243; Ida Clyde Clarke, *American Women and the World War* (New York: D. Appleton, 1918), 298–300. "The [Mississippi] legislature has not to date recognized the work financially," recorded the minutes of the national CND on February 26, 1918. See Minutes of Meetings of the Committee on Women's Defense Work, May 2, 1917–February 12, 1919 (Washington, D.C.: National Archives Microfilm, 1978), 354.

29. *Winston County Journal*, 26 April, 3 May 1918; Emily Newell Blair, "The Woman's Committee, United States Council of National Defense. An Interpretive Report. April 21, 1917 to February 27, 1919" (Washington, D.C.: U.S. Government Printing Office, 1910), 100–101.

30. *A History of the Mississippi Federation of Women's Clubs*. Works Progress Administration. Historical Research Project 38 (1 November 1936): 56–58 (MDAH); *Winston County Journal*, 7, 14 June 1918. Woodward's handwritten notes on a Fourth Liberty Loan bulletin, dated 12 September 1918 and distributed by the Committee on Public Information, indicate that she had access to a steady supply of study material. Copy in possession of Davis L. Fair, Jr., Louisville.

31. *Official and Statistical Register of the State of Mississippi, 1920–1924* (Jackson, Miss.: Hederman Brothers, 1923), 351; *Winston County Journal*, 30 August 1918, 12, 17, 28 November 1919, 23 January 1920; interview with Albert Woodward, Jr., 18 March 1986 (Washington, D.C.); Monroe Billington, *The American South* (New York: Scribners, 1971), 234. Judge Woodward was one of numerous lawyers attracted to eastern Oklahoma after new oil strikes.

Many sought monetary gains in establishing guardianships over minor Indian children and in defrauding Indian landowners by other forms of chicanery. Woodward may have disliked the circumstances he found in Okmulgee.

32. *Greenville Daily Democrat-Times*, 8 January, 28 July 1920, 27 January 1921; interview with Lucy Somerville Howorth, 19 June 1984 (Cleveland, Miss.).

33. *Greenville Daily Democrat-Times*, 15, 21 September, 20 October 1920, 6 June 1922.

34. Joanne Varner Hawks, "Like Mother, Like Daughter: Nellie Nugent Somerville and Lucy Somerville Howorth," *Journal of Mississippi History* 45 (May 1983): 118–19. Somerville is quoted by John Patrick McDowell, *The Social Gospel in the South: The Women's Home Mission Movement in the Methodist Episcopal Church South, 1886–1939* (Baton Rouge: Louisiana State University Press, 1982), 118. See also, pages 89–93; and Noreen Dunn Tatum, *A Crown of Service: A Story of Woman's Work in the Methodist Episcopal Church, South, From 1878–1940* (Nashville: Parthenon Press, 1960), 350–60.

35. *Greenville Daily-Democrat Times*, 18 February, 7 April 1920, 20 March, 7 April 1921, 20 May 1922. The phrase "City Beautiful" was scrapped by professional city planners around 1920, but the term remained current in such popular magazines as *House and Garden* and *Ladies Home Journal* and in GFWC study materials that touted piecemeal aesthetic projects in landscaping, sanitation, home beautification, and related civic improvements. See Jon Alvah Peterson, "The Origins of the Comprehensive City Planning Idea in the United States, 1840–1911" (Ph.D. dissertation., Harvard University, 1967), 199, 206, 323, 420.

36. *Greenville Daily Democrat-Times*, 4, 11 July, 6 December 1921, 26 August 1922; Howorth interview, 19 June 1984. For an explanation of the economic dislocation in the Mississippi Delta, see Robert S. Synder, *Cotton Crisis* (Chapel Hill: University of North Carolina Press, 1984), xv-xvi.

37. *Winston County Journal*, 29 September 1922. A former neighbor describes the house as turn-of-the-century, set eight feet above the ground on a beautiful foundation. Square columns rose from a high porch which completely surrounded the house. The same greystone constituted a four-foot fence around the property, enclosing a tree-filled yard. The interior was noted for its millwork and English-style oak paneling, the dining room walls fitted with beveled mirrors. The house was torn down in the early 1950s as the business district encroached upon the neighborhood. William R. Parkes to the author, 17 July 1986.

38. *Winston County Journal*, 9 March 1923; 11 April, 8 August 1924, 4 May 1928. Today the old city park is the locale of the county library; the community building houses the Louisville Chamber of Commerce.

39. *The Woman Voter*, 23 November 1922, 23 March, 7 December 1923 (microfilm in MDAH); Woodward interview in *Memphis Press-Scimitar*, 6 August 1938; ESW to Susie Selser, 18 March 1941, ESW 1139.1, Box 14.

40. *Winston County Journal*, 10 August, 25 January, 23 April 1924; Minutes of the Board of Trustees of the Matty Hersee Hospital (5 September 1925), RG 25, MDAH. A biographical sketch of Judge Woodward can be found in the *Official and Statistical Register of Mississippi, 1924–1928*, 289–90.

41. *Winston County Journal*, 13, 18 February 1925; interview with Albert Woodward, Jr., 23 June 1983 (Washington, D.C.); interview with Davis L. Fair, Jr., and Dorothy Fair Brown, 4 January 1985 (Louisville).

42. *Winston County Journal*, 27 March, 3 April, 15, 29 May, 14, 31 July 1925; *Jackson Daily News*, 29 March 1925.

43. *Winston County Journal*, 14, 28 August, 11 September 1925.

44. *New Orleans Times-Picayune*, 21 March 1926; Howorth interview, 19 June 1984; Anne Firor Scott, "Nellie Nugent Somerville," in *Notable American Women: The Modern Era* (Cambridge, Mass.: Harvard University Press, 1980), 655; Frank Waldrop, ed., *Mountain Voices: The Centennial History of Monteagle Sunday School Assembly* (Nashville: Monteagle Sunday School Assembly, 1982), 208.

Somerville's and Woodward's terms did not expire until the beginning of the 1928 session; thus they were counted among the total of 127 women serving in 36 state legislatures in 1927. See J. Stanley Lemons, *The Woman Citizen: Social Feminism in the 1920s* (Urbana: University of Illinois Press, 1973), 115.

45. *Jackson Daily News*, 11 January 1926.

46. *Journal of the House of Representatives, January 5, 1926–March 19, 1926*, 165; *Bulletin* of the MFWC, 1 (August 1926): 97 (copy in MDAH); interview with Howorth, 19 June 1984.

47. *Jackson Daily News*, 4, 15 January 1926; William D. McCain, "The Triumph of Democracy, 1916–1932," in Richard A. McElmore, ed., *A History of Mississippi* 2 (Jackson: College and University Press of Mississippi, 1973), 81–82.

48. *Jackson Daily News*, 15 January, 5 February 1926; *Memphis Commercial Appeal*, 21 March 1926; Jeannine Lackey Laughlin, "The Mississippi Library Commission: A Force for Library Development" (Ph.D. dissertation., Indiana University, 1983), 25–26; Madel Morgan Jacobs, "History of the Mississippi Library Commission," in Margarete Peebles and J. B. Howell, eds., *A History of Mississippi Libraries* (Montgomery, Al.: Paragon Press, 1975), 163–65.

49. *Winston County Journal*, 5, 12 March 1926; *House Journal*, 97, 520, 576, 2059.

50. *House Journal*, 638, 664; Christopher K. Curtis, "Mississippi's Anti-Evolution Law of 1926," *Journal of Mississippi History* 48 (February 1986): 19. A related article by Richard Halliburton, Jr., sheds no light on how legislators voted: "Mississippi's Contribution to the Anti-Evolution Movement," *Journal of Mississippi History* 35 (May 1973).

51. *Winston County Journal*, 19 February 1926; *House Journal*, 1330.

52. Eunice F. Barnard, "Madame Arrives in Politics," *North American*

Review 126 (November 1928): 553; Wellington Brink, "Southern Personalities," *Holland's Magazine* 63 (June 1944): 7; *Jackson Daily News*, 4 January 1926; *Winston County Journal*, 26 March, 2 April 1926. Quoted in the *Literary Digest*, 86 (July 1925), 13, the particular reference by the *Albany News* was to Edith Nourse Rogers, New England's first congresswoman. Of the forty-two women in the Mississippi legislature between 1924 and 1981, fourteen succeeded their husbands; of the twenty-eight others, some were widows seeking new directions. Joanne V. Hawks, M. Carolyn Ellis, and J. Byron Morris, "Women in the Mississippi Legislature (1924–1981)," *Journal of Mississippi History* 43 (November 1981), 268.

53. *Winston County Journal*, 16, 23, 30 April 1926.

54. Constitution of the Louisville BPW Club, ESW 1139.2, Box 59; *Winston County Journal*, 3 September 15, 29 October 1926; *Gainesville (Texas) Daily Register*, 28 October 1926.

55. *Winston County Journal*, 25 February 1927.

56. Ellen Bailey to ESW, 14 April 1926, copy in possession of author.

Notes to Chapter 2

1. Margaret Christie, "Southern Personalities," *Holland's Magazine* 60 (March 1936): 64.

2. Pamphlet on the Mississippi State Board of Development, ESW 1139.2, Box 41; *Winston County Journal*, 3 November 1932. Neither George B. Tindall, in *The Emergence of the New South, 1913–1945* (Baton Rouge: Louisiana State University Press, 1967), nor James C. Cobb, in *The Selling of the South: The Southern Crusade for Industrial Development, 1936–1980* (Baton Rouge: Louisiana State University Press, 1982) touches on the MSBD. Their accounts of the BAWI do provide, however, a perspective on the economic climate in Mississippi. Some confusion may result from nomenclature. A new Mississippi Board of Development was created in 1940 by Governor Paul B. Johnson, who had permitted the BAWI to expire; it was not a lineal extension of the former MSBD.

3. *Winston County Journal*, 10 December 1926; interview with Arch Dalrymple, 26 June 1985 (Monteagle, Tennessee).

4. L. J. Folse to The People of Louisville, 26 November 1926, ESW 1139.2, Box 62.

5. *Mississippi Builder* 4 (January 1927): 83. A full run of the journal is in the Mississippi State University library.

6. *Mississippi Builder* 4 (January 1927): 84–86. For a perspective on the progressive tendencies of Southern women at the time, see Anne Firor Scott, "After Suffrage: Women in the Twenties," *Journal of Southern History* 30 (August 1964): 305, 318.

7. *Mississippi Builder* 4 (January 1927): 83–84. The MFWC cotton promotion was still lively in 1931, the year of the MFWC "Cotton Convention," when the wardrobe of every convention delegate was made of cotton. Edward

L. Blake, *A History of the Farm Bureau Federation* (Jackson, Miss.: Farm Bureau Federation, 1971): 101–105.

8. *Mississippi Builder* 4 (May 1927): 16–17; 5 (September 1928): 30; *History of the Mississippi Federation of Women's Clubs*, Works Progress Administration, Historical Research Project 38 (1 November 1936), 85–91, RG 60 (MDAH).

9. ESW, "How Mississippi Women Are Working for the South's Development," *Manufacturers' Record* 92 (29 December 1927): 57.

10. Unidentified clipping in ESW 1139.2, Box 72; *Winston County Journal*, 8 July 1927.

11. Martha Ida Wiseman, "Laura Wilson Wiseman," biographical sketch in possession of the author (New Albany, Miss.); ESW, "Improved Rural Homes Reflect Mississippi Progress," *Mississippi Builder* 5 (August 1928): 81; James Hutton Lemby, *The Gulf, Mobile and Ohio: A Railroad That Had to Expand or Expire* (Homewood, Ill.: Richard D. Irwin, 1953), 43; *Winston County Journal*, 4, 18 February 1927, 3 April 1931; ESW to Thomas Fautleroy [?] 1927, ESW 1139.2, Box 62.

12. *Winston County Journal*, 4 March, 29 April, 13 May, 18 November 1927; "Know Mississippi Products Campaign," undated speech, ESW 1139.1, Box 16.

13. Mrs. Robert Ralston, "Mississippi Women Do Their Part," *Mississippi Builder* 5 (September 1928): 30.

14. Speech, "Why Women Should Take Active Interest in Commercial and Industrial Affairs," Advertising Club (Jackson, Miss.), 1 June 1932, ESW 1139.2, Box 24; *Winston County Journal*, 13 January 1933.

15. *Mississippi Builder* 4 (August 1927): 73; *Winston County Journal*, 16 September 1927; ESW to R. E. Logsdon, 18 July 1927, ESW 1139.1, Box 16.

16. Marie Meloney, "Better Homes in America," *The Delineator* 104 (October 1922): 16–17; Gwendolyn Wright, *Building the Dream: A Social History of Housing in America* (New York: Pantheon Books, 1981), 197–200; Janet Anne Hutchinson, "American Housing, Gender, and the Better Homes Movement, 1922–1935" (Ph.D. dissertation., University of Delaware, 1989): 3, 32–38 (Hoover quotation, 27); Ray Lyman Wilbur and Arthur Hyde, *The Hoover Policies* (New York: Charles Scribner's, 1937): 81. See also, Ray Lyman Wilbur, *Human Hopes: Addresses and Papers on Education, Citizenship, and Social Problems* (Stanford, Cal.: Stanford University Press, 1940), 183–84.

17. Undated speech, 1139.1, Box 16; ESW to Better Homes Chairmen, undated, ESW 1139.1, Box 1.

18. *Winston County Journal*, 17 January 1930, 6 March, 24 April, 8 May 1931; *Jackson Daily News*, 22, 26 July 1931; *New Orleans Times-Picayune*, 21 November 1931; *Jackson Clarion-Ledger*, undated 1923 clipping, ESW Vertical File, Special Collections, Mississippi State University Library.

19. *Mississippi Builder* 4 (March 1927): 21; ESW to Better Homes Chairmen [?] 1932, ESW 1139.2, Box 62; *Winston County Journal*, 7, 14, 1933. In

1934 and 1935, when Woodward was no longer in Mississippi, the state chair position of the BHA passed to Belle Fair. No longer under the State Development Board, the campaign was now jointly sponsored by the MFWC and the extension division of Mississippi State College. *Winston County Journal*, 19 April 1934, 19 April 1935.

20. Craddock Goins, "Recent Mississippi Progress Due to Women's Work," *Memphis Commercial Appeal*, 23 September 1928; ESW to Officers and Directors [?], 1928, ESW 1139.2, Box 62; ESW speeches, ESW 1139.1, Box 16.

21. *Winston County Journal*, 6 January 1928.

22. L. O. Crosby to R. B. Clark, 6 June 1929, copy in ESW 1139.2, Box 3.

23. *Memphis Commercial Appeal*, 30 October 1929.

24. "Lucius O. Crosby," *National Cyclopedia of American Biography* 35 (New York: James T. White, 1949), 517–18; Chester M. Morgan, *Redneck Liberal: Theodore G. Bilbo and the New Deal* (Baton Rouge: Louisiana State University Press, 1985), 224; Martha H. Swain, *Pat Harrison: The New Deal Years* (Jackson: University Press of Mississippi, 1978), 54–55.

25. *Jackson Daily News*, 2 March 1932; *Staple Cotton Review* 32 (January 1954): 1; radio scripts in ESW 1139.1, Boxes 16 and 17; *The Exciter* (Arkansas, Mississippi, and Louisiana Power and Light Companies) 9 (November 1932): 1–5.

26. William D. McCain, "The Triumph of Democracy, 1916–1932," in Richard A. McLemore, *History of Mississippi* 2 (Jackson: College and University Press of Mississippi, 1975), 90–94; J. Oliver Emmerich, "Collapse and Recovery," in McLemore, *History*, 97–100.

27. *Winston County Journal*, 25 July 1930.

28. Daniel C. Vogt, "Government Reform, the 1890 Constitution, and Mike Conner," *Journal of Mississippi History* 58 (February 1986): 43–45.

29. Jane Whiteside Elliott, "Lucy Somerville Howorth: Legislative Career, 1932–1933" (M.A. thesis, Delta State University, 1975): *passim*. Howorth was then legislative chairman of the Mississippi BPW Clubs, chairman of the Mississippi district of the YWCA, and department secretary of the American Legion Auxiliary. Mrs. Gamble held B.A. and M.A. degrees from Columbia University. She had taught political science at Vanderbilt University. Mrs. Foresman was a Meridian businesswoman. "Women Leaders Back Research Commission," *Jackson (Miss.) Daily News*, 7 September 1930.

30. Author's interview with Howorth, 19 June 1984.

31. "Earlene White-Career Woman," *DD* 15 (September 1938): 34; White to Clark, 27 August 1930, ESW 1139.1, Box 2.

32. *Report on a Survey of the Organization and Administration of State and County Government in Mississippi* (Jackson, Miss.: Research Commission, 1932), 3–4, 6. The Brookings recommendations for Mississippi were similar to those made in its other surveys. Standard recommendations for efficiency, reorganization, and better revenue enhancement are discussed by Edward M.

Wheat, "The Bureaucratization of the South: From Traditional Fragmentation to Administrative Incoherence," in James F. Lea, ed., *Contemporary Southern Politics* (Baton Rouge: Louisiana State University Press, 1988), 269–70.

33. James Leiby, "Frank Bane," in Walter I. Trattner, ed., *Biographical Dictionary of Social Welfare in America* (Westport, Conn., 1986), 54–56; ESW memorandum to Research Commission, 24 July 1931; "Trend of the Month" (MSBD newsletter), July 1931 (both in ESW 1139.2, Box 62).

34. *New York Times*, 20 November 1930; *Addresses and Abstracts: White House Conference on Child Health and Protection* (New York: Century, 1931), ESW 1139.1, Box 17.

35. *Winston County Journal*, 7 November 1930; Mississippi Children's Home Society (MCHS), Superintendent's Report, November 1930; Board Minutes, 14 July 1931, 18 October 1932; Program, "Mississippi Follow-Up Conference," in ESW Scrapbook, 1139.2. The author is grateful to Christopher Cherny, present director of the MCHS, who located and made available the fifty-year-old board minutes of the Society.

36. Elizabeth Wisner, *Social Welfare in the South: From Colonial Times to World War I* (Baton Rouge: Louisiana State University Press, 1970), 127–28; 1931 Program, Papers of the Mississippi Conference on Social Welfare, Box 1, MDAH.

37. In 1930, Mississippi received 47 percent of the rainfall of previous years and was the recipient of some Red Cross relief. Nan Elizabeth Woodruff, *As Rare as Rain: Federal Relief in the Great Southern Drought of 1930–31* (Urbana: University of Illinois Press, 1985), 55, 134–35.

38. Albert U. Romasco, *The Poverty of Abundance: Hoover, the Nation, and Depression* (New York: Oxford University Press, 1965), 143, 147. See also, Harris G. Warren, *Herbert Hoover and the Great Depression* (New York: Oxford University Press, 1959), 155, 191. The fullest scholarly treatment of Hoover's relief programs is Jeffrey C. Singleton's "Unemployment Relief and the Welfare State" (Ph.D. dissertation., Boston University, 1987).

39. Members of the Mississippi committee (Tom Brady, Jr., chairman, R.B. Clark, Holt Ross, Ben M. Fulton, Rosabel Foresman, and Vivian Cook) are listed in Theodore G. Bilbo to Frank Bane, 30 November 1930, POUR Central Files 600 (Miss.), RG 73, NA. Cook was the state BPW president at the time.

40. Foresman to Gilbreth, 14 January 1931; Gilbreth to Foresman, 20 January 1931; ESW to Alice M. Dickson, 11 February 1931; Dickson to ESW, 13 February 1931; all in POUR Series 23 (Miss.), RG 73.

41. Warren, *Hoover and the Great Depression*, 196–97. For an account of the limitations of POUR, see William R. Brock, *Welfare, Democracy, and the New Deal* (Cambridge: Cambridge University Press, 1988), 124–34.

42. ESW to Harry Kinnear, 18 May 1932, PECE/POUR Papers, Series 10, State Files (Miss.), Herbert Hoover Library (West Branch, Iowa); ESW to E. P. Hayes, POUR, Central Files 620 (Miss.), RG 73.

43. E. P, Hayes to ESW, 23 January 1932, POUR, Central Files (Miss.),

RG 73; Hayes, *Activities of the President's Emergency Committee for Employment* (Concord, N.H.: Rumford Press, 1936), 28, 121–39. In 1860, prominent church women in Mobile provided employment for needy women by sponsoring a job agency and furnishing sewing jobs to poor women. Harriet E. Amos, *Cotton City: Urban Development in Antebellum Mobile* (Tuscaloosa: University of Alabama Press,1985), 179.

44. Quoted in Harry L. Hopkins, *Spending to Save: The Complete Story of Relief* (New York: W.W. Norton, 1936), 67. The statement may have come from a local report of W. K. Clements, mayor of Greenwood, to the Mississippi POUR Committee. See POUR Central Files 620 (Miss.), RG 73.

45. Roger D. Tate, Jr., "Easing the Burden: The Era of Depression and New Deal in Mississippi" (Ph.D. dissertation, University of Tennessee, 1978), 4, 36–37; Warren, *Hoover and the Great Depression*, 206–207; Romasco, *Poverty of Abundance*, 223–26.

46. *Mississippi Woman's Magazine* (MFWC journal) 7 (December 1932): 56; Daniel C. Vogt, "Hoover's RFC in Action: Mississippi's Bank Loans and Work Relief," *Journal of Mississippi History* 47 (February 1985): 45–46; George B. Tindall, "Business Progressivism: Southern Politics in the Twenties," *South Atlantic Quarterly* 62 (Winter 1963): 104; James Leiby interview with Frank Bane, Regional Oral History Office, University of California (Berkeley), 128–30.

47. Roger D. Tate, Jr., "George B. Power and New Deal Work Relief in Mississippi, 1931–1934," *Journal of Mississippi History* 46 (February 1984): 1–3; John A. Salmond, *A Southern Rebel: The Life and Times of Aubrey Willis Williams, 1890–1965* (Chapel Hill: University of North Carolina Press, 1983), 38–39; Morton Sosna, *In Search of the Silent South: Southern Liberals and the Race Issue* (New York: Columbia University Press, 1977), 69–70. While in Jackson in November 1932, to confer with Governor Conner about Mississippi's compliance with RFC procedures, Bane met with Woodward. Woodward appointment calendar, ESW 1139.1, Box 15.

48. Some SBPW minutes are found in Federal Emergency Relief Administration (FERA) States Files 460 (Miss.), RG 69, NA. On Rowland's Republican affiliation, see Neil R. McMillen, *Dark Journey: Black Mississippians in the Age of Jim Crow* (Urbana: University of Illinois Press, 1989), 65, 67–68.

49. Tindall, *Emergence of the New South*, 374; Vogt, "Hoover's RFC in Action," 46–48; Thomas Williams, "The Dependent Child in Mississippi: A Social History, 1900–1932" (Ph.D. dissertation, Ohio State University, 1976), 47–49.

50. *Winston County Journal*, 8 June, 6 July 1928; *Memphis Commercial Appeal*, 2 September 1928.

51. Roy V. Peel and Thomas C. Donnelly, *The 1928 Campaign: An Analysis* (New York: R.R. Smith, 1931), 83–84; Eunice Fuller Barnard, "Women in the Campaign," *Woman's Journal* 13 (December 1928): 7–9.

52. For a positive account, see Sophonisba P. Breckinridge, *Women in the*

Twentieth Century: A Study of Their Political, Social, and Economic Activities (New York: McGraw-Hill, 1933), 285–86. Less enthusiastic is a recent historian, Elizabeth Israels Perry, *Belle Moskowitz: Feminine Politics and the Exercise of Power in the Age of Alfred E. Smith* (New York: Oxford University Press, 1987), 194–95.

53. Glenda E. Morrison, "Women's Participation in the 1928 Presidential Campaign" (Ph.D. dissertation, University of Kansas, 1978), 67; Dorothy M. Brown, *Setting a Course: American Women in the 1920s* (Boston: Twayne, 1987), 70.

54. *Memphis Commercial Appeal*, 2 September 1928; Brown, *Setting a Course*, 67; *Official Report of the Proceedings of the Democratic National Convention* (Indianapolis, n.d.), 29–30.

55. FDR to ESW, 3 December 1928, ESW 1139.2, Box 8; MWD to ESW, 5 January, 23 November 1931; ESW to MWD, 14 December 1931, all in ESW 1139.2, Box 3.

56. ESW to Harrison, 26 January 1932; ESW to FDR, 30 March 1932; FDR to ESW, 18 April 1932, all in Papers of Democratic National Committee (DNC) 1932 (Miss. Pre-Convention), Box 318, Franklin D. Roosevelt Library (FDRL), Hyde Park, New York; ESW to Stevens, 29 March 1932; ESW to MWD, 27 May 1932; both in ESW 1139.2, Box 14.

57. *Memphis Commercial Appeal*, 7 June 1932. Stevens was the daughter of Anselm J. McLaurin, who had replaced William Van Amberg Sullivan in the Senate. It was ironic that Woodward replaced Stevens on the Democratic National Committee; if there was any rivalry between the two women, it was not apparent to associates, although it was gratifying to Woodward that she replaced the daughter of her father's rival.

58. *Jackson Clarion-Ledger*, 9 October 1932; "Summary Highlights of the Democratic National Committee," in ESW 1139.1, Box 17; *Democratic Bulletin* 7 (August 1932): 21. This title was little more than a letterhead stationery title conferred on all Southern national committeewoman.

59. Record of Minutes, 1930–1936, I, Papers of Democratic Executive Committee, (MDAH).

60. *Jackson Clarion-Ledger*, 16 August, 6 October 1932; Mrs. John A. Clark to ESW, 3 October 1932, ESW 1139.2, Box 59.

61. ESW to Mrs. Mabel Mason, 24 October 1932, ESW 1139.2, Box 5; ESW to MWD, 8, 28 October 1932, ESW 1139.2, Box 3; ER to ESW, 15 September, 1932, ESW 1139.2, Box 10.

62. Desk calendar, ESW 1139.1, Box 15; ESW to Hubert Stephens, 17 November 1932; ESW to John E. Rankin, 14 February 1933; both in ESW 1139.1, Box 2.

63. ESW to George H. Etheridge, 4 February 1933; ESW to Edgar G. Williams, 15 February 1933; both in ESW 1139.1, Box 2.

64. Anne Firor Scott, *The Southern Lady: From Pedestal to Politics, 1890–1920* (Chicago: University of Chicago Press, 1970), 218.

65. H. C. Nixon, "The Changing Political Philosophy of the South," *Annals of the American Academy of Political and Social Sciences* 153 (January 1931): 248.

66. Lillian Symes, "Women Who Work," *Woman Citizen* 12 (October 1937): 21.

67. Lucy Randolph Mason, *Standards for Workers in Southern Industry* (National Consumers' League, 1931): 10–11, 19.

68. Mason, *Standards for Workers*, 37, 45. A search in the papers of the Women's Trade Union League turns up no contacts with Mississippi club-women, public officials, or the State Board of Development.

69. *Winston County Journal*, 10 March 1933. The Lucy Randolph Mason Papers at Duke University contain no correspondence from September 1932 to July 1933, the time when Mason extended the invitation to Woodward.

Notes to Chapter 3

1. *Winston County Journal*, 3 March 1933; ESW, "Account of the Inaugural," ESW 1139.2, Box 27. Woodward's radio address coincided with Governor Mike Conner's arrival in New York to seek a market for the state's bonds.

2. ESW to Chamber of Commerce, 22, 24 June, 8 August 1933, ESW, AES, Box 1; *Jackson Daily News*, 20 December 1953.

3. *Jackson Daily News*, 8 August 1933; Jackson Business and Professional Women's Club Scrapbook, 1933, in PBW Papers, Box 1 (MDAH); *A History of the Mississippi Federation of Women's Clubs*, Works Progress Administration, Historical Research Project 38 (1 November 1936), 109–10, RG 60 (MDAH).

4. ESW to Pat Harrison, 9 August 1933, Pat Harrison Papers, University of Mississippi Library; ESW to FDR, 9 August 1933, ESW 1139.2, Box 16.

5. Ross to ESW, 10 November 1933; ESW to G. H. Lowe, 5 January 1933; ESW to Mrs. A. Y. Malone, 17 February 1933; all in ESW 1139.1, Box 2.

6. ESW to Jeff Busby, 15 February 1933; MWD to ESW [February, 1933]; ESW to Dewson, 10 February, 8 June 1933; Lucile Virden (ESW secretary) to Howorth, 27 February 1933, all in ESW 1139.1, Box 2; Bess Furman, *Washington By-Line: The Personal History of a Newspaperwoman* (New York: Knopf, 1949), 227.

7. Ross to ESW, 19 May 1933, ESW 1139.2, Box 7; "Patronage, 1933, Women," MWD to Farley, 31 July 1933, both in bound patronage volume, Dewson Papers, Box 16; Jean Azulay, "Female Networks for Social Change: Progressive Reform in the New Deal" (M.A. thesis, Sarah Lawrence College, 1980), 91–92.

8. William H. Matthews to HLH, 23 May 1933, FERA Old Subject File (OSF), Box 17, RG 69; Frank Bane to the author, 18 September 1973. When Hopkins sent Lorena Hickok into the field in 1933, he told her, "I don't want the social worker angle." Quoted in John F. Bauman and Thomas H. Coode, *In the Eyes of the Great Depression: New Deal Reporters and the Agony of the American People* (DeKalb: Northern Illinois Press, 1988), 1.

9. Pat Harrison to HLH, 26 July 1933, in Harry L. Hopkins Papers (hereinafter HLH), Box 58; Lucy S. Howorth, "Recollections of Mississippi Women in Public Life Whom I Have Known," copy in author's possession; Howorth interview, 19 June 1984; Paul Taylor, "The Entrance of Women in Party Politics: The 1920s" (Ph.D. dissertation, Harvard University, 1966), 368. "She came, she saw, she conquered," Bane later recalled to the author (23 September 1973).

Maurine Mulliner, who knew Hopkins when she was secretary to New York Senator Robert F. Wagner, reminisced, "Now Harry Hopkins had some very good women on his staff, but they weren't pulchritudinous and they weren't very charming." (Mulliner Memoir, COHC, 152). Bonnie Schwartz describes Hopkins's antipathy to social work methods as applied to federal relief and relates the circumstances that once provoked him to tell social work critics to "Go to Hell!" *The Civil Works Administration: The Business of Emergency Employment in the New Deal* (Princeton, N.J.: Princeton University Press, 1984), 24–25.

10. Paul Kurzman has noted that three of five FERA divisions were headed by Southerners: Woodward, Aubrey Williams of Alabama, and Lawrence Westbrook of Texas, each of whom "represented the new progressive element in the South." William R. Brock has pointed out that most FERA division heads and field representatives were not graduates of prestigious universities and were from rural or smalltown origins. Other than Woodward's surrogate term in a state legislature, none had held elective posts or public office other than in welfare organizations. Howorth, "Recollections of Mississippi Women," 8; Paul Kurzman, *Harry Hopkins and the New Deal* (Fair Lawn, N.J.: R.E. Burdick, 1974), 130; William R. Brock, *Welfare, Democracy, and the New Deal* (Cambridge: Cambridge University Press, 1988), 179–82. In her study, *Beyond Suffrage*, Susan Ware does not indicate that Dewson and Woodward had any prior personal exchange. While Ware wrote that one of Dewson's "proudest placements was Ellen Woodward" [*Partner and I: Molly Dewson, Feminism and New Deal Politics* (New Haven, Conn.: Yale University Press, 1987), 189], Maurine Mulliner credits the appointment to Bane's contact with Woodward in Mississippi. Telephone interview with the author, 2 March 1984.

11. HLH to Clark, 3 August 1933; ESW to HLH, 16 August 1933, both in ESW 1139.2, Box 16; ESW to Lucille K. Boyden, 1 November 1938, WPA State series (Ss) (Miss.): 660, RG 69; *Jackson Daily News*, 26 August 1933; "Personnel Lists, 1933–1935," HLH, Box 83; *Staple Cotton Review*, 32 (January 1954): 1.

12. ESW, "Work for Idle Hands," *DD* 8 (June 1936): 5; George McJimsey, *Harry Hopkins: Ally of the Poor and Defender of Democracy* (Cambridge, Mass.: Harvard University Press, 1987), 58–59. Pyle is quoted by Edward Robb Ellis in the latter's *A Nation in Torment: The Great Depression* (New York: Capricorn Books, 1971), 505.

13. Doris Carothers, *Chronology of the Federal Emergency Relief Administration, May 12, 1933 to December 31, 1935* (Washington, D.C.: U.S. Government Printing Office, 1937), 22; ESW memorandum, 19 March 1933, ESW 1139.2, Box 18; ESW to Mae Cresswell, 13 September 1933, FERA Ss (Miss.): 453.2, RG 69; MWD to ESW, 24 October 1933, Papers of DNC, Women's Division, Box 27; author's interview with May Thompson Evans, 9 September 1984 (Washington).

14. Eleanor Roosevelt, "I Want You to Write Me," *Woman's Home Companion* 60 (August 1933): 8; Frances M. Seeber, "'I Want You to Write to Me': The Letters of Anna Eleanor Roosevelt," *Prologue* 19 (Summer 1987): 95; Ruby Black, *Eleanor Roosevelt: A Biography* (New York: Duell, Sloan and Pearce, 1940), 198–207; Tamara Hareven, *Eleanor Roosevelt: An American Conscience* (Chicago: Quadrangle Books, 1968), 39–62. The letters can be found in the Eleanor Roosevelt Papers (FDRL), scattered throughout the Woodward Papers (MDAH), and in the "White House Correspondence Files," FERA, RG 69.

15. Mary Elizabeth Pidgeon, "Employment Fluctuations and Unemployment of Women: Certain Indications from Various Sources, 1928–31," Women's Bureau Bulletin no. 113 (Washington, D.C.: U.S. Government Printing Office, 1933); "Women Unemployed Seeking Relief in 1933," WB Bulletin no. 139 (1936). For a fuller account of the Woodward-Roosevelt collaboration, see Martha H. Swain, "ER and Ellen Woodward: A Partnership for Women's Work Relief and Security," in Joan Hoff-Wilson and Marjorie Lightman, eds., *Without Precedent: The Life and Career of Eleanor Roosevelt* (Bloomington: Indiana University Press, 1984), 135–152.

16. ESW to Ethel Payne, 18 June 1934, FERA Ss (Miss.): 453.1, RG 69; ESW to ER, 6 June 1934, ER, Box 639.

17. ESW to ER, 10 November 1933; ESW to Helm, 11 November 1933, both in FERA OSF, White House Correspondence, RG 69.

18. *Proceedings of Conference on Emergency Needs of Women*, FERA OSF, RG 69 (also in ESW 1139.2, Box 21).

19. *Proceedings of Conference on Emergency Needs of Women.*

20. *Proceedings of Conference on Emergency Needs of Women.* Among others attending were Mabel Broadman (American Red Cross), Mary Anderson (Women's Bureau), Ethel Swope (American Nurses Association), Mrs. August Belmont (National Woman's Party), Grace Abbott (Children's Bureau), and Hilda Worthington Smith (FERA Workers' Education). Congresswomen Edith Nourse Rogers (Massachusetts), Mary T. Norton (New Jersey), and Isabella Greenway (Arizona) were also present.

21. William F. McDonald, *Federal Relief Administration and the Arts* (Athens: Ohio State University Press, 1969), 46; ESW quotation in *Conference Proceedings.*

22. ESW to ER, 9 December 1933, FERA OSF, White House Conference, RG 69; ESW to State Directors, Women's Division, 24 November 1933, ESW

1139.2, Box 17; Edith Foster, "Mississippi Field Reports, 1933–1934," HLH, Box 58.

23. ESW to Robert Sherwood, 27 October 1947, ESW 1139.2, Box 14; Sherwood, *Roosevelt and Hopkins: An Intimate History* (New York: Harper, 1948), 52.

24. *Washington Post*, 2 December 1933; "W–1" (14 November 1933) through "W–67" (10 June 1935) are in HLH, Box 23. See also, Carothers, *Chronology of the FERA*, 105–106.

25. Thus the CWA did not supplant the FERA entirely. Many official accounts and lay journals used the terms "CWA" and "FERA" interchangeably. More often than not, for the sake of simplicity, CWS (that is, women's) projects were subsumed under the term "CWA."

26. "Excerpts and Complaints about Women's Work," in ER, Box 639.

27. "W–6" (5 December 1933), HLH, Box 23; Theodore E. Whiting, *Final statistical Report of the Federal Emergency Relief Administration* (Washington, D.C.: U.S. Government Printing Office, 1942), 106; Forrest A. Walker, *The Civil Works Administration: An Experiment in Federal Work Relief, 1933–1934* (New York: Garland, 1979), 36, 68, 98; John J. Wallis, "Work Relief and Unemployment in the 1930s" (Ph.D. dissertation, University of Washington, 1981), 85, 149.

28. ESW to Frederick B. Pratt, 5 May 1935, FERA New Subject File (NSF) 375.4, RG 69. It was during the CWA that Woodward's division developed the practice of circulating "Working Procedures" among all states to disseminate information about unique and successful ideas that were reported to the central office. McDonald, *Federal Relief Administration*, 63.

29. *Washington Post*, 3 March 1934. The North Carolina report is quoted by Susan Wladaver-Morgan, "Young Women and the New Deal: Camps and Resident Centers, 1933–1935" (Ph.D. dissertation, Indiana University, 1982), 170.

30. "FERA-CWA-CWS," *American Journal of Nursing* 24 (March 1934): 183. Weed anticipated contemporary arguments for "comparable worth" in her "The New Deal that Women Want," *Current History* 41 (November 1934): 179–83.

31. "W–2" (29 November 1933), HLH, Box 23; ESW to Mr. Bookman, 20 November 1933, CWA Administrative Correspondence (General), RG 69; Alfred Steinberg, *Mrs. R.: The Life of Eleanor Roosevelt* (New York: Putnam, 1958), 225–26; Black, *Eleanor Roosevelt*, 200; *New York Times*, 5 December 1933.

32. "Excerpts from letters to Mrs. Roosevelt," FERA OSF, White House Correspondence, RG 69; Mayme O'Dow to George Power, 16 March, FERA Ss (Miss.): 453.2, RG 69; Richard M. Judd, *The New Deal in Vermont: Its Impact and Aftermath* (New York: Garland, 1979), 42.

33. Walker, *Civil Works Administration*, 82–84; Wallis, "Work Relief and Unemployment," 10, 152. Wallis has a brief but apt assessment on the

relationship of the three levels of government: "The local governments controlled the pork barrel . . . . the state government controlled patronage [and] the federal government controlled the bureaucracy" (162–63).

34. McJimsey, *Harry Hopkins*, 64; ESW to Ethel Payne, 1 December 1933, FERA Ss (Miss.): 453.1, RG 69; ESW to Emma Lindsey, 13 January 1934; ESW to Felix Underwood, 22 January 1934; ESW to Pearl Guyton, 3 April 1934; and ESW to Lucille Wilkins, 6 July 1934, all in FERA Ss (Miss.): 453.2, RG 69.

35. White to Howorth, 18 June 1934; Howorth to White, 22 June 1934, both in Lucy Howorth Biographical File, Archives of the National Business and Professional Women (Washington, D.C.).

36. Richard Lowitt and Maurine Beasley, *One-Third of a Nation: The Reports of Lorena Hickok* (Urbana: University of Illinois Press, 1981), 122; *New York Times*, 26 December 1933; *Washington Post*, 3 March 1934; ESW speech to General Federation of Women's Clubs, 11 January 1934 (Washington), ESW 1139.1, Box 19; ESW, "This New Federal Relief," *IW* 13 (April 1934): 104.

37. Mrs. J. D. Morland, "CWA Women's Projects," *DD* 13 (July 1934): 15.

38. "Signs and Portents," *American Journal of Nursing* 34 (January 1934): 55; "Notes from Headquarters, *American Journal of Nursing* 34:86, 88; Ethel Swope, "The CWA and the American Nurses Association," *American Journal of Nursing* 34 (April 1934): 356–60; "Nurses Prove Their Way," *Survey* 70 (May 1934): 164; ESW, "Federal Aspects of Unemployment Among Professional Women," *American Journal of Nursing* 34 (June 1934): 534–38; Susan M. Reverly, *Ordered to Care: The Dilemma of American Nursing, 1850–1945* (Cambridge: Cambridge University Press, 1987), 177.

39. "News," *American Journal of Nursing* 34 (May 1934): 507; "The Biennial," *American Journal of Nursing.* 34 (June 1934): 613; Ella Best (ANA) to ESW, 15 February 1935, FERA NSF 375.4, RG 69.

40. Woodward learned much from Elizabeth Robinson, head of the Mississippi Library Commission, whose FERA rural library development won national acclaim. See Beatrice S. Rossell, "Book Relief in Mississippi," *Survey* 71 (March 1935): 73–74; and Elizabeth Robinson, "Federal Aid Comes to Mississippi," *Library Journal* 60 (1 February 1935): 95.

41. Beatrice S. Rossell, "New Book Services to Rural Areas," *Rural America* 12 (December 1934): 5–6; Ralph Munn, "Made Work," *Bulletin of the ALA* 27 (April 1933): 189; "Library Projects Under Public Works, Civil Works, and Relief Administrations," *Bulletin of the ALA* 27 (December 1933): 539–551; Edwin S. Goree, "Progress Made in Texas with Federal Aid," *Texas Library Association News Notes* 10 (January 1934): 7; "Civil Works Service and the Library," *Library Journal* 59 (1 March 1934): 212–18; Julia Wright Merrill, "Library Projects under the FERA," *Bulletin of the ALA* 28 (October 1934): 820–26.

42. Tommie Dora Barker, *Libraries of the South: A Report on Develop-*

ment, 1930–1935 (Chicago: American Library Association, 1936), 78–83; Edward B. Stanford, *Library Extension Under the WPA: An Appraisal of an Experiment in Federal Aid* (Chicago: University of Chicago Press, 1944), 27–28; "Uncle Sam's Libraries," *School Life* 20 (April 1935): 182–83; "McGuffeys Forever," *DD* 23 (July 1935): 15.

43. "The Biennial," *American Journal of Nursing* 24 (June 1934): 613; Henry Alsberg, *America Fights the Depression: A Photographic Record of the Civil Works Administration* (New York: Coward-McCann, 1934), 115.

44. The retreat of Hopkins and his assistants to former FERA policies and procedures requiring the means test was the beginning of the alienation between the former New York chief and his social work associates in the state; they were disturbed that applicants for relief work had first to be placed on relief rolls. See William W. Bremer, *Depression Winters: New York Social Workers and the New Deal* (Philadelphia: Temple University Press, 1984), 136–37.

45. Corrington Gill, *Wasted Manpower: The Challenge of Unemployment* (New York: Norton, 1939), 170; John L. Palmer, ed., *Creating Jobs: Public Employment Programs and Wage Subsidies* (Washington, D.C.: Brookings Institution, 1978), 160–61.

46. "Excerpts and Comments About Women's Work," ER, Box 639; "W–3" (14 May 1934), HLH, Box 23.

47. Janet Poppendieck, *Breadlines Knee-Deep in Wheat: Food Assistance in the Great Depression* (New Brunswick, N.J.: Rutgers University Press, 1986), 166–67; Louise Armstrong, *We Too Are the People* (New York: Arno Press reprint, 1971), 306; ESW to ER, 20 September 1934, ER Box 639; ER to ESW, 11 January 1935, FERA NSF 375.3, RG 69.

48. Press release (2 August 1934), ESW 1139.1, Box 19; Carothers, *Chronology*, 71.

49. "Chatham County Centers," mimeographed report (18 February 1935), ER Box 672.

50. E. M. Clement, "A FERA Proving Ground," *DD* 123 (August 1935): 10, 27; Lowitt and Beasley, *One-Third of a Nation*, 173.

51. Theodore E. Whiting, *Final Statistical Report of the FERA* (Washington, D.C.: U.S. Government Printing Office, 1942), 54, 56–57.

52. Federal Emergency Relief Administration, *The Emergency Work Relief Program of the FERA-April 1, 1934–July 1, 1935* (Washington, D.C.: U.S. Government Printing Office, 1935), 62, 65, 82–87.

Notes to Chapter 4

1. ESW speech at inauguration of WPA, 17 July 1935, HLH, Box 26; ESW to Robert Sherwood, 27 October 1947, ESW 1139.2, Box 14.

2. William E. Leuchtenburg, *Franklin D. Roosevelt and the New Deal, 1932–1940* (New York: Harper & Row, 1963), 125–26; Edward A. Williams, *Federal Aid for Relief* (New York: Columbia University Press, 1939), 247–57;

Albert U. Romasco, *The Politics of Recovery: Roosevelt's New Deal* (New York: Oxford University Press, 1983), 65.

3. *Literary Digest* 120 (6 July 1935): 38; *New York Times*, 20, 21, 22 June, 7 July 1935; *Washington Post*, 21 June 1935; "Jobs for Jobless Women," *Equal Rights*, Independent Feminist Weekly (20 July 1935): 154; *DD* 7 (July 1935): 6; John A. Salmond, *A Southern Rebel: The Life and Times of Aubrey Willis Williams, 1890–1965* (Chapel Hill: University of North Carolina Press, 1983), 85 (Hopkins quotation).

4. *Jackson Daily News*, 30 June 1935; Agnes Cronin to Chloe Owings, 25 February 1936, WPA GSF 230, RG 69; ESW to Myra Hazard, 18 December 1935, ESW 1139.2, Box 59.

5. William McDonald, *Federal Relief Administration and the Arts* (Athens: Ohio State University Press, 1969), 71–72, 99–100.

6. Doak Campbell, Frederick Blair, and Oswald Harvey, *Educational Activities of the Works Progress Administration* (Washington, D.C.: U.S. Government Printing Office, 1939), 9, 12; Baker to Forrest A. Walker (27 November 1961), quoted in Walker, *The Civil Works Administration: An Experiment in Federal Work Relief, 1933–1934* (New York: Garland, 1979) 50; ESW telephone conversation with Florence Kerr, 21 February 1936, ESW 1139.2, Box 49.

7. Isabel Kinnear Griffin, "Five Regional Directors," *DD* 13 (June 1936)): 22–23.

8. ESW to Lula Scott, 10 March 1936, WPA GSF 231.1, RG 69; Scott and Kerr Field Reports, ESW 1139.1, Boxes 13, 18; Louise Armstrong, *We Too Are the People* (New York: Arno Press reprint, 1971), 462; Chloe Owings, "Life Is a Cooperative" (unpublished autobiography), 292, Owings Papers, AES. The organizational structure and duties were defined in Bulletin no. 28 ("Women's Activities"), 27 September 1935, HLH, Box 16.

9. Charley Tidd Cole, "Memorandum" [1936], WPA GSF 231, RG 69; Jean Azulay, "Female Networks for Social Change: Progressive Reform in the New Deal" (M.A. thesis, Sarah Lawrence, 1980), 97. For a brief description of the state directors, see "They Know What They're About," *DD* 13 (June 1936): 25.

10. Delta Kappa Gamma, *Adventures in Teaching: Pioneer Women Educators and Influential Teachers* (Richmond, Va.: Delta Kappa Gamma, 1963), 113–26 (copy in Virginia Historical Society, Richmond); Ronald L. Heinemann, *Depression and New Deal in Virginia: The Enduring Dominion* (Charlottesville: University Press of Virginia, 1983), 74; Helen Wolfe Evans, "Ella Graham Agnew: New Occasions, New Choices" (Graduate paper, Duke University, 1988), copy in possession of author.

11. *Vanderbilt Alumnus* 59 (Winter 1974): 32; *Vanderbilt Alumnus* 62 (Summer 1977): 30.

12. Martha H. Swain, "A New Deal for Mississippi Women," *Journal of Mississippi History* 46 (August 1984): 193.

13. Lula Scott to ESW, 16 June 1935, WPA GSF 231.1, RG 69.

14. Michael Holmes, *The New Deal in Georgia: An Administrative History* (Westport, Conn.: Greenwood Press, 1975), 48–49; biographical sketch, Register for Van De Vrede Papers, Georgia Department of Archives and History, Atlanta; obituary, *Atlanta Constitution*, 5 January 1972.

15. Barbara Blumberg, *The New Deal and the Unemployed: The View from New York City* (Lewisburg, Pa.: Bucknell University Press, 1979), 77; clippings on Rider, ESW Scrapbook, 1139.2.

16. Bulletin no. 37 (30 December 1935), HLH, Box 16; Arthur W. Macmahon, John D. Millett, and Gladys Ogburn, *The Administration of Work Relief* (Chicago: University of Chicago Press, 1941), 207.

17. *New York Times*, 17 January 1934; MWD to ESW, 31 December 1936, MWD, Box 7; Charles H. Trout, *Boston: The Great Depression and the New Deal* (New York: Oxford University Press, 1977), 161, 163.

18. Agnes Cronin telephone conversation with Izetta Jewel Miller, 17 January 1936, ESW conversation with Miller, 21 May 1936; both in ESW 1139.2, Box 50; Emma Guffey Miller to ESW, 13 May, 11 June 1936, Miller Papers, Box 2, AES. Dewson on Miller is quoted by Elsie George, "The Women Appointees of the Roosevelt and Truman Administrations" (Ph.D. dissertation, American University, 1972), 59. The birthday card is in the Woodward Scrapbook, ESW 1139.2.

19. ESW telephone conversation with Sarah Krusling, 20 January 1936, and with Wayne McCoy, 21 January 1936, ESW 1139.2, Box 49.

20. ESW telephone conversation with Kerr, 7, 11 January 1936, ESW 1139.2, Box 49; Timothy K. Evans, "This Certainly Is Relief: Matthew S. Murray and Missouri Politics During the Depression," *Missouri Historical Society Bulletin* 28 (July 1972): 219–33; Richard M. Judd, *The New Deal in Vermont: Its Impact and Aftermath* (New York: Garland, 1979), 222.

21. ESW to ER, 28 August 1935, ER, Box 672; ESW to Malvina Schneider, 20 January 1936, ER, Box 704; ESW telephone conversation with Mrs. Harry G. Leach, 290 May 1936, ESW 1139.2, Box 50.

22. ESW to ER, 14 December 1937, 16 July 1938, both in ER, Box 723.

23. Agnes Cronin Oral History, Federal Theatre Project Archives, George Mason University; author's interview with Grace Allen, 23 June 1983 (Washington, D.C.).

24. Merrill is quoted by Elizabeth Robinson to Ethel Payne, 24 December 1936, WPA Ss (Miss.): 660, RG 69.

25. Armstrong, *We Too Are the People*, 302. Armstrong's autobiography is one of the most sensitive accounts of the FERA in print. See Bernard Sternsher and Judith Sealander, eds., *Women of Valor: The Struggle Against the Great Depression as Told in Their Own Life Stories* (Chicago: Ivan Dee, 1990), 202–22.

26. Quoted in Julia Kirk Blackwelder, *Women of the Depression: Caste and Culture in San Antonio, 1929–1939* (College Station: Texas A & M Press, 1984), 126, 192.

27. Press release (15 October 1938), ESWP, AES; James Glenden to ER, WPA OSF, White House Correspondence, RG 69; D. Jerome Tweton, *The New Deal at the Grassroots: Programs for People in Ottertail County, Minnesota* (St. Paul: Minnesota Historical Society Press, 1988), 81.

28. Woodward was one of the Democratic Women's Division activists who petitioned FDR in 1936 for repeal of Section 213. She was a member of the BPW Resolutions Committee at the 1937 annual convention that called for the repeal that eventually came late in 1937. Carolyn Wolfe to ESW, 6 March 1936, WD-DNC, Box 27; *IW* 18 (August 1937): 233; *DD* 14 (August 1937): 36.

29. ESW, "Notes to Mrs. Norton About the WPA Women's Program" [1936], ESW 1139.1, Box 22; press release, ESW 1139.1, Box 24.

30. Grace Abbott, *From Relief to Social Security* (Chicago: University of Chicago Press, 1941), 274–75; Lynn Y. Weiner, *From Working Girl to Working Mother: The Female Labor Force in the United States, 1820–1880* (Chapel Hill: University of North Carolina Press, 1985), 107–10.

31. Doris Carothers, *Final Chronology of the Federal Emergency Relief Administration, May 12, 1933 to December 31, 1935* (Washington, D.C.: U.S. Government Printing Office, 1937), 88.

32. Richard Lowitt and Maurine Beasley, *One-Third of a Nation: The Reports of Lorena Hickok* (Urbana: University of Illinois Press, 1981), 49, 216; Amy Maher, "Unemployed Women" *Social Science Review* 8 (December 1934): 774.

33. Bertha Dunkle to FDR, 5 December 1934; ESW to ER, 11 October, 21 December 1934; all in FERA OSF, White House Correspondence, RG 69. Simkovich is quoted in John E. Bauman and Thomas H. Coode, *In the Eye of the Great Depression: New Deal Reporters on the Agony of the American People* (DeKalb: Northern Illinois Press, 1988), 709.

34. Lena Madesin Phillips to ESW, 6 December 1933; Dorothy Ballanca to ESW, 20 May 1935; both in FERA NSF 375.4, RG 69; MWD to ER, 20 February 1935, copy in ESW 1139.2, Box 13.

35. ER to ESW, 15 October 1934; Aubrey Williams to ESW, 30 October 1934; ESW to ER, 16 November 1934; all in ER, Box 639.

36. The Alabama complaint is in FERA OSF, White House Correspondence, RG 69; the Missouri letter is in ER, Box 704.

37. ESW to ER, 6 October 1934, FERA NSF, White House Correspondence, RG 69.

38. ESW to HLH, 6 April 1936; "Record of Letters Referred by Mrs. Roosevelt" [1938], both in WPA GSF 236, RG 69.

39. ESW to Izetta Jewel Miller, 8 February 1936 (copy), ER, Box 704.

40. ESW to ER, 27 April 1935, ER, Box 672; *New York Times*, 21 May 1935; Maurine Beasley, *The White House Press Conferences of Eleanor Roosevelt* (New York: Garland, 1983), 31.

41. ESW speech (17 June 1935), HLH, Box 26.

42. George McJimsey, *Harry Hopkins: Ally of the Poor and Defender of*

Democracy (Cambridge, Mass.: Harvard University Press, 1987), 87; Charles Trout, *Boston: The Great Depression and the New Deal* (New York: Oxford University Press, 1977), 166.

43. ESW to ER, 8 October 1935, WPA GSF 230, RG 69.

44. ESW to ER, 8 October 1935, WPA GSF 230, RG 69; ESW to Hopkins, 10 December 1935, WPA GSF 230, RG 69.

45. ESW to ER, 21 December 1935, ER, Box 672; ESW to HLH, 10 December 1935, WPA GSF 230, RG 69.

46. John J. Wallis, "Work Relief and Unemployment in the 1930s" (Ph.D. dissertation, University of Washington, 1981), 152; Donald Howard, *The WPA and Federal Relief Policy* (New York: Russell Sage Foundation, 1942), 144–46.

47. McMahon, Millett, and Ogburn, *Administration of Work Relief*, 134; ESW to National Council of Women (New York City), 3 December 1936, ESW 1139.2, Box 25.

48. *Final Report: Feeding*, 7, WPA Professional and Service Division, RG 69; Holmes, *New Deal in Georgia*, 126–27; Resolution, Massachusetts Political Club (27 May 1935), FERA NSF 375.4, RG 69; Final State Report (Idaho), RG 69.

49. ESW to Perkins, 13 April 1936, WPA GSF 236, RG 69; ESW to MFWC convention (5 November 1936), ESW 1139.1, Box 24; ESW, "Women Are Working at Security Wages" (GFWC) *The Clubwoman* (October 1935): 11ff.

50. Frank March to John J. McDonough, 8 April 1937, Division of Women and Professional Projects, Box 12, RG 69. Frances Fox Piven and Richard A. Cloward are extremely critical of the "security wage"; see their *Regulating the Poor: The Functions of Public Welfare* (New York: Vintage, 1971), 95.

51. ESW to Regional Directors, 24 August 1936, WPA GSF 231, RG 69. Many of Woodward's strong directives were drafted, as was this one by Catherine K. Nonamaker.

52. Report on Progress of the Works Program (March 1937), ESW 1139.2, Box 39.

53. Letters to ESW, September 1935–February 1935, WPA GSF 230, RG 69; ESW to J. W. Sanders, 21 July 1936, ESW 1139.1, Box 4.

54. Hundreds of letters are in WPA GSF 230. See especially ESW to Lowenstein and Sons (New York City), 18 August 1936.

55. ESW to MWD, 18 October 1935, WD-DNC, Box 27; ESW to HLH, 3 April 1935, FERA Old Subject File, Box 27, RG 69; ESW telephone conversation with Lebengood, 28 September 1936, ESW 1139.2, Box 50; *Philadelphia Inquirer*, 20 May 1936.

56. Cole and Franklin, *REPORT*, 395–96; ESW memorandum to HLH, 22 January 1936, WD-DNC, Box 27; ESW to ER, 13 January 1936 and ER to ESW, 5 February 1936, both in ER, Box 704; *Mid-Week Pictorial: The Newspicture Weekly* 44 (16 December 1936): 36.

57. Cole to Regional Directors, 23 March 1937, WPA GSF 231, RG 69; Cole and Franklin. *REPORT*, 398–400. In January 1937, the WPA had

thirty-two employees as press and public information agents. Betty Houchin Winfield, "The New Deal Publicity Operation, Foundation for the Modern Presidency," *Journalism Quarterly* 61 (Spring 1984): 48.

58. ESW to Marguerite Wells, 24 February 1937, Papers of the League of Women Voters, Series II, Box 379, Library of Congress.

59. MWD to ESW, 6 February 1935, WD-DNC, Box 27.

60. Quoted in Susan Ware, *Beyond Suffrage; Women in the New Deal* (Cambridge, Mass.: Harvard University Press, 1981), 74. The members of Ware's network are suggested by a lengthy document entitled "Thumbnail Sketches of Women You Hear About in the New Deal" (copy in League of Women Voters, Series II, Library of Congress, Series II, Box 612). The list also appears in the Dewson Papers.

61. ESW to O'Day, 27 July 1935; ESW telephone conversation with O'Day, 8 August 1935, both in ESW 1139.1, Box 3; Anderson to ESW, 28 December 1935, ESW 1139.1, Box 4; Wolfe, *Educating for Citizenship: A Career in Community Affairs and the Democratic Party, 1906–1976* (Women in Politics Oral History Project, Bancroft Library, University of California, 1978), 125.

62. See Ware, *Beyond Suffrage*, 70, for a full description of the reporter plan.

63. Dewson, "An Aid to the End" (unpublished autobiography), II, 79, MWD Papers.

64. ESW to MWD, 18 October 1935, WD-DNC, Box 27; ESW speech, 10 September 1935, ESW 1139.1, Box 17.

65. Dewson, "An Aid to the End," 2:71–72; *DD* 12 (April 1935): 7:12–15; Carolyn Wolfe to Study Leaders, 26 June 1935, MWD, Box 8. The full program of the dinner, "In Honor of the Women of the New Deal," is in ESW 1139.2, Box 21.

66. ESW to Farley, 8 February 1934, ESW to ER, 17 March 1934, both in ER, Box 639; *Jackson Daily News*, 31 July, 1 August, 5 September 1934; Minutes, vol. 1, Papers of Mississippi Democratic Executive Committee (4 September 1934), MDAH.

67. ER to ESW, 31 October 1935, ER, Box 672; MWD to ESW, 26 January 1936, WD-DNC, Box 27; MWD to ESW, 11 April 1936, MWD, Box 4; ESW to HLH, 4 June 1936, ESW 1139.2, Box 17.

68. ESW to Regional Conference, 19 March 1936, ESW 1139.1, Box 19; MWD, "An Aid to the End," II, 118; *Jackson Daily News*, 1 June 1936; *Official Report of the Proceedings of the Democratic National Convention . . . Philadelphia, June 23–27,1936* (61–62, Microfilm 848, Reel 4, Vanderbilt University Library (Nashville); Susan Ware, *Partner and I: Molly Dewson, Feminism, and New Deal Politics* (New Haven, Conn.: Yale University Press, 1987), 217.

69. MWD to ESW, 16 July 1936, MWD, Box 4; Carolyn Wolfe to ESW, 30 September 1936, WD-DNC, Box 27.

70. Congressional correspondence relating to the FERA is in the New

Subject File 375.2, RG 69. The most revealing material is in the telephone transcripts in ESW 1139.2, Boxes 48 to 53.

71. Telephone conversations, 6 July 1935, ESW 1139.2, Box 51; ESW to Williams, 21 November 1936, quoted in Elsie L. George, "The Women Appointees of the Roosevelt and Truman Administrations," 160.

72. Sillers to ESW, 23 September 1935, Walter Sillers Papers, Delta State University (Cleveland, Miss.); ESW to FDR, 25 August 1936, FDR, OF 300, Box 46.

73. ESW telephone conversations with MWD, 13, 18 January 1936, ESW 1139.2, Box 48; ESW conversations with Dorothy Nyswander, 18, 20 January 1936, ESW 1139.2, Box 50.

74. ESW telephone conversation with Disney, 4 August 1937, ESW 1139.2, Box 53.

75. Kerr to ESW, 20 August 1935, ESW 1139.1, Box 3; ESW telephone conversation with Miller, 10 September 1936, ESW 1139.2, Box 50; ESW telephone conversation with O'Day, 13 May 1936, 1139.2, Box 51; O'Day to ESW, 9 November 1936, ESW Scrapbook, 1139.2; Miller to ESW, 11 June 1936, and Miller to Ely, 17 June 1936, both in ESW 1139.1, Box 4.

76. Priscilla F. Clement, "The Works Progress Administration in Pennsylvania, 1935 to 1940," *Pennsylvania Magazine of History and Biography* 95 (April 1971): 259–60. Susan Ware describes Emma Guffey Miller's differences with Molly Dewson (*Partner and I*, 218–19); Leila J. Rupp and Verta Taylor further describe Miller's fractiousness in *Survival in the Doldrums* (New York: Oxford University Press, 1987).

77. Kerr to ESW, 28 October 1935, ESW 1139.1, Box 4; Kerr to ESW, 4, 10 August 1935, ESW 1139.1, Box 3. A grand jury indicted Langer for shaking down federal employees; as a convicted felon, he was, nevertheless, reelected to office. See William R. Brock, *Welfare, Democracy and the New Deal* (Cambridge: Cambridge University Press, 1988), 245–46.

78. ESW telephone conversation with David K. Niles, 3 September 1936, ESW 1139.2, Box 50.

79. ESW telephone conversation with Paul Edwards, 21 October 1938, ESW 1139.2, Box 6.

80. Dorothy Dunbar Brumley, "Chloe Owings: The Story of a Girl Who Exchanged Her Sunbonnet for the 'Bonnet de Sorbonne'," *Woman Citizen* 11 (April 1927): 12; Owings File, ESW 1139.1, Box 13; Owings File, Knox College Archives (Galesburg, Ill.); Owings to ESW, 28 September 1934, FERA Ss (Miss.): 432.2, RG 69.

81. Owings to ESW, 13 May 1936, WPA GSF 230, RG 69; ESW to Owings, 22 May 1936, ESW 1139.1, Box 13.

82. Owings, "Life Is a Cooperative," unpublished manuscript in AES, 272–73, 301, 304–305. Owings returned to New York City, devoted a year to study and writing, and became the faculty dean at Keuka College. From 1943 until retirement in 1952, she was director of the Pasadena Institute for Radio

(later the California Institute for TV and Radio) and served as a Republican precinct chairman in the 1950s (Owings File, Knox College). Owings may have held views like those of her profession who moved from mere dischantment to hostility toward Hopkins's views. See William W. Bremer, "'Along the American Way': The New Deal's Work Relief Programs for the Unemployed," *Journal of American History* 62 (December 1975): 636–52.

83. ESW speech, 5 November 1935, ESW 1139.1, Box 24. Mississippi's excessive restrictions on absentee voting contained no exemption for which Woodward qualified, and thus she was compelled to return home to vote in primary and general elections.

Notes to Chapter 5

1. ESW address, 5 May 1936, copy in HLH, Box 26; *DD* 13 (June 1936): 19; *Congressional Record*, 74 Cong., 2 Sess., 8373–75 (30 May 1936).

2. Lewis Merriam, *Relief and Social Security* (Washington, D.C.: Brookings Institution, 1946), 417. By contrast, of male workers on relief in March 1935, 36.5 percent were classified as unskilled. In RG 69, the Final State Report on WPA Administration and Operation for many states have extensive comments on the unskilled.

3. ESW to HLH, "Justification of Sewing Projects," 23 December 1936, WPA Division Records, WPP, RG 69; ESW to HLH, "Memorandum on Sewing Projects," 13 January 1937, WPA GSF 237, RG 69; *New York Times*, 4 February 1936; Barbara Blumberg, *The New Deal and the Unemployed: The View from New York City* (Lewisburg, Pa.: Bucknell University Press, 1979), 141–42.

4. Charley Cole and Esther Franklin, *REPORT: Division of Women's and Professional Projects, WPA, July 1, 1935 to January 1, 1937*, bound copy (17 February 1937), 264–65, in ESW 1139.2, Box 40.

5. ESW memorandum to HLH, 13 January 1937, WPA GSF 237, RG 69.

6. Ethel Payne to Wayne Alliston, 15 April 1936, WPA Ss (Miss.): 661, RG 69; U.S. Department of Agriculture, "Haberdashers to the Needy, *Consumer's Guide* (1 May 1939): 3; "Report on Progress of the Works Program, March, 1937," bound copy, ESW 1139.2, Box 39; Final State Report on WPA Operation and Administration (Pennsylvania), RG 69; Harry L. Hopkins, *Spending to Save: The Complete Story of Relief* (New York: Norton, 1936), 103, 169–70; Blumberg, *New Deal and the Unemployed*, 142.

7. ESW, "Women at Work Under WPA," ESW 1139.1, Box 22; "Sewing and Weaving," *DD* 13 (June 1936): 8–9.

8. Martha H. Swain, "ER and Ellen Woodward: A Partnership for Women's Work Relief and Security," in Joan Hoff-Wilson and Marjorie Lightman, eds., *Without Precedent: The Life and Career of Eleanor Roosevelt* (Bloomington: Indiana University Press, 1983), 140–41; "Native Arts and Crafts," *DD* 13 (June 1936): 13–14; *Work Relief in Nebraska: Report of the Work Division of the Nebraska ERA*, bound copy in Ernest F. Witte Papers, Box 6, SWHA.

9. ESW to HLH, 14 January 1937, WPA Division Records, WPP, RG 69.

10. Marie Dresden Lane and Francis Steegmuller, *America on Relief* (New York: Harcourt, Brace, 1938), 71–78; Anthony J. Badger, *The New Deal: The Depression Years, 1933–1940* (New York: Noonday Press, 1989), 206 (North Carolina quotation).

11. "Confidential Report," 6 April 1937, WPA Division Records, WPP, RG 69.

12. Susan Wladaver-Morgan in "Young Women and the New Deal Camps and Resident Centers, 1933–1943" (Ph.D. dissertation, Indiana University, 1982) criticizes the sewing room methods as "a conscious throwback to preindustrial forms of women's work . . . [that] contributed to making the women's projects seem contrived, wasteful, and easily expendable" (171).

13. ESW to Green, 19 April 1938, ESW 1139.2, Box 4.

14. ESW to ER, 8 October 1935, WPA GSF 230, RG 69; Erwin Feldman to Lawrence Westbook, 16 September 1935, and John Freeland to ESW, 20 September 1935, WPA GSF 230 RG 69; ESW to Henry E. Weinhberg, 6 September 1935, ER, Box 672; Douglas L. Smith, *The New Deal in the Urban South* (Baton Rouge: Louisiana State University Press, 1988), 131.

15. Drew Pearson and Robert Allen, "Washington Merry-Go-Round," undated 1935 column in ESW Scrapbook, ESW 1139.2; Nels Anderson, *The Right to Work* (New York: Modern Age Books, 1938), 56. The WPA summary history of the Production Projects includes a twenty-six-page list of complainants. "WPA Program Operation and Accomplishment, 1935–1943," Vol. 2, "Clothing" (Exhibit U).

16. For representative files, see that on Martin R. Durkin, attorney for Massachusetts binderies, and the extensive correspondence with Pelham Barr, executive director of the Library Binding Institute, WPA GSF 237, RG 69. For Barr's indictment of WPA mending and for Woodward's reply, see "WPA Mending Again," *Library Journal* 63 (1 December 1938), 900–01.

17. ESW to C. W. Carroll, 14 March 1938; ESW to Clarence J. West, 25 June 1938; Martin R. Durkin to HLH, 16 August 1938; HLH to Henry Cabot Lodge, Jr., 23 August 1938, and Kerr to ESW, 20 September 1938, all in WPA GSF 237, RG 69.

18. George T. Blakey, *Hard Times & New Deal in Kentucky* (Lexington: University of Kentucky Press, 1986), 64; ESW, "WPA Library Projects," *Wilson Bulletin* 12 (April 1938): 518–20.

19. Daniel F. Ring., ed., *Studies in Creative Partnership: Federal Aid to Libraries During the New Deal* (Metuchen, N.J.: Scarecrow Press, 1980), 37, 48, 75, 93, 108; "The Month at Random," *Wilson Bulletin* 11 (May 1937): 620–21; Louise Crawford to Ethel Payne, 16 March 1936, WPA Ss (Miss.): 663, RG 69.

20. ESW to Merrill, 12 June 1936, WPA GSF 230, RG 69; Edward A. Chapman, *Works Projects Administration Record of Program and Accomplishment, 1935–1943*, Vol 6, *Library Service*, 1–2, 11–12, RG 69.

21. Edward B. Stanford, *Library Extension Under the WPA: An Appraisal of an Experiment in Federal Aid* (Chicago: University of Chicago Press, 1944), 47, 56–57, 97; Susan Ware, *Holding Their Own: American Women in the 1930s* (Boston: Twayne, 1982), 69–70.

22. Martha H. Swain, "A New Deal for Mississippi Women," *Journal of Mississippi History* 46 (August 1984): 205–206; Blumberg, *New Deal and the Unemployed*, 142–43; *DD* 13 (June 1936): 14–15, 17; Corinne Reed Frazier, "WPA Serves the Blind," *Commonweal* 32 (11 August 1939): 371–72.

23. Frazier, "WPA Serves the Blind," 371; WPA Final State Reports (Indiana), RG 69.

24. Federal Works Agency, *Final Report on the WPA Program, 1935–1943* (Washington, D.C.: U.S. Government Printing Office, 1946), 68.

25. Kate Adele Hill, *Home Demonstration Work in Texas* (San Antonio: Naylor Press, 1938), 38–39; Mary Jean Simpson report (April 1937), Division of Women's and Professional Projects, Box 9, RG 69; ESW, "The Works Progress Administration School Lunch Projects," *Journal of Home Economics* 38 (November 1936): 592–96; ESW, "WPA School Lunch Program," *School and Society* 46 (17 July 1937): 91–94; ESW, "80,000,000 School Lunches," *School Executive* 66 (August 1937): 474–75; ESW, "The WPA School Lunch Program," *School Management* 7 (September 1937): 8–9.

26. ESW to Clara Littledale, 18 April 1938, WPA GSF 235, RG 69; Dorothy Canfield Fisher, "Get It While It's Hot," *Ladies Home Journal* 55 (November 1938): 104.

27. *WPA Program Operation and Accomplishment, 1935–1943*, vol. 4 Feeding, 3–4, RG 69; Janet Poppendieck, *Breadlines Kneedeep in Wheat* (New Brunswick, N.J.: Rutgers University Press, 1986), 241–42.

28. *DD* 13 (June 1936): 12–13; "WPA Nursing Projects," *Public Health Nursing* 29 (January 1937): 50–51; "WPA Projects for Registered Nurses," *American Journal of Nursing* 27 (January 1937): 35–37; ESW, "Nursing and Public Health Projects Under WPA," *Public Health Nursing* 29 (March 1937): 169–72; Eugene C. Chemine, "The Neighbors Lend a Hand: A Project in Home Hygiene," *Hygeia* 15 (March 1937): 256–57; ESW, "Rural Health," *Southern Planter* (August 1937): 26–67.

29. Edward H. Beardsley, *A History of Neglect: Health Care for Blacks and Mill Workers in the Twentieth Century South* (Knoxville: University of Tennessee Press, 1987), 158–61; "The WPA and Public Health," *American Federationist* 45 (June 1938): 600–03; Mrs. Albert Werthan to ESW, 9 November 1938; Mrs. Edward Abbott to HLH, 8 November 1938; ESW to Mrs. Abbott, 22 November 1938; all in WPA GSF 212, RG 69. Three boxes containing hundreds of letters on the subject of birth control are in RG 69.

30. John Carmody, "The Federal Works Agency and Public Health," *American Journal of Public Health* 80 (August 1940): 892–93.

31. Cole and Franklin, *REPORT: WPP, July 1, 1935 to January 1, 1937*: 301–308; Carmody, "The Federal Works Agency and Public Health," 893–94;

Dorothea M. Argo, "What Housekeeping Aides Do," *Journal of Nursing* 41 (July 1941): 775–80.

32. *DD* 13 (July 1936): 11–12; ESW to Edwin M. Schaefer, 1 February 1938, WPA GSF 236, RG 69.

33. ESW to Alma H. Scott, 15 June 1937; ESW to Ella Best, 14 July 1937; ESW to Mary C. Jarrett, 5 May 1938; all in Division of Women's and Professional Projects, Box 7, RG 69; Phyllis Palmer, *Domesticity and Dirt: Housewives and Domestic Servants in the United States, 1920–1945* (Philadelphia: Temple University Press, 1989), 101–102; Winifred Wandersee, *Women's Work and Family Values, 1920–1940* (Cambridge, Mass.: Harvard University Press, 1981), 97.

34. Folders on Mayflower Conference, WPA GSF 230AAAA, RG 69; *WPA Program of Operation and Accomplishment, 1935–1943*, XI, *Training*, 9–11, RG 69; Ellis Meredith, "Not Lost, But Regained," *DD* 13 (June 1936): 24.

35. George B. Tindall, *The Emergence of the New South, 1913–1945* (Baton Rouge: Louisiana State University Press, 1967), 460. See also, Thomas L. Stokes, *Chip Off My Shoulder* (Princeton, N.J.: Princeton University Press, 1940), 517–18.

36. ESW to HLH, 13 December 1933, ESW to Aubrey Williams, 15 December 1933; both in FERA Ss (Miss.): 432.21, RG 69; ESW note on Payne memorandum (May 1936), WPA GSF 230AAAA, RG 69; Mississippi file, HLH, Box 51.

37. Jean Azulay, "Female Networks for Social Change: Progressive Women in the New Deal" (M.A. thesis, Sarah Lawrence College, 1980), 111.

38. *New York Times*, 29 April 1934.

39. Susan Wladaver-Morgan, "Young Women and the New Deal Camps," 148–50.

40. Joyce L. Kornbluh, *A New Deal for Workers Education: The Workers' Service Program, 1933–1942* (Urbana: University of Illinois Press, 1987), 106; Smith to ESW, [?] January 1951, ESW, AES.

41. ESW to Regional Conference of Democratic Women (Binghamton, NY), 15 April 1936, ESW 1139.1, Box 19: Alfred Edgar Smith, "Report: Negro Clients of Federal Unemployment Relief" (31 December 1935), in Smith Papers, Special Collections, University of Arkansas Libraries (Fayetteville). On Smith's activities, see David Brinkley, *Washington Goes to War* (New York: Knopf, 1988), 79–80.

42. ESW to ER, 31 October 1935, ER, Box 672.

43. ESW-Smith telephone conversations and conference reports, 26 August–6 November 1935, *passim*, Hilda W. Smith Papers, Box 20 (FDRL).

44. ER to ESW, 8 January 1937, ESW Scrapbook 1139.2; ER, "Woman's Work Is Never Done," *Woman's Home Companion* 62 (April 1935): 4; "The Servant Problem," *Fortune* 17 (March 1938): l81–85; ESW to ER, 28 December 1936, WPA GSF 210.13, RG 69; National Committee on Household

Employment *Bulletin* 5 (December 1936), copy in WPA Division Records, Box 9, WPP, RG 69.

Representative of Woodward's several articles in professional journals are: "Household Employment and the WPA," *Journal of Home Economics* 28 (September 1936): 439–42; "The WPA Prepares Women for Housework," *Occupations* 17 (December 1938): 220–22; and "Making Housework a Skilled Occupation," *Journal of the American Association of University Women* 30 (October 1936): 23–25.

45. Genevieve Offcut to ER, 22 December 1937; Aubrey Williams to Ellison D. Smith, 5 April 1938, and other letters filed under "Complaints," Household Workers' Training, WPA, Division Records, WPP, Box 6, RG 69. Both the National Youth Administration and the WPA's Division for Adult Education conducted programs for training household workers. Like those of the WPP, success was intermingled with failure. See Judith Allen, "Help!" *Literary Digest* 124 (11 September 1937): 18–20.

46. Ruth Chalmers to Florence Kerr, 3 August 1939, WPA GSF 212.2, RG 69; Final State Reports, Household Workers' Training, WPA Professional and Service Division, RG 69; *New York Times*, November 1941.

47. Donna L. Van Raaphorst, *Union Maids Not Wanted: Organizing Domestic Workers, 1870–1940* (New York: Praeger, 1988), 236; Doris Faber, *The Life of Lorena Hickok, ER's Friend* (New York: William Morrow, 1980), 198.

48. John F. Jones and John M. Merrick, *Citizens in Service: Volunteers in Social Welfare During the Depression, 1919–1941* (Ann Arbor: University of Michigan Press, 1976), 83, 98–99.

49. Memorandum on Committee on Standards for Household Employment, ESW 1139.1, Box 4.

50. Palmer, *Domesticity and Dirt*, 104.

51. Richard Sterner, *The Negro's Share: A Study of Income, Consumption, Housing and Public Assistance* (New York: Harper & Brothers, 1943), 244; Blumberg, *New Deal and the Unemployed*, 153; Julia Kirk Blackwelder, "Quiet Suffering: Atlanta Women in the 1930s," *Georgia Historical Quarterly* 61 (Summer 1977): 112, 124.

52. Jean Collier Brown, *The Negro Woman Worker*, WB Bulletin 165 (Washington, D.C.: U.S. Government Printing Office, 1938), 1–2; Marion Cuthbert, "Problems Facing Negro Young Women," *Opportunity: A Journal of Negro Life* 14 (February 1936): 47.

53. Margaret Leach to ESW, 15 May 1935, FERA Ss (Miss.): 453.2, RG 69; Report of Alfred E. Smith, "Race of WPA Workers" (31 July 1940), Smith Papers.

54. Alfred E. Smith, "Negro Clients of Federal Employment Relief" (31 December 1935), Smith Papers; Jacqueline Jones, *Labor of Love, Labor of Sorrow: Black Women, Work and the Family From Slavery to the Present* (New York: Basic Books, 1985), 216–20. For a demonstration of Southern fears regarding labor, see Raymond Wolters, *Negroes and the Great Depression:*

The Problem of Economic Recovery (Westport, Conn.: Greenwood Press, 1970), 109.

55. Rev. E. A. Mayes to HLH, 19 June 1938; Beulah Mae McGowen to FDR, 26 July 1938, both in WPA Ss (Miss.): 663, RG 69; "Extracts from 1937 Annual Report of Alfred E. Smith," WPA GSF 230, RG 69; Albert Hayes, "WPA Practices Discrimination, *The Woman's Voice* 1 (February-March 1940): 5–6.

56. Many letters are in the Papers of the National Association for the Advancement of Colored People (NAACP), Administrative Files C, Box 618, LC, and the WPA files at Howard University (Washington, D.C.), two of which are printed in Rosalyn Baxandall, Linda Gordon, and Susan Reverby, *America's Working Women: A Documentary History* (New York: Vintage Books, 1976), 249–51.

57. Pinckney to Smith, 13 April 1937, and Smith to Charles Houston, 13 April 1937, both in Papers of NAACP, Adm. File C, Box 418.

58. Michael S. Holmes, *The New Deal in Georgia: An Administrative History* (Westport, Conn.: Greenwood Press, 1975), 80.

59. *Washington Post*, 20 August 1937; ESW telephone conversation with Jenckes, 7 July 1937, ESW 1139.2, Box 53.

60. In New York City, they constituted 90 percent of the workers; nationwide, in 1938, of the workers, 93 percent were black. In New York City, they constituted 90 percent of the workers; nationwide, in 1938, of the workers, 93 percent were black. WPA news release (22 March 1938), WPA GSF 230, RG 69.

61. Blumberg, *New Deal and the Unemployed*, 134; Julia Kirk Blackwelder, *Women of the Depression: Caste and Culture in San Antonio, 1929–1939* (College Station: Texas A & M Press, 1984), 124; Alfred E. Smith, "Negro Project Workers" (1938) Smith Papers.

62. ESW telephone conversation with Bethune, 7 July 1937, ESW 1139.2, Box 53; Nancy J. Weiss, *The National Urban League, 1910–1940* (New York: Oxford University Press, 1974), 252; Dona Cooper Hamilton, "The National Urban League During the Depression, 1930–1939: The Quest for Jobs for Black Workers" (D.S.W. dissertation, Columbia University, 1982), 127, 143; Phyllis Palmer, *Domesticity and Dirt*, 103.

63. "Extracts From 1937 Annual Report of Alfred E. Smith"; Thomas C. Walker, *The Honey-Pod Tree: The Life Story of Thomas Calhoun Walker* (New York: J. Day, 1958), 249.

64. Holmes, *New Deal in Georgia*, 132; Thurgood Marshall to Brehon Somerville, 5 August 1937, NAACP Adm. File C, Box 418, LC.

65. Richard Lowitt and Maurine Beasley, *One-Third of a Nation: Lorena Hickok Reports on the Great Depression* (Urbana: University of Illinois Press, 1981), 145.

66. Lowitt and Beasley, *One-Third of a Nation*, 350.

67. Agnes Cronin to Regional Directors, 15 July 1936, WPA GSF 231, RG 69; Cronin to Kerr, 12 September 1936, and ESW to Brehon Somerville, 3 September 1936, both in WPA GSF 236, RG 69.

68. ESW to Smith, 14 November, 5 December 1936, WPA GSF 230, RG 69.

69. See Harvard Sitkoff, *A New Deal for Blacks: The Emergence of Civil Rights as a National Issue: The Depression Decade* (New York: Oxford University Press, 1978), 81–82.

70. ESW telephone conversation with Bethune, 26 February 1938, ESW 1139.2, Box 53; ESW to ER, 4 April 1938, ER, Box 741; Cronin to ESW, 30 March 1938, WPA GSF 230, RG 69.

71. "Morning Session Proceedings, Participation of Negro Women and Children in Federal Programs," 89–91, Papers of the National Council for Negro Women, Series 4, National Archives for Black Women's History (Washington, D.C.); *Chicago Defender*, 9 April 1938.

72. ESW telephone conversation with Bethune (26 February 1938), ESW 1139.2, Box 53.

73. "Afternoon Session Proceedings," 17, 20; ESW to ER, 4 April 1938, ER, Box 741. For a fuller description of the effect of eligibility policies on black women, see Donald S. Howard, *The WPA and Federal Relief Policy* (New York: Russell Sage Foundation, 1943), 285–96.

74. ESW to ER, 4 April 1938, ER, Box 741.

75. ESW to Aubrey Williams, 20 September 1938, WPA GSF 237, RG 69.

76. Blackwelder, *Women of the Depression*, 118–23, 172.

77. Hamilton, "National Urban League During the Depression," 111; Dwight Morgan to Thurgood Marshall, 26 August 1937, in Papers of NAACP, Adm. Files C, Box 418, LC.

78. Charles H. Trout, *Boston: The Great Depression and the New Deal* (New York: Oxford University Press, 1977), 191.

79. ESW to E. R. Fryer, [?] October 1936, and ESW to William Zimmerman, 23 December 1936, both in WPA GSF 236, RG 69; Fryer to the author, 9 April 1984, in author's possession; Harry A. Kersey, Jr., *The Florida Seminoles and the New Deal, 1933–1942* (Boca Raton: Florida Atlantic University Press, 1989), 52.

80. Author's conversation with Kenneth Philp (University of Texas, Arlington), 28 June 1984; Sandra Schackel, *Social Housekeepers: Women Shaping Public Policy in New Mexico, 1920–1940* (Albuquerque: University of New Mexico Press, 1992), 150.

81. Schackel, *Social Housekeepers*, 149–51.

82. Forrest, *The Preservation of the Village: New Mexico's Hispanics and the New Deal* (Albuquerque: University of New Mexico Press, 1989), 112–13, 119–24.

83. Lowitt and Beasley, *One-Third of a Nation*, xxiv.

84. Notes on conference (14 January 1937), ESW 1139.2, Box 54.

85. Durant, "Home Rule in the WPA," *Survey Midmonthly* 74 (September 1939): 274. For perspectives on "Social Effects of Relief Policies upon Minority Groups," see the chapter by that title in R. Clyde and Mary K. White, *Research Memorandum on Social Aspects of Relief Policies in the Depression* (New York: Arno Press, 1972).

86. ESW to R. C. Brown, 17 October 1936, WPA Ss (Miss.) 663, RG 69.

87. Chester Davis, quoted in Pete Daniel, *Breaking the Land: The Transformation of Cotton, Tobacco, and Rice Culture Since 1880* (Urbana: University of Illinois Press, 1985), 101.

88. John O'Donnell and Doris Fleeson, "Capital Stuff," *Washington Times*, 24 January 1938; Jerry Mangione, *The Dream and the Deal: The Federal Writers' Project, 1935–1943* (New York: Avon, 1972), 225–26. In an uncharacteristic moment of regret, Bilbo had his diatribe removed from the *Congressional Record* (Mangione, 226).

89. Mellett to ESW, 25 June 1938, ESW 1139.1, Box 5; *Jackson Daily News*, 10 July 1938. Woodward knew Howard W. Odum, the University of North Carolina specialist on regional matters, and attended a banquet of broadcasters with him in Washington in 1936. ESW scrapbook item, ESW 1139.2.

90. *Memphis Press-Scimitar*, 6 August 1938; *Birmingham News*, 26 October 1938; ESW Birmingham speech, ESW 1139.2, Box 63.

91. Ethel Payne, "Mississippi News Letter" (30 November 1938), ESW 1139.1, Box 6.

92. ESW to Louise O. Charlton, 17 January 1938, ESW 1139.1, Box 7.

93. May Thompson Evans to ESW, 12 April 1940, ESW, Box 1, AES; ESW to Niles Trammel, 11 January 1943, ESW 1139.2, Box 14.

94. "Harmon, Francis Stuart," *Who's Who in America* (1932–1933), 1049; ESW to Harmon, 23 March 1944, ESW 1139.1, Box 11; Cohen interview, 7–8, Oral History Project, Lyndon Baines Johnson Library (Austin), copy in Cohen Papers, Box 29, SHSW.

95. ESW to ER, 1 July 1938, ER, Box 741; Beard to ESW, 18 November 1938, ESW 1139.2, Box 2.

96. *Washington Star*, 3 October 1937; ESW to staff, 10 February 1937, ESW 1139.2, Box 54.

97. Interview with Otis Harden, 19 March 1986 (Washington, D.C.).

Notes to Chapter 6

1. ESW to Democratic Women's Regional Conference (Birmingham), July 1936, ESW 1139.2, Box 23

2. *Jackson Daily News*, 27 March 1938; ESW to HLH, 6 April 1938, WPA GSF 210.13.

3. ESW to HLH, 6 April 1938, WPA GSF 210.13; "Women and the WPA," *Woman Worker* 18 (September 1938): 8.

4. ESW to ER, 29 July 1938, HLH, Box 100; *Washington News*, 26 August

1938. ESW to ER, [?] August 1938, ER Box 741; FDR to HLH, 17 August 1938, HLH, Box 100.

5. Price to Mrs. R. R. Hudson, 8 December 1938, ESW 1139.2, Box 4.

6. ESW speech (26 October 1938), ESW 1139.1, Box 19.

7. *REPORT: Division and Women's and Professional Projects,* July 1, 1935–January 1, 1937, ESW 1139.2, Box 40.

8. ESW speech to Good Neighbor League (Columbus, Ohio), 9 October 1936, ESW 1139.2, Box 25.

9. ESW to HLH, 22 September 1937, WPA GSF 210.3, RG 69.

10. Henry L. Kinnear to ESW, 1 July 1936, ESW 1139.2, Box 5; Aubrey Williams to ESW, 3 July 1936, WPA GSF 210.13; *New York Times,* 4 July 1936. There were other federal projects which did not figure as prominently in Woodward's administration as Federal One: Federal No. 2, Historical American Buildings Survey; Federal No. 3, Staffing State Planning Boards; Federal No. 4, Survey of Federal Archives; Federal No. 5, Inspection of Plumbing Installation in Federal Buildings; and Federal No. 6, Historic American Merchant Marine Survey.

11. Owings to HLH, 26 May 1936; Baker to Bruce McClure and Eduard Lindeman, 17 June 1936, both in WPA GSF 230, RG 69.

12. *Fortune* 15 (May 1937), 113; ESW telephone conversation with Kerr, 27 February 1936, ESW 1139.2, Box 49; ESW memorandum to HLH, 27 April 1936, ESW 1139.1, Box 22.

13. Monty N. Penkower, *The Federal Writers' Project: A Study in Government Patronage of the Arts* (Urbana: University of Illinois Press, 1969), 40; Jerre Mangione, *The Dream and the Deal: The Federal Writers' Project, 1935–1943* (New York: Avon Books, 1972); Jane De Hart Mathews, *The Federal Theatre, 1935–1939: Plays, Relief, and Politics* (Princeton, N.J.: Princeton University Press, 1967); and Kathleen O'Connor McKinzie, "Writers on Relief, 1935–1942" (Ph.D. dissertation, Indiana University, 1970).

14. ER is quoted by Holger Cahill, COHC, II, 385.

15. Cahill interview, Archives of American Art (Washington, D.C.), 5–7.

16. William F. McDonald, *Federal Relief Administration and the Arts* (Athens: Ohio State University Press, 1969), 165. There was so much resistance by Four Arts participants to McDonald's completion of a work begun in 1942, that publication was long delayed. Nevertheless, I have relied upon it for dates, names, and events because the book is encyclopedic in that regard. Cahill wrote Woodward of his delight that she "wanted to get into the fight" that he and Flanagan were making against McDonald's manuscript, but nothing else in her papers indicates a role she may have taken [Cahill to ESW, 16 October (?), ESW 1139.2, Box 3].

17. Wolfe to ESW, 11 July 1936; ESW to MWD, 16 July 1936, both in DNC-WD, Box 27. Dewson's comment is penciled in on Woodward's letter.

18. Robert Asher to ESW [?] January 1936, WPA GSF 210.13; ESW statement, 2 July 1936, ESW 1139.1, Box 22.

19. See the many memoranda from ESW in WPA GSF 210.13 (August 1936); ESW to HLH, 12 November 1936, WPA GSF 230; McDonald, *Federal Administration and Arts*, 178–9.

20. ESW to HLH, 30 December 1936, WPA GSF 210.13; ESW to HLH, 14 January 1937, WPA GSF 210AAAA; ESW to Mary Isham, 3 January 1937, WPA GSF 210.

21. McDonald, *Federal Administration and the Arts*, 204–05, 208–10.

22. Elsie L. George, "The Woman Appointees of the Roosevelt and Truman Administrations" (Ph.D. dissertation, American University, 1972), 168–69; ESW to Lula Scott, Izetta Miller, Blanche Ralston, and Florence Kerr, 23 October 1936, WPA GSF 210AAAA, RG 69. As the white-collar adjunct of the Workers' Alliance, City Projects Council members were left-wing. Organized by the Socialist party in 1935, the Workers' Alliance was captured by Communists who came into the Alliance when the latter united with the Unemployed Councils. Malcolm Goldstein, *The Political Stage: American Drama and Theater of the Great Depression* (New York: Oxford University Press, 1974), 287, 290.

23. McKinzie, *The New Deal for Artists* (Princeton, N.J.: Princeton University Press, 1973), 94; ESW telephone conversation with O'Day, 1 July 1937, ESW 1139.2, Box 53.

24. Richard Polenberg, *War and Society: The United States, 1941–1945* (Philadelphia: Lippincott, 1972), 220.

25. ESW telephone conversation with Somervell, 21 September 1936, ESW 1139.2, Box 52.

26. Mathews, *Federal Theatre*, 122–24.

27. Cronin Oral History, FTP Archives, George Mason University; Goldstein, *The Political Stage*, 263; John Houseman, *Run-Through: A Memoir* (New York: Simon & Schuster, 1972), 225, 258; J. E. Vacha, "The Case of the Runaway Opera: The Federal Theatre and Marc Blitzstein's 'The Cradle Will Rock'," *New York History* 62 (April 1981): 138–50. According to a Welles biographer, unconfirmed rumors circulated that Roosevelt personally ordered that Hopkins's ruling to close *Cradle* be respected. Frank Brady, *Citizen Welles: A Biography of Orson Welles* (New York: Scribners, 1989), 114.

28. Richard France, *The Theater of Orson Welles* (Lewisburg, Pa.: Bucknell University Press, 1977), 101–104.

29. ESW to Williams, 25 June 1937, WPA GSF 210.13, RG 69.

30. McKinzie, *New Deal for Artists*, 101; ESW telephone conversation with Ryan, 29 July 1937, ESW 1139.2, Box 53.

31. ESW telephone conversations with Cronin, 5, 8 July 1937; with Hardy, 9 July 1937, all in ESW 1139.2, Box 53.

32. Williams is quoted by Mangione, *The Dream and the Deal*, 168–69; ESW telephone conversation with Niles, 7 July 1937, and with Cronin, 8 July 1937.

33. ESW telephone conversation with Mallon, 21 October 1937, ESW

telephone conversation with Miller, 13 August 1937, both in ESW 1139.2, Box 53; Philip Barber Oral History, FTP Archives, George Mason University.

34. ESW telephone conversation with Margaret Clark (7 July 1937), ESW 1139.2, Box 53.

35. ESW telephone conversation with Niles, 29 July 1937, ESW 1139.2, Box 53.

36. Mathews, *Federal Theatre*, 126–28; Goldstein, *The Political State*, 287; Pierre de Rohan, "Federal Theatre's First Federal Summer Theatre . . . A Report," copy at FTP Archives, George Mason University; ESW telephone conversation with Flanagan, 29 July 1937, ESW 1139.2, Box 53.

37. ESW to Regional Supervisors, 24 February 1938, WPA GSF 231; ESW to HLH, 29 March 1938, WPA GSF 210AAAA; ESW to ER, 27 November 1937, ER 724.

38. McDonald, *Federal Administration and the Arts*, 231–32; ESW to Aubrey Williams, 11 April 1938; ESW to HLH, 27 April 1938, both in WPA GSF 210.1, RG 69.

39. Note to James Roosevelt (11 April 1938) attached to correspondence file of ESW requests, WPA GSF 210AAAA; FDR to ER, 25 February 1938, ER to ESW, 26 February 1938, both in ER, Box 741; ESW to ER, 5 May 1938, WPA GSF 237.

40. Mangione, *The Dream and the Deal*, 653; George McJimsey, *Harry Hopkins: Ally of the Poor and Defender of Democracy* (Cambridge, Mass.: Harvard University Press, 1987), 118–21.

41. McDonald, *Federal Administration and the Arts*, 234–35; William E. Leuchtenburg, *Franklin D. Roosevelt and the New Deal: 1932–1940* (New York: Harper Torchbook, 1963), 249–50, 257; Federal Works Agency, *Final Report on WPA Program, 1935–1943* (Washington, D.C.: U.S. Government Printing Office, 1946), 28–29.

42. George, "Woman Appointees of the Roosevelt and Truman Administrations," 177.

43. Mathews, *Federal Theatre*, 171–77; MWD to ESW, 8 May 1938, WPA GSF 300, RG 69.

44. Mathews, *Federal Theatre*, 178, 191–92, 211.

45. McDonald, *Federal Administration and the Arts*, 565; John O'Connor and Lorraine Brown, *The Federal Theatre Project: Free, Adult, and Uncensored* (London: Eyre Methuen, 1986), 178.

46. *Raleigh (N.C.) News and Observer* 20 August 1938; May Campbell to ESW, 26 August 1938, ESW 1139.1, Box 6.

47. Two unpublished studies of the FWP are Janelle Findlay-Warren's "Of Tears and Need: The Federal Music Project, 1935–1943" (Ph.D. dissertation, George Washington University, 1973), and Cornelius B. Canon, "The Federal Music Project of the Works Progress Administration: Music in a Democracy" (Ph.D. dissertation, University of Minnesota, 1963).

48. Transcript of ESW conference with Arts Directors, 15 September 1937, ESW 1139.2, Box 54.

49. Quoted in Findlay-Warren, "Of Tears and Need," 204.

50. Findlay-Warren, "Of Tears and Need," 258.

51. The origin of the HRS, like that of all Federal One projects, is much more involved than is suggested by this brief sketch. The fullest study on the HRS is Edward F. Barese, "The Historical Records Survey: A Nation Acts to Save Its Memory" (Ph.D. dissertation, George Washington University, 1980).

52. McDonald, *Federal Administration and the Arts*, 764–65. Evans's brief against Woodward is quoted by David L. Smiley, "A Slice of Life in Depression America: The Records of the Historical Records Survey," *Prologue* 3 (Winter 1971): 156.

53. ESW confernece with Arts Directors, 27 September 1937, ESW 1139.2, Box 54.

54. Ray A. Billington, "Government and the Arts: The WPA Experience," *American Quarterly* 13 (Winter 1961): 468–69; George Biddle, "Art Under Five Years of Federal Patronage," *American Scholar* 9 (July 1940): 334–35.

55. Biddle, "Art Under Five Years," 334–35; McDonald, *Federal Administration and the Arts*, 467–69.

56. McDonald, *Federal Administration and the Arts*, 395.

57. Cahill, COHC memoir, 461–62.

58. Hallie Flanagan, *Arena: The Story of the Federal Theatre* (New York: Duell, Sloan and Pearce, 1940), 72; Mathews *Federal Theatre*, 112; ESW telephone conversations with Hassett, Dewson, and Farnsworth (8 September 1936), all in ESW 1139.2, Box 49. The sale of the offending papers was simply moved out to the sidewalk in front of the Biltmore.

59. ESW telephone conversation with Farnsworth, 24 September 1936, ESW 1139.2, Box 49. Regarding an FTP play in Seattle, Farnsworth told Woodward, "the interest of the people in Seattle was to see whether it was dirty or not and that if it wasn't dirty they would feel they were gypped, and if it was dirty there would be trouble." (Telephone conversation, 24 September 1936).

60. ESW telephone conversation with Miller, 10 September 1936, ESW 1139.2, Box 50; Flanagan, *Arena*, 393.

61. ESW, Niles, and Morris telephone conversation, 12 October 1936, ESW 1139.2, Box 50. Mayor Kelly had earlier blocked the opening of "Model Tenements" (1936) which was then abandoned by the FTP. O'Connor and Brown, *The Federal Theatre Project*, 29.

62. ESW telephone conversation with Dunham, 12 October 1936, ESW 1139.2, Box 49.

63. ESW telephone conversation with Hunter, 14 October 1936, ESW 1139.2, Box 49; ESW telephone conversation with David Niles, 14 October 1936, ESW 1139.2, Box 50.

64. ESW telephone conversation wtih Flanagan, 3 September 1936; ESW telephone conversation with Dewson, 9 September 1936; ESW telephone conversation with Hassett, 9 September 1936, all in ESW 1139.2, Box 50.

65. Flanagan, *Arena*, 111.

66. ESW telephone conversation with David Niles, 14 October 1936; ESW 1139.2, Box 50; ESW telephone conversation with Flanagan and Niles, 28 October 1936, ESW 1139.2, Boxes 49 and 50.

67. Mathews, *Federal Theatre*, 99–100.

68. Conference Notes, 12 January 1937, ESW 1139.2, Box 54.

69. Mathews, *Federal Theatre*, 114.

70. O'Connor and Brown, *Federal Theatre Project*, 28; Miller to Lawrence Morris, 21 December 1937, WPA GSF 210, RG 69.

71. ESW telephone conversation with Major L.S. Dillon, 7 February 1938, ESW 1139.1, Box 5

72. ESW telephone conversation with Jerry Voorhis, 18 October 1938; O'Connor and Brown, *Federal Theatre Project*, 28–29; Findlay-Warren, "Of Tears and Need," 249. One FTP employee who regained her job through Woodward's intervention was a woman dismissed to provide a job for a supporter of William Gibbs McAdoo (Jesse E. Jacobson to ESW, 27 September 1938, ESW 1139.1, Box 6).

73. Penkower, *Federal Writers' Project*, 52n.

74. Penkower, *Federal Writers' Project*, 18–19; McKinzie, "Writers on Relief," 171.

75. ESW to Cronin, 17 March 1937, WPA GSF 210.3, RG 69; ESW telephone conversation with Alsberg, 18 September 1936, ESW 1139.2, Box 48.

76. ESW telephone conversation with Reed Harris and Lawrence Morris, 3 August 1937, ESW 1139.2, Box 53; ESW speech to regional arts administrators, 22 June 1938, ESW 1139.1, Box 25.

77. Blair Bolles, "Federal Writers' Project," *Saturday Review of Literature* 18 (9 July 1938): 18

78. Mangione, *Dream and the Deal*, 217; ESW telephone conversation with Harris, 10 August 1937; ESW telephone conversation with Alsberg, 11 August 1937, both in ESW 1139.2, Box 53. Mangione, who seems not to have cared for Woodward, described her arrival "attired in fluttering organdy" and her "last moment" seizure of the book from Alsberg so that she could snare the "limelight" (216). The telephone conversation with Alsberg on August 11 indicates he intended that she make the presentation.

79. ESW speech in ESW 1139.1, Box 29.

80. For accounts of the uproar, see Billington, "Government and the Arts," 477–78; and Penkower, *Federal Writers' Project*, 101–107.

81. McKinzie, "Writers on Relief," 90; Bolles, "Federal Writers' Project," 18; ESW memorandum to HLH, 24 April 1937, WPA GSF 210.13, RG 69.

82. Malvina Schneider to ESW, 13 December 1934; ER, Box 639; ER to ESW, 13 February 1935, FERA NSF 375.3, RG 69; ER to ESW, 14 March 1935, ER, Box 672.

83. Copy of ESW statement, 21 January 1938; Sirovich to ESW, 18 January 1938, both in WPA GSF 210AAAA, RG 69.

84. U.S. Congress, House. 75 Cong., 3 Sess. (1938), *Hearings* before the Committee on Patents on H. J. Res. 79 (Department of Science, Art, and Literature), 107 (Sirovich quotation); *New York Times*, 9 February 1938.

85. *Cong. Record*, 75 Cong., 3 Sess., 9491–99 (15 June 1938).

86. U.S. Congress, Senate. 75 Cong., 3 Sess., (1938), *Hearings* before Subcommittee of Committee on Education and Labor on S. 3296 (Bureau of Fine Arts), 63–70.

87. ESW telephone conversation with Paul Edwards, 14 February 1938, ESW 1139.2, Box 53. For a discussion of opposition among professionals to the bill, see McKinzie, *New Deal for Artists*, 151–55; Grace Overmyer, *Government and the Arts* (New York: W.W. Norton, 1939), 191–207; Flanagan, *Arena*, 325–26.

88. ESW to Bancroft Association (undated), ESW 1139.1. Box 23; ESW to Town Hall Club (7 June 1938), ESW 1139.1, Box 25. Among the many examinations of the New Deal patronage of the arts that authenticate Woodward's prophecies on the legacy of the Four Arts is Gary O. Larsen, *The Reluctant Patron: The United States Government and the Arts* (Philadelphia: University of Pennsylvania Press, 1983).

89. Walter Goodman, *The Committee: The Extraordinary Career of the House Committee on Un-American Activities* (New York: Farrar, Straus & Giroux, 1968), 26–27, 44–45; McKinzie, "Writers on Relief," 205–06 (quotation on Dies); D. A. Saunders, "Dies Committee: First Phase," *Public Opinion Quarterly* 3 (April 1939): 225–38.

90. House of Representatives, 75 Cong., 3 Sess., *Hearings*, Special Committee on Un-American Activities on H. Res. 282, I, 775–829; Mathews, *Federal Theatre*, 200–206.

91. *New York Times*, 17 September 1938.

92. Mathews, *Federal Theatre*, 210, 212; Woodward to MWD (10 October 1938) is quoted by Elsie L. George, "The Woman Appointees of the Roosevelt and Truman Administrations: A Study of Their Impact and Effectiveness" (Ph.D. dissertation, American University, 1972), 143.

93. *New York Times*, 27 November 1938.

94. HUAC, *Hearings*, IV, 3109–21 (19 November 1938). Jerre Mangione provides the McCoy quotation and much of the incriminating dialogue among Dies, Lazell, and others who testified in an executive session. Mangione is convinced that Lazell was an informer "avid to see the Project killed" [*The Dream and the Deal*, 304–06)]. Woodward remained charitable in her opinion of Lazell. When questions about her continuing accusations began to haunt Eleanor Roosevelt, she wrote Woodward in 1939, "I would like to know the truth about the whole thing. Please be honest." Woodward replied that she believed Lazell's allegations were due to a long illness and her being "worried to death about finances." ER to ESW, 13 April 1939, ESW to ER, 10, 14 April 1939, ESW 1139.2, Box 12.

95. Flanagan, *Arena*, 339.

96. George, "Woman Appointees," 183.

97. *Hearings*, IV, 2905 (6 December 1938). For a profile of the committee, see Raymond P. Brandt, "The Dies Committee: An Appraisal," *Atlantic Monthly* 165 (February 1940): 232–37.

98. *Hearings*, IV, 2729–30 (5 December 1938).

99. *Hearings*, IV, 2734, 2750–56.

100. *Hearings*, IV, 2764–65.

101. *Hearings*, IV, 2776–77, 2780–83.

102. *Hearings*, IV, 2796–2807.

103. *Hearings*, IV, 2822.

104. *Hearings*, IV, 2827–28, 2837.

105. *Washington Post*, 6 December 1938; *New York Times*, 6, 7 December 1938; *Jackson Daily News*, 11 December 1938.

106. MWD to ESW, 6 December 1938, ESW 1139.1, Box 6; author's interview with Evans, 15 September 1984 (Washington, D.C.).

107. Flanagan, *Arena*, 339; Cahill COHC, 385; Rhodes, Bosworth, and Barber Oral Histories, FTP Archives, George Mason University. Barber added that Woodward "was a horse's ass anyway," but he had been annoyed by her attempt to involve him in dealing with the *New York Times'* adverse coverage of FTP administrative difficulties. Historians of Federal One are in basic agreement that Woodward's appearance before HUAC was weak. Jerre Mangione described her as "a valiant and sometimes tenacious witness" who simply did not have first-hand information (*Dream and the Deal*, 308). Jane De Hart Mathews wrote that "with good reason" Woodward was not pleased with her performance (*Federal Theatre*, 216), while Richard McKinzie deemed her testimony "a mistake" (*New Deal for Artists*, 157). Kathleen McKinzie considered "Mrs. Woodward's decision to be the chief witness was not a wise one" ("Writers on Relief", 216).

108. ESW to HLH, 17 December 1938, ESW 1139.2, Box 17; ESW to David Niles, 7 December 1938, ESW to Morris, 27 December 1938, both in WPA GSF 210.13, RG 69; ESW to Robert Donner, 5 October, 2 November, 8 December 1938, all in WPA GSF 210, RG 69.

109. Cole to ESW, 28 November 1938, ESW 1139.1, Box 6.

110. *New York Times*, 21 December 1938; *Washington Herald*, 21 December 1938; *Washington Post*, 23 December 1938. Harrington died less than two years later (1940) whereupon *Survey Midmonthly* noted that he had seen the WPA "primarily as work, secondarily as relief" (October 1940, p. 197).

111. Miller to ESW, 29 July 1939, ESW 1139.1, Box 9; Isham to ESW, 15 January 1939, ESW 1139.2, Box 5; Davidson Oral History, FTP Archives, George Mason University.

112. *Jackson Daily News*, 25 December 1938.

113. ESW to HLH, 22 December 1938, HLH, Box 100.

Notes to Chapter 7

1. Altmeyer, *The Formative Years of Social Security* (Madison: University of Wisconsin Press, 1968), 7, 45; AJA to MWD, 6 July 1935, Social Security Board Papers, Chairman of the Board Files (1935–1942), RG 47, NA.

2. *New York Times*, 20 Feb. 1937; interview with Wilbur Cohen, 4 March 1984 (Austin, Texas).

3. *New York Times*, 21 December 1938. For a description of Dewson's tenure on the Board and for the private reasons that she resigned, see Susan Ware, *Partner and I: Molly Dewson, Feminism, and New Deal Politics* (New Haven, Conn.: Yale University Press, 1971), 233–37.

4. MWD to Beyer, 31 January 1939, Clara Beyer Papers, Box 4, AES; Ware, *Partner and I* (other Dewson quotations, 238–39); ESW to MWD, 20 December 1938, in Dewson Scrapbook on Social Security Board; Mary W. Dewson, "An Aid to the End," II, 225 (an unpublished autobiography), both in Dewson Papers.

5. Martha H. Swain, "Pat Harrison and the Social Security Act of 1935," *Southern Quarterly* 15 (October 1976): 1–14; Drew Pearson, "Merry-Go-Round," *Nashville Tennessean*, 25 December 1938.

6. ESW to FDR, 21 December 1938, FDR OF 1710.

7. Pauline Frederick, "Career Women in Washington Fill Men's Jobs," *New York Times*, 18 December 1938, II; *Saginaw* (Mich.) *News*, 21 December 1938, clipping in ESW 1139.2, Box 69; *Pathfinder*, 14 January 1939. Frances Perkins, at $15,000 was the highest paid of the three. Mrs. J. Borden (Daisy) Harriman, as Minister to Norway, also drew $10,000, as had SSB member Molly Dewson.

8. *Washington Times*, 30 December 1938.

9. *Baltimore Sun*, 21 December 1938; R. M. Barrett to W. L. Mitchell, 23 December 1938, General Correspondence, Executive Directors Files, 1941–1948, RG 47.

10. ESW to AJA, 28 December 1938, Chairman of the Board Files, 1935–1942, RG 47; ESW to ER, 28 December 1938, ER, Box 741; *New York Times*, 31 December 1938; "My Day," *Washington Times*, 31 December 1938.

11. Stern memorandum, Chairman of the Board Files, 1935–1942, RG 47; ESW statement (30 December 1938), ESW 1139.1, Box 6; *Chicago Times*, 27 December 1938; *Washington Evening Star*, 30 December 1938.

12. Bernard Braxton to ESW, 30 December 1938, ESW 1139.1, Box 7.

13. *New York Times*, 3, 13 January 1939; *Jackson Daily News*, 10 January 1939; *Cong. Record*, 76 Cong., 1 Sess., 236 (12 January 1939).

14. Edwin E. Witte, *The Development of the Social Security Act* (Madison: University of Wisconsin Press, 1963), 194–95; James Leiby, "Social Security at 50," *Public Welfare* 43 (Fall 1985): 9–10. Further meaning can be attached to the fact that the Committee on Economic Security, at the urging of Harry Hopkins, was quartered in the Walker-Johnson Building where the FERA was located (Witte, 13–14).

15. ESW to ER, 31 August 1938, WPA GSF 236, RG 69. Helpful in understanding work relief vis-à-vis social security are: Eveline Burns, *Toward Social Security* (New York: Whittlesay House, 1936), 148–51; William Bremer, *Depression Winters: New York Social Workers and the New Deal* (Philadelphia: Temple University Press, 1984), 142–43; and Lewis Merriam, *Relief and Social Security* (Washington, D.C.: Brookings Institution, 1946). An illuminating critique is Nancy Rose, "Work Relief in the 1930s and the Origins of the Social Security Act," *Social Service Review* 63 (March 1989): 63–91.

16. Charles McKinley and Robert W. Frase, *Launching Social Security: A Capture and Record Account, 1935–1937* (Madison: University of Wisconsin Press, 1970), 12–13; Altmeyer, *Formative Years*, 45–47; Altmeyer, "Social Security Board," *New International Yearbook*, 1939 (New York: Funk & Wagnalls, 1940), 707–708.

17. Altmeyer, *Formative Years*, vii–x; McKinley and Frase, *Launching*, 385; W. Andrew Achenbaum, "Arthur Joseph Altmeyer," *Biographical Dictionary of Social Welfare in America* (Westport, Conn.: Greenwood Press, 1986), 25–27; telephone interview with Ida Merriam, 28 December 1989 (Washington, D.C.).

18. Author's interview with Abe Bortz, SSA historian, 13 June 1983 (Woodlawn, MD). Hoey "led Woodward," according to Roy Wnykoop [telephone interview, 13 June 1983 (Washington, D.C.)].

19. Altmeyer, *Formative Years*, 90–92, 106; Robert M. Ball, "The 1939 Amendments to the Social Security Act and What Followed," in *Report of the Committee on Economic Security of 1935: Fiftieth Anniversary Edition*, 166–67.

20. Edward D. Berkowitz, "The First Social Security Crisis," *Prologue* 15 (Fall 1983): 133, 137; ESW, "Next Steps in Social Security," *DD* 16 (February 1939): 12, 28.

21. MWD to ESW, 7 August 1939, ESW 1139.1, Box 9; AJA to Albert Woodward, Jr., 17 November 1971, copy in possession of author; author's interview with Cohen, 4 March 1984.

22. Martha Derthick, *Policymaking for Social Security* (Washington, D.C.: Brookings Institution, 1979), 45. The others were the 1935 act and the 1950 amendments that added coverage for domestic and farm workers, some professional and self-employed individuals, and optional coverage for many state employees.

23. ESW to Murphy, 9 August 1939; Murphy to ESW, 2 September 1939, both in ESW 1139.1, Box 9.

24. *Birmingham Post*, 7 August 1939; Radio text, ESW 1139.1, Box 26.

25. Willard F. Bond, *I Had a Friend; An Autobiography* (Kansas City, Mo.: E. L. Mendenhall, 1958), 174–75; J. A. Thigpen, "Twentieth Anniversary," *The Welfare Brief* (Mississippi DPW) 2 (April 1956): 122. The Mississippi act was written with the assistance of Leonard Calhoun, a native son on loan to the state from the SSB.

26. Altmeyer, *Formative Years*, 78–79, 138; Bound copy, Informal Notes of Board Meeting, 13 December 1940, RG 47; Blanche Coll interview with Cohen (19 October 1985), copy in possession of author.

27. *Jackson Daily News*, 22, 23 August 1939; *Winston County Journal*, 25 August 1939; Telephone memorandum for Edwin Watson, 3 August 1939, FDR OF 1710.

28. Informal Notes of Board Meeting, 15, 22 September 1939, RG 47.

29. Sillers to Paul B. Johnson, 14 March 1940, Miscellaneous Folder; Sillers to Harrison, 7 July 1940, "Public Welfare, 1940–1942" folder, both in Walter Sillers Papers, Delta State University Library (Cleveland, Mississippi).

30. ESW to W. L. Mitchell, 27 June 1940, Files of the Office of the Commissioner, 1935–1940; ESW to Hoey, 27 July 1940, Central Files of SSB (1935–1947); Informal Notes of Board Meeting (26, 30 July, 6 Aug. 1940); Transcript, ESW and Bond (1 August 1940), Files of the Office of the Commissioner, 1935–1940, all in RG 47.

31. Sillers to ESW, 17 August 1940, "Public Welfare, 1940–1942," folder, Sillers Papers; Informal Notes of Board Meeting (16 August 1940), RG 47.

32. ESW to Sillers, 17, 21 August 1940, "Public Welfare, 1940–1942" folder, Sillers Papers; Informal Notes of Board Meeting (27 August 1940), RG 47.

33. ESW to Sillers, 21 August 1940; Sillers to ESW, 7 July 1941, "Public Welfare, 1940–1942" folder, Sillers Papers; Informal Notes of Board Meeting (17 February 1941), RG 47. The Board discussed the Georgia imbroglio on April 22, 1941.

34. Sillers to ESW, 12 Sept. 1940, "Public Welfare, 1940–1942" folder, Sillers Papers; Pearson, "Merry-Go-Round," *Nashville Tennessean*, 7 September 1939; ESW to FDR, 17 July 1941, ESW 1139.2, Box 12. An unconfirmed rumor appeared in an unsigned column in a Washington newspaper that friends were touting Woodward as a gubernatorial candidate in 1939. *Washington Times-Herald* (16 March 1938). She apparently took no notice of the matter.

35. *Jackson Daily News*, 5 November 1939; ESW to Jane Hoey, 24 November 1939, ESW 1139.2, Box 4.

36. Bond, *First 50 Years*, 16; SSB Minutes (28 February 1941), copy in ESW 1139.2, Box 17; Frances Fox Piven and Richard A. Cloward, *Regulating the Poor: The Functions of Public Welfare* (New York: Vintage Books, 1972), 116–17.

37. Geoffrey May to ESW, 13 May 1939, ESW 1139.1, Box 8.

38. Author's interview with Cohen, 4 March 1984; telephone interview with Wynkoop.

39. McKinley and Frase, *Launching*, 385–86, 428–29; Author's interview with Wilbur Cohen, 4 March 1984; Informal Notes of Board Meeting 24 March, 22 September, 7 November, 4, 12, 15, 19 December 1939, 23 Feb. 1945, RG 47.

40. Lavinia Engle COHC, II, 122; "Lavinia Engle of the LWV," *Washington Post*, 16 March 1969.

41. Informal Notes of Board Meeting, 26 January 1945, RG 47.

42. Informal Notes of Board Meeting, 17 March 1942; Sadie L. McCain (North Carolina) to ESW, 19 February 1941, ESW 1139.1, Box 10; "Federation Support of the Merit System," undated statement in ESW 1139.2, Box 61.

43. Schlesinger Library interview with Merriam, quoted in *Raleigh* (N.C.) *Times*, 26 November, 1987.

44. Edward Berkowitz, "Wilbur Cohen and American Social Reform" *Social Work* 34 (July 1989): 293.

45. ESW to Cohen, 16 June 1941, Executive Director Files (1941–1948), RG 47; author's interview with Cohen, 4 March 1984. Examining Woodward's correspondence makes clear Cohen's authorship of much of the material that appeared under her name.

46. Mary Anderson, "Women Workers and the Social Security Program," *DD* 13 (July 1936): 40.

47. See Jean T. D. Bandler, "Family Protection and Women's Issues of Social Security," *Social Work* 34 (July 1939): 308; also Gail B. King, "Women and Social Security: An Applied History Overview," *Social Science History* 6 (Spring 1982): 223–27.

48. There are a number of extremely critical retrospective studies on the way in which the 1935 act and 1939 amendments exacerbated the "feminization of poverty" and imposed discriminations against women, vestiges of which remain even today. The most trenchant of the works is that of Mimi Abramovitz, *Regulating the Lives of Women: Social Welfare Policy from Colonial Times to the Present* (Boston: South End Press, 1988), 253; chap. 8 is particularly strong.

49. Blair to ESW, 29 December 1938, Box 6; Huse to ESW, 9 March 1939, Box 8.

50. Dickinson to ESW, 23 March 1945, General Cooorespondence, Executive Director's Files (1941–1948), RG 47. A bound volume of thirty of Woodward's speeches is in the library of the Health and Human Services Department in Washington, D.C., and in the library of the Social Security Administration headquarters, Woodlawn, Maryland. In addition, ESW 1139.1, Box 10 contains copies of many of her SSB presentations.

51. ESW, "Business Women in a Democracy," Virginia Federation of BPW Clubs, 21 October 1939 (Richmond); Informal Notes of Board Meeting, 23 September 1939, RG 47; author's interview with Ewan Clague, 23 June 1983 (Washington, D.C.).

52. Radio text (10 January 1940) in compilation of ESW speeches; ER, "My Day," 12 January, 21 September 1939.

53. ER, "My Day," 21 September 1939.

54. *Washington Times Herald*, 24 July 1940. A tape of the fifteen-minute broadcast (no. 48–388) is in the National Archives.

55. ESW, "A Family Kept Together," *American Way* (organ of the Emigrant Industrial Savings Bank), Fall 1944: 6–7.

56. ESW to ER, 26 August 1940, ER to ESW, 30 August 1940, both in ER, Box 795; ESW, "Schedule for September and October 1940," in WD-DNC (1927–1944).

57. *San Francisco Chronicle* 13 September 1940; *Los Angeles Citizen*, 27 September 1940.

58. *Salt Lake City Tribune*, 29 September 1940; *Denver Post*, 1 October 1940.

59. Witte, *Development of Social Security Act*, 152–53; Thomas H. Eliot in Katie Louchheim, ed., *The Making of the New Deal; The Insiders Speak* (Cambridge, Mass.: Harvard University Press, 1983), 165.

60. Brenda Faye Clegg, "Black Female Domestics During the Great Depression in New York City, 1936–1940" (Ph.D. dissertation, University of Michigan, 1983), 111–13; Abramovitz, *Regulating the Lives of Women*, 234.

61. Merrill G. Murray (Assistant Director, OASI) to ESW, 3 April 1941, ESW 1139.2, Box 17; Memorandum "OASI for Domestic Workers," ESW 1139.2, Box 54.

62. ESW, "Social Security-In War and Peace" (27 January 1943), Bound Speeches; AJA to ESW, 6 February 1943, General Correspondence, Executive Director Files (1941–1948), RG 47.

63. ESW, "Social Security Serves the Home, *Journal of Home Economics* 35 (March 1943): 149–50; ESW, "A Bridge to the Future," *IW* 22 (May 1943): 142ff; ESW, "They Want More Social Security," *IW* 24 (January 1945): 11ff.

64. For example: ESW, "Social Security for the Professional Woman," *Practical Home Economics* 20 (September 1942): 284–86.

65. ESW to Nettie Nimock, 28 February 1945, ESW 1139.2, Box 5.

66. On dual entitlement, see W. Andrew Achenbaum, *Social Security; Visions and Revisions* (Cambridge: Cambridge University Press, 1986), 127–28, and Abramovitz, *Regulating the Lives of Women*, 258–59.

67. *Woman Worker* 21 (November 1941): 7–8; Memorandum, "For Mrs. Woodward's Reply to Miss Dorothy Crook" (November 1941), SSB Central Files, 1935–1937, RG 47.

68. The author is grateful to Blanche D. Coll for making available an advance manuscript copy of several chapters of her book, *Safety Net: Welfare, 1929–1979* (New Brunswick, N.J.: Rutgers University Press, forthcoming). Chap. 5 describes the complex subject of family budgeting vs. flat grants. See also Coll, "Public Assistance: Reviving the Original Comprehensive Concept of Social Security," in Gerald D. Nash, Noel H. Pugach, and Richard F. Tomasson, eds., *Social Security: The First Half Century* (Albuquerque: University of New Mexico Press, 1988), 226–28.

69. The whole question is so complex, and the debate shifted so often, that readers are advised to consult Blanche Coll's writings on the subject of flat grants versus family budgeting.

70. In Altmeyer's words, "Now Mr. Bigge's worries are two, the legal questions and family snooping. Mrs. Woodward, what are yours?" She answered, "My worries are both also." Informal Notes of Board Meeting, 29 June 1940, RG 47.

71. ESW to Gladys Tillett, Tillett Papers, Southern Historical Collection, Wilson Library, University of North Carolina (Chapel Hill); ESW to Bennett Clark, ESW to Eastland, both 3 July 1943, ESW 1139.1, Box 10; *New York Times*, 7 July 1943.

72. ESW Memorandum to AJA, 4 February 1943, General Correspondence (1941–1948), Executive Director Files, RG 47.

73. ESW to ER, 28 November 1942, Central Files, SSB, 1935–1947, RG 47; Informal Notes of Board Meeting, 8 December 1942, RG 47; "My Day," *Washington Times*, 8 December 1942. Although she was no longer with the relief program, Woodward continued to handle the requests for cash and Christmas gifts that Eleanor Roosevelt received. Malvina Thompson to ESW, 13 December 1944; ESW to Thompson, 5 February 1945, both in ESW 1139.2, Box 11.

74. Witte, *Development of Social Security Act*, 153; Derthick, *Policymaking for Social Security*, 49, 263–64.

75. ESW, "What Social Security Can Mean for the South," *Social Security Bulletin* 8 (July 1945), 2–5. The piece was actually written by Martha Ring and Mary Ross under the supervision of Wilbur Cohen. On the South, see Achenbaum, *Social Security*, 42.

76. Martha H. Swain, "Pat Harrison and the Social Security Act," 3, 13; Blanche Coll interview with Wilbur Cohen, 19 October 1985, use by permission of Coll.

77. ESW, "Soil Security and Social Security," *Soil Conservation* (Soil Conservation Service) 11 (December 1945): 128–33; ESW, "Social Security-Today and Tomorrow," speech to Mississippi Conference of Social Work (29 April 1943), Bound Volume.

78. See Jill Quadagno, *The Transformation of Old Age Security: Class and Politics in the American Welfare State* (Chicago: University of Chicago Press, 1988), 115–16, 128–29, 132–37.

79. Altmeyer, *Formative Years*, 146, 154; Derthick, *Policymaking for Social Security*, 26.

80. *Milwaukee Journal*, 19 March 1940. She had spoken to the Milwaukee BPW Club.

81. ESW to ER, 12 January 1944, ER, Box 937; ESW to ER, 22 January 1945, ER, Box 948; ESW to ER, 16 March 1945, ER, Box 3777.

82. Derthick, *Policymaking for Social Security*, 317; *New Orleans Times-Picayune*, 12 March 1943; ESW, "They Want More Social Security," *IW* 24 (January 1945): 11, 26.

83. ESW to ER, 18 May 1939, ER Box 767; Informal Notes of Board Meeting, 18 November 1942, RG 47.

84. ESW to AJA, 1 September 1943, Files of the Executive Director, 1941–1948, RG 47.

85. Robert Huse to ESW, 24 January 1945, Files of the Executive Director, 1941–1947, RG 47; ESW to Wilbur Cohen, 23 February 1944, ESW 1139.1, Box 11.

86. ESW to Francis Harmon, 23 March 1944, ESW 1139.1, Box 11.

87. ESW to Stern, 27 March 1944, Stern to ESW, 14 April 1944, both in Executive Director Files, 1941–1948, RG 47. A number of sharply worded memoranda exchanged between Woodward and Stern.

88. Author's interview with Wilbur Cohen (4 March 1984); ESW to Bane, 20 July 1944, Frank Bane Papers, Box 6, University of Virginia Library (Charlottesville).

89. ESW telephone conversation with Bache, 3 March 1945, ESW 1139.2, Box 69. When the New York State Federation rescinded the charter of one of the clubs that admitted black members, the club instituted a lawsuit. Susan B. Anthony II, *Out of the Kitchen—Into the War: Woman's Winning Role in the Nation's Drama* (New York: Stephen Daye, 1943), 225–26.

90. ESW to Robert Huse, 5 February 1945, ESW 1139.1, Box 11; *IW* 24 (April 1945): 108–09, 118.

91. ESW to Oscar Powell, 7 March 1945, ESW 1139.2, Box 28.

92. *IW* 25 (August 1946): 219–20.

93. ESW to ER, 10 July 1946, ER, Box 3777.

94. ESW, "Informal Remarks at Last Meeting of SSB," ESW 1139.2, Box 61.

95. AJA to Albert Woodward, Jr., 17 November 1971, copy in possession of author; AJA to Elsie L. George, 25 January 1972, AJA 400, Box 1; Altmeyer COHC Memoir, 63.

96. Author's interview with Cohen, 4 March 1984; Mulliner COHC Memoir, 152–53; Mulliner to the author, 3 July 1984, in author's possession.

97. Author's interview with Maurine Mulliner, 17 June 1983 (Washington, D.C.).

98. Telephone interview with Emily Earley, 10 July 1988 (Madison, Wis.). Earley was assigned by Cohen to assist Woodward during 1940–41 in her depositions on Capitol Hill.

Notes to Chapter 8

1. Susan Ware, *Beyond Suffrage: Women in the New Deal* (Cambridge, Mass.: Harvard University Press, 1981), 116–31; and *Partner and I: Molly Dewson, Feminism, and New Deal Politics* (New Haven, Conn.: Yale University Press, 1987), 243–44. On the other hand, historians who have "worked" the papers of a number of women's organizations of the 1940s have found much of vitality in spite of differences among their goals. See Susan M. Hartmann, "Women's Organizations During World War II: The Interaction of

Class, Race, and Feminism," in Mary Kelley, ed., *Woman's Being: Female Identity and Vocation in American History* (Boston: G.K. Hall, 1979), 313–28.

2. Grover Whalen to ESW, 15 November 1937, ESW 1139.2, Box 15; Details of Advisory Committee Duties; ESW to Monica Barry Walsh, 25 October 1939, both in ESW 1139.2, Box 58; *Washington Post*, 19 April 1939.

3. Catt dated the century from the refusal in 1840 of male delegates to seat eight women at the World Anti-slavery Convention in London.

4. Catt to ER, 9 January 1940, ER, Reel 3.

5. Robert Booth Fowler, *Carrie Catt: Feminist Politician* (Boston: Northeastern University Press, 1986), 37; Catt to ER, 3 May 1940, ER, Reel 3; *New York Times*, 24 November 1940; "Suggestions for Covering the Centennial Congress," ESW 1139.2, Box 59. The other Mississippians were Mrs. Frank Wisner of Laurel, Mrs. Samuel Gwin of Greenwood, and Mrs. Birney L. Parkinson of Columbus. (Memphis) *Commercial Appeal*, 8 December 1940.

6. Anne Kimbell Relph, "The World Center for Women's Archives: A Dream Deferred" (independent research paper, George Mason University, 1976), 10, 12 (located in Special Collections, Fenwick Library, GMU); Barbara K. Turoff, *Mary Beard as Force in History* (Dayton, Ohio: Wright State University, 1979), 60; Nancy F. Cott, *A Woman Making History: Mary Ritter Beard Through Her Letters* (New Haven, Conn.: Yale University Press, 1991), 142–44; *IW* 14 (November 1935): 363; Minutes of the Washington Meeting (10 November 1936), AAUW, Reel 148.

7. *The Reflector* (Mississippi State College), 23 September 1936. Woodward was initiated into the Mississippi State College Phi Delta chapter of Chi Omega through her close friendship with Amalie Fair Robinson of Jackson, chapter adviser.

8. ESW to Beard, 30 March 1938, Beard Papers, Box 1, AES. The canceled check is in ESW 1139.2, Box 58.

9. *Washington Post*, 1 March 1938, 14 December 1939; *Jackson Daily News*, 5 March 1939.

10. Beard to ESW, 3 November 1939, ESW 1139.2, Box 2; author's interview with Howorth, 19 June 1984; Turoff, *Mary Beard*, 61. Turoff's bibliography lists eight women, including Woodward, whose correspondence is significant on Beard's role in the WCWA (p. 75).

In 1943, as the NYA faced liquidation, Woodward, at the behest of the White House, explored with Arthur Altmeyer the possibility of placing Bethune with the Social Security Board. Facing a budget reduction, Altmeyer suggested for Bethune the War Manpower Commission or the Fair Employment Practices Committee. Neither job developed for her. ESW to AJA, 13 August 1943; AJA to ESW, 16 August 1943, both in ESW 1139.2, Box 18.

11. Beard to ESW, 24 March 1940, ESW Scrapbook 1139.2.

12. Beard to ESW, 25 December 1940; ESW to Beard, 27 December 1940, both in ESW 1139.2, Box 2. For other problems the WCWA faced, see Ann J. Lane, ed., *Mary Beard: A Sourcebook* (New York: Schocken Books, 1977),

40–41, and Barbara Turoff, "Mary Beard: Feminist Educator," *Antioch Review* 27 (Summer 1979): 277–92.

13. Beard to ESW, 5 June 1944, 17 June 1946, both in ESW 1139.2, Box 2; ESW to Elizabeth Borden, 16 February 1959, ESW 1139.1, Box 12. Subsequently, the Schlesinger Library received portions of Woodward's papers, comprising primarily speeches made in 1946, 1953, and 1959. Woodward retained the vast majority of her papers and memorabilia and later deposited a small collection in the Department of Archives and History of her home state. After her death, her son donated the bulk of the present Woodward collection at the MDAH.

14. Beard to ESW, 18 September, 3 October, 3 November 1939; ESW to Beard, 27 September 1939, 5 June 1946, all in ESW 1139.2, Box 2; ESW speech, "Business Women in A Democracy" (21 October 1939), in ESW 1139.2, Box 26.

15. Bess Furman, *Washington By-line: The Personal History of a Newspaperwoman* (New York: Knopf, 1949), 278; *DD* 17 (April 1940): back cover; ESW statement, ESW 1139.1, Box 26.

16. McAllister to ESW, 12 February 1940, ESW 1139.1, Box 26.

17. ESW to LeHand, 11 July 1940, ESW 1139.1, Box 9.

18. *New York Times*, 18 July 1940; *Washington Post*, 18 July 1940; Woodward plank in ESW 1139.1, Box 17.

19. ESW to McAllister, 24 October 1940, WD-DNC, Box 300.

20. ESW to Missy LeHand, 14 October 1940, FDR Official File 300, Box 49.

21. *Washington Post*, 16 December 1940.

22. *Washington Times-Herald*, undated clipping, ESW 1139.2, Box 69. Nowhere else in Woodward's papers is there any indication that she either sought the job or was considered for it.

23. Unidentified clipping, 30 January 1941, ESW 1139.2, Box 65.

24. *Washington Evening Star* 10 February 1941; *Jackson Daily News*, 11 February 1941. A record of the arrangements is in ESW 1139.1, Box 1.

25. Furman, *Washington By-line*, 284.

26. ESW speech to Richmond BPW (21 October 1939).

27. ESW to Bloodworth, 23 November 1940, ESW 1139.2, Box 2; ESW to Minnie Maffett, 4 September 1940, ESW 1139.2, Box 16.

28. ESW to Hickok, 6 November 1941, WD-DNC, 1937–1944, Box 300. Ruth Milkman in her *Gender at Work: The Dynamics of Job Segregation by Sex during World War II* (Urbana: University of Illinois Press, 1987) provides the keenest analysis of inequities in wartime industries, but her study is limited to automobile and electrical manufacturers.

29. ESW to ER, 6 December 1940, ESW 1139.2, Box 12. On December 3, President Roosevelt had made McNutt coordinator of all health, medical, welfare, nutrition, recreation, and related social service activities pertaining to national defense.

30. Elliott to ER, ESW to ER, both 2 January 1941, both in ER, Box 827.

31. Eleanor Staub, "Government Policy Toward Civilian Women During World War II" (Ph.D. dissertation, Emory University, 1973), 67–72 (Kerr quotation, 72); Richard W. Steele, *Propaganda in an Open Society: The Roosevelt Administration and the Media, 1933–1941* (Westport, Conn.: Greenwood Press, 1985), 88.

32. Staub, "Government Policy Toward Civilian Women," 74–77 (Kerr assessment of work, 77); ESW to ER, 17 July 1941, ESW 1139.2, Box 12.

33. La Guardia to ESW, 18 July 1941, ESW 1139.2, Box 16; VPC press release (19 July 1941), copy in ESW 1139.2, Box 61. Other Region Four members were Blanton Fortson of Atlanta, an insurance executive; W. E. Jacobs of Nashville, a regional Social Security Board manager; and S. E. Roper of Birmingham, president of the Alabama State Federation of Labor.

34. ESW to W. E. Jacobs, 28 July 1941, ESW 1139.2, Box 5.

35. ESW to ER, 31 July 1941, ESW 1139.2, Box 12.

36. EDW to Johnson, 12 August 1941, and to ER, 18 August 1941, both in ESW 1139.2, Box 5.

37. Irvine Belser to ESW, 27 August 1941, ESW 1139.2, Box 2; ESW to ER, 27 August 1941, ESW 1139.2, Box 12

38. Maurine H. Beasley, *Eleanor Roosevelt and the Media: A Public Quest for Self-Fulfillment* (Urbana: University of Illinois Press, 1987), 140–41; Joseph P. Lash, *Love, Eleanor: Eleanor Roosevelt and Her Friends* (Garden City, N.Y.: Doubleday, 1982), 354.

39. ESW to ER, 6 October, 22 December 1941, ESW 1139.2, Box 5; ESW to Blanton Fortson, 20 October 1941, ESW 1139.2, Box 3; Mary E. Judy to ESW, 25 November 1941, ESW 1139.2, Box 5. For a brief description of Mississippi women's homefront activities, see Sandra K. Behel, "The Mississippi Home Front During World War II: Tradition and Change" (Ph.D. dissertation, Mississippi State University, 1989), 85–86.

40. Speech (4 November 1941) in ESW 1139.2, Box 27. Woodward probably drew material from the same FSA team of writers that produced Paul McNutt's "Social Services and Defense," *Journal of Educational Sociology* 15 (October 1941): 69–82.

41. *DD* 18 (December 1941): 26; Tillett to ESW, 10 November 1941; Virginia Rishel to ESW, 4 December 1941, both in WD-DNC, Box 300.

42. ESW to W. E. Jacobs, 6 November 1941, ESW 1139.2, Box 5.

43. ESW to La Guardia, 1 December 1941, ESW 1139.2, Box 5.

44. Joseph P. Lash, *Eleanor and Franklin* (New York: W. W. Norton, 1971), 648–53; Lois Scharf, *Eleanor Roosevelt: First Lady of Liberalism* (Boston: G.K. Hall, 1987), 121–22; James R. Chiles, "Fighting the Battle of America," *Smithsonian* 19 (December 1988): 188–89.

45. Daniels to James M. Landis, 20 January 1942, copy in ESW 1139.2, Box 5; Daniels to ESW, 27 November 1941, ESW 1139.2, Box 3; ESW to Sillers, 21 May 1942, Sillers Papers, Folder on Public Welfare, 1940–42. See

Robert Earnest Miller, "Beyond 'Rosie the Riveter': Wartime Mobilization of Women Volunteers for Civilian Defense, 1940–45," *Forum* 18 (Fall/Winter 1991–92): 8–9 (University of Cincinnati).

46. Tillett to ESW, 31 December 1941, Gladys Tillett Papers, SHC; ESW to Nancy Robinson, 4 May 1951, ESW 1139.2, Box 7; *Women's Work in War Finance, 1941–1945* (Washington, D.C.: U.S. Treasury Department, 1946), 2–3, 26; Staub, "Government Policy Toward Civilian Women," 98–99.

47. Nancy Robinson to ESW, 24 May, 12 June 1946; 10 April, 17 May 1950, ESW 1139.2, Box 7; "To Direct Peacetime Bond Drive," *DD* 18 (August 1946): 19.

48. ESW to ER, 6 April 1951, ESW 1139.2, Box 12; ESW to Nancy Robinson, 4 May 1951, ESW 1139.2, Box 7.

49. ESW radio text (9 April 1941), Chairman of the Board Files, 1935–1942, RG 47.

50. *Washington Times-Herald*, 9 August 1941. For an early popular account of women's war work, see Margaret Culkin Banning, *Women for Defense* (New York: Duell, Sloan and Pearce, 1942).

51. CBS script for ESW (7 June 1942), ESW 1139.1, Box 25; "Woman-power" speech to Chautauqua (NY) Woman's Club (24 August 1942), ESW 1139.2, Box 27.

52. ESW to Altmeyer, 27 April 1942, Altmeyer to William Haber, 7 May 1942, both in ESW 1139.1, Box 10; Staub, "Government Policy Toward Civilian Women," 44–46.

53. ESW, "Womanpower" broadcast (7 June 1942) and "Womanpower" speech (24 August 1942), both in ESW 1139.2, Box 27; Notes on Voluntary Registration, ESW 1139.2, Box 61.

54. *New York Times*, 16 June 1942; *Boston Herald*, 16 June 1942; ESW, "Women on the Production Front—Factory and Farm" (15 June 1942), ESW 1139.2, Box 27. On the registration of women, see Beulah Amidon, "Arms and the Woman," *Survey Graphic* 31 (May 1942): 244–48; *IW* 22 (June 1943): 167; Lelia Rupp, *Mobilizing Women for War: German and American Propaganda, 1939–1945* (Princeton, N.J.: Princeton University Press, 1987), 87.

55. Rupp, 87–88; Staub, "Government Policy Toward Civilian Women," 105–106.

56. ESW to ER, 28 August 1942, ER, Box 855; Staub, 48–51 (Bloodworth quotation, 56); Anthony, *Out of the Kitchen*, 180–81.

57. ESW to Cohen, 1 November 1942, ESW 1139.1, Box 10.

58. Elliott to Tillett, 16 January 1943; ESW and ER telephone conversation, 16 January 1943, ESW 1139.2, Box 53; Doris Faber, *The Life of Lorena Hickok, E.R.'s Friend* (New York: William Morrow, 1980), 282, 294–95.

59. ESW and ER conversation, 16 January 1943; ESW to ER, 20 January 1943, ER, Box 893; Faber, *Hickok*, 294.

60. Tillett to Marvin McIntyre, 26 October 1943, FDR OF 4966, Box 1.

61. *New York Times,* 22 November 1943; *DD* 20 (November 1943): 7, 15; Department of State press release (4 November 1943), copy in ESW Scrapbook 1139.2. Historically, UNRRA dates from November 9, when representatives from forty-four nations met at the White House and signed the agreement establishing the agency.

62. Hoey telegram to ESW, 11 November 1943; ESW memorandum to Acheson, 15 November 1943, both in ESW 1139.2, Box 16 (copy also in ER, Box 896); ESW to ER, 29 November 1943, ER, Box 896.

63. ESW to Acheson, 23 November 1943, ESW 1139.2, Box 55 (also in ER, Box 896).

64. Corson to ESW, 20 November 1943; ESW to Harry Greenstein, 27 November 1943, both in ESW 1139.2, Box 55.

65. ESW to ER, 24, 29 November 1943, both in ER, Box 896; ER to Rosenman, 24 November 1943, ER, Box 1697.

66. ESW to Howorth, 29 November 1943, LSH, Box 12; ESW to Hickey, 27 November 1943, ESW 1139.2, Box 4.

67. Acheson to ESW, 12 January 1944, ESW 1139.2, Box 2; FDR memorandum to ER, 18 February 1944, FDR OF 4966. Notes on meeting, Standing Technical Committee on Welfare (13 January, 6 April, 10 May, 7 June 1944), are all in ESW 1139, Box 1.

68. *First Session of the Council of the United Nations Relief and Rehabilitation Administration, Atlantic City, New Jersey, November 10–December 1, 1943: Selected Documents* (Washington, D.C.: U.S. Government Printing Office, 1944), 128–29, 150–55. Copy in ESW 1139.2, Box 55.

69. ESW to George Healy, 20 December 1943, ESW 1139.1, Box 11.

70. ESW speech to American Association of Social Workers (14 March 1944), ESW 1139.2, Box 29; ESW, "UNRRA-An Answer to Starvation and Despair," *Journal of the National Association of Deans of Women* 7 (March 1944): 99–103.

71. ESW to Howorth, 29 November 1943; ESW to Hickey, 27 November 1943; ESW to ER, 29 November 1943, all previously cited.

72. ESW to Hickey, 27 November 1943; ESW to ER, 27 February 1946; ESW 1139.2, Box 12; ESW to Bloodworth, 30 September 1943, ESW 1139.2, Box 29.

73. ESW to Mary T. Norton, 3 May 1944; Minnie Maffett to ESW, 11 May 1944, both in ESW 1139.2, Box 5.

74. Tillett to FDR, undated copy, ESW 1139.2, Box 18.

75. Williams to ER, 11 June 1944, ER, Reel 20; *New York Times,* 15 June 1944; "Conference at the White House," *IW* 23 (July 1944): 225. In addition to Woodward and Howorth, other Mississippians at the White House were Blanche Ralston and Dera Parkinson, national second vice president of the AAUW. *Meridian Star* [?] July 1944.

76. Lucy S. Howorth, "Women's Responsibility in World Affairs," *Journal of the American Association of University Women* 37 (Summer 1944): 195–98;

Conference program, ESW 1139.2, Box 61; ESW, "My Experience at the UNRRA Conference," ESW 1139.2, Box 29.

77. For a fairly complete file on the preparation of the roster, see AAUW, Reel 122.

78. Lehman to ESW, 26 June 1944, ESW 1139.2, Box 5.

79. "Directory of Second UNRRA Council," in bound volume on Montreal Conference, ESW 1139.2, Box 56; ESW to ER, 14 September 1944, ER, Box 937.

80. G. Howland Smith to Simons, 7 September 1944, Simons Papers, Box 2, SWHA; Biographical data on Simons, Simons Papers, Box 1; Jane Hoey to ESW, 2 April 1945, Executive Director Files, 1941–1948, General Correspondence, RG 47, NA.

81. Transfer assignment, Simons Papers, Box 2, SWHA; Author's interview with Wilbur Cohen, 4 March 1984.

82. ESW, "UNRRA-A Democratic Plan for International Relief," *Social Security Bulletin* 7 (November 1944): 9–12. A copy in the Simons Papers, Box 1 contains a note, "Ghost Written by SMS." See also Simons, "UNRRA on the Threshold of Action," *Social Service Review* 118 (December 1944): 433–43.

83. "William L. Clayton," *Current Biography 1944* (New York: H.W. Wilson, 1945), 95–99.

84. Mulliner to Frank Bane, 22 July, 8 September 1945, in Bane Papers, Box 4, Alderman Library, University of Virginia (Charlottesville).

85. ESW to Gladys Tillett, 14 June 1945, Tillett Papers, SHC; ESW to ER, 21 July 1945, ESW 1139.2, Box 12.

86. ESW to Will Clayton, 5 July 1945, ESW notes on conference with Donald S. Gilpatrick, 19 July 1945, both in ESW 1139.1, Box 28.

87. Will Clayton to ESW, 5 March 1946; C. Tyler Wood to ESW, 9 April 1946, both in ESW 1139.1, Box 28.

88. Will Clayton to John Winant, 22 August 1945, ESW report, "Program for Displaced Persons in Germany" (6 December 1945), both in ESW 1139.1, Box 28.

89. "Highlights of UNRRA Meeting and Trip to Displaced Persons Camps in Germany," *DD* 18 (November 1945): 20; ESW, "UNRRA-Weapon for Democracy," *IW* 24 (November 1945): 342–44; ESW to State Public Affairs Chairmen (BPW), 29 March 29 1946, ESW 1139.2, Box 55.

90. ESW to Mary Anderson, 14 September 1943, ESW 1139.1, Box 11. Marjorie Webster, the D.C. chapter president for 1943–44, wrote glowingly of the year's program, "I think you are wonderful." Webster to ESW, 18 February 1944, ESW 1139.2, Box 59.

91. ESW to Malvina Thompson, [?], ER, Box 937. Obviously, the message was intended for Eleanor Roosevelt.

92. BPW news release (15 April 1945), BPW, Drawer 1; ESW Report on Public Affairs, *IW* 24 (April 1945): 118.

93. "Albert Y. Woodward, Jr.," in *Who's Who in America, 1962–63* (Chi-

cago: A.N. Marquis, 1963), 3452; ESW to Harriet Elliott, 6 July 1943, Elliott Papers; ESW to Alice Doak Temple, 19 August 1943, ESW 1139.1, Box 11; author's interview with May Thompson Evans, 15 September 1984 (Washington, D.C.).

94. Public Affairs Work Plans for 1945–46 (3 October 1946), ESW 1139.2, Box 59. In neither BPW records nor Woodward's papers does a list of members appear for the Committee on Public Affairs. Apparently, BPW national committees were one-woman functions.

95. Report of the Mid-Year Meeting (18–19 January 1946), BPW, Drawer 1 (also in ESW 1239.2, Box 59); *IW* 25 (March 1946): 78.

96. ESW to Banning, 11 December 1945, ESW 1139.1, Box 11; ESW, "Brief Comments on Tentative Legislative Support Program," ESW 1139.2, Box 29.

97. Mary Beard to ESW, 17 May 1946, ESW 1139.2, Box 2; ESW to Margaret Hickey, 26 July 1946, ESW 1139.2, Box 4.

98. ESW, "Public Affairs," *IW* 25 (August 1946): 237.

99. Scharf, *Eleanor Roosevelt*, 95–97, 172–73. "I am influenced in my stand on the Equal Rights Amendment by my labor organization friends," Roosevelt wrote Emma Guffey Miller on September 22, 1941. Miller Papers, Box 12, AES.

100. Quoted by Harrison, *On Account of Sex*, 117.

101. Harrison, *On Account of Sex*, 20.

102. Unidentified statement [1944], ESW 1139.1, Box 11.

103. Geline Bowman and Earlene White, comps., *History of the National Federation of Business and Professional Women's Clubs, 1919–1944* (New York: National Federation of Business and Professional Women, 1944), 74, 85.

104. Minutes of Executive Council, 18–19 January 1946, BPW, Drawer 1; ESW, "Brief Comments on Tentative Legislative Support Program," ESW 1139.2, Box 29.

105. Mississippi BPW "Legislative Program" (September 1943), copy in Susie Powell Papers, Box 2, MDAH. Powell, a firm friend of Woodward, was then the state president.

106. ESW to Nina Avery, 28 June 1946, ESW 1139.1, Box 11. On Avery, see Rupp and Taylor, *Survival in the Doldrums*, 74–75.

107. Marguerite Rawalt, "The Equal Rights Amendment," in Irene Tinker, ed., *Women in Washington: Advocates for Public Policy* (Beverly Hills: Sage Publications, 1985), 52.

108. Telephone interview with Rawalt, 7 July 1987 (Washington, D.C.); Nina Avery to ESW, 28 June 1946, ESW 1139.1, Box 11.

109. George, "The Women Appointees of the Roosevelt and Truman Administrations," 295–96; telephone interview with Hope Ridings Miller, 1 July 1987 (Washington, D.C.).

110. ESW speech (25 April 1938), ESWP, Box 1.

111. ESW to ER, 8 May, 21 July 1945, ESW 1139.2, Box 12.

Notes to Chapter 9

1. Susan M. Hartmann, *The Homefront and Beyond: American Women in the 1940s* (Boston: G.K. Hall, 1982), 154–55; ESW to Elliott, July [?] 1946, in Harriet Elliott Papers, Walter Jackson Library, University of North Carolina at Greensboro; ESW to Bess Truman, 27 February 1946; Bess Truman to ESW, 1 March 1946, both in ESW 1139.2, Box 14.

2. Hartmann, *Homefront*, 148–49; Leila J. Rupp and Verta Taylor, *Survival in the Doldrums: The American Women's Rights Movement, 1945 to the 1960s* (New York: Oxford University Press, 1987), 48, 77.

3. Malvina Lindsay, "Setback for Women," undated clipping in ESW 1139.2, Box 72. Ironically, Lindsay's column bore the name "The Gentler Sex."

4. Interview with Lucy Howorth, 19 June 1984; Howorth to the author, 6 March 1983, in possession of the author.

5. Truman to ESW, 27 February 1946, ESW 1139.2, Box 14; ESW to Amelia S. Copenhaver, 27 March 1947, ESW 1139.2, Box 27; Cynthia Harrison, *On Account of Sex: The Politics of Women's Issues, 1945–1968* (Berkeley: University of California Press, 1988), 54. Harrison attributes Truman's slowness to appoint women to his antipathy toward Gladys Tillett, a holdover in the DNC from the Roosevelt years. After Truman's Missouri friend, India Edwards, succeeded Tillett, the appointment of women to office between 1948 and 1952 increased so much that they surpassed that of Roosevelt, numerically if not substantively. See Harrison, 55, 58, 64.

6. Elliott to ESW, 25 June 1946, ESW 1139.1, Box 11; Lindsay, "Setback for Women."

7. Constance Ashton Myers interview with Howorth, 20–23 June 1975, Southern Oral History Program, SHC.

8. Watson B. Miller, "Federal Security Agency Reorganization: A Second Important Step," *Public Welfare* 4 (December 1946): 266–70. Miller had replaced Paul McNutt in October 1945. It was generally known that Truman wanted federal social services reorganized as a step toward the eventual creation of a new Cabinet department.

9. ESW to Elliott, July [?] 1946, Elliott Papers.

10. Howorth to Elliott, 5 June 1946, Elliott Papers; Howorth, "Recollections of Mississippi Women in Public Life Whom I Have Known," paper in possession of author; Howorth to the author, 1 June 1987.

11. Howorth to Hickman, 31 May 1946, copy in Elliott Papers.

12. Tillett to ESW, 6 June 1946; Tillett to Hannegan, 13 June 1946; drafts of letters to Miller and Truman, 13 June 1946, all in Gladys Tillett Papers, SHC.

13. Copies of the letter, dated 20 June 1946, may be found in ESW 1139.2, Box 61, the Tillett papers, the Somerville-Howorth Papers (Schlesinger Library, Box 13), and the Elliott Papers. William D. Hassett, the President's correspondence secretary, referred all the incoming letters that the women

wrote to Watson B. Miller, OF 59–W, 285–A, Truman Papers, Harry S Truman Library (Independence, Mo.).

14. ESW to ER, 21 June 1946, ESW 1139.2, Box 12.

15. Copies of letters from Mississippi Senator James O. Eastland, Margaret Hickey, and Harriet Elliott, among others, are in ESW 1139.1, Box 11. Others appear in OF 285–A, Truman Papers.

16. Watson Miller to Florence Allen, 10 July 1946, copy in ESW 1139.2, Box 12.

17. Executive Order 9753, OF 7–5, Truman Papers; "The Administrator's Statement of July 16, 1946," copy in AJA-WPP, Box 10; *Washington Evening Star*, 17 July 1946.

18. ESW to Gladys Tillett, 19 July 1946, Tillett Papers.

19. ESW to ER, 10 July 1946, ER Box 3777.

20. For example, see ESW to Robert W. Beasley, 30 July 1946, ESW 1139.2, Box 2.

21. McMillin is one of Susan Ware's figures in *Beyond Suffrage: Women in the New Deal* (Cambridge, Mass.: Harvard University Press, 1981), 51, 122.

22. ESW to Harry Truman, 29 July 1946; Truman to ESW, 2 August 1946, both in President's Personal File (PPF) 2–A, Truman Papers; Tillett to Matthew Connelly, 2 August 1946, OF 7–S, Truman Papers.

23. Swofford to Truman, 29 July 1946; Evans to Truman, 27 August 1946, both in OF 2–A, Truman Papers.

24. Letters to Truman from Congressmen Thomas G. Abernathy, William M. Colmer, Jamie L. Whitten, Will M. Whittington, and Arthur Winstead, dated between August 2 and 9, 1946, are all in OF 2–A, Truman Papers, as is Barnes's telegram to Matthew Connelly (14 August).

25. *New York Times*, 27 August 1946, 9 January 1947; George Martin, *Madame Secretary: Frances Perkins* (Boston: Houghton Mifflin, 1976), 476–77.

26. Directory of the Fifth UNRRA Session, ESW 1139.2, Box 55.

27. ESW to Gladys Tillett, 14 August 1946, Tillett Papers; Clayton to ESW, 7 October 1946, ESW 1139.1, Box 28; ESW, "UNRRA-First International Operating Agency," *DD* 24 (April 1947). The article was actually written by an UNRRA staff member, Alastair M. Taylor.

28. *New York Times*, 7 December 1946; ESW to ER, 9 October 1946, ESW 1139.2, Box 12; ESW to ER, 8 November 1946, ESW 1139.1, Box 11.

29. Agency Order No. 59 (16 July 1946), copy in ESW 1139.1, Box 12.

30. ESW, "Discussions of Functions of My Office with Regional Directors" (18 November 1946), ESW 1139.2, Box 28.

31. ESW, "Discussions of Functions."

32. Maurine Mulliner to ESW, 22 July 1947, Executive Director Files, 1941–1948, RG 47.

33. Ewing to Truman, 11 February 1948, OF 670, Truman Papers; Lally to Simons, 17 August 1948, Executive Directors Files, 1941–1948, RG 47;

Frances Kernohan, Savilla M. Simons, and Charlotte E. Owen, "International Social Work," in Russell H. Kurtz, ed., *Social Work Yearbook 1954* (New York: American Association of Social Workers, 1954), 266–85.

34. *New York Times*, 12 March 1947. The other woman delegate was Mrs. Hansa Mehta of India.

35. ESW to Amelia S. Copenhaver, 27 March 1947, ESW 1139.1, Box 27; ESW to ER, 28 May 1947, ER Box 3777; ESW, Report on the Fourth Session of the Economic and Social Council, copy in Dewson Papers, Box 20.

36. ESW, "Operation 1947," *Survey Midmonthly* 83 (April 1947): 105–107.

37. *New York Times*, 20 July 1947; ESW to ER, 24 August 1947, ESW 1139.2, Box 12.

38. Prospectus on the ICSW (16 April 1951), in Fred Hoehler Papers, Box 68, SWHA; Joe Hoffer (Secretary, ICSW) to ESW, 19 October, 8 November 1949; ESW to Hoffer, 30 November 1949, all in Records of ICSW, SWHA.

39. ESW to ER, 8 October 1952, ER Box 4038. At least no one questioned Woodward's ICSW affiliation, as had friends suspicious of her earlier well-intentioned forays. "Please don't go to any more of these house parties," her publicist Virginia Price wrote in 1938, after Woodward accompanied Emily Blair to a meeting of the Oxford Group on Moral Re-armament in Stockbridge, Massachusetts. Prompted by Mary Woolley, Woodward agreed in 1939 to become a sponsor of the People's Mandate to End War. Nothing came of this, but after Woodward joined in 1944 the women's committee of the Council of American-Soviet Friendship, FBI agents contacted Lucy Howorth to question her friend's motives. Apprised by Howorth of Woodward's proclivity to join organizations promoting internationalism, the matter was dropped, as was Woodward's membership in the Council. Price note on copy of *New York Times*, 5 June 1938 clipping, ESW Scrapbook, 1139.2; Woolley to ESW, 18 April 1939, ESW 1139.2, Box 15; Muriel Draper to ESW, 18 January 1944, ESW 1139.1, Box 13; interview with Howorth, 19 June 1984.

40. Paul E. Smith (USOE) to State superintendents, [n.d.], copy in Truman Papers, OF 7–S; Marjorie E. Pitt, "Exchange Teachers-Ambassadors of Good Will," *IW* 26 (May 1947): 134.

41. For a contemporary account of cultural exchanges, see Ruth Emily McMurry and Muna Lee, *The Cultural Approach: Another Way in International Relations* (Chapel Hill: University of North Carolina Press, 1947), 208–37. A later description is found in Charles Frankel, *The Neglected Aspect of Foreign Affairs: American Educational and Cultural Policy Abroad* (Washington, D.C.: Brookings Institution, 1965).

42. Savilla M. Simons, "Action of Social Significance Taken by United Nations Economic and Social Council Summer Session, 1949," *Social Service Review* 23 (December 1949): 424, 428. For a fuller background on the exchange of persons, see Walter H. C. Laves and Charles A. Thomson, *UNESCO: Purpose, Progress, and Prospects* (Bloomington: Indiana University Press), 93–94.

43. See "International Relations Bulletin No. 1" (23 October 1950) and "Federal Security Agency Participation in International Programs for Health, Education, and Welfare" (FSA: Office of International Relations, 1952), ESWP-AES, Box 2; Annual Report of the Federal Security Agency, 1951 (Washington, D.C.: U.S. Government Printing Office, 1952), 10.

44. The Woodward Papers contain dozens of photographs of Woodward and Simons presenting certificates of program completion to UN fellows.

45. Summary of the International Activities of the Federal Security Agency Office of International Relations, May 1952 (bound volume), ESW 1139.2, Box 55. The author has been unable to locate records of the OIR beyond those in the Woodward Papers and RG 47 (the latter not extending beyond about 1948). The author is grateful to Dorothy Lally for directing her to Stanley Bendet, who, in 1983, was the head of the office within The Department of Health and Human Services that is the "descendent" of Woodward's offices within the FSA and HEW. Bendet located one folder of material, dated September-October 1952, in an old file in his Office of Policy Development-International Affairs, HHS (Washington, D.C.).

46. Simons left government service in 1953 to become the general secretary of the YMCA; after five years with the "Y" she was director of the National Travelers Aid Association until her retirement in 1967. See biographical data, Simons Papers, Box 1, SWHA.

47. Appointment papers for Gates (5 January 1951), ESW 1139.2, Box 60.

48. ESW to Amelia Copenhaver, 27 March 1947, ESW 1139.1, Box 27; AJA to ESW, 15 December 1948, Executive Directors Files, 1941–1948, RG 47; ESW to ER, 2 February 1950, ER Box 3868.

49. Author's interview with Cohen, 4 March 1984; ESW to Elliott, July [?] 1946, Elliott Papers.

50. "Activity Report of the Office of International Relations for the Month of May 1953," in ESW 1139.2, Box 60; interview with Dorothy Lally, 22 June 1983.

51. Interview with Lally. Lally joined the office of the Commissioner of Social Security as his chief adviser on international social welfare upon her return from UNRRA refugee work. She eventually became chief of international activities in the HEW Office of Human Development. See her "International Social Welfare," *Social Work Year Book 1960* (New York: National Association of Social Workers, 1960), 318–20.

52. Mary E. Pidgeon and Janet Hooks, "Women in the Federal Service, 1923–1947," WB Bulletin 230 (Washington, D.C.: U.S. Government Printing Office, 1949), Part I, 5,27, 46, Part II, 71–73.

53. "Women in This First Year of Peace," DD 23 (August 1946): 3–5. Douglas was the United States alternate delegate to the United Nations and Brunauer was the United States representative on the Preparatory Commission to UNESCO and the third woman to hold the diplomatic rank of minister.

54. Edwards to Miller, 9 January 1947, copy in Gladys Tillett Papers, SHC;

Edwards to ESW, [n.d.] 1948, ESW 1139.2, Box 69; ESW to George Healy, 5 March 1948, ESW 1139.1, Box 11.

55. Elliott was still alive when Chancellor Walter C. Jackson notified Woodward of the action of the University of North Carolina trustees. Jackson to ESW, 18 February 1947, ESW 1139.1, Box 11. After Woodward's death, her son placed a brass replica of the full citation on her gravestone.

56. ESW undated [but post 1946] speech to Girls Nation, ESW 1139.2, Box 29; MSCW speech (28 May 1945) and Winthrop College speech (3 June 1951), both in ESW 1139.2, Box 23.

57. *New York Times*, 27 November 1952.

58. ESW to Reading, 1 December 1952, 12 March 1953, both in ESW 1139.2, Box 7; ESW to ER, 4 February 1953, ESW 1139.2, Box 9.

59. Elizabeth Wickenden, "Federal Agencies in Social Work," in Russell H. Kurtz, ed., *Social Work Yearbook 1954* (New York: American Association of Social Workers, 1954), 210–18.

60. ESW to Hobby, 13 January 1953, ESW 1139.2, Box 18; ESW to ER, 4 February 1953, ESW 1139.2, Box 12.

61. *Washington Post*, 27 March 1953; Isidore E. Falk Memoir, COHC, 286. Woodward received a Civil Service rating of E (Excellent), the highest in Civil Service Efficiency Ratings, from 1946 to 1948. For 1950–1951, her rating fell to S (Satisfactory). She ranked at GS–15 with an annual salary of $11,800. The evaluations are in ESW 1139.2, Box 60.

62. "'Mr. Social Security' Loses His Job," *Milwaukee Journal*, 11 April 1953; Hobby to AJA, 7 April 1953, AJA, Box 18; Altmeyer Memoir, COHC, 77–78; Cohen Memoir, AJA Papers, 24–25.

63. ESW to ER, 12 August 1953, ER Box 4134; *New York Times*, 4 November 1953; Robyn Muncy, *Creating a Female Dominion in American Reform, 1890–1935* (New York: Oxford University Press, 1991), 156.

64. *Jackson Daily News*, 20 December 1953; "Ends Service to U.S.," *IW* 33 (March 1954): 119; *Staple Cotton Review* 32 (January 1954): 1–3; ESW handwritten notes, ESW 1139.2, Box 58.

65. Richard H. Lyle (HEW regional director) to ESW, 17 November 1953, ESW 1139.2, Box 5; ESW to Reading, 9 December 1953, ESW 1139.2, Box 12; ESW to ER, 9 December 1953, ER Box 4134.

66. James M. Goode, *Best Addresses: A Century of Washington's Distinguished Apartment Houses* (Washington, D.C.: Smithsonian Institution Press, 1988), 300–306; ESW to Walter Sillers, Jr., 21 May 1942, Sillers Papers; *Jackson Daily News* 11 January 1954.

67. ESW to Stella Reading, 5 May 1952; *Memphis Commercial Appeal*, 9 January 1957.

68. *Picayune (Miss.) Item*, 13 May 1937; *Vicksburg Evening Post*, 27 March 1942.

69. Biloxi *Daily Herald*, 30 September 1955; *Memphis Commercial Appeal*, 12 October 1955; interview with Davis L. Fair, Jr., 4 January 1985 (Louisville, MS).

70. *Washington Post*, 15 April 1956; Jane Dick to ESW, 26 September 1956, ESW 1139.2, Box 3; ESW to ER, 29 October 1956, ESW 1139.2, Box 12; Stennis to ESW, 11 May 1956, ESW 1139.1, Box 12. Lucy Howorth told the author about Harden's dislike of Eastland (19 June 1984). Mona Harden died of cancer before the author could arrange an interview.

71. Howorth to MWD, 19 July 1954, Somerville-Howorth Papers, Box 13; ESW to MWD, 23 November 1956, MWD, Box 20.

72. ER requests to ESW, ESW 1139.2, Box 9; ESW to ER, 27 December 1953, ER, Box 4134; ESW to ER, 9 April 1958, ER, Box 4341.

73. ESW to Howorth, [?] January 1961, Somerville-Howorth Papers, Box 13; *Jackson Clarion Ledger*, 25 January 1961.

74. Susan Ware, *Partner and I: Molly Dewson, Feminism, and New Deal Politics* (New Haven, Conn.: Yale University Press, 1987), 247–48; telephone conversation with Howorth, 15 November 1992.

75. Interview with May Thompson Evans, 15 September 1984; Howorth to the author, 9 March 1988, in author's possession. Woodward retained her membership in Galloway Memorial Methodist Church in Jackson until December 1941, when she transferred her letter to the Washington church nearest her residence. ESW to Board of Stewards, 1 December 1941, ESW 1139.1, Box 10.

76. Pauline E. Mandigo to ESW, 1 February 1954, in Howorth File, NBPW Archives; Howorth to the author, 9 March 1988; author's interview with Howorth, 19 June 1984.

77. Interview with Cohen, 4 March 1984; Altmeyer to Albert Woodward, Jr., 17 November 1971, copy in author's possession; Guest list for Anniversary Program of Social Security Act, copy in AJA 400, Box 18.

78. Interview with Evans, 15 September 1984; interview with Marianne Harrison Cummings, 22 June 1983 (Washington, D.C.); interview with Otis Hardin, 19 March 1986 (Washington, D.C.); telephone interview with Elizabeth Looney, 19 October 1992 and with Howorth, 15 November 1992; Harden to ESW, Christmas 1963, ESW 1139.2, Box 5.

79. *Memphis Commercial Appeal*, 25 September 1971; *Washington Post*, 24 September 1971; *Washington Evening Star*, 24 September 1971; *Winston County Journal*, 30 September 1971.

80. Elbert R. Hilliard to Albert Woodward, Jr., 20 December 1976, copy in author's possession; *Jackson Clarion-Ledger*, 23 October 1977.

81. Hickey to the author, 7 July 1980; author's telephone conversation with Wickenden, 6 April 1986.

Index